Globalisation, Migration and Socio-Economic Change in Contemporary Greece

IMISCOE (International Migration, Integration and Social Cohesion)

IMISCOE is a European Commission-funded Network of Excellence of more than 350 scientists from various research institutes that specialise in migration and integration issues in Europe. These researchers, who come from all branches of the economic and social sciences, the humanities and law, implement an integrated, multidisciplinary and internationally comparative research program that focuses on Europe's migration and integration challenges.

Within the program, existing research is integrated and new research lines are developed that involve issues crucial to European-level policy-making and provide a theory-based design to implement new research.

The publication program of IMISCOE is based on five distinct publication profiles, designed to make its research and results available to scientists, policymakers and the public at large. High-quality manuscripts written by IMISCOE members, or in cooperation with IMISCOE members, are published in these five series. An Editorial Committee coordinates the review process of the manuscripts. The five series are:

1. Joint Studies
2. Research
3. Dissertations
4. Reports
5. Textbooks

More information on the network can be found at: www.imiscoe.org

IMISCOE **Dissertations** include dissertations of IMISCOE members. There are more than 100 Ph.D. candidates in the various affiliated institutions working on doctoral research within the IMISCOE framework.

Globalisation, Migration and Socio-Economic Change in Contemporary Greece

Processes of Social Incorporation of Balkan Immigrants in Thessaloniki

Panos Arion Hatziprokopiou

IMISCOE Dissertations

AMSTERDAM UNIVERSITY PRESS

Cover design: Studio Jan de Boer BNO, Amsterdam
Layout: Fito Prepublishing, Almere

ISBN-13 978 90 5356 873 6
ISBN-10 90 5356 873 5
NUR 741 / 763

Printed and bound by CPI Group (UK) Ltd, Croydon, CR0 4YY

Summary of thesis

The study examines issues surrounding the social incorporation of immigrants in Greece, focusing on a particular city, Thessaloniki, and on two migrant groups, Albanians and Bulgarians. The research is set within the debates about migration and globalisation, and more specifically within the regional context of Balkan transnational migration. The thesis is the outcome of fieldwork research that involved structured questionnaires, in-depth interviews, background sources and systematic observation. It addresses the factors shaping immigrants' lives through combined methodologies and an interdisciplinary approach that goes beyond oversimplifying accounts of exclusion-inclusion; rather, these are seen as dynamic processes connected to the wider social reality. The concept of incorporation is employed in order to analyse both the ways by which migrants organise their lives in the host society and the structural, institutional and cultural contexts that condition them. The analytical framework distinguishes between several interrelated modes of incorporation: social/political responses; labour-market integration; living conditions and social space; coping strategies and community formation. A number of additional factors are also considered: the composition of the migrant populations; migratory patterns and dynamics; the role of social networks; issues of access; and questions of identity.

The findings provide an empirical account of the immigrants' characteristics, uncovering a high degree of heterogeneity that unavoidably determines incorporation patterns. 'Immigrants' become a social category constructed on the basis of the *exclusionary* mechanisms: the restrictive immigration policy, the spread of xenophobic attitudes, and the particular space immigrants occupy in the labour market. However, immigrants *do* make a living in the host society: by adopting certain integration 'strategies'; by relying on (mostly informal) social networks; and by interacting in various ways with the local population. Incorporation is subject to time and place: gradually, immigrants become organic elements of the host society, which shapes, but is also being shaped by, migration.

The findings suggest that the Greek urban experience of immigration is an interesting example of contemporary processes of globalisation, migration and incorporation in urban contexts. Firstly, because some of the chief characteristics of international migration are reflected in the Greek case. Secondly, because the Greek economy and Greek society have experienced immigration during a period of transition and of increasing exposure to the international environment. Thirdly, because of certain features of transnational mobility emerging in the Balkan space, determined by proximity and cultural/historical ties. Within this context, Thessaloniki is becoming a new home for immigrants from the Balkans. With a long past of multicultural coexistence and trans-local importance in the Balkan region, Thessaloniki now searches for new identities and reclaims its old role through the contradictions of a rapidly changing reality.

Table of contents

List of tables

List of figures

Abbreviations used in the text

EKΘ	Thessaloniki Labour Centre
EU	European Union
FDI	Foreign Direct Investment
GATT	General Agreement on Tariffs and Trade
GDP	Gross Domestic Product
GNTO	Greek National Tourism Organisation
IMF	International Monetary Fund
INSTAT	Albanian Institute of Statistics
IKA	Foundation of Social Insurance
ΙΠΟΔΕ	Institute of Diaspora Greeks' and Intercultural Education
MAKINE	Macedonian Institute of Employment
MNC	Multinational Organisation
NAFTA	North American Free Trade Agreement
NGO	Non-Governmental Organisation
NSIB	National Statistical Institute of Bulgaria
NSSG	National Statistical Service of Greece
NTO	National Tourist Organisation (EOT)
ΟΑΕΔ	Organisation for the Employment of the Labour Force
ΟΓΑ	Organisation of Agricultural Insurances
SME	Small and Medium-scale Enterprise
TEBE	Fund for Professionals, Manufacturers and Employers
TNC	Transnational Corporation

Acknowledgements

In the course of my doctoral studies, of conducting the research, writing the thesis, and bringing it to its present version in order to be published as a book, there are a number of people to whom I owe several debts of gratitude; people who have offered valuable help, in various ways and at various stages, during the last five years. Without them the completion of this work would simply have been impossible.

First and foremost, I am deeply grateful to my supervisor, Professor Russell King, for he believed in this research from the very beginning and supported me throughout the whole process, devoting much of his time to checking detail and ensuring quality. His insights have been thought provoking and his feedback extremely useful, but I also owe him a lot for his availability, patience and kindness.

Various people at the Sussex European Institute deserve a word of thanks, as well as the institution itself, for hosting me during all these years of coming and going and for providing both the environment and the resources for this work. Many thanks go especially to Jenny Money, of the Sussex Centre for Migration Research, who has always been there for help or a friendly chat. Two years of my studies were supported by an ESRC Postgraduate Studentship (Award Ref. No.: R42200124239), for which I am grateful. I would also like to thank the research teams at the universities of Sussex (Professor Russell King and Dr Nicola Mai) and Dundee (Dr Gabriella Lazaridis and Ms Maria Koumandraki) for their kind permission and encouragement to use their interview schedule which they had already carefully piloted for the needs of their comparative study into the patterns of social exclusion of Albanian migrants in Greece and Italy (funded by the Leverhulme Trust 2001-2003). I also owe much to my *viva voce* examiners, Professor Jörg Monar, co-director of the Sussex European Institute, and Rossetos Fakiolas, Emeritus Professor at the University of Athens; they went patiently and thoroughly through this piece of work and provided me with useful comments and suggestions on how to improve its quality in both analysis and style.

I would like to thank the publishers at Amsterdam University Press and IMISCOE itself, for supporting this publication. A special word of thanks goes particularly to Dr Maria Berger of the IMISCOE office for taking care of this publication from the very beginning and for providing valuable practical help. The three anonymous referees who carefully read the text and came back with encouraging insights have also helped me to finalise this publication.

As regards to the specificities of immigration to Greece, I would like first to acknowledge how crucially the time I spent as an activist with the Network of Movements for Social and Political Rights marked my academic trajectory and inspired this research. I am also deeply indebted to Professor Lois Labrianidis, my former teacher at the University of Macedonia, for encouraging me to go on with the D.Phil. and for giving me the opportunity to work on two research projects on immigration to Greece, which eventually led to an ongoing fruitful collaboration. The help of Mrs Brikena Brahimi has been of particular importance regarding the carrying out of the interviews and questionnaires; I am indebted to her, as well as to her husband Mr Nadi Kazazi, and his sister Adriana. I am also particularly thankful to Mrs Mimoza Dako and her husband Edi, of the Albanian Association of Thessaloniki, as well as to Mr Dimitri Tsoumas of the language-teaching NGO Odysseas, for trusting me and bringing me into contact with potential interviewees. Odysseas, the Albanian Association and the Anti-racist Initiative of Thessaloniki also deserve a special mention as institutions, for kindly hosting me on several occasions. Various other people were extremely kind in helping me by acting as intermediaries with migrants they knew; I owe apologies to some as space does not allow every single name to be stated. To mention only a few, many thanks go especially to: Mr and Mrs Kambouroglou from Foinikas; Romeo, Hergis and Dimitri, students at the University of Macedonia; and Mrs Liliana, owner of a café-bar that serves a small Bulgarian community. Naturally, I am grateful to all the respondents and interviewees who kindly agreed to talk to me about their experiences; conducting the fieldwork was perhaps the most enjoyable part of the D.Phil. journey. This work belongs primarily to them, even if I have to acknowledge that it may be of little practical use in improving their often difficult lives.

I was glad to have shared some of my time at Sussex with exceptional people: among others, Dr Pontus Odmalm and Dr Nick Walmsley. My friend Enric Ruiz-Gelices offered me shelter several times during my back and forth movements to Sussex, until we lived below the same roof for a year; we agreed and disagreed in endless discussions, we doubted and dreamed, and had a great time.

Back in Greece, I thank my good old friends for being helpful unconsciously: George Ververis, for explaining in uniquely simple ways the most complicated things; Yiannis Poulakis, for doing exactly the opposite, although convincingly; and Dimitri Arapis, for our shared adventures. And finally, my parents, Fotini and Mihalis, who continue to offer their support unconditionally. I have also received practical assistance with the transcription and translation of interviews from Mihalis, Eftychia, Harry and Sofia, who deserve a special thanks.

Last, but not least, I owe a special word of thanks to Eleni Skandali for her valuable help, support and insuperable patience; for being next to me during all these years of 'pain' and joy: this work is dedicated to her, with all my love.

1 Introduction

Migration is nothing new; it is embedded in the history of human societies. However, as a social phenomenon, it reflects, and is determined by, the historical era in which it takes place. At the dawn of the twenty-first century, processes of international migration are characteristic of the present historical context of globalisation. In contrast to migration, globalisation appears indeed as a historical novelty, implying qualitative changes in the dynamics of the world system: the restructuring of the global economy, the interconnectedness between various kinds of networks, the interdependence between states and communities, the increasing interaction, deterritorialisation and fusion of existing cultural forms. Contemporary international migration, its implications and its associated phenomena, are part and parcel of these transformations.

By the end of the past century, Greece had emerged in the European landscape as a new migrant-receiving country. Even in the Greek case, however, this was not new; in fact, migration, in several forms and directions, has long been linked to the fate of the modern Greek nation-state. Soon after gaining independence in 1832, tiny new Greece started attracting Christians from the Ottoman provinces of Thessaly and Macedonia, as well as members of the European and Mediterranean diasporic bourgeoisie. The Balkan wars were marked by displacements and resettlements of people, both voluntary and forced, which peaked with the great population exchange between Greece and Turkey after the former's defeat in the Greco-Turkish War of 1919-1922. Ever since, national homogenisation processes have been marked by conscious policies of the Greek state to assimilate various populations into the national narrative and to stimulate ethnic density, particularly in the 'nationally dangerous' areas of Macedonia and Thrace. Meanwhile, thousands of people were 'on the move': mountain-dwellers from Epirus and Macedonia made their way down to the lowlands, while islanders, as well as peasants from Thessaly and the 'New Lands', moved to the growing industrial centres of Athens and Piraeus; some for a short time only before embarking for the New World. In 1949, the civil war that succeeded the German occupation ended with thousands of those who had fought with the defeated Communists fleeing to the Soviet Union and other countries of the Eastern Bloc. The 1950s and 1960s were marked by large-scale internal and external movements; during this period the main urbanisation phase took place, as well as international migration: initially to the US and Australia, and later intra-European, mainly to West Germany.

By the mid-1970s, emigrants started returning home, followed by repatriating political refugees and ethnic Greeks from the former Soviet Union in the 1980s. In parallel, the first foreign workers were beginning to be recruited, initially in the shipping and fishing industries, later also in agriculture. With the collapse of the Iron Curtain and the developments after 1989, immigration flows intensified, especially from Eastern European and neighbouring Balkan states, with Albania being by far the major sending country. The situation spiralled out of control in the early 1990s as governments failed not only to address, but also to acknowledge the new migratory pressures and the presence of many migrants within Greek territory. The only measures taken were rather reactionary and repressive, resulting in hundreds of thousands of people living under clandestine status, in harsh conditions, and at the margins of mainstream society.

At present, fifteen years later, it appears that many of the initial problems have gradually faded out, while new ones have arisen. Migrants have become 'visible', and currently the public debates raise concerns regarding the issue of integration. Xenophobia, exploitation and social polarisation have been the milestones marking Greece's path to diversity. However, the migrants are 'here', to prove that Greece has de facto become a multiethnic, pluralistic society. They live, work and consume in Greece; their children go to Greek schools; most importantly, they increasingly interact with the local population, producing not only new social tensions, but also new kinds of relationships, new patterns of mobility, new types of cultural expression and exchange. Contemporary trends in migration and integration in Greece differ from any past experience in the history of the country; but they also largely differ from past European and other experiences. On the other hand, there is a range of processes, practices and phenomena resembling other contemporary cases, especially Southern European ones, with which Greece shares many common characteristics, while there are still uniquely Greek expressions and manifestations.

The above concisely suggests the novelty of the phenomenon. This is primarily a study of immigration and the incorporation of migrants in Greece. I focus on the two largest migrant groups, Albanians and Bulgarians, both from neighbouring Balkan countries of different though comparable migration experiences; and on the second largest Greek city, Thessaloniki, geographically close to the migrants' homes and with a longstanding history of multiethnic coexistence and transnational ties. My secondary theoretical focus is to 'read' the patterns and processes of migration and incorporation within the context of societal change in Greece; also, to locate the Greek case on the global map of contemporary social phenomena; and to explore the links between local/national processes and the trends observed at the international level.

The principal aim of this study is to examine the parallel but opposing processes of social exclusion and integration of Albanian and Bulgarian immigrants in Thessaloniki. However, my objective is not to present a series of data to support conclusions of the kind 'immigrants in Greece are well integrated', or 'they live under conditions of social exclusion'. What I consider important is to identify, describe and analyse the patterns and the processes that condition the ways migrants organise their lives in the host country and in the local community where they live and work. To do so, I look at both objective and perceptual factors relating to the characteristics of the migrants themselves; aspects of their lives in different social spheres; their own understandings of their collective and individual experiences and of the various ways they interact with the local population. These issues are to be analysed in relation to the contexts within which different processes of integration/exclusion take place and with reference to the dominant material and ideological conditions immigrants face in the host country.

With respect to the practical achievement of these aims and to the carrying out of the research itself, the first task was to identify the fundamental issues that the study aims to address. Two key sets of research questions were selected:

- What are the conditions and/or the processes shaping immigrants' lives in Greece? What are the obstacles put by structural, institutional or cultural factors?
- How do immigrants overcome such obstacles (if so)? How do they manage to organise their lives (in terms of work, residence, interpersonal relationships, etc.) in the host country and in the specific locality where they are found?

Looking at factors of exclusion and patterns of integration requires first an account of what they involve and of how they can be measured. The explanatory framework ascribes the conditions of exclusion/inclusion to the broader process of 'incorporation', which takes place within interrelated contexts, conceptually 'separated' for the purposes of the analysis. Economy, policy, culture or space can be seen as such contexts, shaping immigrants' lives and determining the dynamics of their incorporation: for instance, the local labour market where immigrants are looking for work; the policy framework that conditions their entry, work and legal presence in the country; racist hostility (or, on the contrary, friendly reception), which affects people's everyday relationships;

the place of residence (or leisure, or work), which becomes the terrain where migrants build their lives and develop their sense of belonging.

However, all these different but interconnected spheres of social existence are not ahistoric, nor unchangeable. They are historically developed and subject to transformation, and they are interacting with the dynamics of migration, whether invisible social structures, faceless institutions, hidden cultural attributes or common daily practices. The informal labour market seems to absorb immigrant labour, but not without serious effects; immigration policy is revised in order to deal with a rapidly changing reality; old perceptions of identity are now challenged by the presence of the 'other among us'; the urban space attains new social uses, creating thus new images of place. In that sense, the study of incorporation gives birth to additional questions that may lie in the background but cannot be avoided completely:

- How are the dynamics of migration linked to the processes of social change? What possible changes related to immigration can we observe in the Greek case? How are these effects manifested in Thessaloniki? Which are the patterns of interaction between immigrants and locals?

Obviously the focus is on a local, urban society; it is impossible though to separate this case from its wider national context. But again, ultimately and increasingly, local and national realities are being restructured and deeply transformed as they are more and more exposed to a changing international environment. Processes related to globalisation and restructuring might be abstractly hidden in the background, but they do influence regional and national contexts, and they are manifested in particular ways in specific localities, whether directly or via the national layer. Migration itself can be seen as one of these forces that produces outcomes where transnational, national and local contexts get fused or interact. Market dynamics are less and less subject to social control; national policies are influenced or directed by international organisations; old certainties of belonging lose their meaning. Space is also transforming, since localities are superseding their regional or national scope, and they are themselves internationalising, with visible alterations in their landscape, while on the other hand their populations are becoming more mixed, culturally and ethnically, and increasingly mobile. Similar patterns of change can be then observed between different countries or different places, although they are expressed in distinctive and concrete ways in each case. Therefore, there is an additional set of secondary questions of a more theoretical direction that are also going to be addressed:

- Can we compare what is taking place in Thessaloniki in respect to migration to the experiences of other countries or to other cases in

Europe or elsewhere? Can we identify common patterns in the dynamics of migrants' incorporation, and which of these forms part of wider global processes?
- How do these broader processes, developments and trends determine the dynamics of migration in the case of Greece and Thessaloniki? In what forms does the global affect the local in respect to migration and incorporation? How can we generalise from our case study, and what theoretical conclusions can we draw?

The answers I seek to find are neither given nor prescribed. The objective is to describe and analyse the *current* situation and to identify and explain the *emerging* trends. Above all, I seek to address the issue of the incorporation of Albanian and Bulgarian migrants in Thessaloniki by identifying the mechanisms of exclusion and the patterns of integration. Finally, my case study aims to provide a basis for comparison and generalisation. Therefore the framework of analysis has been designed carefully in order to apply to other cases without sacrificing its local scope and empirical thrust. Similarly, the methodology is not based on specific principles or epistemological commitments; it rather came out of the practical necessities of the research itself and the theoretical implications underlying the study.

The structure of the thesis is as follows: Chapter 2 is a background chapter. The purpose is to set out a starting point for this study by defining my general perspective and by placing contemporary migration to Greece in a broader context. The chapter elucidates the way I interpret (some of) my findings by developing a perspective to which I am going to return at the end of the book in an attempt to theorise from my results. The discussion then turns more specific and locates the Greek experience within the Southern European 'immigration model' by highlighting its uniqueness – to a great extent due to the country's position in the Balkans – and by briefly overviewing the main socio-economic characteristics and policy developments.

Chapter 3 is about my analytical and methodological considerations. It starts by building up a framework for the analysis of immigrants' incorporation and by specifying my own approach. It proceeds by identifying the limits in the existing literature and the gaps in recent research in order to explain the contribution my thesis has to offer. A description of the research design and the methodological tools used follows, including a personal account of the fieldwork experience. The practicalities of data collection and analysis are discussed, before moving to a brief introduction to the city of Thessaloniki by sketching out its main demographic, socio-economic, socio-spatial and historical features.

In Chapter 4, I start presenting and discussing my findings. I first draw the profile of the migrants, explaining similarities and differences but also highlighting the heterogeneity observed. The characteristics of the participants in the survey research (demographic, geographic, educational, etc.) are presented and discussed. I then analyse the reasons, patterns and dynamics of migration. The migrants' characteristics and the dynamics of migration play a potentially important role in the incorporation process and help us explain similarities and differences between various groups of migrants.

The next four chapters constitute the empirical core of the thesis. Chapter 5 discusses the polity's and society's responses to immigration, as experienced by the migrants themselves. It begins with an account of how the migrants have been affected in practice by the restrictive policy framework, before and after regularisation, identifying common problems of discrimination, bureaucracy and unfair treatment. Their problematic relationship with the authorities is analysed. It then moves to an anatomy of xenophobic discourses and attitudes, commenting also on the emergence of positive initiatives from local civil-society groups.

Chapter 6 deals with the employment of migrant labour. Through the analysis of immigrants' experiences in the Greek labour market, it explains how they satisfy an increased demand for cheap and flexible labour. The evolutionary account of the migrants' conditions from their early years in Greece to the time of the fieldwork allows us to understand their employment trajectories, from situations of extreme exploitation to an overall improvement of their position in the labour market.

Chapter 7 is about space. It examines the basic issue of housing and draws a map of the residential and employment geographies of migration in Thessaloniki. It also looks at the migrants' experiences of urban space in terms of leisure and consumption, and comments on the importance of public space. It shows how, despite exclusionary mechanisms, the city has become a new home for migrants.

Chapter 8 refers to other spheres of the migrants' social life. It starts by addressing the extent to which they have been able to access basic services, like education and health, and the paths they undertook. It also looks at a series of aspects related to their general living conditions. It examines the role and character of formal and informal social networks and describes how migrant communities are beginning to emerge. It then deals with a range of material and perceptual/identificational issues related to the migrants' everyday practices and coping strategies.

Chapter 9 discusses the key findings from a theoretical perspective, returning to the broad issues raised early in the thesis. The multiple and contradictory pathways of immigrants towards incorporation are discussed, and the key explanatory factors are analysed. The narrative then turns to wider theoretical issues regarding the forms through which general processes of migration and globalisation are reflected in the Greek case. Aspects of the global-local interaction are identified with respect to the incorporation of migrants. Migration in the Balkan context is understood in a wider framework of transnational mobility. The spatial and identificational implications of the transformation of Thessaloniki into a multicultural city are finally explored with respect to the city's cosmopolitan past.

The thesis ends with a conclusion, Chapter 10, in which the main arguments are summarised, the strengths and weaknesses of the study are outlined, and important future steps to research are identified.

2 Locating our case in a world of change

After a brief introduction, this much longer chapter sets out the theoretical and geographical background of my thesis in more detail. It is in two main parts. In 2.1, I place immigration to Greece within the broader context of debates on globalisation, international migration and the links between the two. Although migration is increasingly regarded as a global phenomenon (Castles & Miller 1998), the precise linkages between migration and globalisation have rarely been explicitly analysed; I seek to do this here. In 2.2, the focus narrows in on Greece, Southern Europe and the Balkans. I look at the extent to which Greece conforms to what has been described by King (2000a) as the 'Southern European immigration model' and sketch out the main details of Greece's recent experience of immigration, including its (much delayed) policy responses.

2.1 Studying migration in the contemporary world

The objective of this first section is to place international migration within the present historical context and to explore the links between migration and globalisation. To do so, two things are necessary: firstly, to give an account of the major theories of migration; secondly, to define globalisation and describe briefly what it entails. Obviously, it is impossible to include a complete review of the vast literature on both topics. What is important and more relevant to the framing of this research is to build a conceptual framework for understanding globalisation through the critical reading of some key texts, keeping in mind that the target is to link globalisation processes with current migration trends. The explanatory limits of dominant theories are exposed in an attempt to address contemporary phenomena and to reflect on approaches to the study of migration in the global era.

2.1.1 *An overview of migration theories*

How is migration defined? Is it simply the movement of people from one place to another, or does it involve more parameters than the crossing of a distance in space? And how can it be explained? What are the factors producing it, and what are the motives leading people to leave their homes and look for another one somewhere else? There is no single theory for explaining international migration; a starting point, however, requires an understanding of its causes. An introduction to the most prominent migration theories is essential before any attempt to clarify my own point of view. My short overview briefly presents the two traditions that dominated migration theory for years: the neoclassical or voluntarist-functionalist, and the Marxist or historical-structuralist. Despite fundamental differences between the schools of thought that inspired them, both perspectives are characterised by a deterministic account of causes and effects (Papastergiadis 2000); therefore, I proceed by outlining more recent approaches that take into consideration aspects previously neglected. The focus is on the root factors of migration; the effects on, and implications for, host and sending societies and the migrants themselves are not addressed here. They are not underestimated though, and many are touched on throughout the thesis, especially in relation to the empirical findings[1]. I have drawn material from various key texts, but the well-known article by Massey et al. (1993) summarises and categorises most theories and has been used extensively[2].

The voluntarist-functionalist approach, inspired by *neoclassical economic theory*, defines migration as the outcome of individuals' decisions, based on the rational calculation of the factors pushing people out of their countries and/or those attracting them to the destination places. The article by Harris & Todaro (1970) is a key text of neoclassical migration studies. Individuals are assumed to act rationally within a world dominated by the laws of supply and demand; imbalances reach equilibrium through the unhindered operation of the market. At the macro level, the factors causing migration may vary from developmental gaps (e.g. different GDPs per capita), wage differentials and differences in employment opportunities, to international trade[3] and FDI[4]. At the micro level, individuals decide whether to migrate or not on the basis of a rational calculation of the migration costs (costs of travel or adaptation, financial or psychological, etc.) and the expected benefits from migration[5]. It is assumed that after emigration the effects on both host and sending economies (effects on wages, employment, living and consumption standards, human capital, etc.) will reduce the disparities between countries, and a new equilibrium will be achieved. The whole migration issue is thus seen within the wider context of economic development and growth, especially in the countries of origin, and of international trade. Governments should not intervene, according to this approach; the only way to reduce migration flows is through measures promoting the free operation of the market and free trade.

Neoclassical theory has been the target of much criticism questioning in depth most of its assumptions: the extent to which the 'rationally acting individual' is always the key actor in the migration process; the way equilibrium is achieved 'automatically' via market forces; the failure to explain the persistence of migration flows when disparities between countries reduce; the question whether free trade truly reduces migration flows instead of actually enhancing them; the ahistorical analysis that neglects the development of inequalities between regions and countries as an outcome of relations of dependency and exploitation. To an extent, part of this criticism has been developed within orthodox economics. For instance, the *new economics of migration* (see Stark 1991) stresses the role of the family/household in the migration decision: often larger social units, not only individuals, act collectively to maximise income, and most importantly to minimise risks and to loosen constraints associated with a variety of market failures. This approach also clearly distinguishes between the different characteristics of developed and developing economies, and it further explains why migration waves do not stop when wage differentials are eliminated, as they also depend on imperfect markets in the sending countries. The potential role of the government is here emphasised: state intervention for managing migration is welcome not only for regulating the labour markets, but also the credit, insurance and capital markets; the state should also have a more active role in income redistribution. Despite its valuable contribution, however, the 'new economics' theory shares many of the limitations of the neoclassical approach.

The main criticism of neoclassical theory comes from the *Marxist/structuralist* camp. In his own critique of political economy, Marx himself made a small contribution to the study of migration, which he saw as a phenomenon embedded in the capitalist mode of production: capital searches for exploitable labour worldwide, mobilising itself, but also labour, to move where capital needs it. In her classic Marxist analysis, Potts (1990) explained how the development of the world labour market has been connected to global capitalist expansion in two broad phases: firstly, the emergence and development of the world market for labour power under colonialism (with settlers, African slaves, Chinese and Indian coolies, etc.); and secondly, the industrialisation process and the direct incorporation of the capitalist metropole into the world labour market. Dependency and world-systems theorists[6] explained how the industrialised countries of the core tend to need labour for their productive and developmental needs, which is supplied to them from the dependent developing countries of the periphery in the form of migration: the 'surplus population' in the peripheries constitutes an 'industrial reserve army' which is deemed necessary for capitalist expansion. Migration is a result of the dislocations produced through the penetration of capitalist productive relations within peripheral societies and the appropriation of their productive factors (land, raw materials and labour) by capital and its agents (colonial and imperial powers, multinational firms, dependent governments). Moreover, the economic measures imposed by organisations such as the IMF or the World Bank may also have displacement effects, since they expose developing countries to international trade and investment, distorting thus indigenous productive and employment structures.

Further migration is generated through material and ideological links created by the processes of capitalist penetration, like transportation and communication infrastructure, colonial languages and religions, Westernised consumerist lifestyles, etc. (Sassen 1999). In general, once a migration flow has been initiated there are several factors contributing to its continuation, leading to a *cumulative causation* effect (Massey et al. 1993). Out-migration and return may negatively affect the distribution of income or land, the regional distribution of human capital and the organisation of agrarian production in sending countries. The literature on migration, return and development has contributed much in analysing such possibilities (e.g. Swanson 1979; King 2000b). For example, the selectivity of the migration process usually results in the devastation of migration areas in terms of human capital, since these are emptied of the dynamic young and skilled labour force and thus their productivity shrinks. Moreover, return migration may create situations of relative deprivation, i.e. worsening of the position of the poor in relation to the wealthier migrants' families or returnees (rather than becoming actually poorer), which further distorts an uneven income distribution. The unproductive use of land bought by migrants' families and returnees in agrarian communities (e.g. as a symbol of status) distorts the employment structure, leading to local unemployment. All these may result in continuing or reproducing migration flows.

Despite their essential differences, most of the above theories tend to overemphasise the role of supply. Whether limited on the supply side or focusing on the operation of the system as a whole, traditional theories fail to understand a series of existing problems, for instance, the phenomenon of having immigration inflows to countries with high unemployment. A more comprehensive approach has been proposed on the basis of dual labour market theory (Piore 1979), focusing on the demand side by analysing labour markets in receiving countries. M. J. Piore explained why developed countries seem to have a constant need for cheap labour supply, partly covered by migrants, as an outcome of labour-market segmentation, which results from the dual character of the capital-labour relationship. Accordingly, there exist a capital-intensive sector (with stable employment, skilled jobs, better wages, training, trade-union protection, social security and prospects) and a labour-intensive one (with unstable employment, unskilled, low-status and badly paid jobs, no training, no union protection and without social security). Three basic features of developed economies contribute further to this increased demand for migrant workers: structural inflation, motivational problems and the demography of labour supply. Sassen's analysis of labour markets and employment structures in the so-called global cities (1991; 1996) is largely based on this analytical framework. Dual labour market theory generally concludes that governments cannot reduce immigration flows without deep organisational and structural economic reforms. Its weakness lies in the loss of the whole picture of the migration process by neglecting the reasons making people leave their countries; also, it is quite difficult to situate the fragmented structure of labour markets empirically.

Deterministic theories of causes and effects fail to address the determinants of migration once it has started, in time and space, and to link micro issues with the macro level of analysis. Meso-level approaches propose frameworks to connect the structural context and the individual experience by emphasising the role of social ties, social networks and social capital, or even institutions, in the migration process. The institutional school contributed by stressing the role of humanitarian organisations, on the one hand, and profit-making enterprises such as the trafficking networks, on the other, in shaping contemporary migratory patterns as a result of the contradiction between growing numbers of people 'on the move' and increasing barriers to migration (Massey et al. 1993). *Network theory* sees migration as an individual or collective decision process, whereby the acts of migrants at one point influence future migration decisions. Networks reduce the costs and risks of migration and thus increase the likelihood of further migration (chain migration), making it 'progressively independent of the factors that originally caused it' (Massey et al. 1993: 449). Social networks function as 'sources for the acquisition of scarce means, such as capital and information' and as 'social bridges' (Portes 1995: 8, 22): between those who migrated and those left behind, between different members of a migrant community, and between immigrants and locals; they constitute sources of social capital that support migrants in the host country. The recent debates on contemporary diasporas and *transnationalism* are based on the role of networks (Smith & Guarnizo 1998; Vertovec & Cohen 1999; Kivisto 2001). Transnational networks, relationships and practices of today, facilitated by transport, communication and information technologies, point to new patterns of mobility, involving constant movement backwards and forwards, rather than the traditional migration cycle.

Ultimately, there is a tendency in both theory and empirical research to link different perspectives, to look at parallel phenomena from different angles, to take into account various factors and abandon single disciplinary approaches. *Migration systems theories* (School 1998), for example, examine migration between two (or more) specific countries (or two or more groups of countries) by focusing on various factors and by looking at several links (economic, political, social, demographic, cultural). Such links determine migration patterns between the countries involved on the basis of a complex set of push and pull factors and through various kinds of networks and institutions, all playing a role in the ongoing migration process. Clearly then, migration theories have been evolving to follow the development of the phenomena in question, reflecting also the period in which they are born. Ammassari & Black (2001) categorise migration studies into three main generations: (a) studies exploring the push and pull factors for migration; (b) studies emphasising the structural relationship between core and peripheral countries, connected in a system characterised by flows of capital, labour, goods, services and information which are facilitated by historical and cultural links and the operation of migrant networks; and (c) studies on contemporary international migration in the context of globalisation, where areas of origin and of destination are linked together in transnational spaces. The characteristics of migration in the contemporary era and their implications for theory and research are going to be discussed after a brief introduction to the globalisation debate.

2.1.2 *Globalisation: key issues and a conceptual framework*

There are several ways of interpreting globalisation (Held & MacGrew 1999). Within the vast academic literature, various perspectives propose different understandings and areas of focus. Sklair (1999) categorises the main approaches to globalisation according to four main clusters of studies: world systems theory[7], the global culture approach[8], the global society model[9] and the global capitalism perspective[10]. These perspectives are not necessarily contradictory, since they tend to highlight different aspects. Obviously, they come from competing theoretical traditions, and perhaps they imply different political-ideological standpoints; nevertheless, they may all contribute positively to a conceptual understanding of globalisation. In addition, it has been argued that globalisation is only a phase in a wider process of transition towards a new form of social organisation. For example, Castells' (1996: 1-2) description of the 'network society' highlights characteristics that are also addressed by the theories mentioned above: 1) globalisation of strategically decisive economic activities; 2) flexibility and instability of work and individualisation of labour; 3) a culture of virtual reality, constructed by a pervasive, interconnected and diversified media system; and 4) transformation of the material foundations of life, space and time, through the constitution of a 'space of flows' and of 'timeless time' as expressions of dominant activities and controlling elites.

There are strong arguments against the globalisation thesis[11]. Some challenge the exaggerations of globalisation proponents, providing evidence, for instance, suggesting that the current phase of the world economy is actually less 'global' than during the late nineteenth and early twentieth centuries (Hirst & Thompson 1996). Others claim that the concept itself is artificially constructed in order to provide a satisfactory description of the state of the world in the post-Cold War era and/or to serve the dominant ideology of neoliberalism and the interests of the economic, political and intellectual elites (Vergopoulos 1999). In the sceptics' criticism, globalisation is often misleadingly confused with 'internationalisation'; it is therefore essential to distinguish between the two terms[12]. Internationalisation may not involve any qualitative change, but implies a quantitative growth and geographic expansion of national economies, as well as the openness and integration of markets. In fact, internationalisation, mostly concerning economic processes, is both a dimension and an indicator of globalisation, which is a far broader and more multidimensional process. One could observe additional trends indicating that something has indeed changed; such trends cannot be traced by economistic quantitative accounts, nor can they be seen simply as 'constructions' of the dominant rhetoric.

Qualitative changes in the dynamics of the world system are so important as to suggest that we are currently living through a period of transition. Such changes have occurred in the organisation of the production process and the geography of production; in the character of labour and capital, and the relationship between the two; in the declining power of nation-states and the increased role of TNCs and other institutions on the international scene; and in the forms of cultural production and interaction. Globalisation is the prominent term describing the current phase, and as such it certainly serves the prevailing neoliberal ideology in the way it is used by the media, think-tanks and policy makers, though it entails far more than being simply a terminological or ideological tool. Multiplying and intensifying cross-border flows (of capital, goods, services and people, but also of media images, ideas, or pollution) are key indicators of a new historical phase; transnational networks (of corporations, markets, governments, NGOs, crime syndicates or cultural communities) are its key organising structure, and modern information and communication technologies are its key tools (Castles 2000: 271).

Information is now the main source of productivity and power (Castells 1996). Flows of information, as well as capital, goods, services and people, which increasingly characterise the contemporary world, are facilitated and speeded up by technological innovations stimulated by the microelectronics revolution. Money and information can now be moved between distant places by simply pressing a key on a computer. Borders are increasingly penetrable to trade and investment, and some national economic instruments are crucially controlled by supranational organisations; only migration is partly held down, dependent on rigid nation-state regulations. Common cultural values and sets of rules are being disseminated on a global scale. Neoliberalism has emerged as the only dominant ideology seeking to give answers and drive evolution. Neoliberal policies, however, build on the defeat of the alternative paradigm that divided the world until recently and on the successive retreat of anti-systemic movements as a majority choice. The collapse of the authoritarian regimes and centralised economic systems in the former Eastern Bloc (notably without any significant social unrest) and China's transition to capitalism[13] (without major political reforms) have led to the dismantling of the post-war geopolitical balance of the Cold War and made possible the incorporation of these regions in the global market system[14].

Two additional elements are indicative of the contemporary period and are often highlighted as both symptoms and outcomes of globalisation processes. One has to do with the shifting role and significance of the nation-state; the other concerns the new form of the global-local relationship. The nation-state, as a historical model of territorial-political organisation connected to capitalist development, was based on three organic elements: the nation, the state and a corresponding geographic territory (Hobsbawm 1992). Today, these elements are not that distinctly defined: many of the state's traditional powers have been eroded and transferred beyond the national level; its ethnic and cultural homogeneity is undermined, its legitimacy weakens, its autonomy and sovereignty are seriously challenged[15]. This crisis of the nation-state results from its failure to manage successfully matters at the international level, such as capital movements, environmental protection and the guarantee of human rights (Strange 1999)[16]. It now appears 'too small to deal with the big matters and too big to deal with the small ones' (Klein 1997). As a result, the local space seems to separate from the national one and come into direct interplay with the global: places, independently from states, are increasingly interconnected in multilateral networks (Castells 1996); cities and communities now compete directly with each other in an uneven international terrain (Budd 1998). Some emerge as crucial intersections in transnational spaces and become global or regional centres of economic, political and cultural activity. Global flows are filtered through specific places, where international forces are reflected or expressed by taking particular forms. The major cities of the world have achieved global reach (Sassen 1991); they are in more direct contact with each other than with the rest of their national economies; they have become administrative centres of the global economy and concentrate the headquarters of most major corporations. The polarisation between financial/cultural services and labour-intensive activities is represented in these large cosmopolitan centres more than anywhere else.

It is crucial to acknowledge the historicity of globalisation and understand it as a historical process: its historical origins are to be traced in modernity and capitalism[17]. In his pioneering work on globalisation, Robertson (1992) has seen its dynamics developing together with the expansion of Europe (economic, geographic, political, scientific, cultural, etc.)[18], certainly connected to the evolution of modernity. Thus, globalisation can be understood as a consequence of modernity, constantly unfolding to gradually embrace the entire world; Giddens (1991) describes it as a phenomenon of late modernity (which is 'inherently globalising'). Similarly, the economic dynamics of globalisation have been structurally embedded in the process of the development and expansion of the world capitalist system, whose origins lie back in fifteenth-century Europe (Wallerstein 1974). Its seeds can be found in capital's non-national nature (Marx) and in the international division of labour under capitalism (classical economists). The development of a world labour market went hand in hand with capitalist expansion (Potts 1990), passing from colonialism to the industrial revolution, the making of nation-states and the twentieth-century labour migrations. Industrialisation and the development of national economies in Western Europe over the nineteenth century led to the establishment of an international system of nation-states, which enjoyed an early form of economic 'globalisation' (Hirst & Thompson 1996). Imperialism, as a phase of late nineteenth- and early twentieth-century capitalism, had many common features with contemporary globalisation[19], but the period after the First World War was characterised by the prevalence of monopoly capitalism and national economic development.

How has the world economy arrived at its current stage? The basic changes that led to what appears to be a linear trend towards the gradual 'unification' of the globe[20] have been embedded in a wider process of restructuring (of production and consumption, capital and labour) on a global scale. The turning point is almost indisputably located in the changes brought by the economic crisis that followed the 1973 oil shock. The dramatic increases in energy costs in the developed countries generated this crisis, with long-lasting effects: slowing-down of productivity, declining profitability, rising unemployment. The Fordist model[21] had reached a dead-end. The labour process and international economic relations were the basic factors underlying this deep structural crisis (Allen 1996). The first (supply) factor was related to the inability of mass-production methods to realise further productivity gains within manufacturing, as well as their limited applicability to the growing services sector. The latter (demand) factor had to do with the changing patterns of post-war global demand, since, with the devaluation of the dollar (and the breaking up of the Bretton Woods monetary system), international competition intensified (as countries like Japan and West Germany saw their economic power augmenting), leading to increasing global economic instability.

The capitalist system found a way out of the crisis through the radical transformation of its inner dynamic: although capitalist productive relations remain the same, deep qualitative changes occurred in the structures of the system, stimulating productivity and profitability. In the West, the new post-Fordist regime of flexible accumulation presupposes efficiency and adaptability with a focus on technology, quality, planning, innovation and 'just in time' strategies, which now constitute critical elements for the competitiveness of enterprises (Murray 1989). Restructuring involves three major shifts in the structure and organisation of labour and production (King & Rybaczuk 1993: 182-183)[22]: (a) from the Fordist system of mass production for mass consumption (economies of scale) to the post-Fordist regime of flexible production in small and specialised units (economies of scope); (b) from the prevalence of heavy industry to the increasing importance of high-tech manufacturing; and (c) the labour process has undergone important changes, mainly due to increased automation and informationalisation of production. In addition, we can identify three basic dimensions of the transformations brought by the restructuring process.

The first concerns the inner dynamics of the system. Contemporary capitalism is marked by the transition from the industrial to the informational mode of development (Castells 1989), since knowledge and information have replaced energy-machinery as central elements in the accumulation process and have become strategic resources, apart from being products themselves (Castells 1989; 1996; Allen 1996)[23]. Informationalisation shrinks social and spatial distances and compresses time, facilitating the development of networks between corporations (Castells 1996). New technologies intensify the mobility and speed of financial capital and have contributed to the consequent emergence of new financial systems, markets and instruments (Harvey 1989). The bulk of financial capital has grown in relation to the growth rate of the real economy, and it is increasingly invested in 'parasitic' activities (Fröbel et al. 1983; Vergopoulos 1999). In parallel, the tertiary sector grows in size and importance as financial, research and managerial activities become central to the operation of the system, but also as the demand for personal and low-skilled services increases, especially in cities (Sassen 1991; 1996), and the voluntary sector also augments (Rifkin 1995). Informationalisation, de-industrialisation, tertiarisation and the domination of financial capital have led scholars to emphasise the post-industrial character of economic restructuring. To an extent, material production has lost part of its importance, since 'what is increasingly produced are not material objects, but signs', i.e. information, brands, trademarks and labels (Lash & Urry 1994: 4).

The second dimension has to do with changes in class relations as these reflect the transformation of production structures and relations, and they are also manifested in new consumption patterns. Class opposition is no longer based solely on the possession and control of the means of production, but increasingly on the access to information and its uses (Touraine 1971). In addition, the patterns of social stratification have changed significantly and traditional class divisions are not that easily distinguishable today[24]. Increased income aspirations, higher living standards and welfare regimes in developed countries have led to the formation of a wide middle class, in terms of both income and mentality (Gorz 1980), with two important effects on the patterns of demand: consumers now look more at the quality, rather than the cost, of products and services (Reyneri & Baganha 1999), while the demand for personal services, both basic and highly specialised ones, is increasing (Sassen 1996)[25]. This latter development has contributed to the formation of new 'servile' classes, offering personal and other services to middle-class strata as well as to the traditional elites (Gorz 1980; Sassen 1996). As a consequence, labour markets are increasingly characterised by segmentation and dualism[26], which lead to the casualisation of employment relations, to new forms of employment (temporary, part-time) and hence to new types of workers (Sassen 1996; Psimmenos 1995). Together with joblessness and structural unemployment, these developments contribute to new types of social polarisation, which reproduce capitalist productive relations through a situation of constant tension between a narrow economic elite and a growing population at the bottom of the pyramid, with a fragile middle class in between.

The third dimension is political and relates to changes in both governmental policies and forms of social resistance. The mainstream policy discourse and practice shifted from Keynesianism, characteristic of the Fordist era, to neoliberalism. Increasingly, Western governments have adopted policies promoting 'less state' and deregulating the markets. This transition came as an outcome of the ideological and political 'defeat' of the alternative (socialist) paradigm, as it had been practically adopted (in a rather distorted way) in the countries of the erstwhile Eastern Bloc. But it is also connected to the crisis of the state, both material (since it lost its ability to autonomously control the national economy, and it is further undermined by globalisation forces) and ideological (since it is losing legitimacy in people's minds and political behaviour). On the other hand, social resistance and alternative paradigms shifted from traditional working-class struggle to identity politics and new social movements (Touraine 1971; Castells 1997). New claims, which have their origins in the 1960s tradition – women's emancipation, environmental protection, consumers' rights, racial equality, human rights – have emerged in the agenda of contemporary social movements, and are currently interconnecting in a growing global network of grassroots bodies and NGOs to challenge the neoliberal character of globalisation[27].

Identifying the qualitatively new elements that globalisation brings should not lead to exaggerations regarding the importance and role of 'new' phenomena. Endogenous (historical) processes should not be underestimated: states and places are undisputedly shaped by the history of the country to which they belong, and they are linked to its fate; the nation-state is transforming, rather than fading (Mann 1993). In addition, the information-based society 'is no more post-industrial than the industrial society was post-agrarian' (Castells 1989: 367). Even the new high-tech and information industries themselves require some unskilled and semi-skilled labour for both productive and supportive jobs, such as office cleaning, catering facilities, etc. (Sassen 1996; Samers 1998). Capital-intensive strategies, information-based production and automation coexist with labour-intensive activities, often in the same economic sectors. Industrial capital might have lost its centrality, but the global industrial output is augmenting: it is rather industrial employment that shrinks, especially with the de-industrialisation process in the West and the relocation of heavy industry outside the erstwhile traditional centres of industrial development (Samers 1998). On a global scale, mass production has not ceased, but it is technically more automated, organisationally more flexible, and geographically diffused all over the world, so that we can refer to a global Fordist system (Lipietz 1987).

The global economy is being both geographically and institutionally reorganised. The past few decades have been marked by a trend towards the liberalisation of economic activity, trade and investment. Given the international hierarchy of power and development, the main beneficiaries are clearly the wealthier actors, those who control the rules of the game. Investment is relocated in favour of developed economies (Fröbel et al. 1983) and, despite liberalisation, trade takes place on the basis of international agreements (GATT, NAFTA, etc.) that seem to impose a kind of new protectionism and control by Europe, the US and Japan, disadvantaging developing countries (Hettne 1990)[28]. Today, more than ever, capital can choose where to locate: not only as a result of the speed and instantaneity of financial transactions, but also due to the mobility of productive capital. Multinational and transnational corporations have grown enormously in size and 'their global reach has expanded dramatically' (Sklair 1999: 146-147)[29]. Such companies have achieved the spatial and organisational separation of labour-intensive practices and material production from administrative-managerial and research functions (Findlay 1996) through several increasingly popular strategies (outsourcing, subcontracting, etc.). Administration, management and research activities, and the high-tech industries are concentrated mostly in the core areas of the developed world and in global cities (Sassen, 1991). Labour-intensive production is relocated to the peripheries of the traditional industrial centres and increasingly to the South and, since 1989, to the East. Given the mobility of capital, the position of countries or regional blocks within the world system and international migration trends, global economic restructuring presupposes and imposes a new international division of labour (Fröbel et al. 1983).

As the crisis becomes a permanent structural element of the system, the new division of labour generates inequalities both between and within states. The West is the centre of the dynamics of change, but its social net, characterised by relative cohesion in the post-war era, is now undermined. At the same time, globalisation and restructuring affect the rest of the world in similarly contradictory ways. The (erstwhile) 'Second World' faces serious economic and social problems, generated by the process of transition; Western states and multinationals see it as a virgin market with a potentially exploitable cheap labour force. Unemployment has risen and living conditions have fallen below pre-1989 acceptable standards; social polarisation is deepening, with the emergence of small indigenous elites composed of those who have grasped new opportunities or inherited privileges from their bureaucratic past, among them many who have connections with organised crime[30]. On the other hand, the chronic problems of the so-called 'Third World' persist, despite development programmes adopted during recent decades. Conflicts, famine and malnutrition (sub-Saharan Africa), demographic explosion and its consequences (China, India) and the debt crisis (Latin America) are the basic problems that less-developed countries are facing at present (Hettne 1990). Although some areas have experienced positive economic change, resulting in a rearrangement of their peripheral position within the world system[31], in most cases, restructuring has altered production structures with distorting socio-economic effects. The reawakening of aggressive nationalisms and religious fundamentalisms has partly replaced previous ideological paradigms; new oppressive regimes, wars and social conflicts in many areas exhibit few signs of a way out of this crisis.

To conclude, globalisation remains a phase in the ongoing processes of capitalist development, but the qualitative changes it entails are indicative of a period of global transformation. To assume, however, a homogeneous integrated global economy would be an exaggeration; and to take recent developments as consolidated, definite situations suggesting that we live in a brand new world is blindness at best. It is rather wiser to talk about emerging trends consisting of bigger quantities and new qualities: new and old forms coexist in contradictory ways and are fused or interconnected in both time and space. After all, the new always brings malfunctions and destabilisation, creating fragmented patterns of development and producing contradictions; globalisation concerns a set of processes, which at the same time homogenise and differentiate[32]. New and older forms are both part of the system; in times of crises its internal dynamics stimulate new discoveries, new mechanisms, new ways of exploiting labour and natural resources, but also new ways of life and social resistance. Globalisation is more of a trend towards the internationalisation of economies, integration of markets, multiplication of flows, unification of networks, fusion of cultures, etc. Contemporary international migration is part of it: it is shaped by, and partly shapes its époque, and it is impossible for it to be studied in isolation.

2.1.3 *Migration and globalisation: exploring the links*

Scholars have recently suggested that a careful study of contemporary migration should take into account the changes brought by globalisation. Papastergiadis (2000: Ch. 1) has talked about the 'twin processes' of migration and globalisation; Castles & Miller (1998: 5) have written: 'international migration is part of a transnational revolution that is reshaping society and politics around the globe.' At the turn of the century, migration has emerged as a central issue on the international economic and political scene and has become a major factor in societal change and a crucial area of policy for many countries (Castles & Miller 1998; Castles 2000). Globalisation and capitalist restructuring have altered the patterns of international migration, but they are themselves affected by the new multidimensional migration trends. Exploring the links between migration and globalisation is not just one more interesting but useless academic riddle. It can stimulate a worthy debate and provide a framework for a better understanding not only of contemporary migration trends, but also of an aspect of the world in which we live. And it may also reveal certain implications for both policy-making and everyday life.

The causes of emigration from the South and the East of the globe are clearly rooted in the problems briefly mentioned earlier: inequalities between and within countries, together with political (wars, oppressive governments), cultural (gender inequalities, oppression of religious beliefs), and environmental (natural disasters, environmental degradation) factors. But new types of mobility are also multiplying across the globe and remain relatively little analysed by scholarly research: specialised transients and world tourists, skilled migrants, single women, young 'adventurers' and international students[33]. The diversity and intensity of today's population movements, despite barriers to immigration imposed by the West (to migrants from developing and 'transition' countries), suggest that labour, too, seems to follow the rules of the market; though it is not strictly 'the market' that determines contemporary migration patterns, but rather a variety of factors associated with a wide range of causes and motivations. Migrants, in the broad sense of the term, clearly have their position within the new international division of labour (Cohen 1987; Harris 1995), although on their own they do not form a homogenous global work force. Moreover, migrants and a variety of people 'on the move', and their actions, practices and relationships, increasingly characterise and shape societal forms and norms in an ever-growing number of countries, cities and places. Although old forms coexist with new ones, the characteristics of contemporary international migration differ from those of the past. The prevailing trends can be summarised as follows[34]:

1. The increasing heterogeneity of both sending and receiving countries, reflecting a new geography of international migration[35] (King 1993), and the growing interdependence between countries of origin and destination through economic, political and cultural bonds (Castles & Miller 1998; Sassen 1999).
2. The variety of migration channels and routes, such as the role of trafficking networks (IOM 2001; 2002), and the degree and scale of 'illegal' migration (Ghosh 1998), as a result of tightened controls and restrictive polices, and the increasing importance of several forms of migration less represented in the past.
3. The changing characteristics of the migrants themselves: (a) notably, it is not mainly the poorer who migrate (Castles & Miller 1998); (b) 'brain drain' trends are being generated (Harris 1995); (c) mobility of elites and specialists is also on an upward trend (Findlay 1995); (d) the participation of women as independent actors in the migration process is growing (Phizacklea 1998).
4. The shifting patterns of immigrant employment in destination places (Piore 1979), especially in cities, as migrants are increasingly employed in the service sector (Pugliese 1993), and, to a large extent, in personal services (Sassen 1996a), including informal (i.e.

jobs performed in the secondary labour market) or even illegal activities (e.g. sex work, drug-dealing, etc.)[36].

5. The emergence of new ethnic minorities (Castles et al. 1984) challenging the traditional basis of nation-states (Soysal 1994) and giving birth to hybrid deterritorialised identities (Papastergiadis 2000), and the generation of transnational practices and mobility among 'new' and older migrants, leading to the consolidation of 'diasporic' communities across transnational spaces (Smith & Guarnizo 1998; Vertovec & Cohen 1999).

Again, it is important to stress the qualitative aspects: exploring the new trends requires the analysis of structures and processes rather than focusing on numbers. After all, numbers and percentages are very poor means to express social change: despite the increase in the total number of migrants all over the world, from 75.2 million in 1965 to 174.8 million in 2000, their share in the global population grew by only 0.6 per cent (Zlotnik 1999: Table 1; UNPD 2002: Table 1). In recent research, Tapinos & Delaunay (2000) have argued that a comparison of available statistical data does not show any increase in the migration flows, comparing them to the flows of capital, goods and services during the last three decades. As expected, however, statistics are about the registered 'foreign born' or 'migrant' populations; they cannot always count the numerous 'undocumented' nor the children of migrants who have been born and grow up in the host countries. Moreover, there exist several other forms of migration that remain unrecorded: students who work during and/or after their studies; tourists or travellers who stay for employment in the destination place; cross-border 'shuttle' migrants, etc. Apart from the insufficiency of data, the relatively low growth of the global migrant population is explained partly by the paradoxical context in which migration takes place today. While the trend is towards the liberalisation of markets for goods, services and capital, with migration what happens is rather the contrary: although many political and technical barriers to the movement of people have been eliminated, dominant policy trends in developed countries at present clearly restrict immigration. From a historical point of view, the largest (voluntary) migration wave remains the one that took place between 1815-1914. Even so, migration flows are ultimately rapidly increasing: in the last decade (1990-2000) the number of people residing outside their country of birth grew by 13.5 per cent (UNPD 2002: 2).

Contemporary migration is part and parcel of globalisation processes, and the characteristics presented above clearly suggest the multiplication, diversification and transnationalisation of flows. From a geographical point of view, mapping global migration has become an extremely difficult task; if there exists a global migration system, then this is definitely a non-linear one. It would be impossible to draw the turbulent flows of today: the diversity of paths and the complexity of movements would lead us to a rather chaotic map of global migration (Papastergiadis 2000). However, it is not only the structure and patterns of movement that are changing, but also crucially the economic, political and cultural implications of contemporary migration processes. From a geopolitical perspective, migration has now become a global issue: sending countries increasingly need to combine their emigration and return policies with their development projects; receiving states face growing immigration pressures and have to deal with the existing migrant populations. At the economic level, as we have seen, globalisation stimulates important systemic changes (internationalisation, informalisation, tertiarisation, changing structural and organisational patterns, etc.). The key task in exploring the relationship between globalisation and migration is to look for the linkages between these changes and the new characteristics of international migration presented above. Indeed, the changes in immigrant employment, the emergence of new paths and new types of migrants, etc., reflect developments in the global economy that are expressed similarly in different social formations and suggest that migratory processes today take place within an increasingly globalising environment. Migration is thus part of the dynamics of globalisation, as it has a structural function in the dynamics of the capitalist system (Cohen 1987; Harris 1995): although labour is less mobile than capital, contemporary capitalist globalisation creates the conditions for the 'transnationalisation' of labour (Portes 1997).

Moreover, migration 'involves a stretching across space of both the social relations of production and the more personal networks of individual people and ethnic communities' (King 1995: 7). Migrants establish human links between places and their interpersonal networks provide a basis for social action in transnational spaces (Vertovec & Cohen 1999), where cultures are often fused and identities are hybridised (Papastergiadis 2000). Transnational practices increasingly characterise processes of migration and integration, and many migrants today cannot fit within past conceptions of the permanent or long-term 'settler' but actually lead lives between 'here' and 'there'; transnational flows, involving frequent moves between countries or communities, are more and more the case for growing numbers of people (Smith & Guarnizo 1998; Vertovec & Cohen 1999). The advent of transnational migration today has led scholars to refer to a form of 'globalisation from below' (Portes 1997). Clearly, past migrations together with recent technological advances made possible the generation and spread of various forms of transnationalism. Such developments have partly undermined the territorial, cultural and political foundations of the traditional nation-state: not only are national borders increasingly porous to human flows, despite the barriers, but also the homogeneity of Western nations is no more and the patterns of social and political membership are moving beyond the national level (Soysal 1994; Sassen 1996b), questioning the context and content of citizenship (Baubock 2002). Global or 'globalising' cities (Sassen 1991) are attracting various categories of migrants, hence they increasingly become multicultural entities characterised by pluralism and diversity (Papastergiadis 2000). Globalisation and migration forces are uniquely reflected in large cosmopolitan centres, where they produce polarisation and tensions (Sassen 1996a), but also coexistence and fusions that result in 'many cities within a city'. Thus urban societies become mirrors of the world (Mendieta 2001).

In this globalising world, characterised by constant interaction and increasing interdependence between distant societies, processes and patterns of international migration are becoming more complex than ever before. Migration is now a global phenomenon, one of the visible aspects of globalisation and one of its major forces. Talking about 'the globalisation of migration' would certainly be an exaggeration, since much of today's transnational mobility remains local or regional in scale (as the case of Albania and Greece illustrates; see, for instance, Baldwin-Edwards 2004b; King & Mai 2004). However, the brief analysis in this chapter clearly shows that, today more than ever, migration processes have intensified and have far more implications than the simple spatial movement and resettlement of people, whether temporary or permanent. It affects both sending and receiving societies, and the migrants, of course, but also those left behind and the host populations. A multifaceted process in itself, and yet a dynamic one, international migration shapes and is being shaped by globalisation forces, through several kinds of flows and various linkages and forms of exchange between countries or places, cultures, economies and people. The study of migration today can be a challenging and exciting experience, since it may be seen as a ground for understanding broader or related phenomena. But it also constitutes an area that may stimulate rich theoretical discussions and can offer potential for methodological and analytical innovation. Past theoretical traditions, analytical methods and conceptual frameworks now seem inadequate to explain the changing patterns of global migration and the phenomena associated with it. Their understanding of social change is rather poor, as they appear inefficient in describing the various forms of flows, the new types of migrants, the linkages that are being established, the networks operating at several levels, the hybridisation of cultures, identities and social forms.

Massey et al. (1993) have argued that the theories presented earlier are not necessarily contradictory, since they are concerned with different problems, examine different levels of analysis (macro, micro, meso), or are drawn out of different empirical cases. A comprehensive approach to contemporary migration processes should thus be based on a combination of different perspectives, or, at least, of those that are more appropriate to the specific interests of a particular research. The history of migration studies clearly shows an evolution and enrichment of migration theory over time (Ammassari & Black 2001), through influences from both the social context in which it is produced and the useful contributions of various fields in the social sciences. Therefore, interdisciplinary approaches can be useful in enlightening aspects of the phenomenon that have remained in darkness as a result of academic overspecialisation. As King (2002: 101) puts it, addressing the issues of contemporary migration requires a comparative and 'interdisciplinary approach, which also recognises paradigmatic plurality and the value of mixed methodologies'. Comparative research is necessary not simply for assessing similarities and differences between migrant groups, countries or localities. It is crucial for understanding the relevance of the broader context as it might be reflected in common features and processes, and for capturing the intrinsic beauty of possibly unique cases as well as the novelty of potential emerging trends.

As the global context is rapidly and radically transforming, social science should break away from the certainties of the past and from the linear deterministic perceptions of reality. Studying migration today will reveal the complexities of social processes that are increasingly interconnected. As processes of societal transformation across the world take place with the advent of globalisation, it is necessary to understand the dialectics of migration; i.e. the relationship between migration and social change on all possible scales (global, regional, national, local), all levels (economic, social, political, cultural, spatial), and the patterns of interaction between these. Needless to say, it is crucial to incorporate a critical element into any kind of analysis: critical towards those who control economic and political power; to the way 'things work' and to the form they appear in, as well as to the way they are commonly perceived. Lastly, one needs to be careful not to lose the most important element involved in the migration process: the human one. As King (1995: 31) has written, the study of migration may reveal the 'inequalities and human dramas that lie at the heart of the process of globalisation'. Linking the structural context and the individual experience of migration not only underlines the central role of the inequality structures, but also implies that attention should be focused on the personal experiences and the voice of the migrants themselves.

But what is the relevance of the above rather theoretical and abstract analysis to the specificities of recent immigration to Greece and the particularities of the case studied in the thesis? How do globalisation forces affect given social formations and people in specific localities? It should be stated beforehand that such an impact is rather indirect and relates to specific manifestations of global processes at the local/national level (e.g. the way Greece has been experiencing the rise in the global demand for cheap labour; see Psimmenos 1995), or how it is filtered through regional 'layers', which obviously play a more important role than abstract mechanisms of the global economy (e.g. Greece's EU membership and the process of European integration, the Southern European developmental particularities, the new regional position of Greece in the post-1989 Balkan space). These issues are examined in the first few pages of the section that follows and they are revisited at the end of the thesis in Chapter 9.

2.2 The Greek case in international perspective

Several characteristics of contemporary global and European migration can be observed in the Greek case (see Fassmann & Münz 1994; Castles & Miller 1998; Koser & Lutz 1998; Muus 2001). Firstly, the diversity in the origin of the migrants: the 2001 census recorded nationals of more than 200 countries, although the 'East-West' migration patterns (which for Greece are actually from North to South in compass terms) are dominant by far. Secondly, there exist various categories of migrants: returning former emigrants or diaspora Greeks and repatriated political refugees; highly skilled professionals and unskilled labour immigrants; international students and tourist workers; refugees and asylum seekers; sex workers; and transit migrants heading to other EU countries. Women, but also children, constitute important shares in the migrant 'stock', whether as victims of trafficking, dependent family members or independent actors. The channels, routes and types of migration are heterogeneous: visa overstays of tourists and students, family migration, cross-border circular and seasonal movements, trafficking and large-scale clandestine migration. Lastly, immigrants' employment in the service sector appears to be of particular importance and the informal sector plays a crucial role in their economic integration.

The transformation of Greece into a new destination for international migrants coincided with a series of parallel developments that have signalled processes of increasing exposure to global trends. In fact, migration can be seen as one of the factors indicating Greece's particular experience of globalisation; other factors may include:

- The redefinition of the regional position and role of Greece in the Balkans, in the advent of post-1989 developments in Eastern Europe and the former USSR.
- The ongoing process of European integration and the transfer of certain powers to European bodies, especially in respect to Greece's membership in the Common Market, the eurozone and the Schengen Area.
- The general trends of restructuring and internationalisation of the national economy, as expressed, for example, by: the privatisation of key state companies and the process of de-industrialisation; the liberalisation of exchange rates; the growing amount of Greek capital invested abroad and the relocation of production; the further tertiarisation of the economy, particularly regarding banking, finance, business and IT services, etc.

Within this context, Greece is radically transforming into a multicultural society, with all the implications this might have for the economic, spatial, cultural and political spheres of social life. Again, recent trends and developments generally resemble past and present European experiences, including social tensions and xenophobic hostility or socio-spatial segregation and exclusion at several levels, but also informal or organised forms of solidarity and reciprocity, as well as various transnational types of mobility and practice. Above all, however, the Greek experience of immigration shares common characteristics with the rest of the Southern EU member states. This section proceeds with details of the Southern European transition from emigration to immigration. The uniqueness of Greece within the Southern European immigration model (King 2000a), partly resulting from its geographic position in the Balkans, is also addressed. Section 2.2.2 offers a description of current immigration trends with reference to key characteristics of the Greek economy and Greek society. The chapter ends with an overview of the development of the immigration policy framework.

2.2.1 *Greece in Southern Europe and the Balkan dimension*

Much of what is associated today with globalisation takes a particular form in groups of countries sharing similar socio-economic characteristics. The transformation of Southern Europe into a new destination region for migrants during the last few decades is related to the changing character of the international division of labour and the important shift of the region's position within it (King & Rybaczuk 1993; King et al. 1997; Castles & Miller 1998; King 2000a). The parallel emigration histories of Portugal, Italy, Spain and Greece are not the only common feature that has marked their similar patterns of social and economic development. Despite their particularities, regional exceptions and different national histories, these countries share common contradictions indicating their distinct path to capitalist development, reflected in similar productive and employment structures as well as in similar political and cultural characteristics (Giner 1985; Leontidou 1990; Mingione 1995).

Giner (1985: 310) has identified four common historical contradictions of Southern European societies: (a) cultural universalism and local and kinship bonds of patronage; (b) religious legitimation of public institutions and militant secularism; (c) classless and doctrinaire political commitments and uncompromisingly class-bound ideologies; and (d) dependent industrialisation and a substantial degree of national capitalism. On these grounds, Mingione (1995) has argued that Southern European countries provide examples of a distinct model of capitalist development, characterised by late industrialisation, persisting importance of agriculture and traditional activities, heavy reliance on tourism, limited proletarianisation of the labour force, prevalence of family micro-businesses and high rates of self-employment, large underground economies and widespread informal employment arrangements. Leontidou (1990; 1996) has written that this particular Southern European version of capitalism has led to common processes of urban development, historically characterised by spontaneity and informality rather than planning: (a) Mediterranean cities have compact landscapes reflecting their long histories, with narrow streets, tall buildings and suburbs fairly close to the centre; (b) land use is relatively mixed, rather than divided in zones; (c) social classes are generally not horizontally segregated across the urban space, despite a tendency of the more affluent to live in city centres, but there is a 'vertical' expression of social differentiation (the rich on the upper floors). Ferrera (1996) and Symeonidou (1999) have underlined the particularities of Southern European welfare regimes, which can be seen as a distinct model situated between the 'liberal' and the 'conservative'/'corporatist' ones[37], characterised by late development, clientalism, fragmentation and mainly participatory benefits of low value. The role of the family is crucial in social support, and the care of children and the elderly is mostly performed by women, compensating for the insufficiency of the welfare state.

In the course of the past thirty years or so, all four countries have been undergoing more or less similar processes of economic restructuring and political change, which to an extent coincided with their transformation into migrant-receiving states (Hadjimichalis 1994; Mingione 1995; Vaiou & Hadjimichalis 1997). The interaction of internal and external factors has contributed to the gradual formation of the necessary material conditions for the attraction of foreign labour to these erstwhile migrant-sending countries. International economic and political trends, the development of domestic economies, political, historical and cultural factors, demography and geography sketch the basic reasons that explain this transition. Common patterns and features allow us to speak of a distinct Southern European model of immigration (King 2000a); these are briefly analysed in the following paragraphs[38].

On the one hand, there is the effect of *international developments*. By the mid-1970s increasing unemployment and the rise of xenophobia and extreme Right activism combined with the growing concern of the international community and the EU about issues of terrorism, smuggling, drug trafficking, and (later) immigration led the traditional receiving states to increasingly restrictive measures of policing and border control (Salt 1992; Mousourou 1993; King & Rybaczuk 1993). The fact that prospective migrants were facing closed doors at the 'old' destinations is considered one of the chief factors that stimulated the shift of Southern European countries from transit states to 'waiting rooms' and, finally, to host societies (Mousourou 1993; Fakiolas 1995; Solé 1995; King et al. 1997; King 2000a). The collapse of the command economies in Central and Eastern Europe and in the former Soviet Union, and the problems of economic and political transition, generated a new migration trend from East to West (Kupiszewski 1996), whereby Southern European countries became a major destination (Baganha & Fonseca 2004). Political instability and corruption, together with post-1989 conflicts in the Balkans and elsewhere in the former 'socialist' camp, apart from producing refugee and migratory waves, have created a transnational space serving criminal networks involved in the trafficking business (IOM 2001; 2002), through which part of the global movements of today is channelled towards Southern European countries. In the meantime, the persistence of inequalities, unemployment, lack of opportunities etc. on the European periphery (North Africa, the eastern Mediterranean), and also in sub-Saharan Africa and Asia, coupled with demographic explosion, continue to generate population pressures on Southern Europe (King & Rybaczuk 1993; King 2000a).

On the other hand, *internal political, social and economic changes* have been at the heart of this transition. National political environments changed with democratisation and EU membership in Greece, Spain and Portugal, and with the rise of progressive forces into power in all three countries. Despite the persistence of regional inequalities (Hadjimichalis 1994), economic development within the EU has led to rising prosperity and relative convergence of macroeconomic indicators close to EU averages. The widening of the middle classes resulted in rises in personal consumption and diversified consumption preferences. Together with improved living standards, the mass expansion of tertiary education has led to higher employment aspirations, which, given the persistence of strong family bonds, delays the labour-market integration of the young (King & Rybaczuk 1993; Mousourou 1993; King 2000a). The trend towards the feminisation of the labour force has produced a household deficit in child or elderly care and domestic work (King & Zontini 2000). Decreasing fertility and the ageing of the population create labour shortages in specific sectors or areas. The drying up of internal post-war rural-to-urban and intra-rural migration has also left empty vacancies in certain areas in both rural and urban sectors (King et al. 1997).

Such changes explain the rise in demand for the type of cheap and flexible labour now provided largely by migrant workers: with the labour force shrinking and growing old, with no more 'hordes' of unskilled rural residents making it to the cities, with many young people waiting for qualified positions and women increasingly participating in the labour market (both more and more unwilling to accept unskilled manual posts), certain regions and sectors have been left bereft of vital labour supply. In addition, the persistence of strong underground economies and the proliferation of informal economic practices[39] have functioned as an important pull factor for migration (Reyneri 1999; Reyneri & Baganha 1999). The highly seasonal character of certain sectors of crucial importance for Southern European economies (agriculture, tourism, construction), especially, and the fact the many of these activities tend to rely mostly on casual and labour-intensive practices, make it difficult for the state to gain full control and thus provide a space for the employment of unregistered labour.

Moreover, the particular *geographic characteristics and position* of Southern EU member states is a factor of crucial importance (King & Rybaczuk 1993; King 2000a). The northern mountainous borders of Greece, where controlling the entire borderline is an extremely difficult task, are easily crossable, especially on foot. Also, the long coastlines and numerous islands are very difficult to patrol and can be easily accessed by boat, and thus they are in a sense 'open' to clandestine arrivals from the Balkans, Turkey or North Africa. Since Southern Europe has been incorporated into the 'developed block', the Mediterranean becomes Europe's Rio Grande, a dividing line both imaginary (demographic, cultural, developmental) and physical (geographical), unfolding from Istanbul to the Straits of Gibraltar and crossing Cyprus, Crete, Sicily and Sardinia (King 2000a).

Finally, *historical and cultural bonds* between the countries of destination and the sending countries also play an important role (King 2000a). Such bonds originate, on the one hand, from former colonial links, as is the case of immigration from Latin America and the former Portuguese colonies to the Iberian Peninsula (Solé 1995). On the other, there are ethno-cultural and religious ties, for instance in the case of

Pontian ethnic Greeks from former Soviet republics who migrate into Greece, or the role of the Catholic Church in migration to Portugal, Italy and Spain (King 2002a).

Immigration trends into Southern European countries develop as the forces of change related to global economic restructuring gradually take shape (King & Rybaczuk 1993; Anthias & Lazaridis 1999). Both an 'El Dorado' and a 'fortress' (King et al. 2000), Mediterranean Europe turns multicultural, with phenomena of polarisation and exclusion (Anthias & Lazaridis 1999) emerging in parallel to 'new cultural encounters' (King 2001), and with its cities transforming into post-modern multiethnic metropolises (Malheiros & Ribas-Mateos 2002). The Greek case should be understood within this context; its particularity, however, is in the first place determined by its geographic location. The country's position at the south-eastern corner of the EU, its upgraded role in the Balkan region, the generation of various kinds of flows between Greece and its neighbouring countries and the overwhelming shares of nationals from these countries, especially from Albania, in the total immigrant population, are all factors indicating the uniqueness of the Greek experience within the Southern European immigration model. On the one hand, as Labrianidis and his colleagues argue (2004), in the new European geopolitical conjuncture, Greece appears to be playing the role of the 'North' in the Balkans, while at the same time it remains the 'South' in relation to advanced capitalist countries. On the other hand, this geographic dimension appears as an additional aspect of the transnational cross-border dynamics that condition migration in Greece, this time on a smaller regional scale.

Immigration flows into Greece intensified in the early 1990s, i.e. in the post-1989 East-West context, with massive clandestine waves of migrants from Albania. At the same time, it underwent another important shift: from a net receiver of FDI it became a net exporter of capital, with the Balkans being the privileged destination of direct investment abroad (Labrianidis et al. 2004). Factors such as the pursuit of cheap labour and natural resources, the avoidance of tariff impediments, the issue of geographic and cultural proximity and the presence of ethnic Greek communities, the 'virginity' of the local markets and the initial hesitation of large multinationals contributed significantly in attracting Greeks to invest in the Balkans. In 1998, the great majority (81.7 per cent) of about 1,270 investment projects was concentrated in the three countries from where immigrants come, Albania, Bulgaria and Romania, about half of them in Bulgaria. The majority of Greek investment projects are commercial enterprises and industrial plants, with a small but significant presence of service companies (Labrianidis 2000). Although there are numerous investors, the bulk of capital is owned by ten companies only, which account for about 64 per cent of total Greek investments in Balkan countries, while more than half of the total capital is invested by a few publicly owned firms, with Greek Telecom (OTE) having 46 per cent on its own (Labrianidis et al. 2004). We have thus two kinds of FDI: in terms of volume, a few large companies with high-value investment dominate; in terms of numbers, the typical small Greek enterprise prevails.

Greek investment in the Balkans clearly reflects the productive structure of the Greek economy. The vast majority of projects is based on the activities of small and medium-scale enterprises (SMEs), with or without a parent company in Greece, which move to the Balkans in order to overcome competitive problems at home and to avoid high labour costs (Labrianidis et al. 2004). It is the same type of company that mostly employ immigrants in Greece, as a strategy to overcome their competitive problems and to survive in the market by reducing labour costs. The Greek economy relies to a large extent on such small productive units, which are often family run, apply labour-intensive methods, use low- and middle-level technology and are mostly based on indigenous resources (Fakiolas 2000: 60). Faced with increased non-salary labour costs (e.g. high taxation, costly contributions), but also with difficulties in modernising themselves in the face of international competition, such companies 'invest' in cheap labour to overcome their crisis (Labrianidis et al. 2004). Since the early 1990s, the Balkans have been supplying Greece with a cheap labour force, whether domestically, with immigration, or abroad through FDI and relocation, depending on the activities and capacities of individual companies. In that sense, both immigration and FDI appear to be two sides of the same coin, reflecting the demand for cheap, low-skilled, flexible and unprotected labour by Greek capital (Labrianidis et al. 2004).

2.2.2 *Basic socio-economic aspects of immigration in Greece*

Through practices of tax evasion and non-payment of social security contributions, small and medium-sized enterprises and family micro-businesses feed the shadow economy in Greece considerably[40]; to an extent, it is this demand that migrant labour has been covering throughout the 1990s. Taking also into account the high shares of self-employment, applying to nearly one fourth of the labour force at the end of 2003 (NSSG, Labour Force Survey), the potential demand for cheap and unregistered labour increases. In addition, increased living standards, as manifested, for instance, in rises in household consumption[41] also generate part of this demand for migrant labour. With more than one fifth of the migrants recorded in the 2001 census working in the obscure category 'other services' (see Table A1, in Appendix A), the role of private households and the self-employed appears to be crucial, especially for female employment. Other sectors concentrating high shares of migrant workers are construction, agriculture and the primary sector, manufacturing, trade and repair, hotel and catering (again, see Table A1). Clearly, many of the activities involved are labour intensive and some, due to their very nature (agriculture, tourism, construction, small retail trade, work in bars and restaurants, household services) easily escape state regulations through informal arrangements.

With an estimated size of the underground economy at between 30 and 45 per cent of the GDP (Fakiolas 1999: footnote 4), the informal sector has absorbed migrant labour, benefiting from its much-needed flexibility. Among 212,860 regular immigrants in early 2000, 47 per cent were registered with IKA (the largest insurance fund), 26 per cent with ΟΓΑ (the fund for those employed in agriculture), and 1 per cent with TEBE (the fund for service providers and business owners)[42]. A year later, the census counted nearly 400,000 foreign workers; this shows that still, at the time, insurance and hence registered employment was the case for only slightly more than half of the migrants. In that regard, things do seem to be improving, after extensive legalisation programmes and with a more realistic policy approach, as we are going to see in the next section. By September 2003, the number of foreign nationals registered with IKA alone had increased to 245,913 people, which, estimating on the basis of the rates above, means that more than 520,000 immigrants were insured at the end of 2003, mirroring the regularisation procedures. This, however, has been a very recent development.

The needs of small businesses, the self-employed and individual households for flexible, low-cost labour prepared to work informally and hard offer one side of the explanation. The 'accommodation' of migrant labour has been based on gaps and shortages in labour supply in specific economic sectors and geographical regions, in posts that were left vacant or in new ones created by the advent of economic restructuring and social change. Looking at the supply side will help us understand why this demand could not be fully satisfied by the indigenous labour force. Certain jobs that are today performed largely by migrants – in tourism, bars and restaurants, construction, manufacturing, agriculture, etc. – used to be done (and still are, to an extent) by specific segments of the population. For decades, internal migrants from rural areas had been supplying the urban sectors before and after the Second World War (Leontidou 1990). Temporary movements of poor mountain people, Roma or Muslims from Thrace towards the richer lowlands covered the increased seasonal needs of harvesting and other agricultural jobs (Vaiou & Hadjimichalis 1997; Labrianidis & Lyberaki 2001). In the 1970s and 1980s, the work of women supported the flourishing of clothing and garment industries in northern Greek cities (Chronaki et al. 1993; Vaiou & Hatzimichalis 1997). Many young people, some unskilled but also students or recent graduates, still head for work in the tourist industry during the summer or in bars, restaurants and fast-food outlets in urban areas in the winter (Labrianidis & Lyberaki 2001).

Much of this supply has been shrinking over recent decades, while new needs have emerged. Low fertility rates and population ageing are responsible for important decreases in the growth rate of the total labour force (NSSG 2003; see Figure A1 in Appendix A). Fertility rates follow a downward route, decreasing by 0.76 percentage points between 1971-2001. The share of children up to fourteen years old in the total population has fallen by about 10 percentage points since 1971, while the share of people aged over 64 increased by more than 6 percentage points. In the meantime, internal migration has been slowing down since the 1970s, and today it mostly concerns mobility of skilled or highly educated people, while intra-rural seasonal movements have also ceased (Vaiou & Hadjimichalis 1997). Especially in rural Greece, out-migration and population ageing have almost emptied certain areas of people of productive age, not only leaving jobs vital for the communities in the hands of the old, but also leading to the extinction of certain traditional working skills (Labrianidis & Lyberaki 2001; Kasimis et al. 2003). At the same time, women's participation in the labour force and in tertiary education is continuously rising (Linardos-Rylmon 1993; Symeonidou 1999; Fakiolas & Maratou-Alipranti 2000). The expansion of tertiary education, increasingly at a postgraduate level, has created high employment aspirations, leading many young people to late entrance in the labour market, since increased prosperity and strong family ties can support them until the time they will find a 'dignified' job matching their qualifications (Hadjiyanni et al. 1999; Labrianidis & Lyberaki 2001). Additional social and cultural factors also play a role: the continuous enlargement of the housing space, the inadequate number of state kindergartens and care facilities for the elderly, the still low participation of men in housework and middle-class perceptions of status attributing prestige to the employment of a foreign maid (Fakiolas & Maratou-Alipranti 2000).

The above suggest that the transformation of Greece into a host society took place during a period of increasing labour needs, despite rising unemployment rates and relatively slow growth rates. After all, a large percentage of the unemployed (and a growing number of the part-time employed) are young people and women, particularly the most qualified ones (see for instance NSSG's Labour Force Surveys and IKA statistics). Taking into account the jump of GDP growth rates from about 1 per cent annually between 1979-1995 to 3 per cent since then, and despite the fact that this is primarily attributed to the net inflow of EU structural funds (about one third of recent growth; see Fakiolas 2003: 539-540), one can understand how crucial migrant labour has been[43]. This, however, took place under highly exploitative conditions, profiting from the vulnerability of migrant workers partly as a result of their undocumented status. The combination of labour-market structures with an unrealistically restrictive policy framework, police brutality and xenophobic hostility have contributed to the large-scale marginalisation of immigrants: the study of social exclusion was among the first topics that attracted scholarly interest (see Section 3.1.2). Apart from being 'trapped' in the secondary labour market and in hard and badly paid jobs that the locals reject, migrants, and especially Albanians, also became the 'others' whom the collective imagination saw as responsible for many of Greece's contemporary misfortunes: crime, unemployment, falling real wages, etc.

Today, the numbers of foreign citizens in Greece are possibly exceeding one million, counting recent arrivals, ethnic Greek migrants (who are subject to different legal status) and refugees; this means that Greece, and especially certain areas within it, is now a multiethnic society. Between 2000-2002, 14,262 asylum applications were lodged (UNHCR 2003: Table 1). Ethnic Greeks from the former Soviet Union, most of Pontian origin, are estimated at around 110,000 (103,000 of whom were naturalised by the end of 2001), while ethnic Greeks from Albania are thought to be between 40,000 and 60,000 people (Fakiolas 2003: Table 1)[44]. The 2001 census recorded nearly 800,000 foreign nationals living in Greece, making up 7.3 per cent of the total population; more than half are from Albania and another 16.2 per cent are from the Balkans, Eastern Europe and the former USSR; Bulgaria, Georgia and Romania are included in the five main countries of origin, followed by the US, Cyprus and Russia[45] (see Table A2 in Appendix A). The picture seems to have changed slightly since the 1998 regularisation statistics: Albanians and Bulgarians were again in first and second place in shares similar to the present ones, but they were followed by Romanians, Pakistanis, Ukrainians and Poles. According to census data (Table A3, Appendix A), half of the migrants are concentrated in Attica and more than one third in Athens, while about 14 per cent live in the region of Central Macedonia, and 9 per cent in Thessaloniki. The data from the first regularisation vary slightly: about 40 per cent of the applicants were located in the Athens region, with Thessaloniki coming second with 7.2 per cent. The largest regional concentrations, where the share of migrants exceeds 7 per cent among the local population, are in the Southern Aegean and Ionian islands, Peloponnese and Attica, with immigrants in Athens making up 8.5 per cent of the capital's residents (Table A3).

2.2.3 *Greek immigration policy at a glance*

The influx of large numbers of immigrants at the dawn of the 1990s found the Greek government totally unprepared; the existing legal framework at the time dated back to 1929 (Law 4310), and it mostly concerned the out-migration of Greeks, the diaspora and the repatriation of emigrants. In a period of political instability, repeated elections and frequent government changes (1989-1993), the New Democracy (conservative) government introduced a new immigration policy with Law 1975 of 1991, which determined all matters of entry, work and residence of immigrants in Greece throughout almost the whole decade[46]. This was characterised by a strict 'police' logic, since the principal responsibilities fell upon the Ministry of Public Order, and by a failure to address the new situation realistically, as there were no provisions for the legalisation of migrants already present in the country (see Karydis 1996; Kourtovic 2001). The result was hundreds of thousands of immigrants living under clandestine status, hence without any rights and destined to work informally. Before 1998, the number of 'regular' foreigners had not exceeded 120,000 people, one third of them being ethnic Greek migrants or Greek Cypriots. In addition, as Karydis (1996) has pointed out, the law's repressive spirit and emphasis on combating 'illegal' migration through arrests and deportations partly contributed to the stigmatisation of migrants in Greece, by connecting – rhetorically and practically – clandestine status to criminality, building thus the stereotypical equation 'illegal immigrant equals criminal'. At a practical level, the law provided for the establishment of a repressive mechanism for immigration control, which involved frequent police operations and massive numbers of arrests and deportations of undocumented migrants which were dubbed the inventive and deeply offensive term '*skoopa*' (from the Greek word *σκούπα*, 'broom'). Between 1991-2001, the average number of expulsions was 230,000 a year (Fakiolas 2003: Table 1).

The first attempt of the successor PASOK (centre-left) government to address the issue was a bilateral agreement signed between Albania and Greece, regulating the possibility of the invitation of Albanian workers on a temporary (seasonal) contract basis (Law 2482/1997), which in practice affected a very limited number of people. This initial step was followed by the first legalisation programme, decided in 1996 by Law 2434 and launched by Presidential decrees 358 and 359 of 1997[47]. A two-stage process started the following year, with a temporary 'White Card' being issued initially, followed by a longer-lasting 'Green Card' (one to three years) for applicants satisfying certain requirements. The programme was administered by the Organisation for the Employment of the Labour Force (OAEΔ). This separation of the process in two stages, with tight criteria in the second, was one of the issues that attracted criticism and partly resulted in deterring many migrants from applying; another problematic matter was the (large) number of social security stamps required, given that unregistered employment was the only option for the undocumented majority[48]. After various extensions of the period of the programme, 371,641 immigrants had applied, 65 per cent of them Albanians (Cavounidis & Hatzaki 1999). By the end of January 2001, 201,882 had been granted the temporary stay permit (Labrianidis & Lyberaki 2001: 117); in total, 219,024 migrants were issued a Green Card (Fakiolas 2003: Table 4). So far, this first amnesty programme has been followed by another two (2001, 2004), while special arrangements for the renewal of previously granted stay permits have been taking place in the meantime. During the 2001 regularisation, 367,860 people applied and, by June 2003, a total number of about 580,000 immigrants were legalised (Fakiolas 2003: Tables 1, 3). The more recent programme (2004), said to be the last by Ministry of the Interior officials (since the process is going to change after 'as many as possible' immigrants are regularised), was expected to grant legal status to about 250,000 people, bringing the total number of regularised migrants up to about 750,000[49].

The fact that regularisation procedures have been put into a kind of repetitive schedule is indicative of the new, more pragmatic spirit characterising the Greek polity's approach to immigration at the beginning of the 2000s: with Law 2910/2001, the state recognises the presence of immigrants as a de facto reality. The revised legal framework shifts responsibilities from police authorities to the ministries of the Interior and Labour and to local governments: it initiates a more organised management of immigration flows, with emphasis on border control and with provisions for guest-worker invitation schemes through state agencies and bilateral agreements. Immigration is not regarded any more as a purely security/national issue, but it is also connected to the problems of the Greek labour market: the new legal framework separates work from residence permits. In addition, the law includes measures aimed at the integration of immigrants (see Section 8.1) and provisions for family reunification, as well as legal arrangements for the transferability of pension rights. Certain negative features of the previous law persist: the time period stay permits are valid for is short, starting from six-month Green Cards, which apply to the majority, and the regulations for renewals are strict (before one has the right to a two-year permit, s/he has to have five annual renewals, while ten years of continuous legal residence is a prerequisite for a permanent permit). Obviously, arrests and deportations have not ceased, although now they take place at a more organised level: a new police body, the Border Guard, has been established to perform inspections and patrols. In

2001, nearly 220,000 people were arrested for illegal entry/residence, 79 per cent of whom were Albanians (Fakiolas 2003: 548). The costs, however, of enhanced security and control are sky high: Baldwin-Edwards (2004a) reports that, in 2002 alone, 600 million euros were spent on border measures.

In the meantime, a different set of measures applicable to ethnic Greek migrants has been undertaken, pointing to what Triandafyllidou & Veikou (2001) have called 'national considerations in immigration policy'. However, the framework for ethnic Greeks is rather fragmented, containing different provisions for different groups. Pontian Greeks from former Soviet republics were treated as 'returning migrants' (supposedly to their ancestral fatherland) and most were immediately granted citizenship, while some also passed through a special programme of reception and support for integration. For Greek-Albanians, the situation was rather ambiguous in the early 1990s, due to unclear and unstable provisions, but it later developed to its current state: all those who were able to legally prove their Greek origins have now got the 'Special Identity Card for Ethnic Greeks', which gives them certain rights, more a 'half citizenship' status rather than a stay-permit one. Finally, Sarakatsani Greeks from Bulgaria have been granted a special status from the beginning, initially giving them two-month visas, which are now annually renewable.

The development of Greek immigration policy so far has evolved in three phases (Sitaropoulos 2003): (a) from 1991 to 1998 the framework was determined by the particularly restrictive Law 1975/1991; (b) between 1998-2001, it was marked by the first regularisation programme; (c) since then, a more realistic and coherent, although not unproblematic, approach has been initiated with Law 2910/2001. Commentators have acknowledged the impact of Greece's EU membership on the development of the policy framework (Baldwin-Edwards & Fakiolas 1999). In its initial stage, with an exaggerated emphasis on policing, immigration policy-making had been influenced, at least partly and indirectly, by the 'Fortress Europe' ideology that had emerged in the EU policy agenda (Karydis 1996). Greece's full participation in the Schengen system, although a 'blessing' for its citizens, has put serious obstacles to the rights and life chances of newcomers by aiming at effective border control to reduce migration flows (see Samatas 2003); a task that involves collaboration with both EU and third countries (e.g. Turkey). However, as far as integration measures are concerned, Greek policy-making lags far behind the relevant EU legislation and the steps forward made by other member states: in this field, it is only recently and at a limited level that the positive impact of Europeanisation can be traced (Meintanis 2004).

3 Methodology and analytical framework

It is now time to set out the specifics on which the thesis is based, stepping from the macro topics that have dominated the discussion so far to the micro social level of two particular migrant groups in a particular place. As set out in the introduction, the core of the thesis is the presentation and analysis of empirical research concerning the mechanisms of exclusion and the pathways to integration of Albanian and Bulgarian immigrants in Thessaloniki. The analysis is based upon a general explanatory framework that may apply to other cases too. Having outlined in the introduction what the thesis is about, the objective here is to draw the analytical and methodological framework upon which the research has been based and the discussion relies. Moreover, I locate the limits of existing knowledge and approaches and explain my own contribution. Then, I describe the fieldwork itself, its concerns and problems and the way it evolved, as well as the nature of the material collected and the analytical tools used. Finally, I introduce the reader to the economic and socio-spatial specificities of the local context. In other words, here I explain *how* I am approaching my topic (3.1.1); *where* the gaps are in the existing literature and *what* I can add (3.1.2); *by which means* I obtained my data (3.2.1) and *how* I worked with them (3.2.2); and *where* (3.3) the research took place.

3.1 A framework for the analysis of migrants' incorporation

In this section I describe the analytical framework that forms the basis for the discussion later on. The key terms and concepts that I use are defined here, and their theoretical implications are briefly discussed in order to clarify my own perspective and approach to the topic. The limits of the existing literature on immigration to Greece are exposed in order to identify the contribution of my thesis.

3.1.1 *Analytical framework: social exclusion versus integration*

'Exclusion' and 'integration' are simply terms that I use without any theoretical or epistemological commitment, and they have no explanatory power as such. I acknowledge that in the relevant literature both concepts appear to be relative and problematic. Criticism varies from the very fact that, in Europe at least, social exclusion is a fashionable topic for research that attracts funding (Tsiakalos 1998), to the accusation of (policies and projects for) inclusion as a means of 'controlling the poor' (Samers 1998). Therefore it is necessary to briefly reflect on some theoretical implications the two concepts may have and to clarify my personal approach in accordance with the aims of the thesis.

In its general use, the term 'social exclusion' became popular after it was adopted in the discourse and policy guidelines of the European Commission and of a series of EU programmes (Tsiakalos 1998; Room 1999). It gradually came to replace the concept of 'poverty' for describing and analysing various forms of inequality and of social disadvantage for groups or individuals (Room 1999). From a theoretical point of view, exclusion may be vertical, originating from the social structure itself, or horizontal, based on the form and the morphology of society (Alexiou 1999). In addition, it can be understood as a *process* (the set of mechanisms leading to a situation of disadvantage) or as a *condition* (the condition of disadvantage itself). It can also be seen as a lack of means and resources necessary for a 'decent' life or as a lack of access to these means and resources. Such different and sometimes contradictory interpretations are due to several conflicting perspectives on exclusion. Ratcliffe (1999), for instance, outlines the main approaches to social exclusion, which is seen either as a 'determinate and static social position' (with the conservative version attributing it to conscious actions of the 'excluded' themselves), or as a social and economic process, depending thus on forces beyond the individuals which may have differential impacts on different social formations and different social groups. Furthermore, Silver (1994) distinguishes between three main paradigms in the social sciences literature on exclusion. Firstly, the 'solidarity' paradigm, apparent in the French republican discourse, defines exclusion as *rupture* of the social bonds between individuals and social networks, which results in a *lack of access* to solidarity mechanisms and to welfare resources. Secondly, the 'specialisation' paradigm, prominent in the Anglo-Saxon debate, focuses on the *unequal distribution of income and resources* as a consequence of specialisation and of social differentiation, which originate from the economic division of labour. Thirdly, according to the 'monopoly' paradigm, inspired by the Marxian and Weberian traditions, exclusion 'arises from the interplay of *class, status and political power* and serves the interests of the included' (Silver 1994: 543). However, Silver reckons that in some cases the above may not apply, due to historical/political reasons (e.g. dictatorships) but also because of the persistence of traditional structures and of the dominance of vertical social divisions (e.g. kinship ties), as, for instance, in Southern European countries. Finally, some scholars focus on the spatial dimension, whereby exclusion either manifests itself in space, for instance by segregation in cities, or it is directly linked to specific places such as ghettos (Musterd et al. 1998; Ratcliffe 1999).

For obvious reasons, immigrants are one of the groups threatened by, or actually experiencing, social exclusion. 'Integration', on the other hand, is regarded as the reverse process, through which migrants 'adjust', or 'integrate', or are 'inserted', 'included' or 'adapted' into the host society. Here, again, we see various approaches and definitions, which make 'integration' a very relative term. Its interpretations vary from 'a mechanism that activates social participation' (Musterd et al. 1998) to 'a process through which the indigenous population and a minority group settled in the same place gradually intermingle and move towards equality on the socio-economic, cultural and political levels' (King & Rodriguez-Melguizo 1999). Conflicting intellectual traditions are apparent here as well. For neoclassical economists (and theorists inspired by the neoclassical paradigm), integration is the successful economic performance of immigrants (whom they see as rationally acting individuals): this depends on the human capital migrants possess, the length of stay in the host society, their language skills, etc. (see, for instance, Chiswick 1978; Borjas 1994). On the other hand, sociologists tend to approach immigrants as 'members of groups and participants in broader social structures that affect in multiple ways their mobility' (Portes 1995: 24), and locate the process (or processes) of integration accordingly. In general, migration theorists and researchers have addressed the issue of integration from various perspectives. There is a vast empirical literature looking at specific cases of various forms of migrant integration at different levels: labour market, housing, identity, citizenship, etc.

To my understanding, there is a basic problem associated with the use of the terms, related to the ambiguous definition of 'embeddedness' (or non-embeddedness) they imply. Exclusion from what? Integration into what? What is to be conceived as the 'whole' from which certain segments of the population are excluded? Which are the structures, or institutions, or the cultural framework, where distinct social groups like migrants in general are to be included? Should, then, both majority and minority social groups be conceived as static and homogeneous entities? And are, consequently, social formations, whether states or specific localities, to be understood as given and unchanging, into which alien groups or individuals may be inserted or excluded from? These are concerns that should be taken into account in order to clarify my intentions and to set out the analytical framework on which the discussion that follows is based.

Both exclusion and integration should be understood in the first instance as dynamic processes, which are related to the dynamics of the system itself, in general structural terms, but also regarding the specificities of different national and local realities. This is something recognised anyway by scholars from conflicting backgrounds. According to Room (1999: 172), 'social exclusion is a normal and integral part of the power dynamics of modern society.' From a different point of view, Alexiou (1999) locates the dynamics of exclusion in the process of capitalist development: for him, social exclusion refers to phenomena arising from the social structure and its endemic trends, which lead to the marginalisation of certain social groups. Such a systemic interpretation implies that the social margin does not emerge accidentally, but is rather produced by specific forms/structures of economic and societal organisation, within which it plays a specific social role. Therefore, exclusion is not studied here as a process or condition *per se*: the focus is on the trends, mechanisms, reactions and so forth that deny a 'decent' and 'normal' life to immigrants.

Turning now to integration, this can be seen as a process that takes place anyway, because at the end, and in various ways, migrants *do* make a living in the destination places. They can be assimilated, partially integrated, differentially excluded or 'trapped' in ghettos, but they are there and they are 'included', in one form or another and to varying degrees. Immigrants then may or may not be integrated in the *dominant* structures or institutions of the host country, and they may or may not share the *dominant* cultural values, but this is also the case for certain distinct social or cultural groups within the host country's population. In that sense, neither migrants nor locals should be regarded as *homogeneous* entities. It is rather the exclusionary mechanisms themselves (economic organisation, class structures, legal norms, cultural boundaries, etc.) that produce such dichotomies between unified and solid social categories and establish distinctive lines between 'us' and 'them'. Yet, neither 'we' live under unchanging conditions, nor are 'they' coming into static societies. From the very micro-level of the local community to the macro processes of globalisation, our world is made up of many worlds, marked by fluidity and constant motion. Therefore, pathways of integration and processes of exclusion are linked to the dynamics of social change, in our case the patterns of transformation of local and national contexts by internal (historical) or external (international, global) forces of change.

Let me expand a little at this point on the contradiction between the 'system' and the 'lifeworld', that is, between the abstract and general social structures that constitute the system and its internal logic, and the everyday life experiences of people in specific places (referring to Habermas 1984; see also Sayer 2000). On the one hand, there are systemic structures and processes of change, global forces of interaction and transformation. On the other, people's lives are linked to specific places, to everyday experiences and to the happy and sad moments of the life course. In respect to the migratory phenomenon, while it may be reduced to placeless flows of people at a macro-level, on a micro-scale and in respect to each individual migrant's personal experiences, it takes place-specific characteristics (King 1995: 27). Russell King refers to Bourdieu's (1977) concept of *habitus* to highlight the importance of space and address the meaning of place for migrants (King 1995: 28). Living between 'here' and 'there', migrants become human links between places on which their material existence and their images depend: from their working life to their personal time-space experiences and from their geographic and cultural background to their networks of social relationships. The *lifeworld* then of migrants can be conceived as a process which entails all that is 'natural' in everyday life and the perceptions individuals have about it (see Lazaridis & Psimmenos 2000: 170-171): daily experiences, identity, networks and the meaning of place. In addition, it should also embrace the diverse ways by which migrants respond, individually or collectively, to the situations they are faced with. It is therefore essential to move beyond the schemata of victimisation-proletarianisation that were common in studies of the past (Papastergiadis 2000): this conception created distorted views of reality, not because it was not true but because it overemphasised this aspect of the migrant's identity and experience, losing thus other important elements. This requires us to regard migrants as *actors*, according to Touraine's (2000) definition of the term, i.e. 'autonomous beings' and 'agents of transformation' of their immediate environment and their own situation. Such a parallel account of both systemic and more concrete human factors of everyday life allows us to address what King (2002: 101) calls 'the double embeddedness of migration': migration is embedded in societies and social processes, but also in the individual migrant's life course.

Having all these background theoretical points in mind, I refer to the concept of *incorporation* in order to link lifeworlds and systemworlds and to analyse in parallel the ways migrants organise their lives in the host community and the structural, institutional and cultural contexts that condition them. Scholars have employed the term with a variety of meanings. Castles (2001; also see Castles & Miller 1998) generally refers to different 'models' of community formation and incorporation: the history of migration passed from assimilation, dominant in the long-distance pre-war movements, to differential exclusion during post-war labour flows and finally to the pluralist model of today. Portes (1995: 24) talks about 'the process of insertion of immigrants into various contexts/reception levels'. Soysal (1994: 30-31), referring mostly to political participation, defines incorporation as a 'macro-level process whereby a guestworker population becomes part of the polity of the host country', 'a wider process that takes place independently of the integration of individuals or perceptions of such integration'. Despite the differences in disciplines, perspectives, research interests or goals, such definitions have one thing in common: they point to a set of non-linear processes, as well as practices, relations, etc., acknowledging and assigning thus agency and action to the migrants themselves, without implying prescribed outcomes (e.g. 'inclusion' or 'exclusion'), but rather evolving, dynamic, interrelated and interacting phenomena.

To an extent, similar conceptualisations have been proposed through the use of other concepts, or of 'integration' itself as a much more conventional term[1]. It should be acknowledged that 'incorporation' can be an equally vague and relative concept, as its various uses in the literature mentioned above suggest. But there is a need, however, on the one hand, to capture as many elements as possible, and on the other, to distance ourselves from monolithic linear accounts. The conventional understanding of 'integration', especially in policy and public discourses, implies a linear process through which migrants adjust to the host society. The concept of 'incorporation' is being proposed in order to avoid such assumptions; instead, by being a less widely used term, it is value-free and thus allows us to examine the mutual relationship between immigrants and the host society without implying any prescribed outcomes. This relationship is a non-linear one and may have both positive and negative aspects: the process of social incorporation entails both exclusion and integration, as these might apply to different mechanisms, or pathways of different categories of immigrants or different individuals. In other words, the concept refers to a process, or set of processes, through which immigrants are *incorporated* into (i.e. become part of) the social 'body' of a given society, and the mechanisms through which this society responds, reacts, or changes because of this development. The former does not imply that this process will necessarily lead towards a successful integration; the latter addresses the ways the host society adjusts itself to new situations, which might redefine the position of the migrants in various ways. In short, incorporation refers both to: (a) the ways migrants organise their lives in specific localities (a somehow 'natural' process in the real world); and (b) the factors that condition their lives (from the locals' response to forces beyond individuals/communities, whether endemic – historical – conditions in the host country, or exogenous – i.e. influenced by global systemic transformations).

Therefore, the concept of incorporation allows us to look beyond one-way paths through which immigrants are 'inserted' in, or are pushed to the margins of a static host society, as terms like 'cultural adjustment', 'labour-market integration' or 'social exclusion' assume. On the contrary, 'incorporation' rather implies complex processes that take place at various overlapping levels and under conditions formulated in different but interrelated contexts. It is linked to factors originating from different aspects of social life, but which are in constant and dynamic interaction with each other. It entails both the 'obvious', 'visible' side of everyday life, its morphology and phenomenology, and what lies beyond, in the spheres of social structure, social organisation and social praxis, and in the fields of geography, identity and historical/cultural attributes. It has to do with both objective and subjective situations that determine immigrants' lives in host societies, while they simultaneously shape host societies themselves as constantly changing social formations. The study of incorporation may allow us, then, to understand the dynamics of interaction between the global and the local, the macro and the micro, lifeworlds and systemworlds, structure and agency, immigrants and locals. Therefore, it is a useful concept to address the dialectics of migration according to the aims of the thesis.

But how are we to capture incorporation? How can we study, measure and analyse it? Given the above theoretical considerations and in respect to the needs and purposes of my thesis, I draw from the insights, explanatory patterns and empirical approaches presented in other relevant works. Portes (1995: 24-25), for instance, distinguishes between three 'modes of incorporation' which affect individuals through both structural (polity and society) and relational (communities and networks) forms of embeddedness: (i) governmental policy, (ii) civil society and public opinion, (iii) ethnic community and social networks. Similarly, Ribas-Mateos (2000) describes the three contexts that influence the incorporation of immigrants, namely, (i) governmental policy and welfare, (ii) labour market and (iii) the construction of ethnic community and cultural identity; external factors shape these contexts as well, such as the international environment and the conditions in the sending countries. Furthermore, Musterd et al. (2000) write on how the 'modes of integration' – for them, market exchange, redistribution and reciprocity – take place within broader contexts determined by local, regional, national and increasingly global factors: respectively, economic restructuring, welfare state and solidarity/social networks, emphasising also the importance of the spatial context. Also of relevance here is Heckman's (2004) distinction between different 'dimensions' of integration: (i) 'structural integration' means the acquisition of rights and access (legal status, education, housing, labour market, etc.); (ii) 'acculturation' refers to cognitive, behavioural and attitudinal change; (iii) 'social integration' points to private relations and group membership; and (iv) 'identification' has to do with senses of belonging. Finally, Solé (1999), in her account of the impact of immigration on Southern European countries, proposed the following factors that are useful as well: characteristics of the migratory flow; material conditions (labour market, sectors of employment, housing); institutional responses; and the role of the media.

On this basis, and having already outlined the socio-economic context and the policy framework (sections 2.2.2 and 2.2.3), I examine the parallel but opposing processes of exclusion and integration at four different, though interconnected, levels:

- *Governmental policy and welfare.* This has to do with the policy context of immigrants' reception and their degree of integration into the social state. The focus is on the effects of immigration policy and the relevant legal framework (Section 5.1), as well as on the degree of immigrants' access to basic welfare services, such as health and education (8.1).
- *Civil society, public opinion and culture.* This is about the social 'response' to immigration (5.2). The role of various social actors (immigrants' associations, political parties, NGOs, etc.) is discussed and the widespread beliefs of the locals are analysed, touching also on the issue of racism and the role of the media.
- *Socio-economic structures and employment.* The interest here lies in the economic integration of immigrants (Chapter 6). The analysis takes into account the productive structure and employment relations in the local labour market and the implications of the processes of restructuring.
- *Socio-spatial dynamics and place.* The dynamics of urban social geography is of relevance here (Chapter 7). Housing conditions and residential trajectories, as well as broader socio-spatial experiences are discussed in relation to transforming uses and changing perceptions of urban space.

So the multifaceted process of the incorporation of immigrants takes place within the above contexts; to put it in other words, the question of how migrants organise their lives in the host society, in terms of work, residence, relationships, etc., depends on factors born and evolving within these contexts. For each one of them, I am going to identify the exclusionary mechanisms and show how and to what extent they are interrelated. Some of these mechanisms have solely local features, while others are nationally applicable; there are, however, also international forces shaping local and national contexts, whose implications are examined in Chapter 9 in an attempt to revisit the broad theoretical concepts addressed in Chapter 2 and to draw generalisations and theorise from my findings. The analysis is also concerned with the various private and collective practices that migrants commonly employ in order to build a life in Thessaloniki and their own perceptions/understandings of their migration experience. These are discussed anyway in relation to the situations with which immigrants are confronted in each of the above contexts, but there are certain issues requiring special attention. The role of migrant networks is highlighted at several points throughout the analysis; but their character and implications in respect to the emergence of migrant communities are specifically addressed in Section 8.2.2. Additional issues related to the migrants' living conditions, daily practices, coping strategies and negotiations of identity are also crucial to the process of incorporation (Section 8.2.3). But in order to understand incorporation processes, it is first necessary to have an idea of the composition, patterns and dynamics of migration in the specific case studied here; this is done through the description of the basic background empirical findings in Chapter 4.

3.1.2 *Incorporation of immigrants in Greece: the limits of existing literature*

During the past decade, interest in migration to Greece and in a wide range of related issues has been growing, resulting in a large amount of relevant research and publications by both Greek and other scholars. Listing and reviewing this literature in detail would be an enormous task superseding the capacities and escaping the aims of this thesis; therefore, apart from my own readings, a detailed bibliographical essay by Petronoti & Triandafyllidou (2003) has been of great help[2]. The purpose of this section is to briefly overview the main topics addressed and to identify the limits and gaps in the existing literature, especially in relation to the issues that are relevant to my own work. The aim is to locate my study within existing knowledge and to explain the contribution my own research has to offer.

The relevant literature started developing in the early 1990s and focuses on a variety of issues that can be categorised into five main broad themes: (i) migration trends, characteristics and patterns; (ii) immigration policy; (iii) economy and labour-market integration; (iv) social exclusion/inclusion; and (v) issues of identity and culture. Depending on the disciplinary focus, as well as the character and objectives of each study, some of these topics are looked at simultaneously, crosscut by specific issues, whether these are the primary focus or remain in the background: ethnicity, gender, social networks, media, racism, education, etc. Early publications tended to rely on observations, assumptions and estimations, given the lack of available data. With the exception of a few theoretical works (Mousourou 1991; 1993), most publications were mainly descriptive and particularly concerned with either the demographic and/or economic characteristics of immigrants (Petrinioti 1993; Linardos-Rylmon 1993; Katsoridas 1994; Fakiolas 1995), or with their rights and legal status (e.g. Theodoropoulos & Sykiotou

1994). Many studies of this generation failed to understand the transformation of Greece into a receiving country, by assuming that the phenomenon was temporary, thus neglecting the implications for integration until at least the middle of the decade (Glytsos 1995). At the same time, a separate branch of the literature focused on 'returning' ethnic Greeks, especially Pontians from the former Soviet Union (e.g. Kasimati et al. 1992; Markou 1994).

Studies multiplied during the second half of the 1990s, especially after the 1998 regularisation programme and the publication of the first official statistics (Cavounidis & Hatzaki 1999). One can observe a loose disciplinary division between economic studies (Lianos et al. 1996; Markova & Sarris 1997; Sarris & Zographakis 1999; Lyberaki & Pelagidis 2000; Hatziprokopiou et al. 2001), on the one hand, and a series of works on the other that can be labelled as sociological ones (e. g. Psimmenos 1995; 1998; King et al. 1998; Fakiolas & Maratou-Alipranti 2000), combining however a variety of social science traditions ranging from historical accounts (Fakiolas & King 1996) to political economy (Droukas 1998; Fakiolas 1999; Baldwin-Edwards & Safilios-Rothschild 1999) and human geography (Iosifides & King 1998), and from criminology (Karydis 1996) to education (Damanakis 1997; Koiliari 1997; Tsiakalos 2000). In parallel, the interest in the legal framework and the policy implications remained strong (Triandafyllidou 1996; Lazaridis 1996; Baldwin-Edwards 1999; Baldwin-Edwards & Fakiolas 1999; Lazaridis & Poyago-Theotoki 1999), while much research started focusing on specific migrant groups[3]. In the meantime, an increasing number of publications emerged on ethnic Greeks (Pontians and Greek-Albanians) and on refugees. Moreover, migration also featured in studies not directly concerned with the phenomenon[4].

Research output has grown further in the 2000s, spreading across the whole spectrum of the social sciences and involving both qualitative and quantitative studies and interdisciplinary works. The migrants' voice is increasingly being heard as a number of empirical studies are addressed directly to immigrants. Apart from individual or co-authored publications, a number of edited volumes offer combined and comparative accounts on several migration-related topics, including elements previously neglected and factors underestimated, such as gender and agency, respectively (e.g. King et al. 2000; Marvakis et al. 2001; Naxakis & Hletsos 2001; Amitsis & Lazaridis 2001; Tastsoglou & Maratou-Alipranti 2003). Exclusion and integration are now central themes in research agendas and debates. Integration is discussed in relation to the labour market (e.g. Fakiolas 1999; Maratou-Alipranti 2002), language and identity (Koiliari 1997), ethnic mobilisation (Petronoti 2001) and recent policy steps (Fakiolas 2003); often, the focus is on specific migrant groups (e.g. Lazaridis & Romaniszyn 1998; Markova 2001;

Labrianidis & Lyberaki 2001). Exclusion, on the other hand, attracts much of the focus, and criticism is targeted towards the legal framework that led to migrants' stigmatisation (Karydis 1996), the public discourse reflecting the exclusionary construction of Greek national identity (Veikou 1998; Triandafyllidou 2000), socio-economic and socio-spatial mechanisms (Psimmenos 1995; 1998; Mavreas 1998; Iosifides & King 1998; Lazaridis & Psimmenos 2000; Halkos & Salamouris 2003), or education (Katsikas 1998).

However, as Petronoti & Triandafyllidou (2003) note, the patterns of interaction between migrants and locals remain largely under-researched, while the literature generally lacks thorough interpretations and linkages between empirical research on migration to Greece and broad theoretical discussions on globalisation, capitalism, multiculturalism and modernity. In my view, this is because the existing literature approaches the phenomenon mainly from two perspectives, in many cases simultaneously apparent or even fused, but still lacking coherent frameworks and theoretical concern:

(a) *From the perspective of the host society.* The interest here is either in the effects of immigration on the host economy, society and culture, or in the Greek reactions/responses to immigration (policy, xenophobia, etc.).

(b) *From the perspective of the migrants themselves.* This includes studies focusing on the characteristics and living conditions of the migrants, on issues of identity, etc. In a sense, many works can be seen as attempts to 'know' the newcomers, to 'defend' them against xenophobic arguments and to 'respond' to exaggerations and 'inform' the (Greek) public.

No conscious efforts have been made to synthesise dialectically the two perspectives and develop a coherent and prismatic framework of analysis in order to understand the dynamism of the phenomenon, its contradictions and the patterns of interaction. Both the host society and the immigrants are largely treated as unitary and homogeneous entities, limiting our capacity to locate and explain change in either case. Despite their qualities, many studies fail to address the dynamism of migration-related developments and give rather static pictures capturing the 'moment', which are then reproduced in the literature with a distorted version of reality as a result[5]. In addition, despite the criticisms against the policy framework, racism or exploitation, references to Greece as a 'multiethnic' or 'multicultural' society are scarce and only recently have the implications of this started to be discussed. Moreover, the migrant is frequently portrayed as a victim – of the legal framework or the police, of employers, or of xenophobic attitudes and abstract social structures – and agency and action (through informal strategies, social networks, or associational action and unionisation) are underestimated and often ignored. This one-sided 'victimisation' reproduces, to an extent, binaries between 'us' and 'them' and – despite obvious good will towards the migrants – contributes to the consolidation of new stereotypes (e.g. the migrants as excluded, or as destined to perform the jobs Greeks reject)[6].

Furthermore, several elements remain under-researched or totally neglected. Few publications have so far studied the phenomenon in relation to issues of space, and equally scarce are any attempts to understand the relevance of place. Although many of the empirical studies are actually conducted in specific locales, rarely are the implications of the peculiar local socio-economic characteristics taken into consideration, and conclusions are usually generalised at a countrywide level. Apart from rare acknowledgments of the obvious dichotomy between urban and rural migrant employment (see Baldwin-Edwards & Safilios-Rothschild 1999), detailed analyses of the importance of the local setting are rather exceptional, limited to a few recent publications. It is worth mentioning the research of Kasimis et al. (2003) on migrants in rural Greece, which compared the dynamics of migration and development in three different rural areas; also, my own publications (2003b; 2004a) where I highlight the relevance of place to the dynamics of incorporation. Moreover, the relationship between migration and the city and the spatial aspects of exclusion and integration (housing, segregation, public/private space, etc.) are also rarely addressed. The work of Psimmenos (1995; 1998; 2001) has been pioneering: he found that the labour market and housing experiences of undocumented migrants 'entrap' them into exclusionary – 'periphractic' – spaces. Iosifides & King (1998) have also analysed the processes of socio-spatial exclusion of immigrants in Athens. Halkos & Salamouris (2003), in their survey of Pontians from the former USSR in western Attica, also acknowledge the role of the spatial context in social exclusion. In the case of Thessaloniki, Labrianidis & Lyberaki (2001) have a whole chapter on the housing conditions and residential distribution of Albanian migrants, while Pavlou (2001) has studied the implications of local media discourses on crime, city marketing, and the presence of immigrants, regarding the use of the urban space; my personal accounts of socio-spatial issues stemming out of this thesis research should be mentioned as well (2003b; 2004a and b).

In addition, Thessaloniki, the second largest city in Greece, has attracted little interest thus far in respect to its migration experience – particularly striking, if we consider the city's multicultural past (Section 3.3) – with two notable exceptions (Labrianidis & Lyberaki 2001; Pavlou 2001). Also, the issues of identity usually lie in the disciplinary focus of purely sociological or anthropological studies and are examined strictly in relation to cultural attributes, racism or national/ethnic references, without conscious attempts to discuss them with respect to the broader socio-economic context of integration, to investigate the meaning of place and the extent to which transnational or hybrid features are beginning to emerge. Finally, the role of social networks remains poorly researched, and there is one single study on social networks as resources that also determine the patterns of migrant settlement in Greece, emphasising the role of culture and of historical trans-local connections (Sintès 2002). Above all, despite recent efforts, research on migration in Greece lacks coherent theoretical frameworks of analysis and reference, for instance, to understand the role of both market and non-market forces, agency and structure, identity and institutions, space and place. We need an interdisciplinary focus, prismatic views and dialectical understandings in order to capture the patterns of interaction between migrants and locals; to locate the interplay between migration, incorporation and social change; and to explain the impact of global developments, internationalising forces and systemic transformation.

The innovativeness and originality of my research are to be found in the analytical framework outlined in the previous section and in the combination of various methodologies as described in the following one, as well as in the findings themselves and the way they are interpreted throughout the thesis. From an empirical point of view, my research offers an account and comparison of the characteristics of two migrant groups, uncovering a high degree of heterogeneity in all aspects, but also identifying common experiences and patterns that apply to all. It emphasises the role of the local setting and the urban dynamics of incorporation and looks at the relevance of time. It explains the transformation of Greece into a multicultural society through the example of Thessaloniki in its historical dimension and by taking into account its geographic location and its potential role in the wider Balkan area. From a methodological/theoretical point of view, the thesis is an attempt to approach the issue of migrants' incorporation in its totality, by looking separately at different levels, contexts or modes of reception and by identifying the ways these are interconnected. The migrants are seen as actors rather than victims, although much of their experience entails negative aspects (illegality, unfair treatment, racism, exploitation), and the analysis is concerned with explaining how 'they' are 'constructed' as a homogeneous social category through political, ideological and structural mechanisms. The patterns of interaction are understood through a dynamic perspective, linking the issues of incorporation to the dynamics of social change, of which migration now forms part. The relevance of international developments and global forces is explored, in order to understand the extent to which the Greek immigration experience shares common characteristics with other cases and to identify the form that the global-local interaction takes in this particular case of migration, incorporation and social transformation.

3.2 Research design and methodology

The research for this thesis has been based on a wide range of techniques and on a mixture of methodologies. No single approach has been used; my analytical framework provided the basis for a multi-paradigmatic methodological perspective, and the methods finally employed have been designed accordingly to fit the requirements of this particular research. At a technical level, I have consulted general guidelines presented in some introductory textbooks on social research methods: Judd et al. (1991), Bryman (2001), Robson (2002). In this section, I outline the main methods and data collection techniques I used and my sources of secondary data; I then move on to a description of the fieldwork itself and refer to the ethical issues that arose while conducting the research; finally, I discuss the ways I analysed qualitative and quantitative data.

3.2.1 Sources, methods and techniques

The collection of data came from a variety of sources, depending on the nature of the information needed: on-site field investigation, official statistics, press material, documents and leaflets, empirical and theoretical literature. Literature research and reading went on until the very end of the writing of the thesis. In the prior chapters, and in the analysis that follows, there are plenty of references to empirical studies and theoretical texts that provided important background information and were also used in order to confirm findings, draw comparisons, support arguments and generalise. A series of documents, such as laws and governmental provisions, as well as leaflets and brochures from a number of associations, organisations and programmes have also been taken into account, and they are respectively mentioned in the relevant parts of the analysis. A considerable amount of material from the daily press has also been collected and will be used, with respect to specific events, or generally in relation to the discourse about immigration, migrants' living and working conditions, attitudes and perceptions towards them, racism and xenophobia, etc. No structured and detailed discourse analysis of press and other printed material is employed since that would have taken the scope and the purposes of the study too far from its aims. The analysis is largely based on primary material gathered after on-site fieldwork investigation, supported by secondary data and some of the material drawn out of the sources mentioned before. Secondary sources are used throughout the thesis, especially the following:

- Official statistics on immigration, such as the 2001 census (NSSG), data from the first regularisation programme (Cavounidi & Hatzaki 1999), or other sources (NSSG, e.g. Labour Force Surveys, IKA, NTO, various ministries, etc.), including empirical studies using official statistics (Lianos 2001; 2003; Fakiolas 2003) and newspaper articles. In addition to this, I include a series of raw data on hospital admissions of foreign nationals obtained by the administrative offices of one of Thessaloniki's largest hospitals (see Section 8.1.1).
- Published empirical material of relevant surveys and project reports. There are many studies on Albanian immigrants, but of particular value has been the large survey by Labrianidis & Lyberaki (2001), focusing on Thessaloniki. Research on Bulgarian immigrants in Athens was published by Markova (2001) and Markova & Sarris (1997), while at a country level there is the work of Minev et al. (1997). A countrywide survey by Hatziprokopiou et al. (2001) focusing on the demand side (Greek perceptions and experiences), has also been taken into consideration[7].

The fieldwork research aimed exclusively at the collection of qualitative and quantitative primary material, according to the needs and purposes of the research. However, a significant amount of additional information, qualitative in nature, has been gathered in the course of the fieldwork itself through observation and note-keeping. In this respect, my physical presence in the city and my engagement with the field research gave me a first-hand experience of the daily life of immigrants anyway. But apart from this 'automatic' benefit, I went through a rather more systematic observation, which allowed me to map the migrants' lifeworlds in terms of work, residence and leisure, to understand better the actual conditions and to conceptualise social reality relevant to my work. To be precise, systematic observation involved the following:

- Frequent walks and drives all over the city, visits to places with high concentrations of migrants and places of interaction with locals, such as meeting-points in squares, parks, cafés, open markets, etc., as well as informal chats with both immigrants and locals.
- Visits to public services dealing with immigrants, such as the police's Department of Aliens, the prefecture's Department of Employment and Labour (responsible for the issue of work permits) and the Department of Aliens of the Region of Central Macedonia (which controls part of the stay-permit procedure).

- Monitoring of the activities of organisations like the free language courses programme of the NGO Odysseas, the Anti-racist Initiative of Thessaloniki, or the Albanian Association Thessaloniki.
- Information-gathering about the above and other organisations and associations which are run by, provide services for, or deal in various ways with migrants, through (a) the collection of printed material (information leaflets, newsletters and brochures); and (b) informal interviews with representatives and key informants.

The main source of primary data, and the basic original research done throughout the fieldwork, was a survey of 208 Albanian and Bulgarian immigrants living and working in the city, which employed two combined instruments of data collection, namely structured questionnaires and in-depth interviews. In all, 159 questionnaires were administered, with 108 Albanian and 51 Bulgarian respondents, while the interviews totalled 49, with 30 and 19 Albanian and Bulgarian interviewees respectively, although the Albanian interview sample also included people related to the principal interviewees (husbands/wives, children). The questionnaire generated mostly quantitative, 'measurable' data, while the interviews were aimed at producing more detailed and qualitative information. Both techniques were designed to collect information about the demographic profile of the migrants (nationality, ethnicity, gender, age, family) and to address issues such as: the conditions of migration (when, why, how) and the patterns of mobility; the migrants' housing situation and residential trajectories; their labour-market conditions; their education, skills and employment history; aspects of their general conditions and daily lives.

Apart from such 'objective' characteristics, the respondents/interviewees were also asked to give their opinion, to expose their perceptions and subjective understandings of their migration, housing and labour-market experiences, to tell stories of unfair (or fair) treatment by host institutions, services and people, and to comment on cultural aspects of their life abroad. While the main 'unit' was meant to be the individual migrant, the questionnaires were aimed at gathering some information about other people too, basically members of the respondent's family, in order to grasp the general picture of the conditions of the migrant household. The nature of the questions in the interview schedule also stimulated similar responses.

The questionnaire was initially designed in early 2001 in English, then it was translated into Greek and pilot-tested with ten Albanian respondents in April 2001. In its final version, produced after changes and corrections inspired by the testing, the questionnaire was eight pages long and composed of the following six sections: A. Personal Profile, B. Migration Data, C. Housing Conditions, D. Employment

Conditions, E. Living Conditions, F. Additional Information. Most of the items (questions) were expressed in close-ended formats, with boxes to tick corresponding to different answers. Series of categories, dichotomous 'yes/no' formats and simple ranked items like 'friendly-neutral-hostile' were the most common answer formats employed. Where it was necessary, there was also additional space provided for 'other' or 'comments'. There were, however, a few open-ended answers, which provided a vast amount of further detail afterwards. These have been taken into account to an extent, but have not been used in their totality, nor have they been coded. Apart from the profile of the respondents, most of the questions aimed at grasping the condition of the immigrants at the time of the interview; in a few cases, questions addressed their migration history (year of entry, legal status upon arrival, first accommodation in Greece, settlement history and previous occupations). A copy of the original questionnaire that was administered in Greek and its English translation have been included in Appendix B1.

The interviews were based on a guide designed for the purposes of a research project on 'Social Exclusion of Albanians in Italy and Greece', which was funded by the Leverhulme Trust and carried out by two research teams at the universities of Sussex and Dundee. My supervisor, Russell King, was the principal investigator of this project. There was an initial section on demographic data and details of the interview time and place that had to be completed on a form. The rest of the interview was tape-recorded and consisted of five groups of questions: (1) Migration Dynamics; (2) Exclusion (labour market, formal and informal networks and institutions of support/welfare, housing, participation in networks of support/solidarity); (3) Racism and Identity; (4) Cultural Integration/Exclusion (Media); and (5) Future Plans. The interview guide is available in Appendix B2. The schedule was a semi-structured, open-ended one, and the sequence of questions did not always follow the guide, since the aim was to get in-depth information and therefore it was intended to leave the interviewee free to speak without many interruptions. Although it did not really employ the 'life history' interviewing technique, the schedule addressed biographic material also, since all sections contained questions about the personal stories of the interviewees, in respect to their decision to emigrate, their legal status, housing, employment and relationships with locals. All interviews are kept on tape and were fully or partly transcribed into MS Word document files.

3.2.2 *Conducting the fieldwork: a report from the front*

In total, a period of a year and a half was devoted to research in the field. Questionnaires and interviews with Albanian immigrants were done between October 2001 and July 2002, following a one-month pilot phase in April 2001. Questionnaires and interviews with Bulgarian immigrants started in November 2001 but progressed slowly, and a great share of them were conducted between September 2002 and February 2003. The slow progress of the fieldwork has to be attributed to factors such as: problems of coming into contact with immigrants; unwillingness of some to participate; and unavailability due to work/family responsibilities. Most of the meetings had to take place during afternoons and/or weekends, when the interviewees had some spare time and were willing to dedicate it to me and to my research. The chief practical difficulty I faced in the beginning, as well as at some points during the course of the fieldwork, was meeting the desired number of potential respondents and interviewees. I was aware that the 'snowball effect' would solve this problem, but I had to establish some initial contacts first. Therefore, a period had to be spent initially in finding possible sources from where I could ensure a number of first interviewees/respondents. I started by mobilising my personal networks, trying to contact migrants I knew, or people who had some sort of relationship with immigrants (past and present employers, landlords, neighbours, friends, colleagues, etc.). This resulted in unexpectedly many people who were willing to help by bringing me into contact with potential respondents/interviewees. However, apart from these initial individual resources, I found it easy to go through other 'safe' channels, such as NGOs, translation businesses, meeting places, etc. Some important contacts that resulted in significant proportions of the total sample were the following:

- The NGO Odysseas, a free Greek language school for immigrants and refugees hosted by the Macedonian Institute of Employment (MAKINE, home also of the INTEGRA 'Programme for the Reception and Support of Immigrants and Refugees'). I met some of the volunteer teachers involved and gained access to the classes, and so I had the opportunity to speak to some of the students.
- The Albanian Association of Thessaloniki, which runs, among other activities, Albanian language courses for migrants' children every Sunday morning. After being introduced by the association's representatives, it was a good opportunity to conduct questionnaires or interviews with parents who were waiting for their children.
- A group of students from various departments of the University of Macedonia, who are Albanian nationals and who responded positively to an advertisement I placed at the university. They volunteered to help me by bringing me into contact with relatives and friends, and, in some cases, by undertaking to administer a small number of questionnaires themselves.

- A central Thessaloniki café, which operates as a meeting place for a small Bulgarian community in the absence of any formal organisation of Bulgarians in the city. The owner, after having been interviewed herself, offered a great amount of help by introducing me to friends and relatives, as well as customers.

Once some initial contacts had been established, the snowball effect started working, as many respondents/interviewees were able to introduce me to at least one relative, friend or colleague who was eager to participate. I generally tried to avoid contacting migrants directly, being aware of a series of problems that could possibly arise, as they actually did some of the few times I attempted to do so. Such problems were associated with the lack of trust between an immigrant in Greece and a 'local asking questions' without the mediation of a person who could act as a 'referee' for me as the researcher. This can actually be interpreted as an additional manifestation of the 'life in fear' experienced by many immigrants in Greece due to unfair or racist attitudes towards them (see Chapter 5). On a few occasions though, I had no alternative to going out on the street, to piazzas, where immigrants gather every morning to seek work; to cafés, where they meet after work or at weekends; to translation offices; or to the doors of the Albanian and Bulgarian consulates. This strategy was particularly followed when I was facing serious problems in meeting the required number of respondents, especially Bulgarian migrants, in the final stage. In general though, the fieldwork progressed steadily without significant difficulties.

The vast majority of questionnaires and all interviews were conducted personally by myself and were face to face. The questionnaires were completed in open public places, coffee shops, or in rooms at the offices of the organisations involved. On some occasions, more than one questionnaire was administered at the same time. Interviews, on the other hand, were conducted by appointment, and in most cases at the homes of the interviewees. Some of the interviews were joint ones, while in a few cases there were other persons present at the time of the interview (husbands/wives, other relatives, friends/flatmates, employers, etc) who sometimes intervened in the discussion. The time needed to complete a questionnaire varied between fifteen and thirty minutes, while interviews lasted from about thirty minutes to two hours, depending on the willingness of the interviewee to speak. The language used could not be other than Greek. Most of the respondents/interviewees were able to communicate at a comprehensive level of Greek, and I did not face serious problems of mutual understanding. For the interviews though, I tried to ensure meeting only people above a certain level of Greek-language competency. In a few cases, other languages were employed (English, French), depending on the respondents'/interviewees' knowledge, in order to clarify points that could not be well understood. One interview took place entirely in English, because the participant felt more comfortable in this language. In a few cases, third persons who were present during the interview acted as translators in order to clarify my questions or to help the respondents to phrase their answers.

3.2.3 *Ethical considerations*

I decided as a matter of principle to briefly explain to all participants who I am, what I do and what the objectives of my research are. Some people would then ask me questions about the purposes of the survey, who I was doing it for and if it was going to be published and become known and influential to policy makers. In such cases, I tried to keep quite a low profile by explaining that parts of it would certainly be published, and it would be 'a very nice thing' if it had an impact at all; but I felt I should be realistic by sticking to the point that they were actually being asked to help me to do my fieldwork and obtain a D.Phil.

In general, I received a great variety of reactions from actual and potential interviewees, although I can say that most of the people were generally positive, friendly and talkative. Many migrants really wanted to speak for various reasons, mostly to address problems they were facing; some were even more talkative than was actually needed, with a certain degree of exaggeration. On the other hand, there were cases of people who were laconic, or who didn't find it easy to speak about certain things; a young woman burst into tears while recalling her experience of crossing the border illegally. Finally, I came across many who were just hostile or afraid to participate. They would accordingly challenge the importance of the research as a whole, or would express their fears by questions of the kind 'Will I be followed by Interpol?', or 'You are not working for the police, eh?'. I generally tried not to put the interviewees/respondents under pressure and to respect their own will and availability to participate in my research.

The administration of questionnaires, and especially the interviews, presupposed the establishment of a relationship based on mutual confidentiality. I mentioned before the channels through which I moved in order to contact potential respondents/interviewees: these channels, organisations and individuals were my 'guarantee' of confidentiality. Moreover, I felt I should offer my help by spreading information when I could see it was needed: accordingly, I informed some people about the existence of organisations and programmes of support/solidarity (e. g. free language courses, available welfare provisions, etc.). This would usually happen during the discussion that in many cases followed the interviews and contributed further to building relationships of trust. In addition, the assurance of the anonymity of the participants has been a key strategy that helped me in establishing this kind of relationship. The clandestine status of some immigrants was by itself a sensitive issue that required particular care. The questionnaire was anonymous by design, since it did not ask for names or contact details. The interviews were more problematic in that respect, because I had arranged appointments by phone and in many cases visited interviewees at their homes. I had to assure the participants that their contact details would be kept strictly confidential, and that no third persons would have any kind of access to the names, addresses or phone numbers of the people I had interviewed. However, I decided not to change the names of the interviewees in the quotes used throughout the thesis. Given the fact that only first names are used, quite common to an extent, and after having discussed it with some of the interviewees, I am confident that there is no potential danger of the participants being identified.

3.2.4 *Sampling and data analysis*

Despite the differences between the two data-collection techniques, I decided to treat the sample as a whole, as a single quantitative survey, part of which also contains qualitative and detailed information. Therefore, the quantitative material (profile, details on entry, legal status, employment, housing, etc.) that came out of the interviews has been added to the rest of the (questionnaire) data. No particular statistical sample design has been employed. As mentioned already, the sampling process relied almost exclusively upon the snowball effect, and this has been the only available means for assuring a random sample. There are two main reasons for this:

- Firstly, the official statistics are rather poor and were even poorer at the time of the fieldwork: the only published source was the 1998 regularisation statistics, since the 2001 census data appeared online only in late 2003. The Albanian and Bulgarian migrants in Greece and Thessaloniki can be considered, from a statistical point of view, as 'hidden populations'. Even if more complete and accurate statistics were available, the total number of (all) immigrants would remain unknown, since many of them are still undocumented and since a significant number of people are believed to be following circular migration patterns. The existence of a fragmented legal framework, which treats in a differential manner different categories of migrants (ethnic Greeks, seasonal workers, dependent family members, asylum seekers, etc.), affects in turn the collection, availability and accuracy of official data.
- Secondly, because of the objectives of the research itself and its methodological and analytical thrusts. The intention was not simply

> to describe the characteristics of the groups studied, but rather to explore and analyse the processes of *incorporation*, as defined earlier. Thus, there was no overwhelming need for assuring statistical representativeness, since I was not planning to go into sophisticated statistical analysis of the data as such; rather, I *discuss* the data in order to answer my initial research questions on the basis of the analytical framework set out earlier in this chapter. The quantitative data is analysed in relation to the qualitative material and in parallel to my other sources, in an attempt to relate my case study to other cases of migration and incorporation. In that sense, even the over-representation, for instance, of migrants with certain characteristics[8], is not thought to be a serious problem, because it reveals additional factors in the study of incorporation.

Accordingly, the concept of *external validity* should be treated as a very relative one, especially in multi-method non-statistical research like the one employed in my thesis, where quantitative and qualitative elements are constructively combined. Hence, the only criterion used in the selection of the sample was that respondents should be working or have worked in Greece. There has been an effort, though, to keep a balance between the different channels for meeting potential respondents, regarding the share of some of the sub-groups in the sample (e.g. the ethnic Greeks). Having made all these caveats, however, a comparison of the characteristics of my sample with the available statistics and with the findings of other empirical surveys confirms a certain degree of representativeness and allows meaningful statistical generalisations.

All data were processed into MS Excel, which has been used in the first instance to calculate frequencies and percentages. The basic data (quantitative) were coded into key-variables and then transferred to SPSS in order to perform simple descriptive/exploratory statistical procedures more easily. Given the fact that most of the questionnaires had been administered by myself (or had been carefully explained in full detail in the few cases where other people volunteered to help), no problems of misunderstanding or misinterpretation were faced. There were, however, a few difficulties during the processing of the data, as regards the coding of some variables[9]. The majority of the questions were answered; there exists however some missing information, which becomes rather significant in questions concerning money (i.e. rent, wage, household income, remittances, investment, bank account) or regarding some other specific details (accommodation size, floor, etc.).

Apart from frequencies and percentages, I compare means to highlight differences where appropriate and make use of cross-tabulations, chi-square tests and correlations to summarise data and to explore or confirm relationships between variables, when these were implied by the analysis itself, suggested by the qualitative material, or when I had the impression that a relationship could exist. Chi-square was helpful for being a non-parametric, distribution-free test, suitable for categorical variables, while for continuous numeric variables the Pearson's correlation co-efficient has been used. A series of dichotomous variables related to the migrants' living conditions were synthesised into an index in order to summarise the data into one single continuous variable (see Section 8.1.3)[10].

As already stated, interviews were conducted face to face and were tape-recorded. The ones with Albanians were fully transcribed (some with the kind assistance of other people) and then translated into English, as they were also needed for the purposes of the Leverhulme research project mentioned earlier. The rest of the interviews were partly transcribed in accordance with the needs of the analysis. No specialised software package has been employed to analyse the interview material. Being aware of the limits of 'the human as analyst' (see Robson 2002: 460), I decided to proceed by doing the analysis myself after considering the role and the weight of the interviews in my research as a whole. The number of interviews was not so large that it would be difficult or very time-consuming for me to analyse them all. Moreover, the memory of each individual interview was kept alive and was supported by detailed notes, which made it easy for me to go through a careful reading/listening without missing important points. My research is based on a combination of methods anyway, thus it does not rely exclusively on interviews in the sense that a very thorough computer-based qualitative analysis would be necessary. Lastly, any possible bias and misleading first impressions are believed to have been avoided at the end by cross-relating qualitative findings with quantitative data, by testing hypotheses also on a quantitative basis, and by discussing conclusions in the light of other empirical and theoretical works.

As I mentioned earlier, the interview sample itself should not be regarded as statistically representative; after all, quantitative generalisations are made possible by the analysis of the survey as a whole. It rather consists of a rich selection of separate cases, which allow a look at a variety of individual experiences that are discussed and conceptualised in relation to quantitative findings and to what is already known from the literature and other sources. In that sense, the qualitative material drawn out of the interviews has been used in order to frame or re-frame hypotheses, to explore relationships, to construct and/or support arguments and to further interpret the raw numeric evidence coming out of the rest of the survey. Therefore, no special attention is given to the discourse or the wording/phrasing of the answers; what was primarily the focus of the interview analysis was the content of the answers as such, regarding 'objective' conditions and 'subjective' understandings of the interviewees' migration experiences. The qualitative material is incorporated into the discussion, with references to general findings and descriptive summaries of parts of the narratives, while specific extracts from individual interviews are included according to the needs of the analysis.

Ethnographic-like analysis of this kind can reveal interesting qualitative elements, which apply in general to Albanian and Bulgarian immigrants in Greece and to an extent to other migrant groups, especially when discussed in the light of existing knowledge. As King, Iosifides and Myrivili (1998: 159) put it, the 'real experts on migration are the migrants themselves' and qualitative analysis of interviews may thus help us to 'capture the richness of the human experience of migration' (in the words of King, 2002: 101). By 'giving a voice' to migrants, and by analysing their experiences and perceptions on the basis of the structural, institutional and cultural contexts in the specific locality where they live, we can conceptualise their lifeworld. On the other hand, the purpose of quantitative analysis is not simply to describe the characteristics of immigrants in Thessaloniki, but rather to explore relationships, confirm hypotheses and give statistical relevance to arguments articulated on the basis of the qualitative material and/or theory. In general, quantitative and qualitative elements are critically combined and mixed in a constructive synthesis of both methods, with the weight moving from one to the other, depending on the arguments developed. Each method supports, complements and fills in the gaps of the other, or uncovers different aspects of the issues discussed, allowing thus for general and holistic interpretations. In addition, the analysis of interviews provides the biographic material needed for a dynamic account of the migration experiences of the participants, while the questionnaire data give a more static picture of the respondents' characteristics at the time of the fieldwork. The question of time is crucial in the understanding of the dynamics of incorporation and will appear in several parts of the discussion: it is highlighted by qualitative evidence, and confirmed to an extent through statistical comparisons between migrants who came in different periods.

The *unit of study* concerns the two particular immigrant groups studied, although later I refer to migrants in general, in an attempt to theorise my results. The right way of describing the study population would be perhaps 'migrants from Albania and Bulgaria', since both groups include significant shares of ethnic Greek migrants (Greek-Albanians or 'Northern Epirotes' and Sarakatsani Bulgarians). The *unit of analysis*, meaning the chief target of the empirical research and the principal source of information, is basically the individual migrant, although there is also some material pertaining to the migrant household. The *scale of study and analysis* is the city itself. Regarding both the fieldwork and the official data used, what I call *Greater Thessaloniki* is officially called the 'Greater Thessaloniki Area', which is geographically half of Thessaloniki Prefecture, and also includes semi-urban areas. By *metropolitan area*, I mean the peri-urban zone, most likely destined to form the metropolitan area in the near future. Other 'units' that appear are the *Thessaloniki conurbation*, (the built-over urban surface) and the *municipality of Thessaloniki* (basically, the inner city)[11].

3.3 The research setting: a socio-economic profile of Thessaloniki

Greater Thessaloniki is the most important economic centre in northern Greece, and the second most important one in the country, producing more than 11.7 per cent of the total national GDP and about 66.9 per cent of the regional GDP in Central Macedonia in 2002[12]. During the same year, the GDP per capita in Thessaloniki Prefecture was higher than the national one by 18 percentage points. During 1994-1995, manufacturing accounted on average for 25.9 per cent of production and services for 70.5 per cent. At the end of 2003, the area was concentrating about 8 per cent of the total (national) labour force. Vaiou and Hadjimichalis (1997: Table 4.9) describe Greater Thessaloniki as an 'urban-industrial' labour market where traditional, informal, labour-intensive activities coexist with modern, formal and capital-intensive ones. It comprises skilled, 'central' and unionised labour employed in industries and services of both the private and the public sectors, seasonal employment in small- and medium-scale enterprises and in intensive agriculture, 'female' employment in sectors of diffused industrialisation, and informal employment in construction, trade and various services.

Currently, manufacturing accounts for slightly more than one third of the total number of companies in Thessaloniki Prefecture (ICAP 2003), making the area the second most important industrial complex in the country after Athens. In 2000, 16.3 per cent of Greece's manufacturers and 13.9 per cent of industrial employment were concentrated in the prefecture. The principal industries are shoes and clothing, textiles, tobacco, food and beverages, transportation means, furniture and metal machinery. The most dynamic sectors during the early 1990s, with high shares of contribution to the country's industrial GDP, were shoes and clothing, textiles, food and beverages and plastics and chemicals, while the ones declining at the time were the wood and furniture, and metallurgy and metal-machinery industries. The average company size in the mid-1990s was calculated at 6.5 employees per unit (Kafkalas et al. 1996: 55). Chronaki et al. (1993) report that a significant part of industrial activity remains unrecorded, especially for smaller enterprises, often family-owned and family-run, which also tend to apply labour-intensive practices. The tertiary sector is of particular importance for Thessaloniki's economy; trade alone accounted for about 60 per cent of services in 2001 (ICAP 2003: Figure 2). Historically, commercial activities have been the cornerstone of the city's economic life (Moskov 1978).

From the late 1980s, the rise in labour costs and the rigidities of the Greek labour market, increasing international competition and the inability of small enterprises to modernise interrupted the fragile dynamism of the previous decades and led to crisis (Chronaki et al. 1993; Vaiou & Hadjimichalis 1997). The 1990s witnessed many enterprises shutting down and a rapid growth in unemployment. From 8.2 per cent at the beginning of the decade (1991 census), the unemployment rate in the metropolitan area reached 13.4 per cent in 1999, and remains high (10 per cent in early 2003; NSSG, Labour Force Surveys). Restructuring processes combined with the overall 'good' performance of the Greek economy during the second half of the 1990s (reaching EU standards and entering the monetary union) gave way to a new dynamism well manifested in the local economy. Forms of neo-industrialisation have appeared, with an internationally competitive and dynamic industrial complex developing in the area (Komninos & Sefertzi 1998). The urban economy itself is currently undergoing trends of further tertiarisation and informationalisation, and larger companies based on capital-intensive methods are being developed (Giannakou & Kafkalas 1999). Personal consumption increased significantly in the city over the past three decades, and is currently characterised by two major trends (Giannakou & Kafkalas 1999): (i) the persistence of massive demand for 'Fordist-type' products and services, and (ii) the shift towards more individualised forms of demand.

A population of nearly 1.1 million was recorded in the prefecture during the 2001 census; nearly 80 per cent in the metropolitan area, over 70 in the conurbation and over one third in the municipality[13]. One in five prefecture residents have post-secondary or tertiary education. The share of university graduates jumped from 8.4 per cent of the population above 19 years old in 1991 to 11.8 per cent in 2001, with the share of women possessing a degree rising by 4.1 percentage points. Nearly two thirds of the labour force are employed in services: about 20 per cent in trade, 13 per cent in education and health, 7.1 per cent in real estate, 6.3 per cent in transportation, communications and storing, 6.1 per cent in intermediate financial organisations and other service-providing companies, 5.7 per cent in public administration and insurance services, 5.4 in hotels and restaurants. Employment in manufacturing concerns 18.5 per cent of the working population, while 7.7 per cent work in construction and 5.5 per cent in agriculture. Entrepreneurship and self-employment are the case for respectively 12.2 per cent and 12.3 per cent of the labour force (9.4 per cent and 21.3 per cent respectively in 1991). The higher shares of employers are found mostly in the trade sector, but also in manufacturing and the hotel and catering industry, while the self-employed are concentrated in agriculture, trade and real-estate services. The unemployment rate in 2001 was 11.3 per cent, which for women rises to 14.1 per cent, and for young people between 15-29 exceeds 20 per cent. For people aged 15-39 years old, unemployment drops to 16.8 per cent, but it is obviously still high; notably, this is the better-educated section of the labour force, with 40 per cent possessing a university degree (61.5 per cent of women in this group). High shares of part-time employment are also observed among this age group (38 per cent, about 42 per cent for women).

About 80 per cent of the foreign population in the prefecture live in Greater Thessaloniki, more than half in the municipality. The principal sectors for the 31,989 immigrants who are employed are construction (23.3 per cent), manufacturing (21.1 per cent), agriculture (7.4 per cent) and services (41.3 per cent). Compared to the figures for *all* immigrants, employment in services drops to 36.9 per cent among Bulgarians and to 31 per cent among Albanians, while agriculture weighs more for both nationalities (11 and 13 per cent, respectively) and construction is much more important for Albanian nationals (28.3 per cent). About 60 per cent of women work in services, with the 'hotel and restaurants' sector weighing more for Bulgarians (30.2 per cent), and the category 'other services' being more important for Albanians (49 per cent). The share of employment in manufacturing among Albanian women exceeds its equivalent among the total number of foreign workers (24.6 per cent), but it is much lower in agriculture (5.8 per cent), in contrast to that of female Bulgarians (12.5 per cent).

Industrial production is mainly located in two main areas/complexes (Sindos to the west and Thermi to the east), but small manufacturing units can be found all over the city (see Chronaki et al. 1993). Commercial activities are even more diffused, although inner-city neighbourhoods are generally characterised by small retail trade while large commercial outlets tend to concentrate mostly on the outskirts. Similarly, the spatial distribution of other service activities (leisure, finance, public services, etc.) is generally marked by an over-representation in the city centre, followed by the central areas of various districts/municipalities and, depending on the type of activity, certain concentrations in suburban locations. The centre itself concentrates diverse activities, various types of workers and the highest proportion of tenants as opposed to homeowners, since it attracts more people looking for relatively temporary residence (public servants, for example, or students, and increasingly immigrants). This relative diffusion of economic activities is accompanied by a relative mixture of social classes.

As the city geographically spreads along the coast, its social map is divided between the prosperous, more expensive and better-conserved areas of the south-eastern part and the downgraded, poorer and cheaper areas of the north-west, with a socially mixed centre in between (the municipality). There exist relatively 'downgraded' (i.e. overpopulated, with older buildings, cheaper rents, etc.) neighbourhoods within the municipality (in the northern and western districts: e.g. Kassandrou Street, Vardaris) and in eastern Thessaloniki (e.g. Foinikas), but by no means can they be characterised as 'clusters of poverty', while there are also 'nice' areas in the north-west (e.g. Oraiokastro). Tsoulouvis (1996) has noticed a high concentration of social groups living in relatively vulnerable conditions in the north-western part of the metropolitan area (immigrants, Roma, drug addicts, single-parent families, unemployed). Unemployment rates for instance, according to the 2001 census, exceed 12 per cent in most north-western areas (with two exceptions: Pefka and Triandria) and in one case (Efkarpia) approach 16 per cent. However, even in such neighbourhoods the population remains ethnically and socially mixed. In general, social divisions in Thessaloniki are not as sharp as in other urban concentrations, due to the existence of a wide middle class, which is geographically dispersed all over the city (Leontidou 1990: Ch. 5; Labrianidis & Lyberaki 2001: Ch. 7). As shown in Figure A2 (Appendix A), the majority of immigrants recorded during the 2001 census live in inner-city neighbourhoods, with higher concentrations in the north-western districts of the conurbation.

The general feature of vertical social differentiation in terms of residence (the wealthier segments of the population living on the upper floors), noted by Leontidou (1990; 1996), is to an extent evident in the case of Thessaloniki (Labrianidis & Lyberaki 2001: Ch.7). The inner city and the surrounding areas, especially to the north-west, are generally marked by older buildings, more compact urban structure and high population density. According to a study by Velentzas et al. (1996: Table 6.1), the percentage of buildings built before 1970 ranges from 64.3 per cent to 85.2 per cent in the central neighbourhoods (the historical centre and the neighbourhoods at its west and north); only 23 per cent of the blocks in the Thessaloniki conurbation were built after 1980. Also, the north-western districts have resulted from the 'anarchic' urbanisation of the previous decades, while construction patterns in the eastern areas have generally followed a more planned path. Lately, there has been a marked trend of rents going up in most parts of the city, particularly in the centre and the popular eastern districts and suburbs; Velentzas et al. (1996) noted this happening already by the end of the 1980s, but rents have grown very considerably since their study.

Historically, Thessaloniki has been an important commercial port and a major city in two empires: the Byzantine and the Ottoman. Under Ottoman rule it was one of the first industrial centres in both the Empire and the transnational area that later formed the Greek nation-state; in fact, Thessaloniki was the most important centre until Athens took off in the 1870s (Leontidou 1990: Ch. 2). Today it exhibits most of the characteristics of the classic Mediterranean city (Leontidou 1990; 1996), with one notable exception: history. Two peculiarities have to do with that. The first is that what was once the 'historical centre' is now limited to scattered old buildings, while the core of the city is comprised of relatively newly built blocks, as a result of the Great Fire of 1917, the earthquake of 1978, and especially urban-planning policies since the 1960s (Leontidou 1990: Ch. 4-5). The second is that the city's history is no longer visible in the urban landscape, with the exception of some recently restored Byzantine churches and the 'Upper Town', the old Muslim quarter. The historian Mark Mazower (2004: 12) describes it evocatively as 'A forest of densely-packed apartment blocks and giant advertising billboards sprouted where in living memory had been cypresses and minarets, stables, owls and storks.' His description points to the city's multicultural and polyglot history, which lasted for nearly 500 years, from its conquest by the Ottomans in 1430 to the elimination of the erstwhile prevalent Jewish element by the Nazis during the Second World War.

Thus it was not by chance that one of the names the city once bore was 'La Sefarade des Balcanes' (= the Sephardite of the Balkans; Veinstein 1993). Thessaloniki hosted large numbers of Sephardic Jews after the *Reconquista* re-established Christian rule in the Iberian Peninsula, leading to the expulsion of those unwilling to convert. Jews formed the majority of the city's population, followed by Muslims and Christians. For centuries its life was characterised by coexistence between the various communities, on the basis of the hierarchy imposed by the Ottoman elite. At the end of the nineteenth century, it was characterised by contradictory forces of westernisation and tradition; apart from the three main communities, already distinctively identified as Greeks, Turks, etc., it hosted a mosaic of peoples from the Balkans, and also Central and Eastern Europe. Following Mazower, quoting from a novel (2004: 9):

> Leon Sciaky's evocative *Farewell to Salonica*, the autobiography of a Jewish boy growing up under Abdul Hammid, begins with the sound of the muezzin's cry at dusk. Albanian householders protected their Bulgarian grocer from the fury of the Ottoman gen-

> darmerie, while well-to-do Muslim parents employed Christian wet-nurses for their children and Greek gardeners for their fruit trees. Outside the Yalman family home the well was used by 'the Turks, Greeks, Bulgarians, Jews, Serbs, Vlachs and Albanians of the neighbourhood'.

This history, well embodied in the urban landscape until not so long ago, has now faded after less than a century within the borders of the Greek nation-state: the Muslims left with the exchange of the populations that followed Greece's defeat in the Greco-Turkish War of 1919-1922, and the Jews were deported (and most of them killed) by the Nazis during the Second World War. But it was not only modernisation, capitalist development and urbanisation that contributed to this; as Mazower argues, it was also the result of conscious attempts to redraw the city's identity on the basis of national and religious considerations, as well as political and electoral interests. Today, the city seems to be regaining part of its lost multicultural character, as it increasingly hosts people of diverse origins and becomes a new home for migrants from the Balkans and elsewhere. The study of immigrants' incorporation within this urban context may help us to understand the contradictions through which such a process may be taking place.

4 Structure, patterns and dynamics of migration

Thus far I have outlined both the general and the specific contexts of migration and immigrants' integration in Greece. The previous chapter ended with a description of the productive and employment structures and the urban geography of Thessaloniki, with a brief reference to the city's multicultural past. The broad issues related to the Greek experience of migration, including an overview of the basic economic and social features regarding immigrant employment and an account of the relevant policy framework, were addressed in the latter half of Chapter 2. Before starting to analyse the processes of incorporation themselves (what happens once the migrants are in Greece), it is necessary to talk a little about the background factors underlying the specificities of immigration from Albania and Bulgaria, according to the findings of the field research. In this chapter, therefore, I refer to the structure of the migrant population in terms of its demographic characteristics, human capital, geographic and cultural origins, as well as to the reasons for migration, the modes of entering the country, the geographic trajectories within Greece and the patterns of final settlement in Thessaloniki. This information is important not simply as a 'description of the sample' (i.e. who are the migrants questioned, why, when and how they came, from where, and so forth), but crucially because it draws the general picture of the *dynamics* of migration. Migratory dynamics are not only essential to understand the patterns of integration, but also have direct effects on the incorporation process as such. This chapter has this dual task: on the one hand, to describe the sample and sketch the migration profile of the respondents; on the other, to identify the basic patterns and dynamics in this newly formed migration system(s), highlighting their relevance to the incorporation process.

4.1 Immigrants' profile: a description of the sample

The information presented in this section is quantitative and concerns the 'profile' of the participants in the research. Firstly, I describe the demographic composition of the sample, in terms of gender, age and family status, geographic origin, ethnic and religious background. Secondly, I present the immigrants' employment and educational skills; in other words, their human capital characteristics at the time of the fieldwork. Comparisons between the two migrant groups as well as between the subgroups on the basis of gender and ethnic origin are also made.

4.1.1 Demographic characteristics, geographical and cultural background

The sample consists of 138 Albanian and 70 Bulgarian respondents, whose demographic characteristics are summarised in Table 4.1. The share of women is 29.7 per cent among Albanian and 50 per cent among Bulgarian migrants. Approximately half of the persons questioned belong to the 30-49 age group; about one third (36.2 of the Albanians and 31.4 of the Bulgarians) are young people between 18-29 years old. The percentage of older people (of 50 years or more) is notably higher among Bulgarians (21.4 per cent compared to 13.8 among Albanians). This variation in age between the two migrant groups may imply differences in their patterns and reasons of migration, as we are soon going to see. Turning to family status, 61.6 per cent of the Albanian migrants and 52.9 per cent of the Bulgarians are married, with more than half of both groups having children. Slightly more Albanians are single (37.6 per cent), while a significant share of the Bulgarians are divorced (ten people, all women) and one Albanian is widowed. Finally, it appears that only a few of the Albanian respondents have their close family in their home country: only 5 per cent said their husbands or wives live in Albania and about 7 per cent said their children are there. The picture is different for Bulgarian immigrants: for 14.3 and 28.6 per cent of them, their spouses and children respectively live in Bulgaria (with a lower response rate, however).

About one third of the Albanians and 28.6 per cent of the Bulgarians are of ethnic Greek origin (Table 4.1), but, given the lack of official data on ethnic Greek migrants, it is difficult to estimate the relevance of the sample characteristics to their actual population in Thessaloniki. With respect to their religious background, the overwhelming majority of immigrants from Bulgaria are Orthodox. Albanians appear to be a much more heterogeneous population in terms of religion: 60 per cent said they are Orthodox, 11 per cent declared themselves Muslims and 6 per cent Catholic, while a significant share (21.5 per cent) declared 'not religious'[1]. Notably, about 10 per cent of both groups have been baptised in Greece, which might reflect specific integration 'strategies', as we will see in Section 8.2.3.

It is interesting to have a closer look at the differences between the subgroups in the sample, namely in respect to gender and ethnic origin. Regarding the former, we observe that females are more repre-

Table 4.1 *Immigrants in Thessaloniki: demographic characteristics*

	All			*Ethnic Greeks*			*Non-Greek Origin*		
	female	*male*	*total*	*female*	*male*	*total*	*female*	*male*	*total*
					Albanian Migrants				
age									
18-29	36.6	36.1	36.2	36.8	17.9	25.5	36.4	43.5	41.8
30-39	31.7	24.7	26.8	36.8	17.9	25.5	27.3	27.5	27.5
40-49	24.4	22.7	23.2	10.5	28.6	21.3	36.4	20.3	24.2
50+	7.3	16.5	13.8	15.8	35.7	27.7	0.0	8.7	6.6
family status									
single	34.2	39.2	37.7	36.8	17.9	25.5	31.8	47.8	44.0
married	63.4	60.8	61.6	63.2	82.1	74.5	63.6	52.2	55.0
widowed	2.4	–	0.7	–	–	–	4.6	–	1.1
all									
Total (N)	41	97	138	19	28	47	22	69	91
Total (%)	29.7	70.3	100.00	40.4	59.6	(34.1)*	24.2	75.8	(65.9)*
					Bulgarian Migrants				
age									
18-29	20.0	42.9	31.4	25.0	33.3	30.0	18.5	47.8	32.0
30-39	34.3	25.7	30.0	37.5	16.7	25.0	33.3	30.4	32.0
40-49	22.9	11.4	17.1	12.5	16.7	15.0	25.9	8.7	18.0
50+	22.9	20.0	21.4	25.0	33.3	30.0	22.2	13.0	18.0
family status									
single	25.7	37.1	31.4	37.5	16.7	25.0	22.2	47.8	34.0
married	45.7	60.0	52.9	37.5	83.3	65.0	48.2	47.8	48.0
divorced/widowed	28.6	2.9	15.7	25.0	0.0	10.0	29.6	4.4	18.0
all									
Total (N)	35	35	70	8	12	20	27	23	50
Total (%)	50.0	50.0	100.0	40.0	60.0	(28.6)*	54.0	46.0	(71.4)*

* Share of ethnic group within each nationality

sented among Bulgarians, a picture not that far from the reality of available statistics and other sources[2]. The sample thus reflects a 'dependent' pattern in Albanian female migration: women usually follow men, as dependent family members, or are left behind. This is particularly true for non-ethnic-Greek Albanian migrants: the share of women is higher among Greek-Albanians (40.4 per cent), perhaps due to the more 'familial' character of this group's emigration patterns. On the other hand, the higher participation of women in the Bulgarian section of the sample implies a more 'independent' pattern of female migration in their case. The significant share of people who are divorced in the Bulgarians' case consists exclusively of women, which might imply a hidden aspect of this particular migration stream: migration arises as a solution for divorced women, usually themselves responsible for their children, who decide to go abroad in order to improve their situation[3]. In total, while more than half of the female Bulgarians are single or divorced, this is the case for only one in three Albanian women; also, non-ethnic-Greek female Albanians are more likely to be married, which adds to the argument about dependent migration patterns in their case. Bulgarian women, on the other hand, appear to be generally older (than both their male compatriots and female Albanians), with an average age of 38.8 years (36.4 for men), in contrast to the Albanian migrants' characteristics (Albanian migrant women are generally younger than men, but here the age gap is not that sharp).

Albanian ethnic Greeks appear to be on average older than the rest of the Albanian nationals (and are the 'oldest' group in the sample): half of them are 40 years old or more, compared to about 30 per cent of the rest who belong to this age group. This is mostly the case for male ethnic Greeks, contrasting with their non-ethnic-Greek male compatriots, who form the youngest section with nearly 45 per cent being less than 30 years old. Notably, the only women above fifty are of ethnic Greek origin. The percentage of Greek-Albanians who are married is also higher, and this is basically the case for male ethnic Greeks, while women show similar characteristics with the rest of the Albanian sample. On the other hand, the majority of Bulgarian ethnic Greeks (seventeen out of twenty) belong to the Sarakatsani cultural group: eleven are men, in their forties on average, and all but one are married but without having their families in Greece; despite the small number of people in this group, which does not allow for statistical generalisations, their characteristics (together with other elements that will appear later in the thesis) indicate a predominantly male-dominated migration in their case. One man and one woman are of (what is perceived in Greece as) 'local Macedonian' origin: Slavophones, whose families crossed the border after the civil war. The last one is the daughter of a (now separated) mixed couple (Greek father and Bulgarian mother).

Regarding the geographic origin of the participants, 30 per cent of the Albanian immigrants come from the city of Korçë, in south-east Albania, 23.5 per cent from the capital Tirana, and nearly 8 per cent from Elbasan in the centre of the country. Another 16.2 per cent are from the south, mostly from Gjirokaster and Sarandë, where the ethnic Greek minority is mainly concentrated, but also from Vlorë on the coast. The rest come from various central areas, while the northern regions are far less represented (8.8 per cent, one in four from the city of Shkodrë). The share of Albanian women coming from the north is far lower than that of men; a greater percentage comes from southern Albania, reflecting the higher representation of female migrants among ethnic Greeks. All Greek-Albanians come, or originate, from the southern part of the country and many are from Korçë, usually those of Vlach background. Bulgarian immigrants have a more diverse geographical origin: 13 per cent come from the capital Sofia, 13 per cent from the city of Sliven and 10 per cent from Plovdiv. Another 13 per cent are from big and medium-sized cities of the north (more than half of them from Ruse), and 7.1 per cent from Varna on the north-east coast. There is a greater representation of females from Sofia, Varna and the Burgas-Yanbol-Sliven area to the east. Sarakatsani come from various places on the southern side of the long mountainous line that divides Bulgaria (Pernik, Samokov, Karlovo, Plovdiv, Chirpan, Kazavluk, Sliven), while the two Greek-Macedonian interviewees are from the border town of Petrich.

To summarise: the figure of the 'young single male Albanian' no longer represents the 'typical' immigrant in Greece – at least not in the case of Thessaloniki, according to my findings. By contrast, the sample is characterised by a great heterogeneity: gender, age and family status play a role, as well as ethnic origin or geographic and religious background. In addition, many migrants have urban roots: both in the capitals of the respective countries and in other towns. In the following paragraphs, I highlight the similarly heterogeneous human capital characteristics of the respondents, which, again, seem to challenge common Greek stereotypes.

4.1.2 *Human capital: education level and professional experience*

Given the considerable period most of the migrants had already spent in Greece, possibly also due to bias in the selection of the sample, the respondents' language skills seem to be quite good. The majority spoke and understood Greek at an intermediate level (56.5 per cent of the Albanians and 45.7 of the Bulgarians), and significant shares were fluent speakers (33.3 per cent and 42.5 per cent, respectively). Some of the respondents had the opportunity to take language courses in Thessaloniki (see Section 5.2.2). The educational level of the respondents at the time of the fieldwork is shown in Table 4.2.

Slightly more than 30 per cent of the Albanians are university graduates (with five people possessing postgraduate degrees), about one fourth have had some sort of secondary technical or post-secondary professional training and another 30.4 per cent have completed secondary education; only 15.3 per cent had not finished secondary school. Although fewer Bulgarian immigrants hold university degrees (21.4 per cent, three people having done postgraduate studies), a greater share has technical/professional qualifications (41.4 per cent), and there are fewer people who have only completed primary education (5.7 per cent). Women from both countries appear to have better educational qualifications than men. Nearly 40 per cent of female Albanians are university graduates, and some 12.2 per cent hold post-secondary

Table 4.2 *Immigrants' education level*

	Albanian Immigrants				*Bulgarian Immigrants*			
	female	*male*	*all*	*GR**	*female*	*male*	*all*	*GR**
primary	2.4	5.2	4.4	–	–	8.6	4.3	10.0
not completed secondary	14.6	9.3	10.9	4.3	2.9	–	1.4	–
secondary	19.5	35.1	30.4	23.4	31.4	31.4	31.4	25.0
technical	12.2	16.5	15.2	10.6	22.9	37.1	30.0	35.0
professional	12.2	6.2	8.0	10.6	11.4	11.4	11.4	5.0
university	36.6	23.7	27.5	42.6	25.7	8.6	17.1	25.0
postgraduate	2.4	4.1	3.6	8.5	5.7	2.9	4.3	–

* GR = ethnic Greek migrants

professional degrees, compared to 27.8 and 6.2 per cent respectively in the case of men. The equivalent figures for Bulgarian migrants are 31.4 and 11.4 per cent for women and 11.5 and 11.4 per cent for men, respectively. The share of university graduates exceeds 50 per cent among ethnic Greek Albanians and four out of five Albanians with postgraduate qualifications belong to this group, in which men appear to be better educated than women. A much lower percentage of non-ethnic Greeks, especially men, are university graduates; far more have technical/professional qualifications. Among ethnic Greek Bulgarians, only four have university degrees: two men used to be teachers, now retired, and one young woman came to Greece to study law (assisted by a special scholarship for Sarakatsani).

Regarding the respondents' employment skills before emigration, key data are summarised in Table 4.3. A significant percentage of Albanian migrants had not been working before coming to Greece, and this has to be attributed to their young age at the time of emigration: many were school pupils or university students. Of those working, and given the above figures regarding education, the shares of skilled workers and qualified employees in both groups are quite important. Approximately one quarter were skilled or specialised workers, whether in factories or as technicians, craftsmen, drivers, nurses and policemen. One in four Albanians and one in five Bulgarians used to be office employees, teachers, or army professionals. One in four Albanians was a highly qualified professional (senior public servants, scientists, engineers, artists, etc.); only 11.3 per cent of the Bulgarians belonged in this category. A significant percentage of Bulgarian migrants (25.8 per cent) worked as waiting, restaurant and hotel staff or as store clerks in Bulgaria, sectors much less important for the employment of Albanians before emigration (8 per cent). The shares of unskilled factory and other blue-collar workers are relatively low, at 10.3 and 12.9 per cent for Albanians and Bulgarians respectively. Previous work in agriculture was also limited – 8 per cent for Albanian respondents and 3.2 per cent

Table 4.3 *Main occupation in the country of origin*

Sector/Profession of Those Employed		*Albanian Migrants*	*Bulgarian Migrants*
agriculture & cattle-breeding		8.1	3.2
unskilled factory & blue collar		10.3	12.9
skilled factory & drivers		11.5	19.4
leisure & catering, retail trade		8.1	25.8
technicians & craftsmen, nurses, policemen		13.8	6.5
white collar, teachers, army professionals		24.1	21.0
highly qualified/specialised professionals		24.1	11.3
total employed (N)		*87*	*62*
total employed (% of total)		63.0	88.6
not working (N)		43	3
of whom (% of total)	*school pupils*	*23.9*	*1.4*
	university students	*7.3*	*2.9*
missing data		8	5

for Bulgarians. What the table does not show is that 3.6 per cent of the Albanians and 7.1 per cent of the Bulgarian migrants had had various jobs before emigrating; of them, two Albanians had been self-employed and one Bulgarian used to run a bar.

It is worth looking in detail at the differences observed in the sample. Higher shares of Albanian men had been working in skilled positions: slightly less than 30 per cent were highly qualified employees (ten of them engineers, two economists, the rest were senior public servants and other specialists) and another 20.6 per cent used to be teachers (seven), accountants (three) or army professionals (three). More than 22 per cent were factory workers, half of them skilled, including two drivers; nearly 15 per cent were technicians and craftsmen, plus two policemen; 8 per cent worked in retail shops or in restaurants and cafés; the share of former farmers and agricultural workers is low, 6.3 per cent. Male ethnic Greeks had higher shares of highly skilled/qualified positions before emigration and the percentage of those among them who were never employed is far lower than the rest of the respondents in the Albanian sample. Female Albanians used to work as white-collar employees (two secretaries, an accountant), schoolteachers (four), specialised professionals (a university teacher, a social scientist, an engineer), nurses/midwives (three), retail shopkeepers (two); six worked in factories, three of them as skilled workers; three worked in agriculture (one was a supervisor in a state-owned farm). The picture is different in the case of Bulgarian migrants. Bulgarian women used to work as highly qualified professionals (five), white-collar employees (seven), teachers (two), retail shopkeepers (six), waitresses and hotel staff (three) and factory workers (four, three of them skilled); there was also a driver, a technician and a nurse. Only two male Bulgarians fit in the 'highly qualified' category: a musician and an engineer. The share of blue-collar workers among Bulgarian men is significant, as is that of bar, café and restaurant staff (six, one was the owner himself); five were drivers, and there were also two factory workers, two electricians, two army professionals, two teachers, one street-trader and two cattle breeders. These latter were of Sarakatsani origin, having their own animal stock and occasionally working in factories; all but one were employed in Bulgaria before emigrating. Finally, five Bulgarian participants, four of ethnic Greek origin, are retired and receive their pensions back in Bulgaria: for those, the decision to emigrate was in order to supplement their income (e.g. to support their children's studies).

The findings presented above reflect some of the chief differences in the labour markets of the two countries, suggesting how one should understand the dynamics of migration in each of the two cases. For Albanians, who witnessed a massive devaluation of their professional attributes after the collapse of the system, emigration arose as a solution to an immediate necessity: initially at least, they had to go abroad simply because they could not do otherwise, and the scale of the phenomenon was so massive that it touched all sections of the population. For Bulgarians, the situation was rather different: some may have lost their previous jobs, usually jobs in factories, especially in northern Bulgaria (Markova 2001); most would have made a living in Bulgaria, but they decided to emigrate in order to improve their financial situation. In this case, those with a high educational level and qualified jobs form a special category and can be described as 'elites': this consists of women related to or involved with Greek men before leaving Bulgaria, and thus their migration has been directed by reasons of love and marriage; and of specialised professionals (two musicians, a businessman-engineer, a swimming coach), whose decisions came as a career option. These differences between the two migrant groups, and the particularities observed in smaller groups of people, are picked up in the coming section in the light of additional issues concerning the participants' migration decisions and routes.

4.2 Migration patterns and dynamics

Here, I give an account of some key features of the respondents' migration histories: the main reasons that shaped their decision to emigrate, when they entered Greece, the way they crossed the border and the routes they followed before settling in Thessaloniki. I outline both the similarities and main differences between the two migrant groups, and compare the heterogeneous experiences of men and women, ethnic Greeks, etc. Some qualitative elements drawn from the interview material are also incorporated into the discussion, to highlight aspects that quantitative data are unable to capture and to bring out the migrants' own perceptions.

4.2.1 *Reasons for and patterns of migration to Greece*

General economic reasons (push factors) dominated the decision to migrate: 74.6 per cent of the Albanian respondents and 81.4 per cent of the Bulgarians mentioned economic problems in their countries as being at the heart of their decision to emigrate. For some Albanians of the initial wave though (5.8 per cent), political reasons were also important. Quite surprisingly, only half of the Greek-Albanians considered their ethnic origin as a crucial factor that bore upon their decision to leave Albania. Their Greek origin was even less important for Sarakatsani, although most of them mentioned that their knowledge of the Greek language played a role in deciding to come to Greece. Furthermore, an important minor share of respondents selected the option 'other' to state additional factors that shaped their decision. For 7.2 per cent of the Albanians who did so, such reasons comprised joining relatives who were already abroad, studies, or simply the desire to see the 'outside world'.

The picture becomes clearer if we look at the reasons for migrating to Greece in particular (and not to some other country). Economic reasons (pull factors) are not that significant any more, while other factors play a more important role. Only 37.7 per cent of the Albanian migrants and 51.4 per cent of the Bulgarians considered economic conditions in Greece that favourable. Instead, geographic proximity emerges as the most important reason for half of the Albanian respondents and for almost one third of the Bulgarians. Over 28 per cent of the Albanians mentioned 'ease of entry' as an important factor, but this was much less crucial in the Bulgarians' case (5.7 per cent). Thus, emigration may have arisen as a *necessity* for many people, but migration to Greece became an *option* mainly because of the easy-to-cross borders and the geographic closeness to a relatively more developed country. In addition, ethnic origin did play an important role for 68 per cent of the Greek-Albanians and for fifteen of the Sarakatsani: for most of them Greece was a first choice, and it was easier anyway, due to governmental policies that were more favourable towards ethnic Greek migrants. There is a small share of Albanian migrants (6.5 per cent) who consider Greece as a transit country, and who intend to migrate later for a second time to some other state[4]. Finally, many respondents mentioned network factors, namely friends and/or relatives who had migrated earlier, which seem to have conditioned their patterns of settlement within Greece, as we are soon going to see in more detail. On the other hand, the 15.7 per cent of Bulgarians who mentioned additional factors uncovered more 'hidden' features of the migration patterns in the Bulgarian case. As already mentioned, there is a minority of qualified professionals who had contacts in Greece, which, together with their professional achievements, played an important role in their migration, which can be seen as a 'career development' strategy. Another aspect of Bulgarian mobility is also migration because of love/ marriage: five women got married to Greek men and four more people said that they came because their mothers were married to Greeks[5].

This multiplicity of reasons and factors for migration to Greece, which suggests a more complex migration story than that told by 'push' and 'pull' accounts, is highlighted in the following interview quotes (the first five are from Albanian migrants and the remaining three are from Bulgarians):

> We decided to come to Greece because we were not in a good economic situation. We had stopped working in Albania ... In the beginning, my husband came alone, he came with a forged passport ... he worked for a year, then he returned to Albania. We were thinking of starting a business with the little money he had earned here, but we realised we couldn't do anything ... so then we were forced ... we couldn't live separately because we were married, with two children, so we decided to take the children and come here, all the family. (Lela)
>
> I can say that it was not a purely economic motivation, but also a psychological one ... For instance, I was a student, my parents were working. I didn't have a direct need to work ... But, back at that time ... everybody was leaving, that was it. And we students could see that in the future, when we would graduate, there wouldn't be any jobs, nothing ... So we decided to leave. (Dalina)
>
> One reason to come to Greece was for economic reasons. Secondly, because we are close, Greece to Albania; and thirdly and most basic, because we are of Greek descent, I believed we would find the lost homeland ... This was the basic reason why I came to Greece, besides the economic ... cause. (Spyros)
>
> The basic reason is that, before I came to Greece, some other guys had come. They said that Greece is fantastic ... Relatives, people from my village, friends ... And I said to myself 'Why don't I go to try my luck there?' I was single, I was not married ... so I told my mother 'I'm going to Greece.' (Maria)
>
> I came here because Nadi, my brother, was here ... back then there was an insurrection – how can I explain this to you? – in our country ... It was in 1997... With pyramids [referring to the collapse of pyramid banking schemes in Albania, and the subse-

> quent financial crisis]. So, my father and my mother were afraid, and Nadi was here. (Adriana)
>
> [Because of] lack of work in Bulgaria ... I have chosen Greece because I am of ethnic Greek origin, I knew the language, and then I also knew some people here who could help me. (Soultana)
>
> The job was the leading factor. The market was closed and any development in a professional way ... was completely impossible ... On the other side, the company for which I was working decided that my potential to cover this territory was quite good ... I was already working with Greece two years before I came. (Alexander)
>
> There were many reasons, but ... the most important one was that I wanted to change myself and my life, basically. To have a change, because ... things there, as I could see, were not going to get better and I was young, I wanted to try ... And then, I had another thought: to come to Greece, to make some money and then set out for some other place, basically it was not that much that I wanted to come particularly to Greece. (Milen)

In total, 68 and 56 per cent of the Albanian and Bulgarian participants respectively had been in Greece for five years or more, and approximately one third of both nationalities had already spent a period of more than nine years; long-term residence plays a crucial role in incorporation and the impact of time will reappear throughout the thesis. Figure 4.1 illustrates schematically the migratory waves followed by the participants, according to the year they entered the country. More than one third of the Albanian respondents migrated during the 'great Albanian exodus' of the early 1990s (1990-1992). After 1992, the migratory wave slowed down, but continued steadily and reached a second peak after the financial crisis that followed the collapse of the pyramid banking schemes in 1997: another 21.4 per cent came to Greece between 1997 and 1998. Since then, the numbers of people emigrating each year have declined notably. Women seem to 'follow' men, confirming again the initially male-dominated character of Albanian migration and the dependent female migratory patterns. The majority of ethnic Greek Albanians came during the early phase: their migration continued to have small peaks in the following years, mostly due to later arrivals of women.

Bulgarian migration followed a different pattern. Firstly, because there never was a large emigration outflow, apart from the Turkophone Muslims who left the country in large numbers for Turkey at an early stage. The first shock of 1989, as expected, produced outward movements (see Figure 4.1): 18.6 per cent of the interviewees emigrated dur-

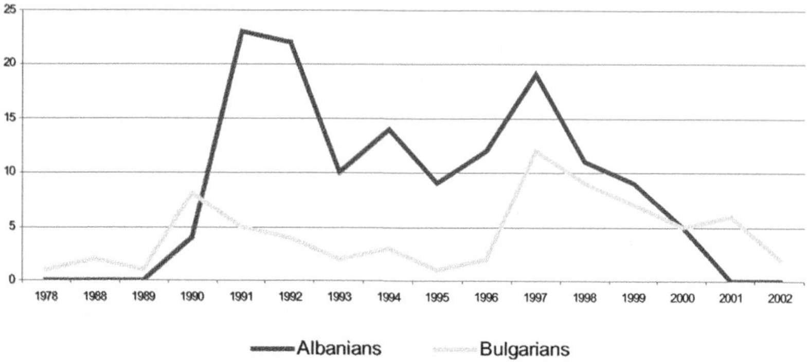

Figure 4.1 *Immigrants' year of entry by nationality (N)*

ing 1990-1991. The numbers decline considerably throughout the decade, but they pick up again in 1997-1998, with 28.6 per cent of the survey's participants having emigrated in these particular years, as a result of Bulgaria's 1996 crisis that led many factories to close. Secondly, in contrast to the Albanian case, Bulgarian migration goes on in relatively significant numbers after 1998: despite the time difference between the administration of questionnaires and interviews with Albanians (finished July 2002) and those with Bulgarians (went on until February 2003), it is rather notable that 30 per cent of the Bulgarian respondents arrived between 1999 and 2002. Thirdly, what the figure does not show is the feminine side of Bulgarian migration: in this case, women do not clearly 'follow' men. Only a relatively small proportion of them followed a pattern similar to the Albanian one, with male 'pioneers' and female 'followers'. Finally, another difference between the two migrant groups is the existence of mobility between Bulgaria and Greece before the 1990s. Four Bulgarian respondents had migrated before 1990, three of them during 1988-1989, when the signs of change were quite apparent, and one much earlier, in 1978, following her Greek husband after he finished his studies in Sofia[6]. As for the other three people who came before 1990, they are all professionals from Sofia. What these specific cases reveal is the different outward mobility patterns between Albania and other Eastern European countries: the Iron Curtain was 'harder' in the Albanian case, while in Bulgaria people belonging to certain social classes had more opportunities to move abroad.

Regarding the conditions of entering Greece (see Table 4.4), about 30 per cent of all immigrants crossed the border illegally; of them, one in five said that they went through trafficking networks and had to pay. The percentage of Albanians who entered the country illegally was 37.5 per cent, while the share of Bulgarian immigrants is much lower (17.1

per cent)[7]. The relatively higher percentage of Bulgarians who used trafficking channels corresponds to both men and women and should be attributed to the organised cross-border criminal networks that increasingly developed throughout the 1990s. These networks also controlled other illicit activities (smuggling, prostitution), sometimes in collaboration with corrupt state and police officials. Prices varied from 177 euros in 1996 (Pantelis) to between 200-300 euros in 1997 (Kostas, Lefteris, Ivan); payment was in German marks or US dollars, sometimes in drachmas as well. A broad idea of how this worked is given in the following quotes:

> We travelled, five or six people together. We came on foot, we passed through Skopje [Macedonia] ... all the way to Polykastro ... then we took a taxi, for which we paid 50,000 drachmas [150 euros] ... until Thessaloniki ... We paid a guy to bring us here, someone like a 'trader' – how can I say it? ... we left our village, and he brought us all the way down here ... We paid him two hundred dollars each ... half the money, I paid it then ... the rest ... I was working, and I paid it after a period, because then I didn't have all the money. (Ivan, came in 1997.)
> There was a guide. There are Albanians who collaborate with the Greeks. We crossed your border, we entered your country, then we'd been travelling for two days and two nights. We'd been walking during the night and we were hiding during the day, because we were afraid that somebody could see us and tell the police to arrest us ... A lorry was waiting for us in the street, there, on the mountain, in Greece, and all twenty-seven people got in the lorry. All of us came to Thessaloniki. (Pandelis)

It should be noted that what is commonly understood as 'trafficking' is not necessarily connected to criminal syndicates; this was especially true during the early phase of intra-Balkan mobility. It was common for Albanians in the early 1990s to travel in groups of people originating from the same place; the guides, however, who helped them to cross the mountainous border-zone on foot, were often people who just 'knew the way through the mountains'[8]:

> The first time, I came on foot. We were walking for five or six days ... We had my brother with us, who had come in 1991, he knew the way and we came. (Gjion)
> We came illegally. We came through Skopje [Macedonia]. We crossed the border on foot ... That night there were nine people ... relatives ... and friends ... My cousin ... knew the way. (Valbona)

Table 4.4 *Immigrants' mode of entry into Greece when they first migrated*

	Albanian Immigrants			*Bulgarian Immigrants*			*All*
	female	*male*	*all*	*female*	*male*	*all*	
illegal entry	12.2	39.2	31.2	11.4	8.6	10.0	24.0
illegal entry (trafficking)	-	8.3	5.8	5.7	8.6	7.1	6.3
falsified documents	9.8	6.2	7.3	-	-	-	4.8
tourist visa	48.8	38.1	41.3	40.0	31.4	35.7	39.4
non-tourist visa	29.3	5.15	12.3	2.9	2.9	2.9	9.1
married to a Greek	-	-	-	8.6	-	4.3	1.4
seasonal worker	1.0	0.7	-	-	-	-	0.5
Greek origin	2.1	1.5	17.1	37.1	27.1	10.1	
stay permit	-	-	8.6	5.7	7.1	2.4	
free (legal entry)	-	-	5.7	5.7	5.7	1.9	

However, the majority of all respondents (about half) entered Greece legally with a visa. Coming with a tourist visa (and extending the stay after it had expired) was the case for 41.3 per cent of the Albanians and 35.7 per cent of the Bulgarians, especially for women. A common strategy for Bulgarian migrants was to travel in organised groups, coming by coach as tourists. Some Albanians (7.3 per cent) used forged travel documents, passports and visas bought on the black market, a strategy absent in the Bulgarians' case. Some 12.3 per cent of the Albanians came with non-tourist visas: only two people gave details and they had come to study. In the Bulgarian case, the issue of non-tourist visas was limited to the professionals mentioned above, or to women who were married to Greeks and therefore had a special status. Greek-Albanians who benefited from special provisions for people of ethnic Greek origin are rather statistically insignificant (two people): ethnic Greeks initially followed the same migration paths as the rest of their co-nationals, despite their 'privileged' treatment by the authorities[9]. Bulgarian Sarakatsani, on the other hand, received special treatment from the very beginning, since they were entitled to special temporary visas. Two further differences between Albanian and Bulgarian migration can be observed: (a) 7.1 per cent of the Bulgarians entered Greece already possessing a stay permit, as a result of their professional status or because they were related to a Greek citizen; (b) a small number of Bulgarians who entered Greece during the last couple of years were not subject to border controls, since after 2000 Bulgarian nationals were entitled to travel within the Schengen Area without visas. In general, it appears that gradually, the patterns of migration have become more institutionalised: 'trafficking' peaks during the mid-1990s, and, since 1998-1999, legal entry has become the case for the majority of the migrants.

4.2.2 *Migration routes and settlement in Thessaloniki*

The research implicitly assumed the absence of previous migration experience among the respondents; the small number of people who had indeed been in other countries, however insignificant as a percentage of the sample as a whole, may represent an interesting aspect of East-West European mobility patterns in general[10]. What was expected, by contrast, was that many migrants would have passed through different places in Greece before settling in Thessaloniki. Apart from the various routes some took when they first entered Greece, reaching border villages initially and then arriving at their destination with several stops on the way (to work or visit relatives and friends for assistance), it was also common for some to settle in a specific place for a period and then re-migrate within the host country itself, in many cases with a rural-to-urban direction. Although the majority (61.5 per cent) came directly to Thessaloniki, 23.6 per cent had spent considerable periods in some other place, while 16 per cent had been to two or more places since they first arrived in Greece. The patterns appear to be similar for both groups with one notable exception: the higher share of Bulgarian migrants who had stayed in more than three places (11.4 per cent, compared to only 3.6 per cent among Albanians) is due to the weight of Sarakatsani, who had been following 'cyclical' migration routes, coming and going frequently for seasonal, usually agricultural, work in various rural areas, before moving to Thessaloniki. Given this, how are we to understand Thessaloniki as a final (?) destination in the migratory 'journeys' of the respondents? This question is not only a rhetorical one, since the place of settlement, as will be extensively argued throughout the thesis, shapes the migrants' incorporation patterns.

It has been argued that the decision of immigrants to move to a specific locality within the host country is subject to push and pull factors similar to the ones conditioning their decision to migrate to a particular country anyway (see, for instance, Stark 1991). More specifically, Lianos (2003: Ch. 3) has attempted an econometric estimation of the factors conditioning the geographical distribution of immigrants in Greece, based on official statistics. His conclusion highlights the importance of regional GDP rates, urbanisation level versus agricultural production, and distance from the border in conditioning the place of settlement of immigrants in Greece. Immigrants can probably be fully aware of the last-named factor only, which, however, is rather overestimated in Lianos' study. Avoiding border regions, which are more tightly controlled and thus a migrant is more likely to get arrested, does not necessarily mean avoiding big towns or rural areas close to the border and does not apply equally to the whole migrant population anyway (cf. legal immigrants, women, ethnic Greeks). In addition, people don't have 'perfect' information about economic indicators (like regional GDP rates): they can only have impressions about how 'rich' a place is from their own experience or from the words of others. Thus the only source of information about the economic and social features of a particular place is first-hand experience, and, most importantly, the feedback of others, via their social networks. As we have seen, Thessaloniki is far behind Greater Athens regarding migrants' concentration, but this is more likely to reflect the centralised character of the Greek state and the prevalence of Athens in the economic geography of the country; after all, Thessaloniki remains the second major destination for immigrants in Greece.

From one point of view, this is logical: immigrants enter a country which has given geographic characteristics and for Thessaloniki, the second largest Greek city, it is reasonable to expect it to attract large numbers of migrants. But the issue of *proximity* should not be underestimated, and this refers to both geographical *and* cultural closeness. If we look at the origins of the migrants of a given nationality, it appears that migrants from specific areas in the sending countries are more represented in particular localities within the receiving state. In Thessaloniki this seems to be true, for example, for Albanians coming from the city of Korçë. The links between places of origin and destination can be economic or geographic, cultural or relational. Sometimes there are old historic bonds connecting places, and this is also a factor that determines migrants' final destination. Also, sometimes social networks are based upon the remnants of old links: first-comer migrants are attracted to particular localities within the host country for historical reasons, and their settlement there is a reason for others to come. In the Albanians' case, an interesting study by Sintès (2002) suggests that modelling the diffusion of the immigrants within Greece according to the country's economic and population geography cannot alone give an adequate explanation for high concentrations of people in certain places. Sintès studied the migratory trajectories of different groups of Albanians (Muslims, Orthodox, Vlachophones, Grecophones) from specific villages and found that they had been directed towards particular places in Greece, initially at least, either where they had relatives from whom they had been separated by the border for decades, or of which they 'knew about' due to trans-local contacts dating from before the Second World War. He argues that kinship and identity, when activated through the migrants' networks, may be used as a resource in the migration process, determining thus the patterns of settlement in ways that push and pull factors are unable to interpret. In the Balkan region, which historically saw various groups of people (e.g. Vlachs, Sarakatsani, Roma, but also merchants, shepherds, travellers, etc.) moving for several reasons between places within the common space of the Ottoman Empire and was later divided by the borders of nation-states, this should not be surprising at all. This argument is to be developed further in the next section, taking the Albanian city of Korçë as an example.

Thus, answering the question 'Why Thessaloniki?' requires us to take into consideration all of the above matters: demography, economic and social geography, productive and employment structures; but also, the location of a city quite close geographically to the sending countries, or to certain localities of origin, with some of which there have been pre-existing links, due to the city's erstwhile role in the Balkans, now reinforced by the migrants' networks of social relationships. These are well reflected in the participants' accounts of the reasons that led them to Thessaloniki. More than half of all respondents said that they came because they had friends and relatives who had settled in the city earlier, from whom they received help in the beginning. Nearly 80 per cent, slightly more in the case of the Albanians, had some initial contacts in Thessaloniki, usually relatives or friends, and many women followed their husbands who had emigrated before, while about 10 per cent of both migrant groups came after they had been invited by Greek friends or employers, and less than 10 per cent came 'alone'. In addition, 18.8 and 31.4 per cent of the Albanians and Bulgarians respectively mentioned that their contacts had informed them specifically about working opportunities, and some of them actually came after a job was already guaranteed. Geographic proximity to countries and places of origin was also a reason; in the words of Ivan from Bulgaria: 'If something happens ... I can be home in five hours.' Three ethnic Greek Albanians (two from Korçë and one from Gjirokaster) had ancestral origins in Thessaloniki, and they had distant relatives or even property in the city. A small number of migrants also highlighted some of the features of the city itself: a 'big city', but 'much quieter than Athens', a 'nice city by the sea', etc. The city was also 'imagined' in historical terms, according to some individuals' family history, or simply their knowledge and perceptions about it:

> In Bulgaria, we call Thessaloniki 'Solun' ... Kyril and Methodi ... who made the Bulgarian alphabet, we call them 'the Solun brothers'. (Albena)
>
> I came to Thessaloniki because one of my grandfathers used to live in America. He had worked there for many years and made a small fortune ... He had some properties here [Thessaloniki] ... I stayed in the islands, until those [people] who were renting our house moved, and when they moved, we came here and stayed in our property. (Stavros)

Proximity is thus a crucial factor shaping both mobility between Greece and its neighbouring countries and – to an extent – the incorporation of immigrants in Thessaloniki. Apart from conditioning people's initial migration decisions, it also facilitates contact between migrants in Greece and their places of origin. Despite the barriers, visits 'back home' have been frequent for a significant number of people, either for holidays (see Section 8.1.3) or for reasons of necessity. Quite significant are the numbers of those who have been to their home countries for reasons other than holidays and for periods exceeding three months: 22.5 per cent of the Albanians and 21.4 per cent of the Bulgarians mentioned such experiences of temporary return migration. In the case of the Albanians, for five people it was not an option: they had been expelled. Another five had to sort out matters concerning their travel documents or visas. Four people returned after having faced financial difficulties or unemployment in Greece, while another three returned to work for a period. Some were coming and going because of their studies or for professional reasons. In general, though, family reasons can be seen as the main factor making immigrants return for significant periods. This was mentioned by some of the Bulgarians as well, but some of them also referred to an additional factor: that of illnesses or health problems, which they prefer to address in their homeland where health services are cheaper and possibly covered by social insurance (Section 8.1.1). However, the percentage of Bulgarians who have returned temporarily is higher because of the 'back and forth' movements of the Sarakatsani.

4.2.3 A case study: Thessaloniki and Korcë, a tale of two cities

In general, social networks appear to have conditioned the migratory routes and patterns of settlement of the majority of respondents. Migrants' networks form 'human links' (King 1995: 27) or 'social bridges' (Portes 1995: 22) between places, which in our case becomes easier because of the proximity of neighbouring countries and border regions. As we have seen, when the locality of origin has particular cultural and historical links with the destination place, social networks are built upon the remnants of an erstwhile cross-border relationship. In the historically common Balkan space there have been several examples of links and bonds of various kinds between different localities[11]; today, new kinds of flows (migration, trade, capital investment) and new geographies of exchange redefine those historical ties. A unique example of such a place-specific, cross-border, interactive migration system based on newly formed transnational networks and old patterns of mobility and exchange is represented in the case of Thessaloniki and Korçë. Not only do many Albanians in Thessaloniki come or originate from this particular town, but also over two thirds of those who came directly to Thessaloniki are from Korçë. Nearly one third of the Greek-Albanian participants are Korçëans, although most stressed their Vlach origins[12].

Korçë was never a centre of the ethnic Greek minority in Albania, but rather a town with a large Vlachophone population[13]. Thessaloniki, on the other hand, used to be one of the cores of commercial activity in the Balkans, with links to major Balkan cities, especially those in the southern part of the region. It provided an exit to the sea and was a key transit place on the west-east route to Istanbul; moreover, its annual trade fair, held every September, was of transnational significance (see Todorov 1986; Katsiardi-Hering 2003; Stoianovich 2003). In some cases, bonds superseding the economic level were formed because of population mobility and settlement, and this seems to be the case in Thessaloniki's links with Korçë, among other towns. The relationships between Korçë and Thessaloniki are rooted back in the nineteenth century and were shaped by commercial links and by the presence of small Greek, and Vlach or Albanian populations in both cities respectively. The geographic location of Korçë and the commercial routes in the Ottoman era directed Korçëan merchants towards Thessaloniki, with Florina and Kozani being in-between destinations.

In my interview with representatives of Epirote House (see Section 8.2.1), I was told that one of the issues that arose after Korçë's autonomy from Ottoman rule (in 1917) was to twin the city with Thessaloniki, and also that in 1940 there were approximately 350 families of Korçëans registered with this association. Contact remained 'frozen' for nearly half a century following the Second World War, and was re-established again in the 1990s, this time through migration, but also other forms of mobility (trade, investment, business travel, etc.). As mentioned by some of the respondents and highlighted by Epirote House's representatives, the opening of the borders re-established a tradition of migration to Thessaloniki, which had been among the chief destinations of Korçëans' abroad, along with North America and Istanbul. In 1999, this special relationship between Thessaloniki and Korçë was institutionalised by the formation of a cultural association named the 'Union of Friendship between Korçë and Thessaloniki', which forms part of Epirote House.

Such historical bonds are reflected in the personal stories of Korçëan interviewees. Andreas, for instance, told me the story of his father, who was born and grew up in the city: 'He used to come to the market in Thessaloniki ... [for] trade ... After the borders closed, this stopped.' As his narration unfolds, it uncovers particular cultural bonds between the two cities:

> They are similar. I speak about Korçë, not about Tirana or Shkodrë ... They [the locals] ... are very much like the people of Korçë ... and the music is similar, there are songs that we sing in Albanian, songs that my father used to sing, and I listen to them now in Greek ... All things are similar, songs, food, houses.

The account of Emil is very similar. Of ethnic Greek origin, his family history had likewise passed through Thessaloniki:

> From what we had heard, some other people had been here before us, we had more [familiar] elements here ... My mother, fifty years ago, had lived here for a period. And she had relatives too. Her first cousin was here, so there were many reasons for coming here ... And there were, traditionally, relations between Korçë and Thessaloniki. I mean that most people from Korçë come here, to Thessaloniki, it is closer than Athens and the traditions, the way of life is similar ... I grew up in Korçë, there we used to have the old traditions, as you had them here in Thessaloniki, the songs and the feasts.

Another Albanian interviewee's family not only originated in Thessaloniki, but possessed property as well, a house belonging to her grandmother, which she was not able to claim back due to usufruct laws:

> All our roots are found here in Thessaloniki. My grandfather was from here, he was a merchant and then he exercised his profession in Albania. The Turks were after him for some reason and that's how he settled in Albania. (Kaiti)

On these grounds, one could arguably confirm the existence of cross-border, trans-local social networks (see Guarnizo & Smith 1998: 13) between Thessaloniki and Korçë. Rooted in historical and cultural bonds and facilitated by geographic proximity, such networks have shaped initial decisions about migration and settlement in the host country, and they also determine the continuation of the migration chain and the persistence of various kinds of relations and flows between the two cities[14]. Regarding Albanian immigrants' incorporation in the local society, this specific relationship is important, since both the size of the Korçëans' community in Thessaloniki (larger than any other migrant group) and the density of interpersonal ties are crucial factors in respect to the effectiveness of the operation of a migrant network (see Portes 1995: 9), as we will see in a later section (8.2). The possibility of similar interplays between history, communities of origin, social networks and settlement in Thessaloniki for other groups (Vlach Albanians, Bulgarians from Plovdiv, Sarakatsani) remains a challenge for future research.

4.3 Some comments on preliminary findings

What do the above findings tell us about the dynamics of migration between Albania, Bulgaria and Greece? How are we to interpret them in relation to the processes of incorporation of migrants in Thessaloniki? A first outcome is a picture of the composition of the Albanian and Bulgarian migrant populations in the city. The figure of the 'typical' migrant has been drawn to the extent that common features apply to the majority, but it appears that this figure is neither a single one, nor is it unique: in the new era of mobility, 'typical' migrants are no more. Despite dominant characteristics, we see differences between the two migrant groups, between males and females in each nationality, between people of the same sex and different nationalities, ethnic Greeks and 'others', urban and rural residents, highly educated and the low-skilled, professionals and workers. Beyond the general and common picture of male-dominated Albanian migration, the survey sample uncovered other features of Albanian and Bulgarian mobility that are equally important in the understanding of incorporation, despite their lower representation. For instance, a more independent female migration pathway in the Bulgarian case; or a certain number of educated professionals from both countries that challenges the dominant perception of the 'poor, rural, illiterate Balkan migrant'; or specific categories of people that keep coming and going to satisfy immediate needs and thus they might not be 'here to stay'.

Moreover, there are some additional elements that come out of this first account of the survey's background findings which show us 'hidden' aspects of the dynamics of migration within this three-country system: network factors and historical links, family strategies and the importance of place. We have seen, for example, how migration can be an 'option of necessity' for divorced women; how factors such as love and marriage play their role in what is usually seen as movement due to economic reasons; how places of destination are not always a casual choice or an estimation of benefits and losses, but depend on historical or relational factors. Proximity has been highlighted as a distinct feature of the migration system between Albania, Bulgaria and Greece that determines mobility patterns, certifying the importance of geography and suggesting that the dynamics of migration involve elements of transnationalism.

The *heterogeneity* observed in the composition of the sample, as well as the variety of reasons, modes and routes, suggests a multiplicity of individual migratory journeys, strategies and plans that explain the diversity we are later going to 'discover', despite – or together with – the common and general patterns in the incorporation process. In addition, *proximity* between Greece and the countries of origin of the groups studied here not only has conditioned the reasons for migration (e.g. Greece being an 'easy' destination), and the structure of the migrant population as a whole, but also continues to play a role (and will do so in the future), with back and forth migratory flows inducing other forms of mobility, including the development of transnational networks and practices that are part and parcel of the incorporation pathways of these migrants in Thessaloniki.

Finally, there is the question of *time*. As the years pass by and migrants settle in the city, many of their background characteristics lose the significance they might have had at an initial stage, since experiences now refer to 'here', or at least 'in-between'. Practices are changing, adapting or reacting, new relationships are formed and old ones break down, identities are constantly renegotiated, while the host society, its structures and institutions, but also its population, values and ideologies are transforming as well. Migration, after all, is a process of transition.

This picture does not point to a homogenous and unitary category of 'immigrants'. On the contrary, even by simply looking at general background characteristics, the sample uncovers a high degree of heterogeneity between and amongst the two migrant groups, which mirrors the diversity characterising the indigenous population as well. The explanatory framework presented in the previous chapter provides the basis for 'treating' analytically such a diverse and heterogeneous population. As will be argued in the conclusion to the analysis that follows, the term 'immigrants' refers more to a socially constructed category than to a distinct social group (see Petrakou 2001). The unifying elements producing this category – in Greece still an ongoing process – are to be found in the exclusionary mechanisms that can be located in each of the different contexts of incorporation: policy, society and culture, economy and space. The migrants themselves respond individually or collectively to these, and they develop certain practices and understandings of their position within the host society. This dual account of incorporation processes forms the core of my analysis, which starts in detail in the next chapter.

5 Confronting the state, facing society

The focus of this chapter is on the effects of Greek immigration policy on the process of migrants' incorporation: in other words, how their legal status and the practical implementation of policy influence immigrants' lives. The discussion draws mostly from the qualitative analysis. The chapter is in two parts. The first section, 5.1, begins with an account of the period when the migrants were undocumented and of their experiences regarding the first regularisation programme. It then turns to details about the respondents' legal status at the time of the fieldwork and criticises the policy framework by locating its contradictions and the practical problems that arose. The second section, 5.2, is on socio-political reactions and the public discourse. Like 5.1, it is in two subsections, dealing first with party rhetoric, the media discourse on immigrants and the issue of racism in Greek society, and, second, with the civil-society responses.

5.1 On the controversies and problems of a restrictive policy framework

5.1.1 *From illegality to regularisation: problems and prospects*

Probably the most outstanding feature of Greece's exclusionary policy framework in its initial phase was the issue of prolonged illegality. The vast majority of immigrants had either crossed the border illegally, or they had overstayed their visas and had not had any opportunity to apply for regularisation until 1997. The only exception, apart from the ethnic Greeks, was a minority of 'elite' migrants, professionals who had been invited to work or who had managed to make their way towards highly skilled positions, many of whom had come to Greece before 1991.

The lack of documents had certainly contributed to the large-scale absorption of migrants by the informal sectors of the economy and to their exploitation by Greek employers, as will be discussed in the next chapter. But living under clandestine status involves much more than working informally: it affects a person's everyday existence. Irregular migrants live a life in fear, and they have to 'hide' themselves. They experience a constant insecurity, afraid of being arrested by the police. Many have not seen loved ones for years; they will not take the risk of travelling back home because of the difficulty and risk of clandestine re-entry. They become 'invisible' and limit their public presence to what is necessary. The analysis of interviews uncovers many such experiences and feelings, highlighting the effects of Greek 'non-policy' on the lives of individual migrants. In their own words:

> It was a different life then. We were living 100 per cent in fear. I was illegal until 1997, when we started applying for our papers. (Gjion)
> There was this fear, this insecurity. Today you were here, working ... and tomorrow a policeman could expel you. We didn't have any protection. (Ani)
> From 1992 to 1998 we were hiding ... maybe I was lucky because I was never stopped by the police. (Nadi)
> Since we were illegal, we were always afraid of the police ... because they used to have these blocks [where] they used to collect us and send us back. (Ivan)

Obviously, direct confrontation with police authorities was not the case for all; however, many were affected. Stops by the police for document checks were daily routine; inspections also took place at the workplace, or even at migrants' homes. Deportations were frequent, and some of the respondents had experienced being arrested in one of the so-called '*skoopa*' operations, or they had such a story to tell about a relative or friend. In addition, when a period of detention before deportation was involved, conditions were far from appropriate[1]. Migrants' treatment depended largely on the attitude of individual policemen, and it was often offensive; incidents of verbal, and even physical, violence were not rare. Among the respondents, 30 per cent of the Bulgarians and 40.6 per cent of the Albanians described the attitude of police authorities towards them as 'hostile'. Some, mostly Albanians, said they had been expelled. The following testimonies of some of the interviewees give an idea about such experiences:

> I was working for one or two years, without going back to Albania ... I was arrested by the police ... Fine, we didn't have papers, you know, they sent us back. I returned here again. OK, this has happened many times. I have been arrested about twenty or thirty times ... It's better now, but then [at the beginning] it was very difficult (Ferin).
> They arrested us on the bus. I was with my girlfriend ... they kept us at the police station for a night ... there were some peo-

> ple [policemen] who were playing the tough guys ... to scare the people inside ... Then ... they took us to a building like a prison, where all the immigrants were [the Police Transportation Department – *Metagogon*]. We stayed there for another night, and then they sent us to the border on a bus. (Milen)
> Something serious happened to my parents-in-law ... They didn't have the Green Card. The police made an inspection, as they should do, and they said 'You don't have papers, deportation to Albania, OK?' Fine, deportation. At least ... don't be so cruel ... My father-in-law was having lunch and the policeman forced him to stop eating and stand up ... And he said to my mother-in-law 'Now you stand up too.' And they got dressed, and they were taken to the police station. (Spyros)

It appears that female migrants were not as vulnerable to the possibility of being arrested and expelled. In the words of Dalina, an Albanian interviewee, for women, 'I don't think it was that hard, but for men, in general, it was difficult.' But even for women, there were definitely exceptions: as Liliana, from Bulgaria, said, 'A woman alone in the street is more likely to attract the policemen's attention.' And the testimony of Maria, an Albanian interviewee, reflects experiences many immigrants have gone through, when undocumented. She had problems with policemen chasing her at work, a nightclub where she was employed as a cleaner, and she had inspections even at her apartment. She has been arrested and deported three times, and three times she has returned illegally the same way.

Within this context, the news regarding the first amnesty programme (in 1997) was welcomed; a way out of fear and insecurity could now be envisaged. Among migrants surveyed in 2001, 46 per cent said that legalisation would allow them 'to walk around freely, without fear', 34 per cent said they could now 'work legally', 29 per cent that they could 'travel back home and return' and 16 per cent responded that they would have access to social insurance and public health[2]. In addition, the regularisation programme gave the opportunity to those left behind, usually women, to rejoin their relatives in Greece, in some cases by taking the risk and paying the high cost of another illegal entry, in order to apply:

> It was in 1998, when we started doing our papers for the first time. I was in Albania at the time. I went there to give birth to my daughter ... We had decided that I would stay there alone and my husband came back here ... I came on the twenty-first of May ... I left my daughter there, she was forty days old then. I entered illegally again. I bought a [forged] passport and a visa in

> Albania, 220,000 drachmas [about 645 euros], and I came by plane, from Tirana to Thessaloniki ... They asked me what I was doing there and I replied 'I am a student.' ... I used a different name, a different passport ... I had to enter the country by any means, in order to be on time for applying for my papers ... and I went directly to apply. (Valbona)

Many of the respondents had applied during this first phase, but talked also about their more recent experiences of the second regularisation programme. As mentioned earlier (Section 2.2.3), the process itself was marked by several problems. The most common ones, according to the interviewees' experiences, concerned the following[3]:

- The financial costs of legalisation: each applicant, including minors above fourteen, had to pay a fee of 50,000 drachmas (150 euros) every time s/he applied (even if it was for a renewal of the stay permit)[4].
- Several documents required for the application (birth certificates, etc.) had to be issued by the home country authorities, thus forcing immigrants to travel to their country and complicating the whole process; certified translations of numerous documents added to the total cost.
- Unregistered employment, often on a casual basis, which is still the case for the majority of migrants, forced many to buy the social security stamps required, increasing the total cost of legalisation even more[5]; those who did not manage were excluded from the amnesty programme.
- Bureaucracy and delays in the issuing of the Green Cards, lack of information about the programme itself and about the application process, plus the language problem, generated difficulties and excluded many from the process.

Nevertheless, despite problems and constraints, it seems that the two first regularisation programmes gave the majority of migrants the opportunity to obtain legal status. Table 5.1 shows the distribution of respondents according to their legal status at the time of the fieldwork. Only four people were undocumented, all with less than three years' residence in the country (three of them from Albania). Another three migrants from Albania had a temporary visa, again, with less than four years of residence in Greece. The majority (62 per cent) were holders of the so-called 'Green Card', the stay permit applying to all third-country nationals; about one quarter of them, though, had not yet received the card itself, but were issued instead with a special temporary document (a certificate of application). About 30 per cent were documented under an ethnic Greek status: 31.9 per cent among Albanians and 25.7

Table 5.1 *Immigrants' legal status, by nationality and gender (N, %)*

	Nationality				*Gender*				*Total*
Status	*Albanians*		*Bulgarians*		*Female*		*Male*		
Illegal	3	2.2	1	1.4	2	2.6	2	1.5	*1.9*
Visa	3	2.2	–	–	1	1.3	2	1.5	*1.4*
Stay permit not issued yet	22	15.9	10	14.3	14	18.4	18	13.6	*15.4*
Valid stay permit	64	46.4	33	47.1	29	38.2	68	51.5	*46.6*
Ethnic Greek status	44	31.9	18	25.7	22	28.9	40	30.3	*29.8*
Greek spouse	–	–	2	2.9	2	2.6	–	–	*1.0*
Greek citizenship	2	1.4	6	8.6	6	7.9	2	1.5	*3.8*

per cent among Bulgarians (all the Sarakatsani). Eight people had been granted Greek citizenship, six of them Bulgarians with long periods of residence in Greece or women married to Greek nationals (all but one of those who were granted citizenship had been living in Greece for eight years or more). Two more women had the special status for those married to Greek citizens, again, both had been in the country for eight years or more.

Apparently, the minority who lacked regular status at the time of the fieldwork did unregistered work, and thus lacked social security stamps:

> Now I found myself without papers ... I used to have a stay permit for six months, now it has expired ... I'm going to apply again, but I don't have insurance, so I don't know if I'm going to get the papers, without social security stamps ... if you don't have them, you can't get one. (Mira)

By contrast, the acquisition of citizenship solved all institutional problems for the few who did manage to get it:

> It was a little paper ... which finally changed so many things in my life ... It has opened the doors. (Stefania)

However, citizenship requires five years of proven legal residence in the country, the relevant application fee is quite high (1,470 euros), and national identity considerations may create obstacles for particular migrant groups, especially economic migrants who are not of ethnic Greek origin and who are not connected to a Greek citizen (e.g. by marriage). All interviewees appear fully aware of the exclusionary policy framework; interestingly, this also applies to 'elite' migrants who, having to undergo the same procedures as most other foreign nationals, comment on this as the only problem they face in Greece:

> [The legal framework was] always related to a conservative policy to keep the country clean. The law changed three or four times, but it was never clear, never correct. The law does not differentiate between highly educated people and unskilled migrants. Now, after ten years here, I still have to renew my stay permit every year (Alexander).

The only differentiation exists for ethnic Greeks, although with them too the legal framework is extremely fragmented. The polity's selectivity according to 'national' criteria privileges ethnic Greeks in comparison to other migrants. However, the state created a 'hierarchy of Greekness' on the basis of national interests related to the Greek minorities in neighbouring and other states (see Triandafyllidou & Veikou 2001), which resulted in different statuses for migrants of ethnic Greek origin coming from different countries. In that respect, Greek-Albanian interviewees saw themselves as 'betrayed' by a state that initially 'invited them to return'. They compared their situation with that of the Pontians from former Soviet countries who were immediately granted full citizenship. Similarly, Sarakatsani Bulgarians expressed their bitterness and compared themselves to both the other groups. Their narratives brought out complex national identity feelings, of being 'foreigners in their motherland', and also revealed practical problems regarding certain rights, free mobility and permanent settlement.

In general, the most controversial feature of the existing legal framework is that it does not guarantee a stable and long-term feeling of security. The law is being constantly revised; long-term residence is still denied to the majority; there is no established system for permit renewals running throughout the year; bureaucracy and delays generate problematic situations; prejudices and discriminatory attitudes by officials are rare, but exist; immigrants' informal employment and lack of insurance make it difficult for them to remain regular; the list of existing and/or potential problems in detail could be endless. What they highlight in sum is that the development of a coherent, realistic immigration policy in Greece, which solves more problems than it creates, is currently at the nursery stage. Meanwhile, things are evolving slowly, with the majority of the migrant population being in a state of uncertainty, as the following quote suggests:

> When I came we were all illegal, then this changed. We became legal. Now it's all a bit confused again, you cannot make decisions ... you cannot make plans. (Milen)

5.1.2 *Immigrants and the state: a problematic and controversial relationship*

In respect to the incorporation of immigrants in Greek society and the everyday reality faced by many after the implementation of legalisation measures, we can distinguish between three main categories of issues that appear to be important. The first one is connected to the practical problems of bureaucracy, lack of information, inexperienced public servants, delays, and so forth, which, although to an extent involve prejudices and/or discriminatory attitudes, mostly reflect the more general negative characteristics of public services in Greece, which equally affects the local population. The second relates to the implications of the specific criterion of (proven) registered employment as an essential prerequisite for being eligible for regularisation: by this the state neglects one of the most problematic features of the Greek labour market (informality) and puts total responsibility on the individual applicant, without touching the root of the problem (regulating the labour market, penalising employers). The third has to do with the difficult relationship between immigrants and certain representatives of the state whom they have to confront on certain occasions: although not all immigrants have had a negative experience of their own, most would agree that police and border officials generally exaggerate the power they are given.

Starting from the first issue, although the procedures have changed with the legalisation programmes that followed the initial one, certainly now including positive features, some of the initial difficulties do not seem to have disappeared. According to most interviewees, delays and repeated payment of fees are among the main problems:

> You have to pay every time. There is very much delay, even if you just want to renew your Green Card and have a normal job ... In Greece there was not any law, any legislation about this issue, but four years have passed now since 1998 ... In four years' time, more or less, the process should work better, I don't understand why there are so many delays. (Nadi)

Delays in the issuing/renewal of stay permits lead to abnormal situations. For instance, a card valid for a year could be delayed more than six months; there are numerous cases where the expiry date stated on the card is earlier than the date of issue. A solution has been adopted since the second programme (June 2001) by issuing a Green Card certificate: an official document confirming application, which can be used until the issue of the Green Card itself. However, owners of this document are not in reality able to travel abroad and return; they have the legal right to remain in the country, and they can travel to their home countries, but in many cases border authorities have not let them re-enter Greece. This was a common problem among respondents/interviewees from both nationalities. Pandelis, an Albanian interviewee, talked about that with bitterness, since his wife and child live permanently 'back home', and he had not been able to visit them for some time:

> My Green Card expired last January, and I have applied with the new system ... They gave me this certificate ... until we get the normal thing. My only complaint is about the papers ... well, apart from the delays, that is another issue ... But with these papers, I mean, with this certificate they gave us ... they don't let us go to our country ... we can't go and come back. I've asked about this at the department in Athens, at their central offices, and they replied, 'Up to now we don't have an order to let you go.' These papers are only for staying legally here. (Pandelis)

In that sense, it would not be an exaggeration to say that such conditions keep immigrants 'hostages' of the state (see *Eleftherotypia*, 23 July 2003). This is reflected in the narratives of the interviewees: the expression used by Vilco, from Bulgaria, is characteristic: 'Now they've locked us in here,' he said. In addition, the breakdown of responsibilities among different public bodies (Police Department of Aliens, regional administration, prefecture, municipality), without much coordination of activities between them, creates abnormalities and confusion. For example, there seems to exist much contradiction regarding the information provided by different departments on the above matter (travel), as the same interviewee's testimony suggests:

> If you go to the council here, they tell you: 'You have documents, you can leave and go back to Bulgaria and stay and then come back.' Then you leave, you go through customs ... and they tell you 'No, you can't.'

Obviously such problems are usually overcome in practice, and some migrants manage to travel without problems, as long as they possess the necessary documents. But even when a solution is finally found, this is usually after much time spent waiting, with the resulting unnecessary suffering:

> The last time I crossed the border I had to wait for twenty-four hours. My card had expired on the fifteenth of July, and I had ... the certificate proving that I had an extension for six months ...

> They told me that my name, which was written on the card, was not on the computer. I was trying to tell them that since my card had expired it was normal that my name did not appear on the computer ... And they kept me there until a [new] certificate was sent from ΟΑΕΔ ... They contacted ΟΑΕΔ, they sent a fax, asking about my name, information about me ... [This was] when I was returning here. The problems are always then. (Valbona)

The regularisation process itself (application for the first time or for renewal) involves direct confrontation with the bureaucratic services of the Greek state for the acquisition of the various documents required and for their submission to the relevant local offices. Despite a few positive steps towards the modernisation of the relevant services at the practical level (decentralisation of services, a multilingual telephone helpline), several problems exist. The interviewees' narratives paint a picture of a chaotic situation that is not uncommon in the Greek public sector, with much confusion about the required criteria and the documents needed, huge queues, frustration, significant delays, etc. The responsible staff are not always patient or even properly trained; many work on six-month or yearly contracts, and they are usually seconded from other posts, since regularisation services operate on an ad hoc basis. For individual migrants, the result may be simply frustration, or, worse, loss of one day or more of paid work[6]:

> When you have to go there, you lose the whole day ... you lose the daily wage ... you get so stressed. (Ivan)

The fact that the process takes place once a year rather than being a continuous service creates excessive concentrations of people who have to be processed within a short period by an inadequate number of public servants. Based on recent research, Psimmenos & Kasimati (2003) argue that as the legal framework develops, immigration control becomes largely the responsibility of individual public servants, who in most cases consider Greece as a culturally homogeneous country and migrants as 'foreign elements' that have to be 'assimilated' otherwise they constitute a 'danger'. Another recent survey recorded widespread xenophobic attitudes among public servants: further restrictions on the entry, residence and work of immigrants in Greece was supported by 90, 61 and 40 per cent respectively; 76 per cent think there are 'too many' immigrants, about 28 per cent consider them 'a threat to their personal security'[7]. But while the quality of the services provided and the treatment migrants receive by clerks may depend on individual stances and moods, they might also reflect a more general 'culture' characteristic of each department. Border and police authorities especially have been reported by many interviewees as the most problematic ones:

> That was the worst thing that has ever happened to me ... the fact that I had to go to the Department of Aliens ... I used to be sick a week before and a week after that ... It was very difficult ... I had to renew my stay permit every year ... Everything was confusing, I could never understand what they needed ... They [the officers] were not treating you as a human being. And they wouldn't make a distinction, you know, somebody may have come and committed crimes ... But for you, who came here because you needed to, what's the problem? (Stefania)

In some cases, the practical difficulties arising from the exclusionary character of the legal framework are coupled with confusion created by misleading information offered by officials. A specific example is given below; although (re)married to a Greek, Liliana had problems legally inviting her daughters from Bulgaria:

> I mostly had to deal with the Department of Aliens, for the documents I had to do at the time, when I got married, and the problems I personally had mostly concerned my children, when I wanted to invite them here for a visit ... At the Department of Aliens they told me ... that my children cannot stay in the country for more than three months. But this is not true ... the law says that ... up to the date they become twenty-three, the child can stay in this country, since I have a stay permit. (Liliana)

National identity considerations and increased responsibilities that put pressure on public servants to be in line with regulations may create additional unnecessary obstacles:

> I needed to get a stamp on a family certificate and I went to the Ministry of Macedonia and Thrace to do this. My husband's name is Lefteris, a Greek Orthodox name, ... although ... his origin is Muslim ... Anyway, I get to the Ministry of Macedonia and Thrace, I meet this person and he told me, 'This is not the right certificate, because this name is fake.' ... Bear in mind that this same paper, I had had it stamped by the same person dozens of times. (Valbona).

Coming now to the second issue: this arises from the requirement for a certain number of social security stamps as proof of registered employment, which is a prerequisite for application. This has been a major constraint that not only resulted in unsuccessful applications, but also deterred many from applying in the first place:

> In 1998, I applied for the Green Card, but we couldn't get it because we didn't have social security stamps. This is the problem here: you can find a job, [but] only a few Greeks register the people [their employees] ... but other people are not interested, they say 'If you want, come,' and we go because we are in need ... But when the day comes to apply for the card ... (Flora)

To overcome this problem, many immigrants bought the necessary number of social security stamps from the main insurance fund (IKA) and finally managed to obtain the Green Card. However, those among them who had not got their insurance guaranteed by their employers, or were not able to find registered employment elsewhere, found themselves in an insecure situation regarding the renewal of their stay permits, despite having acquired legal status in the first instance:

> I got the Green Card, which I have [had] until now, but I will have difficulties renewing it because I need ... social security stamps ... I had to renew it ... last year, and I didn't have the social security stamps required ... I had to pay for them. (Edri)

The state has thus failed to address one crucial aspect of immigrants' presence in Greece: informal work. The central aim hidden behind the requirement for social security stamps was to ensure that only applicants who are formally employed could obtain a permit. In that sense, the state's attempt to regulate the labour market shifted the responsibility from employers (who escape labour legislation through informal employment arrangements and exploitation of the vulnerability/invisibility of migrant labour) to foreign workers (who have no other option but working informally, partly because of their illegal status). The findings show that lacking the insurance needed for regularisation, immigrants would either pay for the social security stamps required in order to apply themselves, or would not apply at all. In the latter case, no progress has been made; but even in the former case, the possibility for remaining legally is ambiguous. In addition, this criterion establishes a relationship of dependency between immigrants and their employers: the possibility of a migrant being able to regularise or to maintain regular status (card renewal) depends directly on the willingness of their boss to pay for social security contributions. As one of the interviewees put it, immigrants should 'belong' to a specific employer in order to be eligible for regularisation:

> Well, you should have a boss, somebody for whom you work, to whom you belong ... [You need a] solemn statement from your boss ... that you work for him, you are not on the streets. (Ferin)

However, with the acquisition of regular status, more and more migrants find access to formal employment and to social security, although the numbers of those not being insured are still rather high (see Section 6.1.2 for further details).

Turning now to the third issue, the relationship that has so far developed between immigrants and some representatives of the state, namely police and border officials, appears to be highly problematic. The excessive sense of duty of some of these officials and their, often offensive, attitude towards immigrants reflects the repressive logic of the legal framework, especially in its initial phase. The years of widespread illegality with the emphasis on policing and mass expulsions, together with chronic deficits in democratic values dating back to the post-civil war period and the dictatorship years, seem to have generated a xenophobic culture among many policemen. Operations like the ones previously described continued to affect immigrants after regularisation, with their treatment depending largely on the attitudes of individual officers. Such incidents appear in the narratives of some of the interviewees and are characteristic of similar experiences of offensive or unfair treatment experienced by many[8]. They indicate the emergence of a power relationship between immigrants, who are de facto suspects for having offended the law, and police officers, who have the right to exercise the power the law entitles them to, in order to 'protect' the country from illegal aliens and potential criminals. The weak position of the migrant in this relationship is highlighted by statements such as the one that follows:

> You have to talk gently, to bow the head... They will tell us how to behave, how to talk, they don't understand that we do have papers, we work here. (Nicolas)

An idea of the experience of a migrant's confrontation with the police may be offered by the story below, told by Lazaros, another Albanian interviewee:

> I was coming back from Albania ... by car ... It was after midnight ... so we decided to stop at the side of the road and sleep for a while ... But I couldn't get myself to sleep, so I got out of the car to smoke a cigarette. Suddenly, the cops came, they told me, 'Lie down on the road,' ... I asked them 'What have we done?' They were shouting at me, so I got down on my knees.

> They told me to show them my passport, I also showed them the visa that I had just got, plus the Green Card ... They started searching the car, asking us things, taking our stuff out of the car ... Finally they calmed down, they asked us, 'Where do you live? Where do you work?'... They wrote down our details ... and then we left. That day was one of the very few times I have been afraid in my life.

Cases of police brutality are not rare and reports of such events appear quite often in the press. One of the Albanian interviewees (Gjion) mentioned that his wife had once been stopped on her way home: after checking her permit, the policeman threatened to tear it up. Another Albanian interviewee (Lefteris) had such an experience himself. Verbal abuse during inspections or arrests was reported by many:

> I have personal experience ... We were arrested once, on our way to visit my brother. It couldn't have been worse ... It was one of these operations. And despite the fact that we had our papers in the car, they handcuffed my husband, and before I reached our car they had already taken him in the police van. I brought the papers that we had at the time, and, well, they finally let us go, but they treated us very badly, they were insulting us. (Dalina)

However rare these incidents might currently be (after several revisions of the legal framework and with increasing numbers of legalising immigrants), they are characteristic of the repressive spirit embedded in the polity's approach to immigration and of the way this affects migrants' lives daily. More common 'adventures' than the ones just mentioned relate to the frequency and personal cost of inspections taking place in the city, which disrupt the life of individual migrants and may cost them a day out of work. There are many cases of people being arrested even when they had their documents with them, and being taken to the police station to confirm that their documents were valid:

> They arrested me once. I had a copy of my [Green] card, stamped by the police, and they didn't believe that it was legal. They arrested me ... they kept me ... until the afternoon, and then they let me go. (Dimitris)

The establishment of the Border Guard might have been a positive development with respect to the distribution of competencies, or perhaps to the training of officials. But the Border Guard often exaggerates its responsibilities in terms of the frequency of inspections and arrests, especially in certain places (city districts) where the same officers confront the same immigrants on a daily basis:

> Well, these last one or two months, a new police body has appeared. You go out in the morning to go to work, and they arrest you. They ask for your papers and even if you show them your papers, they'll take you to Thermi [where a large police station is located] ... If you run and try to escape they may hit you sometimes ... They take us there to check us ... they keep us there for five or six hours and then 'You may go now, you are free.' But ... next day 'Here are my papers, have a look, I have everything,' because it's not fair, I may lose my job ... I'll lose the day's wage ... And the thing is that this ... happens continuously. (Ferin)

On the other hand, for many immigrants who might not have had such negative experiences with the police, direct confrontation with the authorities is limited to customs when they travel to their home countries. There, especially during periods when mobility takes place on a massive scale (summer, Christmas and Easter holidays), lack of organisation and insufficient members of staff contribute to the generation of problematic situations, while, most importantly, the behaviour of officials is far from being professional. Many interviewees reported incidents of offensive treatment, while some commented on this as one of the most difficult situations they continue to face after years of legal residence in Greece. Below I quote some of the interviewees' responses to my question on 'unfair treatment by the Greek authorities':

> I can only tell about the border ... I don't like it there, not at all ... We are humans, we are not animals ... But there, they may take a piece of wood in their hands and shout 'Back! Back!' ... When we go there, with our papers, we are legal, we have our Green Card and everything. Why should they behave like that? (Mira)
>
> Well, at the border, at customs, there are many problems. Going from here to Korçë, without any stop, it takes four hours [by car], it's close. But at customs they don't let you go. I don't know why, you may stay there for six, seven, twelve hours ... When you come back it's worse. (Dimitris)
>
> On the border this is something usual ... Well the bus has priority ... but by car, especially at Christmas and the Easter holidays, because it is so crowded, you may be waiting day and night to cross the border. And to tell you 'Go back, you Albanian.' This is the kind of behaviour on the border. (Kaiti)

Albanian immigrants reported that most problematic incidents take place at the Krystalopigi customs office (the eastern one, closer to Thessaloniki, and mostly used by those travelling from Korçë). The last two quotes in the set above are from interviews with ethnic Greek migrants, showing that there is not much differentiation in their treatment or the conditions they face. The situation at the Bulgarian border appears to be similar, despite the recent liberalisation of movement between Bulgaria and the EU:

> At the borders, this attitude is quite bad ... even now ... even if you just go on holiday ... It's not everybody, it's just a few specific people. (Milen)

5.2 On socio-political reactions and the public discourse

5.2.1 *The public discourse: party rhetoric, the media and some notes on racism*

Despite their restrictive policy agendas, parliamentary parties nowadays increasingly take into consideration migrants' presence and voice, whether this is done on the basis of policy measures, ideological agendas, or electoral interests. The two main governmental parties have obviously been directly involved in policy-making: the first 'aliens' law' to appear was introduced by the conservative (New Democracy) government (Law 1975/1991), and it was characterised by the strict 'police' logic described earlier. This framework did not change much when the socialists (PASOK) came into power, although there has been a difference at the integration level, particularly with the regularisation measures. Although it is rather early to make such assumptions, it currently seems that the return of New Democracy to government in March 2004 has not much affected the positive steps made under socialist rule.

Both parties seem to have developed a 'managerial' approach to immigration, aimed at effective border control and combating 'illegal' migration, on the one hand, and at measures for the smooth integration of immigrants already present in the country, on the other. Migration and immigrants are now part of the policy agenda in Greece; obviously, this does not refute the criticism and the problems outlined earlier. In addition, the rhetoric of the main parties, particularly with respect to the stances and statements of individual politicians and local party branches that sometimes escape official lines, is much influenced by calculations of the political cost involved in provoking the 'national sentiment' of citizens, contributing thus to the reproduction of widespread prejudices. Traditionally, the conservative New Democracy party in

Greece represents the Right, a notion connected to traumatic historical memories of the period that followed the civil war and lasted until the fall of the dictatorship, and it is much more prone to nationalist ideology. PASOK, on the other hand, is located on the centre-left side of the political spectrum, with strong union representation, and it is inclined towards a more populist discourse. To give an example of such a conflict between nationalist and populist considerations between the two parties, it is worth mentioning the fears of New Democracy before the last elections regarding the supposed intention of the (then) socialist government to grant citizenship to 300,000 (!) Greek-Albanians in order to attract votes and be re-elected (*Kathimerini*, 10 June 2003); an intention which was obviously never realised. The nationalistic discourse of the Right is particularly apparent in the local environment of Thessaloniki, with about fifteen years of conservative control of the municipality and, ultimately, with the election of a New Democracy politician, representing the nationalistic Orthodox section of the party, as head of the prefectural council. In general, however, at the local level, especially in Athens but also in Thessaloniki, both parties have tried to build a liberal multicultural profile, by including 'foreigners' in their electoral lists (mostly migrants of ethnic Greek descent and people who had acquired citizenship after long-term residence in the country).

Regarding the rest of the parliamentary parties, the democratic left (Coalition of the Left, of Movements and Ecology – ΣΥΝ) has perhaps been the most active mainstream political force advocating for migrants' rights and organising public events, giving voice also to migrants' representatives. The Communist Party (KKE) has included 'foreign workers' in its rhetoric and has managed to mobilise individual migrants in union participation, particularly in the branches it has a strong influence in nationally or locally (e.g. construction sector, tobacco industry)[9].

Of particular interest (and a reason for concern) is the recent rise of LAOS, a newly formed party of nationalist-populist and religious ideology, led by a former conservative MP, which has a clear anti-immigrant/anti-Muslim stance[10]. It took a 2.2 per cent share in the recent national elections (March 2004) and reached 4.1 per cent in the European elections (June 2004); even more successful were its electoral results in Greater Thessaloniki, with 4.4 and 7.7 per cent in the national and European elections respectively. It has a potentially strong influence due to its ownership of a small Athens-based TV channel (Telecity) and its support of TV programmes on local Thessaloniki channels. These particular programmes, as well as the overall discourse of the channels on which these appear, point to the existence of a small but strong minority of extreme Right propagandists and activists at the local level who engage in certain 'open' events (protests, clashes with left-wingers); they formally asserted their presence for the first time in the last local elections, with a local party inventively entitled 'Thessaloniki: City of Greeks' (which gained 1.2 per cent of the votes), and ultimately found political expression in the LAOS party mentioned above. Apart from other factors related to the phenomenon, populist media of this kind should be regarded as major contributors to the spread of xenophobic perceptions and attitudes that have resulted in the successful electoral performance of the far Right. This particular side of the local media discourse had been noticed by some of the immigrants questioned/interviewed, especially the Albanians:

> Only on Telecity ... they say, 'We want the Albanians to leave the country' ... Only there. I don't listen to what they say. I watched it once. (Mira)
>
> There is somebody who speaks, on this TV channel ... Best [channel's name]. He says 'They [Albanians] are going to rape our wives.' (Nicolas)

Despite the rather marginal presence of such openly racist perceptions, however, xenophobic prejudices and attitudes are quite widespread within contemporary Greek society. Traditional stereotypes about 'the Turks', 'the Blacks', or the country's northern neighbours have been reinforced, or have given place to new ones directly related to the presence of immigrants (see Tsimouris 2003). The initial, and to a certain degree expected, xenophobic reactions towards the massive influx of immigrants have unfortunately led to openly racist feelings. Problems such as the high unemployment rate and the rise in criminality during the 1990s have been the main arguments used in racist discourse, connected directly to the coming of immigrants. The experiences of Albanian and Bulgarian immigrants in Thessaloniki clearly confirm this situation. The detailed interviews uncover experiences of discrimination or offensive treatment of both nationalities. In the case of Albanians, this is more evident, due to their generally negative public image, which connects them to dirty, hard work, illegality and hence criminality, and backwardness. Albanians have been the victims of a widespread 'Albanophobia', in some cases manifested in very extreme ways by both the state, as we have seen, but also by locals (massive deportations, violent attacks). Negative experiences among Bulgarians are clearly less common; offensive language, in their case, is inspired by historically originating hostility (e.g. the Balkan wars) or from the recent 'connection' of Bulgarian women, along with other Eastern European women, to prostitution. The slogan 'Bulgarian women forthcoming' was a common 'joke' during the mid-1990s, after it was written on the advertising boards of nightclubs in rural Greece to promote events with strippers and prostitutes. Such expressions of racism and xenophobia are reflected in the experiences of most of the people questioned and highlighted in a variety of ways in the interviewees' narratives:

> People were saying, 'What do you want here, you immigrant?' I mean, particularly regarding Albanians, there is something here, not that all Greeks say such things, but there are some reactions against us ... And I have felt this personally. Many times they told me, 'What do you want here? Go back to your country, find a job there. You can't stay here.' (Pandelis)
> Well, people say that all Albanians are thieves, that they are bad. (Ferin)
> Swear words ... 'Fuck your Albania.' They don't like Albanians at all. (Maria)
> There is this other thing, 'You came from up there and took our jobs.' They say this without thinking about that ... We may hear it on the bus. (Adriana)
> [She was told once:] 'All Bulgarian women are whores ... How much money do you want me to pay you so that you sleep with me?' (Maria)

How are we to explain xenophobia and the growth of racism in the Greek context? To an extent, it has appeared as a spasmodic reaction to the 'immigration boom' and the massive arrival of Albanians in the early 1990s. The transition of the country towards a de facto host society took place quite suddenly, and the migrant population is often perceived as alarmingly large, especially compared to what is referred to as the 'demographic problem' in Greece, i.e. the declining fertility rate and the ageing population (especially noticeable in rural areas). Research on xenophobia in northern Greece has identified a widespread feeling of 'excessive numbers of foreigners' among the local population (Kafetzis et al. 1998). Another factor that contributed significantly to the rise and spread of xenophobic sentiments, as noted earlier, has been the legal framework itself: the 'police' logic of governmental policy stigmatised migrants through the criminalisation of their clandestine status, thus building the stereotype of the 'illegal immigrant = Albanian criminal' (Karydis 1996).

Such stereotypes have been widely used in the mass media, especially television, through 'the common use of an overtly racist and offensive language' (Triandafyllidou 2002: 157). The media in particular have cultivated sentiments of alarm by exaggerating the numbers of 'foreigners' living in the country, by focusing on their harsh living conditions and highlighting the 'invasion of the poor', by showing repeatedly images of mass arrests of clandestine migrants, and by emphasising the contribution of immigrants to rising criminality. Stereotypes and prejudices about people from Balkan countries in particular are the most common[11]. The contribution of the media in creating a negative image of immigrants in Greece, particularly among Albanian interviewees, is highly emphasised:

> People believe what they see on TV. The news may exaggerate with a simple event. People don't think that good Albanians may also exist ... 'All of them are like that, since the TV and the newspapers say so.' (Gjion)
> You know, they insult them [Albanians] ... they say that they are bad people, to tell you the truth. I watch TV a lot, at nights, when I don't go out, and they insult everybody, not only us. They insult the Pontians too, the Romanians. (Ferin)
> I believe that in the beginning, the media created an initial impression ... I mean that something that was done, by an Albanian or by anybody, would be given priority, in order to impress the public opinion and attract the audience. And this has passed to the people ... What is left is the first impression. (Ani)

From the petty thefts of hungry newcomers in the early 1990s to the isolated actions of desperate people who had seen their lives devastated (e.g. the May 1999 incident of the hijacking of an intercity bus, which resulted in the deaths of the young Albanian protagonist and one of the hostages; see Papailias 2003), and from images of '*skoopa*' operations, or arrests of trafficked Eastern European women forced into prostitution, to endless TV debates on the right of locals to protect themselves with the use of arms against foreigners who stole 'a bag of potatoes', the media discourse is largely responsible for the spread of the myth of immigrants as criminals. As Pavlou (2001) has noted in the case of Thessaloniki, local media have created this negative image in four ways: by being selective with the information they publish, choosing to promote news of foreign nationals involved in crime; by 'inventing' daily affairs through references to past events as if they were current; by adopting a style of reportage much resembling police reports, focusing on the nationality of the offender; and by presenting high concentrations of immigrants in specific districts as worrying situations. On the other hand, TV series passed from their initial neglect of migrants' presence in Greece to the reproduction of dominant perceptions and prejudices, cultivating the new exclusionary ideology of xenophobia and racism. The figures of the immigrant appear in a stereotypic way, but always remain in the background, playing the role of the domestic servant in middle-class homes, the prostitute, the worker, or the criminal, and occasionally being either used as a tool for comedy, or portrayed as victims or victimisers.

But what do the facts tell us about the supposed connection of immigrants to criminality? Certainly, the participation of foreigners in illicit activities is beyond dispute: crime has nothing to do intrinsically with nationality, and there is no doubt about the involvement of nationals of various countries, including customs and police officers or public officials, in transnational criminal syndicates. However, the contribution of foreigners to criminality does not greatly exceed their share in the country's population, with the exception of serious offences. Even this difference fades if we take into account the criminalisation of the migrants' undocumented status, the authorities' prejudices towards them, and the socio-economic and legal conditions that push desperate people to illegal activities (see Karydis 1996; Kourtovic 2001). An additional explanation could be the flourishing criminal syndicates and the emergence of new 'Mafias' in countries of the former Eastern Bloc (often connected to Western organised crime), as a result of political and economic instability and of sharpening inequalities; instability, ethnic conflict and war in the Balkans have offered a fertile ground for the proliferation of such activities. In the Albanian case specifically, the 'pyramid crisis' of 1997 led to a collapse of law and order and resulted in large nuumbers of convicts fleeing into Greece. According to official data (NSSG 1999), among 8,885 prisoners in Greece in 1998, 25 per cent were foreign nationals (one third of them Albanians), of whom 24 per cent were facing charges related to 'illegal entry and residence in the country' (29 per cent of them Albanians). According to statistics published by the police in 2002, the share of offenders of foreign nationality was high regarding document falsifications (85.9 per cent), smuggling (49.3 per cent) and sexual exploitation (41.8 per cent), that is, in the kind of illicit activities most related to international criminal syndicates; regarding other serious offences, foreign nationals were also involved in murders (32.7 per cent), in rapes (31.2 per cent), and in thefts and robberies, including vehicle thefts, (30.6 per cent), while their share was very high among offenders charged with 'begging' (68.9), which is regarded as a minor offence and more reflects harsh socio-economic conditions. Two further points need to be clarified when interpreting crime statistics: firstly, many of the most serious offences are actually of an 'intra-criminal' nature (affecting people involved in crime anyway); secondly, offences by 'foreign nationals' do not necessarily point to 'immigrants'.

The interviewees themselves acknowledge a certain degree of participation by their co-nationals in crime, but they distance themselves and they feel offended at how generalisations are made on this basis against all immigrants in Greece:

> We should say the truth, not all Albanians are good, there are bad ones too. (Nadi)
> I believe that this has to do with politics, not with what we do, because they may turn a simple, small event into something very important. (Pandelis)

Above all, the public discourse on immigration reflects the exclusionary construction of the Greek national identity, which defines the concept of 'Greekness' on the basis of religious, linguistic and genealogical criteria, rather than civic ones (Triandafyllidou 2000). As Lipovac (1993) writtes, Greek political culture is based on the conception of Orthodox religion as an integral part of the national myth, which identifies itself in a line of historical continuity from ancient Hellas to the modern Greek nation-state, directly passing from, and incorporating, the Byzantine Orthodox tradition. Research in northern Greece located widespread sentiments of mistrust towards distinct national and religious identities of the migrants, particularly 'the Albanians' and 'the Muslims' (Kafetzis et al. 1998). This finding not only points to the fear of the 'other' in a society that had long and largely perceived itself as a homogeneous one, but also highlights the particular weight of elements prominent in the Greek national self-image (ethnicity, religion) which crucially determines stances towards immigrants. Religion (Orthodoxy), for example, has returned as a value commonly shared by many during the 1990s, while the present Archbishop's attempts to play an important political/ideological role reminds us of the controversial reality of a Church never separated from the structure of the (modern) state (see for instance Lipovac 1993). On the other hand, the nationalist paroxysm of the early 1990s, stimulated mainly by the 'Macedonian question' and by a crisis in Greco-Turkish relations (Triandafyllidou et al. 1997)[12], has indicated a revival of nationalistic ideology at the turn of the millennium, which coincided with the transformation of Greece into an immigrant host country and significantly influenced the population's perception of the 'other within'. But apart from its overall negative effect in the social 'reception' of the migrants, there are cases where nationalism directly defines 'host-stranger' relations, drawing from particular historical disputes between Greece and some of its neighbouring Balkan countries; 'traumas' of the past are symbolically brought back into the collective memory in a selective way (see Lipovac 1993). Such elements are reflected in the experiences of the interviewees regarding the reactions of Greek people towards them: Albanian migrants are treated with mistrust or thought to be criminals, while Bulgarians have also faced negative attitudes, articulated in the context of the Balkan wars; both are expected to 'look' physically different, although they are obviously not:

> Many times, when I used to socialise with a lot of people and go out with them ... 'Where are you from?', 'Albania,' I was telling them. 'No way,', 'Why no way? I am Albanian,', 'Are you a Christian?', 'No, I'm a Muslim.' Then they looked at me in a strange way ... 'Well, not everybody is like you, Maria.' (Maria)
> In any case, what happened in the past, happened then ... Especially here, in northern Greece, you might have discussions like 'Do you know what Bulgarians did then?' Well, yes, I know, but it's not my fault. (Stefania)

Furthermore, there is also a socio-economic, class-related, aspect of xenophobia: the 'other' is not simply different from 'us', ethnically and culturally; the 'other' is also, and primarily, recognisable because of the conditions s/he lives in, and, crucially, the work s/he does. As we are going to see in the next chapter, most immigrants do dirty, badly paid jobs unwanted by most Greeks. As the Balkans are now imagined in Greece as the country's 'hinterland', largely due to 'poor' Balkan immigrants 'here' doing the dirty work and 'clever' Greek businessmen 'there' exploiting opportunities and people, xenophobic attitudes may imply feelings of superiority which are born through relations of dependency[13]. Thus, despite widespread prejudices, towards Albanians mostly, the roots of racism lie in class relations as well; as Balibar & Wallerstein (1990) have argued, racism is embedded in the inner logic of the capitalist system itself. The inclusion of 'elite' migrants in the sample has been useful in order to capture such differentiations on the basis of class and/or status: Albanian and especially Bulgarian professionals with a high socio-economic status mostly face the problems posed by the legal framework, not so much discriminatory or racist treatment as such, as they generally tend to be better accepted and certainly more respected. By contrast, the majority of the interviewees of both nationalities complained about offensive attitudes expressed by locals, in respect to their or their countries' socio-economic conditions:

> People think that because we speak about poverty in Bulgaria, we are also of a lower class ... and sometimes they offend us. Some really mean it, and they do it on purpose, and some people do it without really intending to offend ... For instance, there was this lady that I used to go to, to clean her place. In the beginning, she kept telling me 'What do you Bulgarian women know about houses? You don't have houses up there in Bulgaria, how do you know to clean them?' (Liliana)

> In the shops, in the street, many times people tell me 'You don't look like [an Albanian]' and I'm getting angry, I say 'What do I have to do in order to look like one, do I have to write it on my face?'... When we go on holiday, we rent a room next to two or three other families, they start asking you details ... questions that insult you, 'How can an Albanian go on holiday?' (Mimoza)

Nevertheless, there is a certain degree of ignorance connected to the novelty of the phenomenon that should be taken into account in order to understand the particularities of xenophobia in Greece. In the words of Milen:

> I wouldn't call it racism, but to some extent it exists. And I think that this is quite natural ... There are some people who have never been abroad, who are quite closed, who have not read many things, and they don't understand.

Additionally, almost fifty years of separate histories and closed borders imposed by the Iron Curtain have resulted in a certain degree of ignorance regarding Greece's northern neighbours. This formed the terrain on which prejudices and stereotypes were built during the 1990s, under the influence of governmental policy, due to exposure to negative media images, and on the basis of the explanatory factors analysed here.

However, as contact between immigrants and locals is enhanced and interpersonal relationships are developed over time on the basis of mutual trust, collaboration, friendship, etc. (see Section 8.2.2), perhaps also as a result of regularisations that gave migrants an opportunity to lead normal lives and acquire a public presence, xenophobic sentiments gradually fade and racist attitudes become characteristic of only a small minority among the local population. The curative effect of time should be considered as an element of crucial importance regarding immigrants' incorporation. Not only do policies move towards a more comprehensive set of measures which facilitate integration, as already stated, but also the material conditions of immigrants as well as other aspects of their lives in Greece improve over time, as we are going to see in later chapters. In respect to the social perceptions and attitudes towards the migrant 'other', a similar pattern of the smoothing of host-stranger relations can be observed in both the public discourse and the experiences of the migrants themselves. The media, for instance, now take more seriously the relevant anti-discriminatory regulations, and positive portraits of migrants are more frequently pictured[14], while some state TV and radio channels have included multilingual programmes for immigrants (e.g. ET3 TV channel has a Sunday afternoon programme in Russian and Albanian). This overall positive development in their level of acceptance was mentioned by some of the interviewees and is highlighted in Nadi's testimony below:

> That was mostly in the beginning. Now it still happens, but it is not that strong. The first years, people here were not prepared for this, there were many negative reactions. Now it's different, gradually the situation gets better. People start understanding what's going on, they start learning how to distinguish who is good and who is bad ... Before, we were all the same, people could not distinguish who was a criminal and who was an economic migrant, a normal person, anyway ... The Greeks are hospitable after they get to know you.

5.2.2 *Non-state actors in support of immigrants: the response of civil society*

Some of the gaps in governmental policy for the welfare of immigrants have been covered to an extent by non-state initiatives: community associations, NGOs, left-wing parties, anti-racist groups, trade unions, the Church, etc.; in short, what can be described by the term 'civil-society organisations', the community, voluntary and non-profit sectors. Since the early 1990s, there have been growing positive responses from such initiatives, whether state-funded institutions or grassroots collectives, aiming to support immigrants and to defend their rights. Their activities vary as much as the types and nature of the organisations themselves[15]: initiatives offering welfare services directly (medical treatment, provision of food and shelter, counselling and psychological support), vocational training (language and other courses) or legal assistance exist, as well as institutes researching migration, racism and related issues, and organisations advocating immigrants' rights, or launching campaigns which involve mobilisation and/or participation of the migrants themselves. A listing of such organisations in Thessaloniki is provided in Table A5, Appendix A. The outcomes of such attempts are rather limited in scope, in geographical scale and in the numbers of people they affect; but their role should not be underestimated, especially regarding their growing potential and particularly with respect to their importance at the local level. In addition, the moral/political but also practical support from these sections of the host society encouraged and/or assisted migrant groups to get organised in associations and hence to acquire their own institutional 'voice'.

The number of participants who had benefited from, or simply were aware of, such initiatives is rather low. However, it would be an important omission not to take them into account. During the fieldwork research, background information was collected on the principal initiatives of this kind that were active in Thessaloniki at the time, and this was kept updated until late 2004, with material appearing in the daily press or on the Internet. We can categorise these initiatives into two groups according to the type of services they provide, or the main actions they undertake: (i) social and welfare services; and (ii) vocational training and Greek language teaching.

Language and vocational training courses. Within the framework of relevant EU programmes (e.g. INTEGRA, EQUAL), the Greek government funds non-profit initiatives offering courses of vocational training to migrants and other target groups. 'Returning' ethnic Greeks, immigrants, refugees and asylum seekers comprised 11 per cent of the EQUAL budget for vocational training programmes for vulnerable social groups[16]. The Ministry of Labour funds special Greek language educational programmes for legal migrants and 'returning' ethnic Greeks; courses are organised by private (non-profit) Centres of Vocational Training (KEK). In late 2002, the prefecture of Thessaloniki had-provision for fourteen such programmes, with a total capacity of 664 benefactors and a budget of 2.1 million euros (*Macedonia*, 11 December 2002). But apart from state-funded programmes, there have also been independent (self-funded) initiatives, such as the NGO Odysseas, composed of a group of volunteer teachers, which provides free language courses to immigrants, refugees and other foreign nationals, in rooms provided by the Macedonian Institute of Employment (MAKINE), a research and training body of the city's labour centre. In 2002, there were 350 regular participants in their three levels of classes (*Macedonia*, 11 December 2002). Another example encountered during the fieldwork is a group of volunteers of anarchist/libertarian ideology (*Steki Viologikou*) offering free language courses in an squatter university room. In addition, there are similar language programmes for regular immigrants only, run by bodies of the social services divisions of the council and of the prefecture. Finally, there is the Greek language school at the Aristotle University of Thessaloniki, which charges tuition fees and mostly serves foreign students.

Social and welfare services. Here the landscape appears more diverse. Well-established local branches of international NGOs such as Médecins Sans Frontières, Doctors of the World and the Red Cross are active in providing health services, as well as counselling and psychological support. The former two run clinics which provide free medical treatment to low-income people, including immigrants and refugees, whatever their legal status. In addition, some church parishes used to provide shelter and food for a period, and assist in finding jobs, or support people in need, including migrants, by collecting and distributing used clothes or household equipment. Since the early 2000s, the Refugee

Reception Centre has provided food, temporary accommodation, counselling and other forms of support for asylum seekers in the city. Additionally, a number of organisations exist that focus specifically on counselling, advice on employment and insurance matters, and legal support (including assistance with stay-permit applications). Apart from NGOs, organisations working in this field include community associations like Epirote House, EU-funded projects such as the Centre for Reception and Support of Immigrants and Refugees (hosted by MAKINE and funded through the INTEGRA Community Initiative), initiatives by trade-union bodies such as an office for migrant workers at the Thessaloniki labour centre, left-wing groups and networks, as for instance the local branch of the Network for Social and Political Rights or the European Social Forum.

Obviously, the vast majority of immigrants in the city are not necessarily aware of all those activities aimed at supporting them. Among the respondents in my survey, one fifth of the Albanians and 15 per cent of the Bulgarians had benefited from Greek language programmes. Another six Albanian migrants had participated in vocational training seminars. One (Bulgarian) interviewee mentioned the Médecins Sans Frontières clinic as her way of accessing health services. Two respondents said they had received the help of their local church parishes at an initial stage. Based on this, the impression one gets is that civil-society organisations do indeed play an important role at the local level, but the number of people they affect is fairly marginal. Not only are the capacities and infrastructures of the initiatives mentioned above rather limited as far as the numbers of potential benefactors are concerned, but also immigrants' access to information about the existence of such programmes is problematic. Linguistic obstacles play a role in this, as well as the migrants' legal status, that keeps them 'hiding', as we have seen, or that makes them ineligible for many of these services; but there are factors that make it far more difficult for immigrants to participate in or find out about such initiatives. These range from the spatial concentration of most of these organisations in the central areas of the city, to the everyday reality migrants face in respect to their working hours, family duties and leisure time, as well as to their availability, interest and willingness to participate. Crucially, also, the services provided are not of the same nature: medical treatment for instance, or legal support and assistance/information regarding the documents required for regularisation, are services much more needed and thus more welcome, than, for example, increasing the human capital potential through vocational training and language courses. Nevertheless, however limited the scope of such activities by civil-society organisations, the number of benefactors seems to be gradually growing: for instance, the language-teaching initiative Odysseas, who started with less than ten students during their first steps in 1997, has seen student numbers jump to a few hundred in 2002, upgrading its status from a grassroots collective of volunteers to a registered NGO. According to my information, it is reasonable to assume that any assessment of the experience of other organisations would find similar progress, in addition to the very fact that the number of such initiatives in the city has multiplied.

In parallel, the influence of the activities of a diverse range of organisations[17], which advocate for immigrants' rights, campaign on behalf of individual cases and try to spread a spirit of tolerance among the local population has been growing. Initially, they took the form of solidarity with 'immigrants' in general, focusing on anti-racist and pro-migrant propaganda, through the organisation of public debates, publications related to issues of migration, human rights, xenophobia, etc., or through demonstrations and other forms of activism. In the recent past such activities were rather marginal, often trapped in the political isolationism of traditional radical Left activism, on the one hand, or in the limited influential power and elitism of small think-tanks, on the other. However, through networking and the coordination of activities, but most importantly through the mobilisation of migrants and the formation of associations, there are currently signs of an emerging anti-racist, pro-migrant social movement in Thessaloniki, characterised by organisational, political and ideological diversity (see Glarnetatzis 2001). It is the local equivalent of the (now) well-consolidated Network for the Support of Immigrants and Refugees, based in Athens, with which it maintains links; that was the first attempt in Greece, in terms of wide participation and successful campaigning and lobbying, which also managed to mobilise individual immigrants and migrant organisations.

This movement currently comprises many of the above-mentioned organisations, plus other NGOs (e.g. *Antigone*, part of the EUMC RAXEN network, the local branches of Amnesty International and the International Helsinki Federation for Human Rights), trade-union bodies (e.g. MAKINE), left-wing activist groups (e.g. Network for the Support of Social and Political Rights, the Anti-racist Initiative of Thessaloniki – one of the principal coordinators of activities), etc. Its public presence in the city seems to be increasing and is not solely based on marginal demonstrations and radical propaganda any more; rather it focuses on coordinated protest and advocacy activities embracing wider sections of organised civil society. It engages itself in other actions that apply to a wider public and include immigrants. For instance, public lectures and open debates are organised in collaboration with academics and researchers working on immigration, racism, intercultural education, etc.; relevant press releases appear quite frequently in daily newspapers, and some of the participant organisations, including migrants' associations, have a voice in the above-mentioned local Sunday TV programme for immigrants and ethnic Greeks. Furthermore, cultural events celebrating diversity take place from time to time in various districts of the city, sometimes with the support/funding of local councils, and with the participation of both immigrants and locals (e.g. the annual Anti-racist Festival, an international food festival, musical events, art exhibitions, etc.). By such means, the movement has contributed significantly to bringing immigrants' problems and rights to the forefront of the public discourse, denouncing state policy (particularly events of police brutality), as well as to responding to racist propaganda. In that sense, and despite the fact that the majority of immigrants in the city are neither aware nor part of the movement as such, the overall outcome could be assessed as a positive one, and its contribution, existing and potential, should not be underestimated.

6 Employment and labour-market integration

The economic integration of immigrants is perhaps the most crucial aspect of their experience, to the extent that it determines most of what can be described as the material dimension of their existence, their living conditions and the fulfilment of life-projects and migratory plans. Addressing the processes of economic integration presupposes an insight into their occupational characteristics, their position in the labour market, their working conditions, payment and so on. On the other hand, the patterns of migrants' labour-market integration tell us much about the host economy itself, the indigenous demand for migrant labour, and even the dynamics of class relations: the local productive and employment structures form the socio-economic context whereby migrants are 'inserted', and they are affected subsequently by the presence of the migrant labour force. However, as we have seen, many migrants had previously lived and worked in other parts of Greece before moving to Thessaloniki; their employment history is thus crucial in order to understand their pathways in the Greek labour market. In this chapter, I follow the migrants' employment trajectories, starting from the occupations they held at the time of the fieldwork. Looking back into their past experiences, I develop a dynamic perspective to explain the process of labour-market integration. Findings are also to be understood within the context of the basic socio-economic features of Greece and Thessaloniki as already described in Section 2.2. The narrative builds around an analysis of the survey data, which are backed up, enriched and extended by the use of extracts from the in-depth interviews.

6.1 A cheap and flexible labour force

Exploring the quantitative material from the questionnaire survey allows some initial key observations regarding the basic characteristics of immigrant labour in Thessaloniki: the kind of jobs they perform and the types of companies that employ them, the sectors of the economy they mostly work in, and the differences between male and female migrant labour. The discussion then turns to a description of the migrants' employment conditions, with the focus being on the length of their working days, their payment, whether they are registered or not, and their relationships with employers and colleagues. An overview of the migrants' job-finding strategies and their period of employment in the position held at the time of the interview closes this section.

6.1.1 *Sectors of employment and types of work*

The vast majority of the respondents are waged employees (77.9 per cent). A share of 12 per cent are self-employed (or freelance professionals), 3.4 per cent (seven people) are entrepreneurs and 1.9 per cent (four people) work in the family business. Unemployment concerns only 2.9 per cent (six people), all of whom had been working until shortly before the fieldwork. Four respondents (1.9 per cent) were not working at all: two men were pensioners though who had worked some years in Greece, and two women were housewives. The employment position and skills of those working at the time of the interview are presented in Table 6.1[1] according to their sector of employment. More than two thirds were employed in permanent full-time positions, while 10 per cent said their job arrangements were temporary. Seven per cent were doing casual or part-time work and an equal share were holding more than one position (combining either two part-time jobs, or a full-time one with part-time work or self-employment). A detailed account of the respondents' professions by sector can be found in Table A6 in Appendix A.

Table 6.1 allows for a first key observation concerning the concentration of migrant labour in two basic types of jobs: either manual positions in construction and manufacturing, or posts on the lowest rungs of the service-sector ladder. The principal sectors of migrants' employ-

Table 6.1 *Employment position and level of skills by sector (%)*

	Employment Position			*Nature of Post (skills)*			*Total*
	*employer**	*self-employed*	*waged*	*minimum*	*skilled manual*	*white collar***	
manufacturing	9.1	8.0	29.6	20.8	47.1	4.5	*25.8*
construction	–	12.0	18.5	18.4	19.6	–	*16.7*
personal services	–	32.0	15.4	24.0	5.9	–	*16.7*
maintenance & repair	9.1	20.0	3.7	1.6	19.6	–	*6.1*
hotel & catering	18.2	–	9.9	12.8	3.9	–	*9.1*
trade & retail	27.3	12.0	13.0	20.0	3.9	–	*13.6*
other services	36.4	16.0	9.9	2.4	–	95.5	*12.1*
Total	*5.6*	*12.6*	*81.8*	*63.1*	*25.8*	*11.1*	*N=198*

* Including assistants in family businesses
** Including professional posts, businessmen and entrepreneurs

ment are *manufacturing* (25.8 per cent, including small workshops, carpentry, etc.), *construction* (16.7), *personal services* (16.7 per cent), *trade* (13.6 per cent, both retail and wholesale), *hotel and catering* (9.1 per cent), *maintenance and repair services* (6.1 per cent)[2] and other branches of the *tertiary sector* (12.1 per cent)[3].

A second observation relates to the nature of work migrants do, which is usually physically demanding, often of a servile character, and, for most of them, in low-skilled positions. The vast majority of the respondents work in jobs requiring either *no skills at all or very basic ones* (63.1 per cent). One quarter of them are domestic workers (cleaners, carers, maintenance/repair workers), about 40 per cent are manual labourers in manufacturing and construction, and one fifth work as assistants in retail stores and trading companies. Of the 25.8 per cent who do skilled manual work, almost half are employed in factories and workshops (machine operators, craftsmen), about one fifth in construction (skilled builders, painters, cement mixers, etc.) and another fifth are technicians (electricians, plumbers) or workers specialising in maintenance and repair tasks (painters, etc.). Professionals, entrepreneurs and white-collar workers form a share of 11.1 per cent, and all but one are employed in services.

A third observation has to do with the types of employers that tend to rely on the work of immigrants: these are usually *small- or medium-sized enterprises*, in many cases family-owned, on the one hand, and *individuals or households*, on the other. Among those in industrial employment, few work in big factories (metal machinery, clothing); for most, small- and medium-scale manufacturing is the case, especially in sectors that were at a 'take-off' stage fifteen years ago (shoes and clothing, plastics and chemicals), or in those that were then in decline (metallurgy, metal products), as well as small units such as carpenters' and metal-processing workshops[4]. Employment in the construction sector for the majority is also mostly with small workshops where the employer is usually a Greek foreman, rather than with big building companies undertaking large projects. Similarly, trade concerns mostly (for 9.6 per cent of the total) small retail trade (corner-shops, small stores, bakeries, petrol stations, etc.), and to a lesser extent larger trading companies and storerooms (3.5 per cent). Most of those in the hotel and catering industry work as waiters/waitresses, kitchen assistants and delivery boys in restaurants and fast-food joints (5.1 per cent), waiters/waitresses in cafés and bars (4 per cent), plus one working room service in a hotel.

The increased participation in 'personal services' for individuals or households, mostly in 'reproductive' activities such as care work (33.3 per cent among those working in this sector), domestic help and cleaning (42.4 per cent), and house-repair tasks (18.2 per cent), leads us to a fourth observation regarding the different employment niches male and female migrants cover in the local labour market. Table 6.2 shows, among other things, immigrants' employment by gender. Of all the men in the sample, most work as manual labourers on construction sites (25 per cent), in factories (22.7 per cent) and workshops (7.6 per cent), in maintenance and repair (7.6 per cent),and in trading companies and storerooms (6.1 per cent). Another 7.6 per cent are assistants or shopkeepers in small retail stores, bakeries and petrol stations, while 6.1 per cent work in cafés and restaurants. A share of 4.5 per cent, who are casual manual workers, perform 'personal services'. The rest are employed in various branches of the tertiary sector, as businessmen and/or professionals, with the exception of three working as manual assistants in services. Women, on the other hand, comprise more than one third who are domestic servants and carers, factory workers (14.5 per cent, almost exclusively in small- or medium-sized clothing manufacturers) and waitresses or assistants in cafés, bars and restaurants (13.2 per cent), while 7.9 per cent of them work in retail shops. Thus, they are mainly concentrated in traditionally 'female' sectors. The percentage of women (18.4 per cent) who work as white-collar employees or professionals is far greater than men[5]. Finally, four out of the six unemployed respondents were women.

Extracts from some interviews presented below highlight both the variety of job types performed by migrants, and the contrast between male and female employment:

> This is what I chose, and it suits me because now I keep my entire wage ... I don't pay rent, for phone calls. (Lioupa, looks after an old man as a live-in carer.)
> Well, what I do now I have been doing since the beginning. Houses ... cleaning houses and stairs ... many houses. (Melina, domestic cleaner.)
> Now I work in this office, I help with the translation ... I mostly do admin work. (Dalina, secretary in a translation office owned by a Greek-Albanian.)
> I still work now ... in a clothing factory as a packer ... I've worked there for one year and two months. (Valbona, manufacturing worker.)
> I work in the field I studied, as a mechanic. In the machines department, in an aluminium factory ... it employs about fifty people. Eight hours per day, five days per week and my wage is satisfactory. (Ani, mechanic in a factory.)
> I am a construction worker, a skilled worker, a builder. I've learned the job here; at the beginning I was only helping, but I

Table 6.2 *Immigrants' employment by nationality, gender and ethnic origin (%)*

	Albanian Migrants			*Bulgarian Migrants*			*All*		
	women	*men*	*EGR**	*women*	*men*	*EGR**	*women*	*men*	*EGR**
manufacturing	17.1	29.9	21.3	11.4	31.4	5.0	14.5	30.3	16.4
construction	–	22.7	6.4	–	31.4	40.0	–	25.0	16.4
personal services	39.0	4.1	17.0	31.4	5.7	15.0	35.5	4.5	16.4
maintenance & repair	2.4	6.2	2.1	2.9	11.4	10.0	2.6	7.6	4.5
hotel & catering	4.9	7.2	6.4	22.9	2.9	15.0	13.2	6.1	9.0
trade & retail	9.8	17.5	17.0	5.7	11.4	10.0	7.9	15.9	14.9
other services	19.5	8.2	21.3	17.1	5.7	5.0	18.4	7.6	16.4
unemployed & inactive	7.3	4.1	8.5	8.6	–	–	7.9	3.0	6.0

* EGR = migrants of ethnic Greek origin

had to learn the job, I had to get some more money. (Gjion, construction worker.)

I am in charge in that bakery now. There are three people, and in the morning the boss comes and says 'We have to prepare this and that, bread, this amount in kilos ...' (Spyros, works in a bakery.)

I drive around all the construction projects and I buy the supplies required for each. I also supervise some workers, Albanians, Bulgarians, who I train on the job ... It's quite a responsible position. (Milen, driver/foreman for a large construction company.)

Many things, I do ... gardening, painting, stone-setting, fences, doors. (Kostas, casual manual worker.)

Table 6.2 also shows some differences in the sectoral employment of immigrants by nationality and ethnic origin. For female migrants, manufacturing work is more common among Albanian women, who also work to a great extent as domestic servants and cleaners. The hotel and catering industry is much less important for them, compared to its significance for the employment of female Bulgarians. Bulgarian women are far less likely to be employed in manufacturing. Personal services for them almost exclusively concern caring for elderly or ill people (the five live-in carers of the sample are all Bulgarian women). The largest shares of Bulgarian men, on the other hand, work in construction, and maintenance and repair tasks, mostly due to the weight of the Sarakatsani, half of whom are employed in these sectors. More Albanian men work in bars, restaurants, retail shops and trading companies. The large share of (non-ethnic-Greek) Bulgarian migrants in the tertiary sector may reflect the over-representation of highly skilled professionals in the sample. The highest percentage of employment in the tertiary sector though is observed among ethnic Greek Albanians:

about one fifth of them are white-collar employees or professionals, and this is largely because of the women. By contrast, Sarakatsani men are far less likely to do white-collar work.

Entrepreneurship and self-employment are more common among men: five out of the seven business-owners are men. Managers of larger companies are exclusively men, while women entrepreneurs (two, both from Bulgaria) tend to run smaller companies. Four women are assistants in the family business; for two of them, their Greek husbands are the owners. Most entrepreneurs (five out of seven, plus two assistants in family businesses) are of ethnic Greek origin. Among the self-employed, one third (six people) are women. For men, self-employment refers mostly to migrants undertaking small-scale construction, painting or house-repair projects (tiling, roofing, etc.), or to specialised technicians (electricians, plumbers), often in partnership with relatives or friends, and after 'learning the art' during their previous years in Greece[6]. This explains the high degree of self-employment among those in personal services and maintenance and repair, as shown in Table 6.1. Examples from the interviews offer an idea of how some migrants see their involvement in self-employment/entrepreneurship:

> Regarding our job, several tasks ... painting, plaster ... [I work] with my brothers ... One of them is an electrical engineer ... The other is a mechanical engineer ... We work at construction sites. Our elder brother does the studies [the projects] ... For instance, currently we are renovating a building opposite the White Tower. It's a good job ... We never run out of work. (Louzim, self-employed in construction, undertakes repair/renovation projects with his three brothers.)
>
> I got married ... I stayed at home for a period ... and then we decided to start this business ... This is why we started this business, so I wouldn't have to seek work somewhere else, I could be together with my husband. (Liliana, running a café-bar together with her Greek husband.)
>
> I am the owner of this [translation] service ... I have faced the same problems that a Greek can face when he starts his own business. I have five full-time employees and many external collaborators. The external collaborators are mostly Greeks. Well, some of them are foreigners, because we offer translation services and we need people who speak foreign languages. My employees are all ethnic Greeks and Albanians, because they have to know the Albanian language, since the big bulk of our work has to do with translations from Greek to Albanian and from Albanian to Greek. (Stavros, owns a translation office.)

> For all these ten years, I have been working in a kiosk ... I was working as an assistant in the kiosk for four or five years, then I rented it together with my brother. During the last six years, I've been working there ... In the beginning I had a problem with the papers [the permit to open a kiosk], because in order to get the papers you have to have a stay permit, which they wouldn't issue during those years. (Emil, runs a kiosk together with his brother.)

6.1.2 *Access to employment and working conditions*

The working conditions and payment of the respondents reflect to an extent the *cheap and flexible labour* offered by immigrants. The main issues addressed here concern the respondents' daily working hours, payment and social security, as summarised in Table 6.3. To start with, working days for most of the interviewees are in line with the usual Greek standards (five or six days per week), depending on the nature and the needs of each job. However, for men in construction or in casual manual work, and for women in care work and domestic service, work can be highly seasonal or occasional, respectively, sometimes involving long working weeks and employment during weekends and bank holidays. On the other hand, as shown in Table 6.3, for many the working day is much longer than the usual eight-hour one. A working day of up to eight hours is the case for 38.1 per cent. For an equal share, the working day usually exceeds eight hours (about 15 per cent actually work for more than ten hours a day, including the female live-in carers). The remaining 23.8 per cent, who said their daily working hours were not fixed but varied, were mostly men employed in manual jobs requiring minimum or no skills (construction and casual house maintenance/repair workers, retail shop assistants), or women working as domestic servants/cleaners and shop assistants.

Furthermore, according to Table 6.3, slightly less than half of the respondents earn between 20-29 euros a day, and about one third makes more than 30 euros, with 12.4 per cent earning 40 euros or more[7]. A daily wage of less than 20 euros is the case for about 10 per cent of the respondents, while 11.9 per cent said their wage is not fixed but depends on the availability and hours of work, or if the 'business goes well'. Payment below 20 euros a day mostly concerns Albanian domestic servants and cleaners, since employment in personal services is generally less likely to pay well. Employment in construction and maintenance/repair usually pays between 30-39 euros a day, but these sectors are also the ones where wages fluctuate more, especially for the self-employed. As expected, those working in white-collar employment and in highly skilled positions (other services) are far more likely to receive

Table 6.3 *Working conditions by sector of employment*

	Hours of Work per Day (N=181)			*Daily Wage (in Euros) (N=154)*					*Social security*
	8 or less	*8+*	*not fixed*	*< 20*	*20-29*	*30-39*	*40+*	*not fixed*	
manufacturing	60.0	33.3	6.7	4.0	74.0	16.0	6.0	–	68.6
construction	27.3	45.5	27.3	3.0	24.2	48.5	6.1	18.2	75.8
personal services	12.9	45.2	41.9	33.3	33.3	18.2	3.0	12.1	30.3
maintenance & repair	33.3	11.1	55.6	9.1	36.4	27.3	–	27.3	75.0
hotel & catering	40.0	33.3	26.7	5.9	52.9	5.9	17.6	17.6	66.7
trade & retail	36.0	56.0	8.0	7.7	53.8	19.2	3.8	15.4	59.3
other services	47.8	21.7	30.4	4.2	20.8	4. 2	58.3	12.5	83.3
Total	38.1	38.1	23.8	9.8	45.4	20.6	12.4	11.9	64.1

Note: Percentage within sector of employment

higher wages. Now, comparing the average daily wages (means) of the 158 respondents who did state the actual amount of their wage, we find significant differences in terms of gender and ethnic origin. Men earn about 30 euros a day, women about 26. Ethnic Greek migrants earn more than 30 euros, but this accounts mostly for men (Greek-Albanian women make 29 euros on average). Non-ethnic-Greek female Albanians as a group have the lowest average daily wage (21.2 euros a day). Figure 6.1 represents these differences schematically.

Clearly the sample shows a certain degree of heterogeneity; the interviews reveal that wages first depend on the type of occupation and the position held, but also on the period a person was working for the same employer, the hours of work and the kind of relationships with bosses. The daily wage for a manual worker in (metal- or wood-processing) workshops and on construction sites (general manual tasks, building, cement-mixing, painting) varies from 23 to 32 euros. For a domestic servant/cleaner it lies between 10-30 euros per day, depending on the hours of work and the good will of the employer. Care work (looking after children or old people) can start from 90 euros per

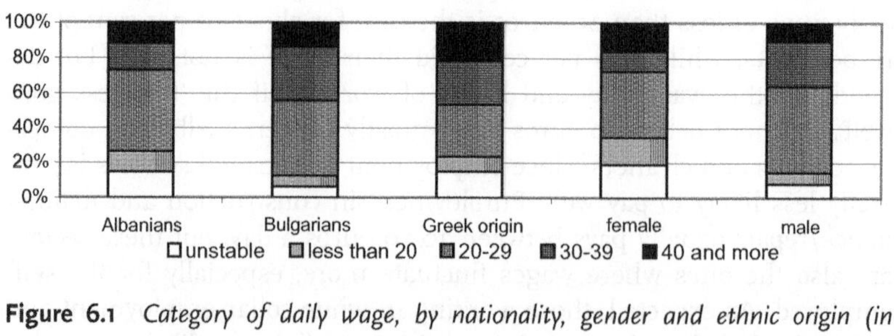

Figure 6.1 *Category of daily wage, by nationality, gender and ethnic origin (in euros)*

month for a part-time position and rise up to 380 euros per month for a full-time one, or stay at 300 euros for a live-in maid (since accommodation and food are provided). Unskilled workers in small manufacturers get paid around 20 euros for eight hours of work; skilled ones in bigger factories may receive more than 700 euros a month, depending on the employee's position and qualifications and on the period of working for the same employer. Low payment was one of the problems commented on by the majority of the interviewees, while a comparison with Greek workers' wages is unavoidable, especially when it concerns the same type of work[8]:

> To tell you the truth, for the job I do, I don't get the money that I deserve. (Ferin, manual worker in a metal workshop.)
> Now I get 11,000 drachmas [33 euros]. Again, this is not the daily wage a skilled worker should take, but I profit again, and the employer profits, because we have a deal. (Gjion, construction worker.)
> We can't earn what a Greek skilled worker earns. We get paid a bit less, but we are satisfied. (Kostas, casual manual worker.)
> There is a slight difference [between Greeks' and Albanians' wages], there always is one, but it's not as big as it was in the beginning. (Nadi, mechanic in an aluminium factory.)

Another interviewee commented on both the longer working hours done by immigrants and the lower payment they receive as an 'advantage' for being preferred by Greek employers:

> [The Greek] at ten o'clock wants to have a coffee break ... at 12 o'clock he wants to eat for half an hour ... at two o'clock, a fifteen- or twenty-minute break for coffee and a cigarette ... Here all the Greek bosses don't want Greek workers ... at all small factories ... this is why they hire Albanians, Russians, Bulgarians, because we work for less money. (Raicko, skilled worker in a metal-processing workshop.)

Unregistered work is still the case for many – only 64.1 per cent had social security at the time of the fieldwork. Even for those who did, in some cases there is no fixed-term employment contract, while many had managed to register only shortly before the fieldwork. There were many examples of interviewees having bought their social security stamps from IKA in order to be able to apply for regularisation or renewal of their stay and working permits. Some, especially those with previous experience in agricultural work, prefer buying ΟΓΑ stamps because they cost less. A small number of people who were self-employed and entrepreneurs were registered with TEBE. Another strategy, most common amongst people who work on a freelance basis, such as self-employed construction workers, electricians or plumbers, and domestic servants/carers, is to get self-insured at IKA, sometimes paying part of the fees themselves while the rest is covered by their employers. In many cases, social security is partial, covering health insurance but not pension contributions[9]. Since registered employment is a prerequisite for the issue of stay and work permits, one understands why insurance is one of the migrants' greater concerns:

> [I am] a stitcher-sewer. It is a small one [manufacturer]. I am worried, because I can't go [leave the job], but I want to go because the money is not good. I want to find a job offering social security. (Katerina)
> I work ... for eight hours per day, and I get 130,000 drachmas [390 euros] per month ... I take care of the children, I iron, I wash dishes ... I am not insured. (Kaiti)

As also shown in Table 6.3, registered employment is more common among those in white-collar/professional employment, followed by construction and maintenance and repair. For people working in personal services it drops to 30.3 per cent, and this obviously particularly affects female migrants: 61 per cent of Albanian women and 48.6 per cent of female Bulgarians were lacking social security at the time of the survey. Finally, unregistered work was also high among ethnic Greek Albanians, with 51.1 per cent of them not being insured, again mostly due to the preponderence of women.

Union participation rates are extremely low: only eight people, or 4 per cent among those employed, were members of a trade union. Notably, seven of them have been in Greece for nine or more years, six are married and four are between 30-39 years old, while only two are women. Five were employed in manufacturing, all in the metal-machinery sector, one in construction and two were white-collar service employees. Certainly, the widespread informality and the nature of the jobs migrants do (casual work, domestic service) partly provide the explanation for such limited union membership, together with fear, lack of information, limited language competence and perhaps a degree of mistrust towards collective organisations. What fieldwork findings failed to capture is an increasing number of migrant construction workers registering with syndicates in this sector and sometimes actively participating in strikes/campaigns; this is revealed by the construction workers' trade union's statements and articles in the daily newspapers, and was also mentioned by an Albanian interviewee who works as a translator:

> The only exception is the construction workers' trade union. I know this because I have done their translations. There are many registered there, Russians, Albanians and everything. It's a very big trade union ... because of the Communist Party. The people I met were from the Communist Party. (Adriana)

Membership though seems not to mean active participation. Two Albanian migrants, Nadi and Ani, both working in metal-machinery factories, stressed this fact, since the only thing they do is to go on strike when the union decides to, or otherwise to just 'count as a member'; an elderly Sarakatsani Bulgarian who is a construction labourer spoke with bitterness of the way his union 'does nothing' in practice and expressed his willingness to opt out. On the other hand, the precarious character of migrant labour is precisely what makes it so flexible, and thus so in demand, while the immigrants' vulnerable position and insecurity makes them reluctant to organise themselves in the face of highly exploitative working environments and conditions. Lazaros' story below is self-explanatory:

> This is one of the bad things in Greece [the way syndicalism works and the way employers react]. I'll tell you a story, about a guy who used to work at Pizza Hut with me. He was a university student ... He used to work there and he had contacts with a union. Some people from the union came once to speak to us. The result? The guy was fired. The bosses found an excuse to fire him. I was new there, but I could understand what was going on. And those people from the union never came again.

Furthermore, regarding access to employment, the findings suggest that migrants tend to rely largely on informal relationships of support and solidarity in order to make their way through the local labour market. Only 16.8 per cent said they found their job at the time of the fieldwork 'alone', and other job-finding strategies appear even less significant. Some 5.3 per cent of the sample, exclusively men, were in a position they found through the so-called 'piazzas' – meeting points where immigrants gather and where Greek employers know that they can find labourers to work for them. Few made use of the newspapers' job pages (3.4 per cent, mostly women), or of official employment agencies, whether public (OAEΔ, 2.4 per cent, again mostly women), or private ones (another 2.4 per cent, exclusively Bulgarian women who work as carers and domestic servants). A lower percentage of women looked for work alone (12.7 per cent, compared to 20.6 per cent of men). More than half of all respondents (58.1 per cent) found their current jobs through information provided by, or through direct help from, relatives and friends, or sometimes also by Greek people they knew. Some differences, though, are evident between the two nationalities: greater percentages of Albanian immigrants made use of their social networks (68 per cent, compared to 46.9 per cent of Bulgarians) or looked for work alone (20.8 per cent, compared to 12.5 per cent of Bulgarians), while more Bulgarian migrants went through vacancy ads, or through OAEΔ. Finally, the higher percentage of Bulgarian respondents who found their current post through job-finding piazzas (12.5 per cent, compared to 2.4 per cent of the Albanians) has to be attributed to the Sarakatsani, who work mainly on a casual basis and in temporary positions. In conclusion, it appears that the main sources of information about job opportunities, or of assistance in job finding, are the migrants' own social ties and relationships. Sometimes they are even necessary, in order to facilitate access to employment, as shown in the example below:

> I found it from an ad. I went for an interview and they told me ... 'We will call you.' I waited for two or three weeks. I had no reply, so I called and they told me, 'We haven't decided yet,' and finally I pulled a few strings ... Somebody I know, who knew the boss, spoke to him and said, 'Take him, he is good for this job.' (Ani)

Temporariness in working arrangements is the case for many immigrants in Thessaloniki, adding more fuel to the argument about the *flexibility* of migrant labour. Apart from the earlier mentioned 10 per cent who said their employment agreement was for a (fixed) limited period, there are also many who had started working not long before the time of the field survey[10]. For the majority (43.4 per cent), their current occupation dates back no more than a year. Slightly more than one third had been working at the same job from one to five years, while only one in five had been in more stable positions for more than five years. The average (mean) period in the last job was three years, with a fluctuation of five or six months more for men and less for women. Ethnic Greek Albanians tended to have more stable positions, working in a single post for 4.5 years on average – unsurprising, perhaps, as most of them were among the first to migrate.

6.2 Immigrants' trajectories in the Greek labour market

Most of the respondents have worked in various occupations during their stay in Greece. Looking at their employment history, we find that individual migrants have done many different jobs in different parts of the country. Not surprisingly, white-collar work or entrepreneurship weighted much less in the overall employment profile of the sample. On the other hand, agricultural employment has been the case for many, especially during their first years in Greece and obviously before moving to the city. This heterogeneity of immigrants' working experiences, despite their concentration in particular labour-market niches, uncovers two basic characteristics of foreign labour in Greece, both related to migrants' *trajectories* in the Greek labour market:

- Firstly, a single migrant is likely to have changed occupations many times while in Greece, performing various different tasks, in many cases unrelated to one another. This means that, being in urgent need, immigrants had to accept *any job* that was offered to them, despite their qualifications and experience back home. Thus, apart from constituting a 'pool' of cheap, hard-working labour, unregistered for the most part, they are also extremely *flexible* regarding the types of jobs they do. These are the issues discussed in the rest of this section.
- Secondly, there are significant shifts in the occupational structure of the sample. Initial conditions were harsh, including high levels and various forms of exploitation by employers. At the time of the fieldwork, none was working in agriculture and fewer people were working in the leisure and catering industry, in personal services, or were employed as general manual workers. Now there are more industrial workers, shop assistants, skilled workers, technicians and white-collar employees, including some in highly skilled positions. This suggests that, after a period in Greece, immigrants in Thessaloniki tend to find *better jobs*, a fact that points to a certain degree of occupational, and possibly socio-economic, *mobility* over time. This is the topic of Section 6.3.

6.2.1 *Doing 'any' job: trajectories and pathways of access*

At the time of fieldwork, only 26.9 per cent of the respondents had been practicing the same profession since they arrived, but even in such cases it was exceptional to have been doing this for the same employer. And for people who had been working continuously for one employer, their responsibilities and type of work did not remain the same over time. Some of the interviewees recalled numerous different jobs they had done, sometimes at many places. For obvious reasons, the earlier a migrant had come to Greece, the more likely s/he was to have done many different jobs. Frequencies among 144 detailed responses give the following shares[11]: 29.9 per cent were previously employed in hotels, cafés and restaurants, 25.7 per cent as general manual workers, gardeners, painters and technicians, 22.9 per cent in cleaning and domestic work, 22.2 per cent in construction, an equal share in agriculture, cattle-breeding and fishing, 16.7 per cent as general manual workers, 13.2 per cent as carers and nurses, 10.4 per cent in manufacturing and another 10.1 per cent as shop assistants. Women were more likely to have done the same profession since the beginning (32.9 per cent), and this adds to the argument of labour-market segmentation according to gender and the existence of purely 'female' sectors of employment. Women of both nationalities have mostly worked in the leisure and catering industry (48.8 per cent), as carers and nurses (41.5 per cent), as domestic servants (31.7 per cent) or cleaners (26.8 per cent), but also in agriculture (26.8 per cent), manufacturing (14.6 per cent) and in retail trade (14.6 per cent). Bulgarian migrants are less likely to have been doing the same profession since the beginning (17.7 per cent, compared to a 31.1 per cent of Albanians); most have worked in cafés, hotels and restaurants (39.2 per cent, compared to 26.9 per cent of Albanians), as general manual workers (38.1 per cent, compared to 20.4 per cent of Albanians), or as carers and nurses (23.5 per cent, compared to 9.7 per cent of Albanians). Also, higher proportions of Bulgarians have worked in agriculture, cattle-breeding and fishing (39.2 per cent, compared to 19.4 per cent among Albanians), but the percentages rise to an extent due to the presence of the (male) Sarakatsani. Ethnic Greeks of both nationalities have changed jobs many times (only 15.6 per cent of them have been in the same profession since the beginning): many have worked in the leisure and catering industry (31.5 per cent). Examples from the relevant section of the questionnaire follow some respondents' *trajectories* in the Greek labour market:

- *Female Albanian from Tirana, 24, married, came in 1999:* 1. cleaning houses → 2. waitress in a café → 3. room service in a hotel → 4. domestic service.
- *Female Albanian from Sarandë, 27, single, came in 1993:* 1. advertising leaflets → 2. waiteress → 3. cleaner → 4. assistant in a beauty parlour.
- *Female Bulgarian from Chirpan, 46, divorced, one child, came in 1994:* 1. agricultural worker, picking olives → 2. agricultural worker, picking tomatoes → 3. cook in a hotel → 4. bar in a hotel → 5. live-in carer of an ill woman.
- *Female Bulgarian from Kazavluk, 38, single, came in 1992:* 1. worker in a fruit-canning factory in Kavala → 2. agricultural worker (olives, tomatoes, grapes), various places → 3. room service in a hotel in Rhodes → 4. waitress/cleaner in a café → 5. assistant/cleaner in a fast-food restaurant → 6. kitchen assistant in a restaurant.
- *Male Albanian from Elbasan, 27, married, came in 1992:* 1. agricultural worker, harvesting olives → 2. assistant in a store selling bath-

room equipment → 3. harbour worker → 4. agriculture worker, tobacco → 5. worker in a confectionery supplier.
- *Male Albanian from Korçë, 22, single, came in 1992 with his parents:* 1. manual worker in a plaster materials company → 2. kitchen assistant in a restaurant → 3. carpenter's assistant → 4. carrying boxes for a transport company → 5. working in a factory producing plastic boxes.
- *Male Albanian from Korçë, 28, single, came in 1991:* 1. waiter in a fish restaurant in Athens → 2. agricultural worker in Larisa for six years → 3. construction worker in Lamia for two years → 4. builder for a small construction company in Thessaloniki.
- *Male Bulgarian from Ruse, 60, widowed, came in 2001:* 1. cattle-breeding → 2. agricultural worker (tractor) → 3. worker in a small factory producing detergents.

It is also interesting how some of the respondents emphasised the specific details regarding the numerous jobs they had in different parts of the country:
- *Male Sarakatsani from Pernik, 59, married with two children (who live in Bulgaria but come occasionally to work), came in 1990 for the first time and initially followed a 'back and forth' path.* He worked in agriculture, in various places: picking peaches in Veroia, apples in Agia (Larisa), oranges in Argos, olives in Korinthos, watermelons, grapes, tomatoes, peaches in several villages around Larisa. For six months he was a gardener in a big hotel in Halkidiki. Currently he works casually as a gardener and manual worker in Thermi.

Many of the barriers potentially imposed by the market, or by the limited knowledge migrants have about its geographies and its conditions, as well as language barriers, are overcome in practice, not only by the flexibility and the low cost of their labour, but also because they posses a particular 'advantage' in terms of social capital. This refers to the strength and density of their social networks, i.e. the informal ties and interpersonal relationships that are naturally developed between individuals. In the case of immigrants, networks played an important role in their decision about migration and determined their 'journey' and settlement in Greece, as we have seen; when the question turns to their labour-market integration, networks also function as an important source of information about job opportunities in particular places, or are of direct assistance in finding employment. Among the multiple answers given by the respondents, at least half of them recognised that their main way of finding work since they arrived in Greece has been through the help of relatives, friends or acquaintances. Only 21.2 per cent had previously found work through newspapers, and 16.2 per cent (exclusively men) mentioned the piazzas. Social networks appear to be even more important among ethnic Greek migrants (79.7 per cent). One third of the respondents said they had also found work 'alone' (i.e. on their own initiative), but this answer has probably a limited explanatory value, since it fails to capture the function of networks as sources of information. In that sense, the 40 per cent of women who said they had found employment 'alone' may be hiding other strategies of job-finding, especially newspaper advertisements and private agencies, both appearing more significant for female respondents. But again, the nature of many of the jobs migrant women do, especially those working as domestic servants, cleaners and carers, is more individualistic and does not allow for much socialisation at work. By contrast, men in construction, for example, might be asked by their employers to tell their friends that there is a need for workers.

The in-depth interviews highlight better the crucial role of social networks, because, going into more detail, they help to clarify such obscurities. For instance, even those interviewees who complained about the lack of solidarity and support among their compatriots acknowledged the fact that, between relatives and friends at least, information exchange about job opportunities can be a help in smoothing individuals' pathways into the labour market. Social networks provide a guarantee for securing access to employment, especially for those who have been in Greece for longer periods and who also have contacts with locals. Some relevant quotes from the interviews:

> My acquaintances helped me ... when I came to Greece I knew some people here that helped me very much in order to find this [first] job. (Soultana).
> Mostly through friends, Greeks ... 'Andreas, come here, there is work,' ... 'How much?' ... and I work. (Andreas).
> Since I was working there, I could ask the boss 'I have a friend, he's a nice guy, can he also work here?' So my friend would start working, then he might bring two, three, four, or more friends of his, to work there too. (Lazaros)
> Well ... everything I did, I did it on my own, myself and my husband. We didn't have any great help, except the help my cousin offered us in the beginning, as I told you. And, OK, my husband found employment through an Albanian ... Me too, at the factory where I worked for one or two days per week, where there was necessity. [I found this] through some Albanian women. (Valbona)
> Well, usually it happens between friends, Albanians, who help each other ... For instance, the boss at work says, 'Bring me

> more people,' and he's going to tell some relatives first ... then friends. (Flora)
>
> Brother, cousin, friend, somebody we know from the village [in Albania], anybody we can help, we do. For example, I don't work, my brother-in-law does, or he knows about some jobs for me, that's the way we help each other. (Gjion)

On these grounds, long-term and/or structural unemployment has not been the case so far. However, during their period in Greece and in between different occupations, many migrants have experienced shorter or longer periods of unemployment. Almost half of the respondents have found themselves unemployed for periods longer than one month. Almost exclusively, such an experience can be described by what economists call 'natural', rather than 'structural', unemployment. For men, that would usually mean a temporary lack of work availability, particularly between two jobs (when fired, or abandoning a post to look for something better), or because of a move to another place in Greece. In a few cases, unemployment came as a result of coming back to Greece after a short return to the home country. For women it was also connected to the female life course, birth and maternity, involving a necessary absence from employment during the pre- and post-natal period, and the difficulty of finding work immediately after taking the decision to return to the labour market. For a limited number of people of both sexes, there were periods of 'voluntary' or 'strategic' unemployment in order to find a job according to their qualifications or simply offering more in terms of pay and security than their previous one. Finally, some respondents mentioned problems finding employment at an initial stage, when they first entered the country, connecting their experience to their limited knowledge of the language and local conditions:

> At the beginning, I didn't have a job, I didn't know the language, nothing ... for about two months ... Then I worked at a firm producing slippers, I worked for twenty months there. Then... that was in 1998 ... there was a problem with our papers, the factory shut down and I found myself unemployed again. (Pandelis)
>
> Between the two jobs, there was about one year of unemployment ... I was looking for something better, I couldn't find anything, until I found this one. (Ani)
>
> We left there [Kastoria] and we came to Thessaloniki. And then I found a job here ... but I spent about a month and a half unemployed. (Liliana)
>
> There was a period I was looking for a job and could not get any. I don't remember now for how long. That was after my

> daughter was born... because I had to stay with her when she was a baby ... But then I started looking for a job ... I was looking in the yellow pages. I was looking for a job in an office, or a saleswoman, this kind of job, and I couldn't find any until I found this one. (Dalina)

6.2.2 *'I'm not afraid of hard work': 'de-skilling' and work as a 'value'*

Generally, however, immigrants in Greece have not faced serious difficulties of *access* to the labour market. What seems to be the norm for the overwhelming majority is concentration in specific sectors of the economy, at the margins of the formal labour market, in badly paid manual jobs of a deeply 'servile' character, for which indigenous labour supply is insufficient and which would not be done in the absence of foreign labour. But while this might be true for migrant job-seekers who go for unskilled or low-skilled positions, it does not seem to be the case for migrants who look for more qualified posts in sectors where competition is sharper, even among Greeks. We have seen that employment in non-manual skilled jobs is the case for just one tenth of the respondents, while only one quarter work as skilled manual workers, technicians and craftsmen. These figures contrast sharply with the educational and professional background of the migrants: indeed, a significant number of the respondents are specialised or qualified. As shown in Chapter 4, the shares of those with a university or technical/professional education reach 27.9 and 29.3 per cent respectively. Also, keeping in mind the high percentage of people without previous work experience in their home countries (23.8 per cent, excluding missing cases), about two thirds of the respondents who used to work were occupied in skilled positions: one fifth in skilled manual jobs or posts involving certain skills and responsibilities (drivers, nurses, policemen), and more than 40 per cent in white-collar employment or as teachers, scientists and professionals.

Migrants are thus 'forced' to do the jobs available in Greece, despite their educational qualifications and professional experience. In that sense, it would not be an exaggeration to suggest that migration involves a significant *devaluation* of the individuals' employment profile and occupational status. It has a deep 'de-skilling' effect, since what used to be a rich educational capital in the countries of origin becomes almost useless and obsolete in the Greek labour market, where the high demand for foreign labour is for the bottom-end jobs in the employment pyramid. In that respect, the experience of migration can be seen as downward social mobility at the individuals' level[12], as shown in the following examples:

- *Dimitris, 39*: Accountant in Korçë, construction worker in Thessaloniki.
- *Spyros, 36*: primary school teacher and part-time journalist in Sarandë, assistant in a bakery in Thessaloniki.
- *Valbona, 30*: primary school teacher in Burrell, now works in a clothing factory on the outskirts of Thessaloniki.
- *Gjion, 35*: policeman in Mirdita, construction worker in Thessaloniki.
- *Mimoza, 39*: office secretary in Tirana, occasionally cleaning houses and shops in Thessaloniki.
- *Lioupa, 54*: Nursery teacher in Petric, live-in carer of an old man in Thessaloniki.
- *Kostas, 52*: Former army officer in Plovdiv, retired, now a casual manual worker in Thessaloniki.

How can a skilled worker or a qualified person move towards low-status, low-skilled occupations? In some cases, this appears to be partly a result of linguistic or cultural obstacles, or due to 'outdated' qualifications:
- *Soultana, 36, worked as a secretary at Karlovo:* Initially, it was difficult for me, because I couldn't speak the language very well ... of course, I couldn't practice the profession I was doing in Bulgaria ...
- *Panoraia, 36, was an accountant in Gjirokaster*: Well, in Albania we didn't use computers at work ... So if some day I decide to work as an accountant I'll have to learn computers first ...

The language factor obviously plays an important role: while more than one third (36.3 per cent) of the sample speaks Greek perfectly, as already mentioned, less than 10 per cent write fluently as well. For university graduates, there is also an 'institutional' factor concerning the highly bureaucratic procedures for the recognition of foreign degrees. The process also involves written examinations in certain subjects, making things even more difficult because of the language barrier (although the process itself is the same for all, including Greeks who study abroad). And certainly, there are the problems arising from the uncertain legal status of immigrants in Greece, as we have seen. Such problems are highlighted in the following interview extracts:

> I work ... as a mechanical engineer ... But my boss cannot register me as an engineer, since my diploma is not yet recognised here ... which is impossible to do, as far as I know ... The system with the Green Cards is not stable yet, it changes every year ... since the Green Card is not sorted out yet, which is the most basic thing ... you can't go further, take exams, anything ... So, I

> work in my profession, but I am not registered as an engineer. (Nadi, studied engineering and practiced his profession before emigrating.)
>
> I thought about that [working in his profession] in the beginning, but it was quite difficult to get a job here, I had to take some exams. It was difficult. (Emil, studied economics and statistics in Albania and now runs a kiosk in Thessaloniki.)
>
> I finished my degree and I waited for three years to get the ID card for Northern Epirotes. I had already applied to ΔΙΚΑΤΣΑ [the centre for the recognition of foreign degrees] and I had to be examined in four courses. I was registered at the university, and I got the books and I started studying. Once I went to the university for information, and I was asked where I came from. Then I was told that the examinations were very difficult even for native Greeks. It would be more difficult for me since Greek is not my mother tongue. Also, I'd been out of school for some years. I didn't have much time because I was working. So finally I gave up. (Kaiti, biology graduate, works as a childminder and domestic worker.)

But these factors seem inadequate to fully explain the phenomenon. Is it really a direct outcome of the migrants' educational capital and knowledge of the Greek language that they tend to work in low-skilled manual jobs? It would be quite naive to overestimate such parameters at the expense of the structural conditions that seem far more important for understanding the patterns of immigrants' insertion in the Greek labour market. Throughout this chapter, it has been made evident that the demand for immigrant labour in Greece is precisely for the low-skilled manual and servile posts where most of the respondents work. When immigrants seek to get out of the space 'reserved' for them in the labour market, they face difficulties of access, structural and institutional obstacles, discrimination and sometimes complete exclusion. Especially for migrants who have a university education, institutional barriers together with linguistic difficulties make things even harder. Working in the public sector is not an option, partially due to recruitment procedures but mostly to the legal framework that excludes non-Greek/non-EU nationals from public-sector employment[13]. And many of those employed in 'personal services', especially men, as we have seen, are in most cases manual workers or assistants. So the proportion of migrants who do non-manual work in skilled posts in 'mainstream' economic sectors is even lower. Thus, the step towards better positions is not an easy one, particularly for qualified migrants.

But, apart from the highly qualified positions, this is also true for certain specialisations for which competition is sharp in the local economy. Such is the example of Edri, an Albanian interviewee who, being a medical school graduate from Tirana University, was employed in Greece as a private nurse, a profession which she abandoned after deciding that she wanted a change in her career. She re-trained in a private professional institute in Thessaloniki and became a hairdresser, but when she tried to look for a job she faced only closed doors: 'There is too much supply, and I know that I am the last one because I am a foreigner.'

Kaiti's experience was similar. A biology graduate from Korçë who speaks four languages, Kaiti currently works as a childminder and domestic helper:

> I tried to learn computers and languages to work as a secretary ... I have taken computer courses ... But I have not found a job as a secretary. I have told our friends, our relatives, but up to now nothing. I am still on a waiting list.

So the question posed earlier should be put in a different form: why do qualified migrants *accept* this type of work? The answer then looks simpler: the economic conditions in the home countries, which have been at the root of people's decision to emigrate, and the family or personal needs generated by the transition to a market economy push people to 'throw away' – at least for a certain period – what can be characterised as acceptable standards of dignified employment. Hence, they accept any job in order to survive or to support their family back home, by sacrificing the present to gain a future life of dignity. As it emerges in the qualitative material, work seems to have become an important value for immigrants, an indicator of their virtue and dignity and a path to well-being, something that 'you shouldn't be ashamed of'. This probably explains the relatively low percentage (28.3 per cent) of the respondents who said they were not satisfied with the working conditions they met in Greece. Hard work is connected to both the condition of the migrant, and his/her status as a foreign (non-EU) national in Greece, described in legal documents and in policy discourse by the term 'alien'. In answer to my question 'What does it mean for you to be an Albanian in Greece?', Ferin, 22, from Albania, replied: 'Well, an ΦalienΦ as you say here, somebody who works for the [minimum] daily wage.' This phrase reflects both the dominant idea about the position of immigrants in Greece and their own perception of this idea: the immigrant as a worker. Obviously, this relates to the propensity of migrants to accept *any* job; but it also shapes, partly at least, their identity, as well as the way Greeks 'see' them. Similar views were highlighted by many interviewees:

> My only thought was to start working, to get paid what my boss would pay me. (Pandelis)
> I've worked as a construction worker since the beginning. It's a heavy job, as you know. It was difficult for me, because I had never performed any job of this kind, but I needed to work and I wanted to live in Greece ... that's why I don't mind working in any job. (Dimitris)
> Any job, I can do it, tiles, painting, everything ... I'm not afraid of hard work ... (Andreas)
> We foreigners, when we came here we came for work ... any work. We did heavy jobs here, jobs that Greeks don't do at all. All of us, I'm not talking only about the Bulgarians [but about], all foreigners. (Lioupa)

Such narratives reflect the very nature of Albanian and Bulgarian emigration: economic necessity and the need to work and secure an income were the main reasons for leaving the home countries in the first place; hard work is thus a necessity for migrants in order to survive and realise their plans. But hard work might affect their daily lives in very precise ways, if we pay closer attention to individual experiences. The interview quotes below are only moderate examples of the problems emerging as a result of hard work, for instance in the migrants' family lives and regarding personal health[14]:

> *Ivan, 35, now a driver for a transportation company, speaks about his experience of health problems at work*: Then I started having health problems. Lifting lots of heavy things in and out of the refrigerators ... my hands started giving me pain ... and I decided to stop, so as not to sacrifice my health.
> *Lazaros, 40, now a delivery boy for Pizza Hut, recalls the problems during the period he and his wife spent working as shop-keepers*: We worked there for a period. Too many hours, my kids could not see me. I was leaving in the morning and coming back in the evening. And we finally reached a point when the kid asked 'Who is he?' ... He was not seeing his father at all. And we said enough, it's better be in a more difficult economic situation than destroy our family.

6.3 Stories of exploitation and stories of success

The aim of this section, as already indicated, is to compare and contrast the immigrants' employment characteristics described earlier in the chapter, with the situation they faced initially. A relative improvement of their position is generally evident, including some particularly 'successful' trajectories, pointing to a process of upward socio-economic mobility overall. Yet, this finding should not divert our attention far from other essential features of migrant labour in Greece, its exploitation being certainly one, especially during the first years, but still the case for many.

6.3.1 *Initial conditions: various forms of exploitation*

Initial conditions were harsh for the vast majority of the respondents. Living under clandestine status and with little money in their pocket, with limited knowledge of Greek and needing to survive, most migrants felt vulnerable, afraid and insecure, so that they were forced to accept the situation they were faced with. Employment was not scarce, but it would offer little in terms of payment, it would be very demanding, and it was not a matter of choice. Employment arrangements were temporary or seasonal; in many cases, migrants used to work for a few days here, a few days there, changing frequently not only employers, but also tasks and types of work. Job-finding was based on word-of-mouth strategies of information exchange between relatives, friends, or simple acquaintances from the same place of origin. However, it often involved days of wandering around, or hours of waiting at piazzas. Many of the interviewees recalled these first years by referring to their need for pure survival, to their extremely low wages, and to their lack of previous experience of the work they were asked to do:

> I found this small workshop ... the boss understood I was Albanian. She invited me inside, she started speaking to me, but I didn't understand anything that she was saying ... I started working there. She offered me the job, and I was living with her parents, her father and mother. They had a little house. I stayed there for a year and a half. I worked at their daughter's small business. She was paying me very little money, 1,000 drachmas [3 euros] per day ... and I used to work for twelve hours, sixteen hours sometimes. (Maria)
>
> Well, at the beginning I worked ... in a small factory. I was sewing, at the machine ... I didn't know [the job] ... [It] was paying me very poor money ... for me, it was fine, because in Albania I wouldn't earn any money, so it was fine ... I was working for

> twelve hours and earning 3,000 drachmas [9 euros], very little money ... without social security stamps, without anything ... I worked there for a year and a half ... and at the end, they owed me 100,000 drachmas [300 euros] ... Finally I got it, with a lot of difficulties. I was lucky ... Then I quit that job. (Lela)
>
> The beginning was ... very difficult, with the language especially ... In the beginning, I worked at a butcher's, I was cleaning the place. Later, I got the knife in my hands. I was also carrying the meat, I was cutting it, everything. (Lazaros)
>
> In Veria I used to work at a small clothing firm ... When we first came, it was much less. To tell you the truth, in the workshop I was getting paid 2,000 drachmas [6 euros], from the morning until three in the afternoon. But I didn't know anything, I was tidying up, I was cutting thread, such things, until I learned ... and then it reached 3,000 drachmas [9 euros] ... after five years I was almost like a technician, because I was working with all the machines. (Flora)
>
> I went to Crete, I lived there for seven months. I worked in several jobs. I didn't know you see, I was used to living in a town, I didn't know what a hoe was ... I've learned to work with that, this is the kind of job I did in Crete ... [In Albania] I used to work in a factory ... In Crete I worked in the fields ... I was cutting grass, clearing the fields. Fields, mud, I used to pick olives too. (Nicolas)
>
> For four years, I was cleaning houses, staircases, and I was ironing ... The salary was, and still is, ridiculous. For a job I had in Panorama, six days a week, Monday to Saturday, from 8 a.m. to 4 p.m., after one year [of work] I was receiving 100,000 drachmas [300 euros] per month, about 3,800 drachmas [11 euros] per day. (Kaiti)

Accounts like these confirm the *flexibility* of migrant labour and clearly indicate its high degree of *exploitation* by Greek employers. In the relevant section of the questionnaire, more than half of the respondents themselves acknowledged that they had received poor treatment by employers, in terms of low payment, long working days, no social security, etc. The in-depth interviews confirmed this situation with many examples of the migrants' experiences:

> This is something I don't like here ... if they could [the employers], they would take your soul ... it's just not fair to work that much and get paid only 5,000 drachmas [15 euros] a day. (Maria)

> The employer wants to make profit out of you, that's why he employs you, because he doesn't pay for your social security stamps. That's how it is. I know ... people who have worked, let's say, five years for the same employer ... and when they start asking for social security stamps, they are fired. They [employers] fire them and threaten that they are going to call the police if they complain ... They want to make profit out of us, that's for sure. There is exploitation. (Dalina)
> We could make 20-30,000 drachmas [60-90 euros] per day, but I would get only 5,000 drachmas [15 euros] and I would leave home at 9 a.m. and return at 9 p.m. Once, we made a deal, 75,000 drachmas [225 euros] for a week, I would do the whole electricity installation in a week. I finally got only 25,000 drachmas [75 euros] for this, the maximum I could get was 30,000 [90 euros]. The materials didn't cost that much, I was buying them myself, I knew the prices. The guy would make 400,000 drachmas [1,200 euros] out of it and I would get only 25,000 drachmas [90 euros] ... Come on, I'm not a jerk, this is called exploitation. (Lazaros)

Employers have profited greatly from the migrants' desperate need to work. For the majority, exploitation has been expressed in many hours of work a day, lack of insurance and poor wages; however, it used to be particularly intense and far more common during their first years in Greece, also as an outcome of their weak bargaining position[15]. This was certainly connected to their clandestine status, but it can also be attributed to their poor level of spoken Greek, their limited knowledge of the conditions in the host country, and their urgent need to work to survive and to support their families. There are stories of semi-slavery conditions, with employers not paying migrant workers and threatening to inform the police about their clandestine status. As Emil, one of the interviewees reported, 'There are people who work at construction sites or in the fields and they don't get paid.' The cases below are identical:

> My nephew who came here with his family ... they worked in a village. The boss would give them food everyday ... but he never gave them money for those six months ... He finally gave them a cheque, he said: 'Go to Thessaloniki and get the money.' They came here to Thessaloniki, to me, but we went to the bank, and he had no money in the bank. (Lioupa)
> In all the shops he had [his previous boss], I did the electricity installation myself ... In my next life they may pay me ... so far, they haven't ... Because we knew him, he could exploit us ... He

> was like 'We are all one single family, guys, I'll pay you when I can.' (Lazaros)

Exploitation towards women has also taken the form of sexual harassment by (male) employers. Such experiences appear to have been limited among the female participants in my own survey; nevertheless the experience is indeed cruel and, apart from leaving traumatic memories and bitterness for those who face it, it creates additional problems to female migrants' employment. As we have seen in the previous chapter, such attitudes come out of particular expressions of racism related to feelings of superiority towards immigrants and an imaginary connection of foreign women, especially Eastern Europeans, to prostitution. Lela, an Albanian interviewee who had such an experience at the workplace, decided to leave her job in order to escape. A young Bulgarian woman, one of the unemployed respondents, was so disappointed by continuously encountering such incidents at several bars she had worked in, that she lost the will to look for a job, and was facing serious financial problems at the time of the interview. The story of Maria, from Bulgaria, might give a more precise idea of the issue:

> Once I found this job at Hortiatis, five or six years ago, in a taverna ... The guy told me, 'I had a Bulgarian woman working here before, we had a relationship.' Well, I was supposed to work there Fridays, Saturdays and Sundays, and because it's quite far, we had agreed that he would drive me up to Panorama, from where I could get a bus. So, one night he told me: 'You'll stay here to sleep.' I asked, 'Where can I sleep?' I was thinking he meant there, in the taverna. But he said: 'At home ... my wife is not in.' ... When I complained ... he started shouting at me ... 'Who are you, you dirty Bulgarian!'

6.3.2 *Integration dynamics: the issue of socio-economic mobility*

In general, however, things seem to get better over time. It is clear from the material presented so far that there are significant changes in the types of jobs and in the level of remuneration of immigrants in the city. Many of the questionnaire respondents and most of the participants in the in-depth interviews have experienced a gradual improvement of their position in the labour market, and their wages have risen – even in real terms – since their arrival. The rather humiliating initial conditions are not the case any more for the people interviewed. There is strong evidence of many successful employment trajectories, as the following examples clearly indicate:

- *Male Albanian, 29, single, came from Bulqiza in 1994*: 1. seasonal agricultural worker → 2. casual manual worker → 3. builder → 4. technical assistant in a hotel → 5. plumber in a company.
- *Female Albanian, 31, married, one child, came from Tirana in 1992*: 1. cleaning staircases → 2. cleaning storerooms → 3. cleaning a workshop and a coffee shop → 4. domestic service → 5. assistant to a craftsman making ceramics for tourists → 6. baby-sitter → 7. NGO secretary.
- *Female Bulgarian, 35, married, one child, came from Samokov in 1991*: 1. agricultural worker, picking tomatoes → 2. brick-layer → 3. domestic worker → 4. kitchen assistant and cleaner in a restaurant → 5. owner of a taverna (renting the business from her previous boss).
- *Male Bulgarian, 29, single, came from Sliven in 1996*: 1. worker in a metal workshop → 2. plumber in a company → 3. live-in manual worker (house-maintenance/repair, gardening) together with girlfriend → 4. worker in an aluminium-processing workshop → 5. construction worker → 6. driver and foreman in a large construction company.

Many interviewees expressed satisfaction about their progress in the Greek labour market. A gradual improvement in conditions seems to compensate for (although never justifying) the years of hardship. Hard work in that sense has not been for nothing: as the years pass by, conditions get better, certainly due to regularisation, but also because of social security, language fluency, more effective networks and relationships with Greeks, or a combination of all these factors. Some comments by the interviewees themselves:

- *Kostas, 24, from Albania, came in 1997*: In the beginning, when I couldn't even speak, I could only understand a few things. I was getting [paid] 80,000 drachmas [240 euros] per month ... without social security ... Now, gradually ... it has risen and I reached 580 euros per month, or 180,000 drachmas, with social security.
- *Nadi, 37, from Albania, came in 1992:* Before the legalisation law came out, before the migrants could register with IKA and get social security stamps, there was a huge difference in wages. Now, after all these years ... this difference has been reduced, because now they pay the immigrants the same as the Greeks. There is a slight difference, there always is, but it's not as big as it was back then. In the beginning we were getting paid 3,000 drachmas [9 euros] and a Greek doing the same job was getting 6,000 [18 euros]. Now the difference is very small, how can I tell you, 1,000 drachmas [3 euros].
- *Ferin, 22, from Albania, came in 1993*: When I came, I couldn't communicate with people here ... I used to work in the fields, in gar-

dens and such things. After that I worked with a foreman at construction sites, then I left. For two and a half years now I've worked in a metal workshop. I've learned many jobs here ... in the beginning my wage was 3,500 drachmas [10.5 euros per day] ... not eight hours, just the whole day. Now it's fine, I work eight hours, I'm getting paid 10,000 drachmas [about 30 euros], plus the social security stamps.

- *Soultana, 36, from Bulgaria, came in 1991*: In the beginning, I used to work in a small clothing business ... I was assistant to the head of the department. After that, because the visa was for two months ... I had to come and go all the time, in order to be able to go on ... After this factory, where I worked for a couple of months, I went back to Bulgaria, and then I came here again and started working in a shop selling furs, downtown. I worked there for a period as a saleswoman, because I knew the languages, Bulgarian, Russian, Serbian, etc. I was dealing with customers from these countries. After that ... I met my husband ... who owns a [jewellery] store, and I started working in his store.

Sometimes, what has been previously described as a devaluation of the individuals' human capital, imposed by necessity and by conditions that force migrants to accept any low-skilled post, is succeeded, after a period, by a reverse process of re-skilling, although in a different field. Immigrants who stay in the same trade tend to specialise and become skilled workers. This is true in the case of construction workers, who start by doing general manual tasks, often on a casual basis, but later acquire certain skills related to their profession and improve their condition in terms of responsibilities and payment:

> Now, I am a construction worker, a skilled worker, a builder. I've learned the job here. At the beginning, I was only helping, but I had to learn the job ... I had to get some more money. (Gjion)

In some cases, as we have seen, such an experience may lead to self-employment or entrepreneurship in small construction projects and house-repair work. Similarly, qualified migrants gradually make their way towards more responsibilities and duties that correspond more closely to their academic and professional experience, even if the institutional problems remain, putting obstacles in the way of a higher status and wage:

> Since 1992, when I came, I have been working in the same factory. I started there, I'm still there ... I don't do the same job ... my duties have changed ... In the beginning ... I was doing very

> heavy jobs, then, gradually, I started working at the machines. Now I work ... as a mechanical engineer ... But my boss cannot register me as an engineer, since my diploma is not yet recognised here. (Nadi)

Finally, there is a minority of highly educated people who have managed, over time, to work in their profession or find some other solution for building a career. Such is the case of Pyrros, 63, of ethnic Greek origin, who holds a Ph.D. and has worked as a researcher in architecture and as a preserver-restorer of Byzantine/post-Byzantine monuments, churches and traditional houses (an occupation that cost him internal displacement in the years of Enver Hoxha's dictatorship in Albania). After a period spent working on construction sites, he met colleagues in Greece who acknowledged his work, and he finally managed to become a partner in an architectural office undertaking projects for monument restoration. Another example can be drawn out of Stavros' experience: of ethnic Greek origin as well, 44 years old at the time of the interview, he worked at the National Library of Albania in Gjirokaster. His migratory route, although exceptional, epitomises in a sense the pathways of many immigrants in the Greek labour market: he has done numerous different jobs, in various places, and he managed to continue with his studies and to build a successful entrepreneurial career. He told me:

> Up to now I have had twenty-nine professions. First of all, I worked in a pizza house, then as a waiter, as a construction worker, as a cleaner, twenty-nine different jobs ... In 1998, I used to work in a café ... as a waiter. But the business shut down ... and I had to look for another job. I already had a postgraduate degree, and then I realised that I should use ... all my qualifications. So, I started doing a Ph.D., and in parallel, I ... thought of starting a translation business, which today covers all Balkan languages ... Recently I've worked on several university projects as a tutor ... until last year I used to teach – that was part of a project run by the University of Athens, reception classes for Albanophones. And I also teach Albanian at the School of Balkan Languages at the Institute of Studies of the Aemos Peninsula (IMXA) ... [Now] I am the owner of this service [a translation office, with five employees and some external collaborators].

Obviously such examples are rather isolated cases; but, coupled with the other positive experiences of many, they confirm the process of upward occupational mobility, which is sometimes equivalent to an upgrade of the socio-economic conditions of individuals and households.

Apart from an improvement of the migrants' material position in the labour market, one should also consider the more general amelioration of factors not directly related to the market that are however crucial in order to understand the patterns of integration over time. Thus, it is not only mobility towards better posts, payment and working conditions that time brings, but also better relationships with employers and colleagues, as well as satisfaction and fulfilment from work.

> With my colleagues I have nice relationships ... well, not with everybody, but generally, it's nice. I mean, I am satisfied, in comparison to other workshops [I have worked in]. This is the first one, the only one, I can tell, where I feel comfortable, and I can talk more. (Valbona)
>
> In the beginning ... I was simply a labourer, like everybody. They used to treat you in a quite different way, but now, as time passes, when they get to know you, especially when you work with the same people ... they've started understanding who I am. (Milen)
>
> My boss is a very good man, and the working conditions are good, and I'm doing a job that I like. This is basic, to do the job that you like ... Until recently, I was doing a job that, well, I didn't like, but I needed to work in order to survive. (Ani)

Nevertheless, this does not mean to say that migrants always overcome the obstacles put by the legal framework and the labour market, or that they do not face exclusion, discrimination and exploitation in several forms and at various levels. Neither do such examples of upward employment trajectories imply any idealising stereotype of the 'successful immigrant'. But assuming that immigrants in Greece are eternally destined to perform the same types of jobs in the same exploitative conditions is equally misleading, and 'victimises' the migrants' experience. The phenomenon of socio-economic mobility rather reflects the fact that immigrants form a dynamic section of the labour force and also recognises an important temporal factor in their labour-market integration. At the individual level, the migratory route might lead to an improvement of the migrant's condition over time, even if this is not necessarily accompanied by a shift towards 'decent' employment within mainstream sectors of the economy. This is clearly evident in the interviewees' narratives, as shown above, but it is also supported by statistical evidence from the sample as a whole. The following tables show that, for individual migrants, things might get better over time.

I have applied chi-square tests and correlations between the migrants' period of residence in Greece and a number of variables related to their labour-market integration. In Table 6.4a, chi-square values are

Table 6.4a *Evidence of upward socio-economic mobility: Cross tabulations and chi-squares*

Years in Greece	*Nature of Post (skills)*			*Position*			*Social Security*	
	minimum	*skilled manual*	*white collar**	*employers***	*self-employed*	*waged*	*yes*	*no*
up to 2	13	10	2	–	2	23	12	16
3-4	29	13	2	1	3	40	24	23
5-8	45	13	2	–	7	53	39	22
9+	38	15	16	10	13	46	53	19
Total	*125*	*51*	*22*	*11*	*25*	*162*	*128*	80
Pearson's	χ^2 *value*	*Df*	*Sig.*	χ^2 *value*	*Df*	*Sig.*	χ^2 *value* *Df*	*Sig.*
chi-squares	19.87886	6	0.00291	22.25803	6	0.001087	10.88893 3	0.012342

* Including professionals and entrepreneurs. ** Including assistants in family businesses

statistically significant, indicating thus some sort of relationship between the period migrants have spent in Greece and the nature of their occupation (in terms of skills), their position, and the likelihood of them being insured. Chi squares do not tell us much about the nature and strength of the relationship, but the figures in the table clearly indicate that migrants who have long been in the country are more likely to do skilled and white-collar work, to be self-employed or entrepreneurs, and to have social security. In addition, the correlations confirm significant, although not particularly strong, statistical relationships between the number of years migrants have lived in Greece, the period they have been working in the post held at the time of the interview, and the level of their daily wage. In other words, what Table 6.4b actually shows is that migrants who have been in Greece longer tend to have more stable jobs and earn slightly higher wages, while the longer a migrant has been working in a single post, the better payment s/he receives. Interestingly, this is confirmed by other studies (e.g. Labrianidis & Lyberaki 2001). The survey of Hatziprokopiou et al. (2001), which was addressed to employers, found that immigrants' daily wages in Thessaloniki grew by 68 per cent between 1990-1998 (more than in any other place); in 1998, employers paid on average 22.1 euros (higher than in the rest of the country apart from Athens).

Table 6.4b *Evidence of upward socio-economic mobility: Correlations*

	Months in Current Job	*Daily Wage*
years in Greece (N=158)		
Pearson Correlation (R=)	0.409	0.267
Sig. (2-tailed)	0.000	0.001
months in current job (N=125)		
Pearson Correlation (R=)		0.437
Sig. (2-tailed)		0.000

Obviously, 'time' as such, i.e. the period migrants have lived in Greece, is not an explanatory variable *per se*. It rather reflects the influence of other factors that develop over time, and which are crucial for migrants' well-being and pathways to incorporation. The acquisition of legal status is certainly one of them, as we have already seen. With legal documents in their hands, migrants feel secure, and they are more likely to move towards registered employment, escaping the highly exploitative conditions of the informal sector. Higher wages are then possible, while migrants may also move towards better jobs that suit their home-country qualifications or the skills they have learned in Greece. The interaction between migrants and locals and the new relationships and social networks formed locally may function as effective social capital, given the crucial, although informal, role of acquaintances and 'mediators' in the Greek labour market. In addition, the enrichment of the human-capital potential of individual migrants may also lead to upward social/occupational mobility; for example, as a result of the use of working skills acquired in the host country, or simply due to greater language competency over the years.

Regarding the latter, fieldwork findings allow an assessment of the effect of language skills on immigrants' position in the labour market. As shown in Table 6.5, fluent Greek speakers are more likely to work in services, in white-collar and highly skilled positions, with daily wages exceeding 30 euros and with social security.

To conclude, the temporal perspective on Albanians' and Bulgarians' incorporation into Greek society is clearly very important, despite the short span of time that has elapsed since these post-1989 migrations

Table 6.5 Language fluency as an asset in the labour market (%)

	Level of Spoken Greek			*Pearson's Chi-Squares*	
sector	*beginner*	*intermediate*	*fluent*		
construction	28.6	16.3	13.7	Value	19.0
personal services	33.3	32.7	13.7	df	6.0
manufacturing	23.8	16.3	15.1	Sig. (2-sided)	0.004
trade & other services	14.3	34.6	57.5		
skill level					
minimum skills	71.4	68.3	53.4	Value	11.1
skilled manual	23.8	26.0	26.0	df	4.0
white collar & highly skilled	4.8	5.8	20.5	Sig. (2-sided)	0.026
wage scale (euros)					
20	17.6	13.7	5.1	Value	19.1
20-29	58.8	60.0	35.6	df	4.0
30+	23.5	26.3	59.3	Sig. (2-sided)	0.001
social security				Value	6.7
yes	36.4	63.6	65.8	df	2.0
no	63.6	36.4	34.2	Sig. (2-sided)	0.0

began. Too often, comparative analyses of migrants' 'performance' – either before and after migration, or comparisons of different migrant groups (e.g. Iosifides & King 1998) – are based on cross-sectional 'snapshots' which miss out the dynamic element of continuous change and (possibly) improvement. My evidence of Balkan immigrants' trajectories in Thessaloniki certainly vindicates the value of a dynamic time-based approach. The impact of the two regularisations that had preceded my fieldwork has certainly been important and should be emphasised, since this development clearly highlights a turning point regarding the position of immigrants in Greece. But the role of other factors brought about over time, some of which have been mentioned in the analysis above, should not be underestimated.

7 Housing and socio-spatial integration

The story of migration unfolds in specific local communities; it is told through people's everyday lives, practices, experiences, relationships, etc., which are attached to particular places. We have seen so far that the conditions of immigrants' incorporation are determined by the particular local environment where they settle: their labour-market integration depends on the structures of the local economy; the degree to which they are generally accepted, or not, is related to local socio-cultural peculiarities, to the form the public discourse on immigration takes, and to the level of development of inclusive civil-society institutions. But, for the migrants themselves, the locality where they settle becomes *their* place. Therefore, the socio-spatial level of migrants' integration is about their area of residence and housing conditions, i.e. what is generally related to the *private* sphere of living; but it also refers to their lives outside of home, at places of work or leisure, at spaces of action and interaction amongst themselves and with the locals. In other words, it has to do with both their *socio-spatial conditions* and the way space is *experienced* and *perceived*. Apart from affecting the living and working conditions of migrants, we will see in this chapter how space also reflects broad socio-spatial mechanisms of exclusion and discrimination, while, at the same time, it constitutes the terrain wherein migrants build their lives.

7.1 Spatial distribution, housing conditions and residential trajectories

7.1.1 *Access to housing and residential conditions*

The vast majority of the respondents (80.8 per cent) live in rented flats; home ownership is the case for only 9.1 per cent. The remainder live in accommodation provided by their employers, or are hosted temporarily by relatives or friends. Among those who rent, 40.7 per cent pay less than 200 euros per month; those paying more than 250 euros constitute 29 per cent of the sample. Nearly 71 per cent of the respondents live with their families, especially women (73.2 per cent), Albanians (75.8 per cent) and ethnic Greeks (77.3 per cent). The rest live with

Table 7.1 *Immigrants' housing conditions (%)*

Period in Current Property (N=175)		*Housemates (N=192)*		*Rent (N=145)*	
less than 6 months	29.6	family	70.8	50-150	17.9
6-11 months	12.6	other relatives	12.0	151-199	22.8
1-3 years	20.1	friends	13.5	200-249	30.3
3-5 years	17.0	employer	3.6	250+	29.0
5 years or more	20.8				
Size of Property (N=207)		*Floor/Type (N=170)*		*Heating (N=208)*	
up to half room per person	32.9	inappropriate/ground	25.9	central heating	26.9
half to one room per person	31.9	1st	25.3	no heating	10.6
one room per person	22.2	2nd	19.4	oil/wood stove	62.5
more than one room per person	13.0	3rd & higher, house	29.4		

other relatives (12 per cent) or friends (13.5 per cent) and a small section with their employers (3.6 per cent, mostly female live-in carers). The percentage of immigrants who live in inappropriate/bad-quality accommodation, such as basements and storerooms converted to flats, or on the unpopular ground floors, exceeds one quarter of the sample[1]. The majority though (about 45 per cent) occupy flats on the first and second floors and nearly one in four lives on the upper floors (with some of the wealthiest ones living in quite luxurious apartments in the historical centre or by the seafront). There are 5 per cent who live in houses, which perhaps mildly distorts the data since, for many, this relates to old inner-city properties or inappropriate dwellings on the outskirts, rather than comfortable suburban middle-class residences. Properties with central heating are enjoyed by only 26.9 per cent, while 10.6 per cent had no heating at all; the majority uses oil/wood stoves or, in a few cases, electric heaters. Regarding accommodation size, most of the respondents (nearly 65 per cent) have less than one room per person, while only 13 per cent have a living space of more than one room per person. These details are summarised in Table 7.1 for the sample as a whole.

There are some differences between the different subgroups of the sample and according to certain characteristics of the respondents, i.e. by nationality, ethnic origin, gender, family status, fluency in Greek, education level, etc. However, no clear pattern can be observed apart from a general tendency among some categories of migrants to enjoy better housing conditions (Greek-Albanians, Bulgarians and women in general, but also the highly educated and those speaking Greek fluently, etc.), but this stands more as a fact rather than providing any direct explanatory elements. One explanation could be that this information concerns the household, not the individual, and thus depends on household types and sizes. Other elements might also play a role: e.g.

the presence of 'elite' migrants among Bulgarian respondents, different migration strategies or even lifestyles. Rather, the quality of the migrants' housing conditions seems to depend on, and reflect, their position in the labour market[2].

Figure 7.1 illustrates immigrants' residential distribution in the city (see also Table 7.3 in Section 7.2.1). The majority (53 per cent) of the respondents live in the municipality of Thessaloniki and another 30 per cent in the rest of the conurbation; in total, 94 per cent live in the metropolitan area[3]. Albanian immigrants appear to be spatially dispersed all over the city, though more than half (60.2 per cent) are in the central part (municipality), mostly in areas just outside the city centre, and neighbourhoods to its north and east. The percentage of Bulgarians in the municipality is lower (38.5 per cent). North-western districts, where rents are relatively cheaper, are expectedly popular – one third of the Albanians and 37.2 per cent of the Bulgarians live there. Migrants liv-

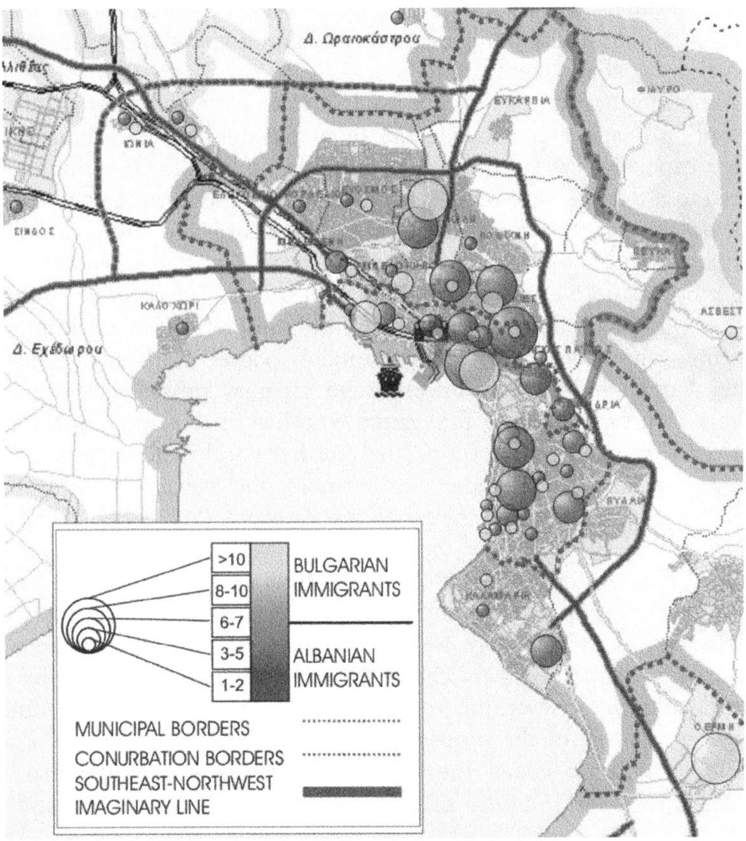

Figure 7.1 *Areas of residence of Albanian and Bulgarian immigrants in Thessaloniki*

ing in the municipality, especially its central, northern and eastern parts, and in the north-western districts of the Thessaloniki conurbation, tend to occupy smaller properties, and higher shares of them rent bad-quality accommodation in basements or on ground floors. On the other hand, the presence of immigrants in 'nice' areas, mostly in the south-east, where 12.5 per cent of all respondents live, is related to factors ranging from work availability to the role of social networks. This confirms both their spatial diffusion and the mixed social geography of the city. Ghetto-like situations, i.e. the concentration of large numbers of immigrants in specific 'downgraded' neighbourhoods, displacing locals, have not been observed so far. The only notable concentration is to be found among Bulgarian migrants: 22 per cent, almost exclusively Sarakatsani, live in the wealthy suburban area of Thermi (in the south-eastern part of the metropolitan area – see Figure 7.1); this case is given special attention in Section 7.2.2[4]. In general, despite a tendency for the affluent classes to relocate to suburban areas, especially to the east, the inner city remains popular for diverse categories of the population, including many migrants, so we cannot speak about any manifestations of sharp segregation.

Although the findings do not imply a clear pattern of rent gradients according to specific areas, they do show that the inner city tends to be more expensive, with an average monthly rent of 225.6 euros (compared to a total average rent of 209.2 euros for the sample as a whole). But do the monthly rent immigrants can afford and the area where they live correspond strictly to what they earn? The share of those earning more than 40 euros a day who live in central Thessaloniki is about 10 per cent lower than in the whole of the sample; half of the migrants on this wage scale live in the (presumably poorer) north-west. On the other hand, amongst the lowest wage category (people earning less than 20 euros a day), we find many who live in the municipality (68 per cent), most in the overpopulated northern and eastern parts where the houses are usually older. Furthermore, the average monthly rent paid by migrants in the highest wage category (215 euros) does not really exceed that paid by those in the lowest wage category (214.5 euros). This evidence suggests that the level of the rent might determine more the specific properties that migrants tend to occupy than the location of the property itself. It also leads us to consider additional factors that shape migrants' choice of a property and an area to live in. The detailed interviews uncover reasons such as the quality of homes, the size and age of the properties, but also the location of the workplace or children's school, the number of household members that are wage-earners, the presence of relatives or friends in the area, and so forth.

To an extent, the narratives of the interviewees mirror perceptions and realities of urban social geography; for instance, in the way the better educated and better off among the migrants feel a need to justify their choice of a specific area:

> *Konstantina, a Greek-Albanian graduate in economics from the University of Thessaloniki, works for a financial (stock exchange) company*: It is ... only recently that I moved there. I've always lived in the eastern part of the city. Now I live in Stavroupoli [western Thessaloniki] ... The apartment is nice, but the neighbourhood is not ... It has a lower level, which is apparent at the shops, in the way the salesmen, the saleswomen behave ... they treat you as 'an Albanian'.
>
> *Nikos, a highly educated ethnic Greek from Tirana, has worked as a university lecturer and at the time of the interview ran a consultancy and trade business*: Well, I live in western Thessaloniki, but this was my choice. I have also bought a flat in the centre, but I live there, at Diavata. I chose it because it's not overpopulated, the building is new ... and I know the area, because my [first] job was close ... and we got used to it. Anyway, I see it as a temporary residence. We rent it, we haven't decided yet where we will live after my daughter finishes her school, but we are definitely going to move then.

The second of these quotes suggests that knowledge of a neighbourhood, convenient distance from the workplace, or the location of the children's school might also be important factors that migrants take into account when looking for a property. Closer attention to some details in the interviewees' stories reveals further elements that play a role in the decision of individuals which are rather common for all immigrants. Kinship ties, for instance, keep people together. The quality and size of a particular property suitable for family needs sometimes compensates for a higher rent and makes people indifferent to a specific area in favour of the conditions of the property itself. The interview quotes below highlight some of these factors:

> I've lived in Stavroupoli for a year or so ... I went there because my daughter lives there, and she has two children and we go to help. (Andreas)
>
> I've lived there for two years. Now, why I did choose this property? Well, the building is relatively old, I can tell, but the apartment is nice, it is big. When I was looking for accommodation, I had been searching for four months, on a daily basis. All the apartments were very expensive, while they were quite old, badly

> constructed, etc ... I liked this one very much, it was big, comfortable. (Valbona)
>
> The rent is a bit expensive, but what can we do? It is expensive, and every year, as he [the owner] told us, it's going to be more expensive ... It's not that fair, because there is no central heating, no elevator, nothing, and he intends to increase it, year after year, but what can we do? I mean, we work, and we just about survive, that's how it is. It is difficult ... We've chosen this place because we needed an extra room for the children to study and we didn't have [space] in our previous apartment. It was a basement, it was not healthy, but we had financial problems then ... Now we are a little better off ... we rented this apartment in order to be more comfortable, for the children, so they don't feel like 'Oh, Mum, we came from Albania and we live in the basement.' (Lela)

Still, of course, the price of the rent plays a crucial role in deciding about the area, and even more so about the property itself. Cheap accommodation is preferred by the majority, and low rents, expectedly, usually mean bad-quality housing (e.g. in the areas within and around the inner city), properties lacking basic facilities (e.g. central heating), or small, inadequate apartments (often on ground floors or in basements). These are among the most frequent problems mentioned in the interviews and confirmed by the percentage data presented earlier in the chapter; they tell us that the vulnerable socio-economic conditions of the majority of immigrants lead them to cheap and therefore bad-quality housing, usually on the lower floors of inner-city buildings and dwellings on the outskirts of the city, mostly in north-western Thessaloniki. Home-sharing strategies and overcrowded accommodation have also been observed in individual migrants' attempts to reduce the cost of living expenses. The following cases give a more vivid picture of the situation:

> *Katerina came in 1999 and lives in a one-bedroom basement in Neapoli (north-western conurbation) with her brother and sister:* I don't like the house at all, there is much dampness ... but we can't move to some other place because we couldn't afford to pay more. We have a certain income, and part of it should go to the house. If we moved somewhere else, if we rented another flat we'd have to pay 70,000-80,000 drachmas [205-235 euros] ... and we can't afford that.
>
> *Melina came in 1999 and lives in a basement in the northern part of the historical centre (Ag. Dimitriou) together with her husband and their three children; apart from the bathroom and kitchen, there is*

> *only a living room and a bedroom*: I am not satisfied, the apartment is very small, but moving somewhere else would cost too much money. We have a lot of problems, we could not rent another property now.
> *Raicko came in 1998 and lives in Stavroupoli (north-western conurbation), in an 'old and humid' house without central heating; he shares a bedroom with his wife and son, while the other two rooms are occupied by another couple and a single man*: I don't earn that much per month, it's not only the rent that I have to pay ... So I went for something cheaper ... And we live many people together ... six people in this house, we pay 60,000 drachmas [190 euros].

The quality of a property, though, is not always clearly associated with the rent. What has been reported by many, bad-quality housing that is expensive at the same time, points to *exploitative conditions* in the housing market which favour the landlord rather than the tenant. In the words of Kaiti, one of the Albanian interviewees:

> They ask extraordinary prices. It has happened to me. I've called about an apartment and the rent mentioned was 100,000 drachmas [300 euros]. No furniture, no telephone, no central heating.

This is a distinctive feature of a housing market where rents follow an upward trend and many buildings, particularly in the inner city, are old and/or lack basic facilities. Taking into account that Thessaloniki has a large number of students who also search, like many migrants, for temporary accommodation, it seems that many landlords increase the rents without repairing or refurbishing their properties until a temporary tenant (a student or a migrant) does so at their own expense. Obviously, this form of exploitation applies to both migrants and locals, but its degree varies, since the former are in a more vulnerable position, especially when they are undocumented. The experience of Maria, among other interviewees, clearly reflects this practice:

> I have many complaints about that ... All the landlords I've met owned 'rotten' places. I had to paint them myself ... the kitchens and everything ... I repaired all those places ... but the landlords, after I had repaired the properties, they told me to leave ... So, I had to go, I didn't have papers.

Moreover, the interviewees' testimonies uncover other forms of exploitation in the housing market. A common practice that has been reported is that of landlords who avoid signing a tenancy agreement, or even sign false ones, to escape taxation for renting the property. This clearly puts immigrants in the vulnerable position described above, making them unable to claim any rights. Their undocumented status was sometimes used as a means to convince them to accept the terms of tenancy, or even to vacate the property without notice in some cases, under the threat (or simply the fear) of the authorities being informed about them. Renting properties that were not built to be used for accommodation, such as storerooms in the basements of inner-city buildings, de facto exempt from the relevant (higher) taxation, is another practice experienced by some interviewees. And certainly the splitting of properties in order to host a higher number of tenants, often without providing basic facilities in the separated spaces (kitchens, bathrooms), again serves the landlord in multiple ways, through the exploitation of a situation of high demand and the vulnerability of this special category of tenants.

The field survey generally shows that, as far as *access* to housing is concerned, migrants in Thessaloniki depend almost exclusively on private-sector lettings and face exploitative conditions in the housing market itself. Access as such is not prevented, but the vulnerable position of the migrants in the market usually leads them towards specific city areas and specific types of properties, often in flats or on floors unwanted by the majority of locals. However, the interviewees' residential experiences suggest that non-market obstacles also exist, which create difficulties in the migrants' pathways of access to housing. By this I refer to the common prejudices about immigrants in Greece, and to xenophobic attitudes that are apparent in their daily interaction with (some) locals. So one of the most important features of immigrants' experiences is the *discrimination* they face in the housing market. Some landlords refuse to rent their property to a foreigner, particularly to Albanians (and especially to young unaccompanied males). The share of respondents who said that they had had such an experience is nearly 40 per cent, but this rises up to 43 per cent among people who are single or divorced, 43.2 per cent among men, 43.7 per cent among people aged between 18-29, 44 per cent among those who are not of ethnic Greek origin and 44.2 per cent among all Albanian immigrants. In their own words:

> They don't want to rent their place to a foreigner, they don't want to make a contract, or they make false contracts. (Maria)
> I had difficulties because I'm an Albanian. Maybe because I was a foreigner ... other foreigners have problems too. I mean, the Bulgarians, the Romanians and the others have problems too ... After six or seven years, they didn't notice that I am a foreigner, because of my accent, and they told me 'It's nice you're not a for-

> eigner, otherwise I wouldn't let you the property.' He didn't understand, but I left, without telling him anything. I said 'I'll drop in tomorrow,' but I didn't go. What could I tell him, that I am an Albanian? (Nadi)
>
> They do not want to rent the apartment to you. When they hear that your Greek is not good they tell you to go away. If you tell them that you are an Albanian, they won't rent the house to you. (Kaiti)
>
> Well, what impressed me was when we had found a nice big apartment ... we had signed a contract too, through a common friend, but when the landlord realised that we were from Albania, he hesitated. He said, 'No, I won't rent this to Albanians.' Well, this is his right, he didn't want to rent it to Albanians, what can I say about that? I could not get angry, this can happen to anybody. Some people don't rent their properties to students, for instance ... We saw many apartments, and when we said 'Albanians', they'd shut the door. So we got this one after telling the landlords that we are Italians. (Mimoza)

As the last quote illustrates, the heavy discrimination exercised by landlords leads migrants to develop specific practices: some, mostly Albanians, introduce themselves as ethnic Greeks, or foreigners of other nationalities that are generally welcome; others make use of their social networks, especially Greek employers, friends or acquaintances, as intermediaries that might speak to the landlord and facilitate access to a particular property. Prospective tenants who take care to present themselves as ethnic Greeks, 'family men' or 'stable breadwinners' have better chances than young single men and women. However, what we are facing here is not an absolutely *exclusionary* phenomenon; the housing market, as any other market, operates in terms of exchange, of supply and demand: if a landlord refuses to rent his/her property to a migrant family, someone else will accept. And in most cases, any initial prejudice will disappear over time, when the relationships between migrants and landlords or neighbours reach a more personal level, as the experience of Dimitri, among many others, illustrates:

> In the beginning, the landlady told me 'There are only Greeks living here ... the rest of the residents don't want Albanians.' ... Now, two years later, the landlady and the neighbours are happy with us, they love our kids, they help us.

7.1.2 *Immigrants' residential trajectories in Thessaloniki*

A more dynamic analysis of the residential experiences of immigrants in the city would lead us to take into account their housing conditions *before* the fieldwork took place. Many of the interviewees talked about negative experiences in *the past*; they spoke about harsh conditions *initially* and problems they had encountered in the course of their residential pathways in the country and in Thessaloniki. Whatever their housing quality was at the time of the fieldwork, things had been worse in the beginning for the majority, especially for unaccompanied males during the first ambiguous years of their migratory journey. Initial conditions, clandestine status, uncertainty and fear had pushed people to sleep at the workplace, or even out in the open air. To mention only a few examples from the interviews: Ivan, from Bulgaria, used to sleep in the lorries where he used to work loading and unloading stock; Raicko and Nadi, from Bulgaria and Albania respectively, stayed for months in the factories they had been working in, with permission from their bosses; Kostas and Maria, from Bulgaria, spent their first few days in a wagon owned by their employer; Nicolas and Ferrin, from Albania, slept out in the fields before finding stable jobs. In total, the share of respondents who had been offered a place to sleep initially by their employers (usually at the workplace itself) exceeded 10 per cent; 30.5 per cent had been hosted by relatives or friends, while another 31.6 per cent, almost exclusively Albanians, had stayed in cheap hotels during their first few weeks in Greece. Some had lived with many others in overcrowded properties in order to save money on the rent. Some others, especially among the pioneers, had received the kind help of locals, who offered them a place to sleep for a few days. Two migrants from Albania said they had spent a period in the state reception camps the government had set up at the border to respond to the emergency of the initial immigration 'boom'. Five people said they had slept out in the open air, on construction sites or in fields, before making their first money that allowed them to rent a property. The following selection of interviewees' narratives sheds light on some details regarding initial experiences:

> I lived in another flat, two families together ... This was when I first arrived, for a short period until I settled, I found work. My brother-in-law had come first with his wife and his kid. Before I brought my wife here, I was looking for a place so that everything was ready. Everywhere we would go, he would take his wife with him, because they would not rent a flat to singles, only to families. Once they told us that they would not rent their flat

> to Albanians. It is different when they see all the family together. (Gjion)
>
> We were living in an apartment ... it was in the basement ... There were four people there, we used to pay 50,000 drachmas [about 150 euros] for rent and it was 55 m2. It had a lot of dampness. (Valbona)
>
> This is the second one [property]. When I was alone I used to live in another place, close to the one where we live now, with two cousins of mine. It was in the basement. There was humidity, it was bad, so when my family came I had to change accommodation. This is why I chose this other one. (Dimitri)

This evidence underlines the dynamic element apparent also in the socio-spatial level of immigrants' incorporation. As in the previous chapter on employment, it points again to the *trajectories* that individual migrants follow in the destination place, this time in terms of residence and housing conditions, suggesting that, for many, situations *do* change over time. Following these trajectories, we see that not only do immigrants experience a high degree of residential mobility, much higher than that of the locals[5], but also that the quality of housing conditions gradually improves.

> *Soultana, 36, came in 1991*: Being an ethnic Greek (Sarakatsana) she knew people in Thessaloniki who helped her and her father to rent a small apartment in Foinikas (eastern Thessaloniki, a working-class area). When her sister joined them, they all moved to Peraia, on the eastern outskirts of the city (near the airport), where they lived in a basement with no heating. When she met her (Greek) husband, they stayed for a period in his flat in the western part of the centre, before moving to a property they bought by the seafront (Faliro).
>
> *Andreas, 49, came in 1991*: In the beginning he arrived at Anghelohori, a village in the prefecture, where he stayed, together with his brother and sister, in a little house on their employers' farm. After six months he moved to Thessaloniki, where his wife and daughters joined him. He changed accommodation five times: initially he stayed in the eastern part of the city (Italias/Makedonias), later he moved closer to the centre, where he works, and after that to western Thessaloniki (Stavroupoli) in order to be close to where his older daughter lives.
>
> *Konstantina, 30, came in 1992*: As a student, initially, she had spent some time in university accommodation. She has lived in four properties, all in the eastern part of the city, before moving to the one she lives in now in the west (Stavroupoli), together

with her husband, her daughter and her mother-in-law. This property was bought by her husband's family.

Nadi, 37, came in 1992: Initially he stayed at the apartment of a friend, as a guest. Then for three years accommodation was provided by his employer in the factory where he still works (located in the industrial complex of Thessaloniki). After that, he rented a flat and lived alone until he got married. Now he lives in a rented apartment in Neapoli (western Thessaloniki) together with his wife, sister and, recently, baby son.

Maria, 52, came in 1992: She first went to the Peloponnese and stayed, together with others, on the farm where she used to work. A friend invited her to Thessaloniki and offered her a room at her place, in eastern Thessaloniki (Martiou), initially. She later spent a period looking after an old lady, during which she was living at her employer's flat in a different area (K. Toumba). When her daughters came from Bulgaria after graduating from school, they all moved into an apartment close to the railway station, in the western part of the centre.

Now, what about the factors determining the residential trajectories of the migrants? If the axiom 'things get better over time' suggested in Section 6.3.2 might seem too generalised, perhaps oversimplifying and idealising actual situations, the analysis of the in-depth interviews does reveal, here as well, a number of key developments that often take place with the passage of time. The acquisition of legal status in this case seems to have played a rather indirect role: it offered migrants a feeling of security necessary in order to invite over family still abroad, and it has been crucial for improvements in the migrants' employment conditions. The main factors though appear to have been family matters (e.g. dependent family members joining from abroad, the birth of children), and the overall improvement in the migrants' position (move to more stable and rewarding jobs, increase of the household income). Other developments may range from children's schooling to changing lifestyle values.

Quantitative evidence supports the argument. Table 7.2 illustrates significant relationships between the number of years immigrants have spent in Greece and certain characteristics of their housing conditions. The data confirm what has been sketched by the qualitative analysis, suggesting that the longer a migrant has been in the country, the longer s/he tends to settle in a particular property and the more likely s/he is to own a property or to live on upper floors. Also, greater shares of those who have been in Greece for nine years or longer stay with their families and enjoy a large housing space. In addition, there is a weak correlation between the number of years migrants have lived in Greece and the monthly rent they pay (Pearson correlation value 0.145, 0.079 significance level, N=198 cases). The share of respondents who declared themselves 'satisfied' with their housing conditions at the time of the fieldwork is notably high: 73.1 per cent, which reaches 74.4 per cent among men, 74.4 per cent among those who are married, 76.3 per cent among people aged 30 and over, 81.7 per cent among fluent Greek speakers and 83.3 per cent among Bulgarian immigrants. Although no significant relationship between 'satisfaction' and 'period in Greece' appears at the statistical level, the shares of those who said they were satisfied with their accommodation increase as the number of years migrants have been in the country rises: from 69.6 per cent among migrants living in Greece for up to four years, to 70.5 per cent among those who have lived there between five and eight years, and finally to 78.2 among people with nine or more years in the country.

All this evidence reinforces exactly what was argued in the previous chapter: it is not *time* as such that 'improves' migrants' housing conditions; neither are all migrants 'naturally' destined to lead successful lives. The analysis has showed that immigrants in Thessaloniki still tend to occupy specific spaces of residence within the urban fabric and the local housing market, just like they cover a particular 'space' within the labour market; for many, these are far from being acceptable standards of living. But again, one has to develop a dynamic perspective and to address the changes that have gradually taken place over the

Table 7.2 *Housing conditions improve over time*

	Period in Greece (years)					*Pearson's Chi-Squares*	
	up to 2	*3-4*	*5-8*	*9+*	*Total*		
period in property (N=175)							
up to 6 months	10	14	14	11	49	χ^2 *value*	13.7270
7 months to 2 years	11	6	15	19	51	*Df*	6
more than 2 years	4	19	23	29	75	*Sig. (2-sided)*	0.03283
type of property (N=208)							
own	1	–	2	16	19	χ^2 *value*	28.5355
rent	21	41	53	53	168	*Df*	6
guest/employer	6	6	6	3	21	*Sig. (2-sided)*	0.00007
floor (N=170)							
inappropriate*/ground	12	13	10	9	44	χ^2 *value*	13.1105
1st, 2nd	11	18	19	28	76	*Df*	6
3rd & higher/house	3	9	17	21	50	*Sig. (2-sided)*	0.04131
% of those living with their families	12.5	20.6	27.9	39	70.8		
% of those enjoying a housing space of one or more rooms per person	39.3	23.4	34.4	42.2	35.3		

* basements, storerooms, wagons, etc.

past fifteen years, including important improvements in the lives of many migrants, which have happened despite their vulnerable position in a quite unfavourable environment and with practically no formal assistance at all. And despite all the trials and tribulations, migrants are making Thessaloniki their new home, changing in turn the nature of the city as a 'place'. This last point will be further supported by the analysis in the next section.

7.2 Space as place: towards a new urban geography

The previous section discussed the residential and housing situation of immigrants in Thessaloniki and explained them in the context of the urban geography of the city. However, the map of immigrants' residential distribution only partly sketches the local geography of migration; and their experiences and uses of space are not solely limited to their housing conditions. The interviewees' own accounts of their migratory journeys in Greece reveal interesting elements regarding their experiences and perceptions of urban space. There are places of work, leisure and socialisation, spaces of action and interaction, which also determine the migrants' sense of place and characterise the urban experience of migration for the city itself: the changes brought by the presence of immigrants, the conditions affecting their own lives, the ways people – immigrants and locals – perceive them and respectively act. Here I examine some of these other aspects of the socio-spatial incorporation of immigrants. A case study of a specific neighbourhood has been included as an example of the interplay between migrant settlement, local economic structures and urban dynamics.

7.2.1 Mapping immigrants' residence and the geography of migrant labour

Let me start from a mapping of migrant labour in the city. Fieldwork findings suggest that the place where immigrants work does not generally depend on where they live (or vice versa). The location of the workplace rather reflects Thessaloniki's economic geography as well as the peculiar nature of migrant labour in respect to three of its chief features: its *flexibility*, its concentration in specific economic *sectors* (construction, personal services, manufacturing) and the importance of *social networks* as a means of accessing employment. Table 7.3 shows how weakly the location of the workplace coincides with the area of residence; it also illustrates the relationship between where in the city migrants work and what type of job they perform.

Clearly, the results reflect key features of the urban economic geography, as described in Section 3.3. Firstly, we have a relatively centralised

Table 7.3 *Job location, area of residence and sector of employment (%)*

		*Workplace Area**											*Total***
		CN	*E*	*W*	*CNW*	*CSE*	*MNW*	*MSE*	*GNW*	*GSE*	*home*	*varied*	
Area of Residence*	CN	8.0	1.1	0.5	0.5	0.5	1.1	–	–	–	1.6	6.9	*20.2*
	E	3.7	5.9	2.7	0.5	0.5	2.1	0.5	–	0.5	1.6	7.4	*25.0*
	W	1.6	0.5	1.6	0.5	–	0.5	–	–	–	–	3.2	*8.0*
	CNW	4.8	–	3.7	3.2	–	5.9	2.1	–	–	1.1	4.8	*25.5*
	CSE	–	–	–	–	2.7	–	1.1	–	–	0.5	–	*4.3*
	MNW	0.5		–	–	–	1.6	–	0.5	–	–	–	*2.7*
	MSE	–	–	–	–	–	–	6.4	–	–	–	1.6	*8.0*
	GNW	–	–	–	–	–	–	–	4.8	–	–	0.5	*5.3*
	GSE	–	–	–	–	–	–	–	–	0.5	–	0.5	*1.1*
Sector	manufacturing	1.1	1.1	2.7	2.7	1.1	8.5	3.7	4.8	–	–	1.6	*26.6*
	construction	1.6	–	–	0.5	–	–	2.1	–	–	–	12.2	*16.5*
	personal services	1.6	2.1	–	–	0.5	0.5	1.6	–	0.5	3.7	5.9	*16.0*
	maintenance & repair	0.5	0.5	–	–	–	–	0.5	–	–	0.5	3.2	*5.3*
	leisure & catering	3.2	1.1	1.6	1.6	–	0.5	1.1	–	–	–	0.5	*9.6*
	trade & retail	4.3	2.7	2.1	–	1.6	1.6	1.1	0.5	0.5	–	–	*14.4*
	other services	6.4	–	2.1	–	0.5	–	–	–	–	0.5	1.6	*11.7*
	Total	**18.6**	**7.4**	**8.5**	**4.8**	**3.7**	**11.2**	**10.1**	**5.3**	**1.1**	**4.8**	**25.0**	**100.0**

* CN=Municipality Centre and North, E=Municipality East, W=Municipality West, CNW=Conurbation North-West, CSE=Conurbation South-East, MNW=Metropolitan Area North-West, MSE=Metropolitan Area South-East, GNW=Greater Thessaloniki North-West, GSE=Greater Thessaloniki South-East.

** Sums in the sector column differ from figures in Table 6.1 due to twenty missing cases.

structure: the city centre concentrates numerous activities, mostly services of all types. Secondly, the main industrial complex is located in the north-western part (Sindos area) and a second manufacturing zone is found in the south-east (Thermi airport area). Smaller-scale activities in all sectors (retail trade, cafés, bars and fast-food restaurants, small manufacturing units, etc.) are spatially diffused all over the city. Immigrants employed in construction are not based in a fixed working place; of those who stated their employment area at the time of the fieldwork, significant concentrations are located in the historical centre (for renovation/repair works mostly) and in the south-east (where new construction activity is intense). Lastly, immigrants working in personal services (house repair, cleaning, domestic work, care work) tend to concentrate in the – more affluent – central and south-eastern areas, but many of them work for more than one employer and thus in different places (working from 'home' mostly refers to live-in domestic helpers/carers).

Job location and place of residence do not coincide for the majority. This appears to be more common among the inner-city residents, while those living in the outer city tend to work closer to home; again, there are variations according to different subgroups (nationality, ethnicity, gender, age, family status, education level, etc.), but no direct one-way relationships arise. The findings point, once again, to the *flexibility* of migrant labour: not only are immigrants prepared (or forced by necessity) to accept *any type* of job, but also they are ready to travel *anywhere* in (and around) the city for work. This has to do with what Sassen (1995: 113) refers to as immigrants' 'sensitivity to job location' in the context of a local labour market. Albanian and Bulgarian immigrants in Thessaloniki are generally looking for work; and almost any job is welcome, wherever the workplace is located. Furthermore, the kind of jobs they do, such as construction and repair work, cleaning and domestic service, or other types of casual employment, means unstable or diverse locations. In addition, the ways through which many find employment – waiting in the job-finding piazzas, for instance, or through friends/relatives and word-of-mouth strategies – makes them indifferent to the workplace location itself, perhaps even more than to the type of work as such.

On the one hand, piazzas represent a fixed 'market place', where migrants gather to look for work and employers know that they are going to find cheap labour. But the work can be of any type, and it can be located anywhere. On the other, migrants' social networks, the basic way of accessing employment for most, could also be seen as a non-market factor partly determining the location of jobs. What Sassen (1995: 106-107) calls the 'place-based knowledge about jobs that immigrants are most likely to do' (again, related to the function of local labour markets) is confirmed by the findings, but is manifested in our case in a peculiar way. Firstly, there is generally a weak connection between immigrants' residential area and the location of their workplace. The former reflects to an extent the urban social geography and the conditions of the local housing market, but it is also related to individual/household factors (condition of property, family needs, social networks, etc.). The latter mirrors the urban economic geography, but is also related to the 'space' migrants occupy in the labour market (certain types of jobs, in certain sectors) and to the character of their labour (flexibility, low cost). Secondly, migrants' decisions about moving to a particular place to take a job are not as much a factor of wages or of the job itself, but rather more a factor of where their contacts are located. For many, their contacts are so widely diffused around Thessaloniki that they could practically work in a job found in any part of the city. For some, whose networks are denser and spatially concentrated in particular areas of the city, the place of residence is usually close to the place of work. An example of such a neighbourhood-based interplay between social networks, job location and area of residence is given in the following section.

7.2.2 *A case study of Sarakatsani Bulgarians in Thermi*

Thermi is a suburb at the south-eastern corner of Thessaloniki and forms part of the metropolitan area. It used to be a village inhabited initially by locals and later (early twentieth century) by refugees from Asia Minor; today it increasingly attracts middle-class households that have moved out of the inner city. It is located in the area near the airport, where a series of different activities are being concentrated: places of leisure and mass entertainment (nightclubs, multiplex cinemas), large supermarkets and shopping malls, offices of large Greek and foreign firms, hi-tech companies, research institutes and techno-parks, medium-sized factories, manufacturers and small workshops. The 2001 census recorded slightly more than 16,000 inhabitants in the municipality of Thermi (i.e. 1.5 per cent of the population of the prefecture and 1.8 per cent of the metropolitan zone). More than 60 per cent are less than 40 years old and 45.2 per cent are economically active. Of those, 56.5 per cent are between 15-39 years old, and 30 per cent have a university education; the majority works in the tertiary sector, 24 per cent in manufacturing and 6 per cent in agriculture. Unemployment in 2001 was far below the city average (8.7 per cent). Thermi contains 1.7 and 3.2 per cent of the non-EU nationals in the prefecture and the metropolitan zone respectively; non-EU nationals in Thermi account for 6.3 per cent of the residents. There is a significant number of immigrants from Bulgaria, the great majority Sarakatsani; there are also Albanian migrants.

Among the seventeen Sarakatsani in my sample, fifteen were living in Thermi or in surrounding places (Nea Raidestos). Interviews uncovered network factors that explain this phenomenon: Sarakatsani are a 'closed' cultural group, who tend to socialise mostly with each other, so that it is reasonable that they chose to settle in a district where people of the same origin are concentrated. Obviously, the availability of work played a crucial role. According to Soultana, one of the Sarakatsani interviewees:

> Let me explain to you ... Thermi is outside Thessaloniki, it is an industrial area. There are many manufacturers there ... So for migrants, it's more convenient there, also because houses [rents] are lower ... Some people settled there initially, one or two. My father for instance was one of the first who went there and then he was followed by many others ... because they can find work there. (Soultana)

People who arrived first found employment easily, and this attracted compatriots from various places in Bulgaria (from the regions of Plovdiv and Sliven mostly). The fact that the Bulgarian Sarakatsani are in Greece under a status of temporary residence (they are entitled to a special annual visa) makes many among them follow a cyclical migration path: they come to work for a period and then go back to Bulgaria, where many continue working in their traditional activities (cattle-breeding, agriculture), then returning again to Greece after renewing their visa.

In Thermi, Sarakatsani work in the surrounding small industries, workshops and commercial businesses, but also in construction activities, repair tasks, gardening, and domestic service in the case of women. The patterns of their integration in the local labour market are explained on the basis of the particularities of the local socio-economic structures. On the one hand, there are businesses that need immigrant labour. On the other, there are relatively wealthy residents with an increased demand for personal/household services who can afford to employ a migrant manual worker or a domestic servant. The 'closed' character of immigrants' employment in Thermi (mostly Sarakatsani and some Albanians who work for locals) keeps daily wages at a fixed rate for manual and construction work: 25 euros at the time of the fieldwork. The older respondents in my sample, usually male household heads, work in order to support the household and to finance specific plans (the purchase of a new house, the further education of the children). Younger males follow their fathers, and they usually work together. The (few) women in this (small) section of the sample exhibit some degree of socio-economic mobility and of 'exodus' from closed family networks, due to studies in Greece, marriage to Greek citizens or entrepreneurship.

The residential situation of Sarakatsani in Thermi appears quite varied, depending on the migratory routes and plans of individuals. Males whose families are in Bulgaria tend to occupy bad-quality properties, in many cases storerooms or basements that are not liable for tax as rental accommodation: these are the properties they can afford to rent in a quite expensive area. Couples and families tend to live in proper accommodation in flats or houses, in a few cases provided by their employers.

The presence of immigrants is visible in the central square of the suburb, where many gather in the mornings in order to look for work, and in the afternoons and evenings for socialising and chatting. Immigrants from different nationalities occupy different parts of the square (as Maria told me, 'The Bulgarians are on one side ... and the Albanians are separate ... each with his group,'). The square used to be a piazza for seeking casual employment during past years, but this activity has now been relocated to the outskirts of the residential area (on the way to the airport); lately (summer 2004) it was undergoing a process of regeneration. Most of the interviewees talked about good relations with the locals, but they have problems with the police because of the frequent checks (although local police officers well know that Sarakatsani Bulgarians are granted special status and thus cannot be clandestine). The police have forced them to move out of the square, denying them its use as a job-finding piazza initially, but ultimately also as a meeting place; the justification for this is the 'protection of the public image' of this particular space located right in the centre of Thermi:

> We sit here, the police come, they tell us 'Come on, you Bulgarians, pick up your stuff and get out of here.' ... Why? (Ghiorgos)

7.2.3 *Beyond residence and work: leisure, consumption and the urban space*

I have talked so far about spaces of residence and of work, as these two seem to crucially characterise migrants' lives in the city; and indeed, to an extent, they certainly do, constituting the places people tend to spend most of their time. But what happens with the space *in between*, out of home, but not at work? How do migrants experience the public space and to what extent do they make use of private spaces of consumption and entertainment? And which are the new geographies and relationships produced by their presence in the city? The majority does indeed go out, consume and socialise, despite facing the financial burden of their situation and, sometimes, discrimination and non-acceptance. Perhaps not as often as the locals do, or in different, less costly ways, immigrants nevertheless make use of their free time to meet with friends, entertain themselves, or consume: in this, the city provides the terrain.

Some material, both qualitative and quantitative, was collected about migrants' entertainment options and 'going out' in particular. At the time of the fieldwork, 39.1 per cent of the respondents used to go out at least once a fortnight and 18.8 per cent at least once a month; 33.7 per cent said they went out only 'rarely' and the rest (8.4 per cent) would never go out. Naturally, there is a high degree of diversity, in terms of age, family status, the area where they live, their employment conditions, etc. Young people below 30 tend to go out more often (65.2 per cent of them said they go out at least once a fortnight, compared to only 8.8 per cent among people aged over 50 years old); the same holds for singles (61.1 per cent) and those who don't have children (53.8 per cent). Migrants who go out that often are also found in higher numbers among those who speak fluent Greek (46.7 per cent, while only 1.7 per cent said they never go out), who socialise with Greek people (45.8 per cent, compared to 26.8 per cent among those who do not have Greek friends/acquaintances), or who have a working day of eight hours or less (45.5. per cent). Women, possibly due to household/family roles, tend to go out less frequently: 36.5 per cent of them go out once a fortnight (40.6 per cent among men); also, 16.2 per cent of women said they never go out (3.9 per cent among men).

More than one third of the respondents seem to prefer the town centre, confirming the relatively centralised leisure industry of the city. Apart from those living in the centre, residents of the western part of the municipality and the north-west districts in particular prefer to go downtown rather than choosing among their limited and 'closed' neighbourhood-based entertainment options. By contrast, the eastern part of the city tends to concentrate numerous entertainment places of various types, and migrants living in these areas are more likely to choose among their local options. The majority though (37.2 per cent) answered that they would go 'anywhere' in the city, depending on 'the company' or 'the mood'. Again, we can observe differences among the different groups. The city centre, for instance, appears to be more popular among people who are between 18-29 years old (46.9 per cent) or who are single (46.3 per cent) – even for those living in the outer neighbourhoods – and people who socialise with Greeks (38.5 per cent); on the other hand, ethnic Greeks, people aged 40 and over, and married people tend to prefer the neighbourhood (the respective shares among these categories are 32.1, 40.7 and 37.8 per cent). Despite the concentration of bars, cafés, etc. downtown and in certain other parts of the city, neighbourhood life is far from disappearing. The in-depth interviews contain a plethora of different individual leisure/entertainment options and habits, which are too detailed and case-specific to be quoted in their entirety here. The examples are perhaps as many as the interviewees themselves; to quote only a few:

> I came here for economic reasons ... I try not to go out that often and spend a lot of money ... I stay mostly at home, watch TV ... I fancy *bouzoukia* and the like. I've been twice with Greek friends, but it's too expensive there. (Ivan)
>
> I go out, to walk ... anywhere ... Not that much in my neighbourhood. Where can I go there? There are no places ... I go out with my brother ... downtown ... But I don't stay very late ... To the movies, I have only been once. (Mira)
>
> I am 'locked' at home ... I can't go out, because this is the nature of my job, they always need me there, they are old people ... and they don't want me to leave ... On Sundays, I am free and then I go to my cousin's. (Lioupa, live-in carer)
>
> Elias [his brother] goes there, me too, but not every week ... Many Albanians meet there, they play pool basically ... We don't

> talk that much about work, mostly we play [pool], we just have company and enjoy ourselves. (Andreas)
>
> I don't go to coffee shops. Sometimes I go to tavernas ... with these two Greek friends that I mentioned ... wherever ... I have been to Pyli Axiou [nightclub with live Greek music] three times ... Again, with my Greek friends. (Valbona)

Clearly, the financial burden explains the limited frequency of 'going out'; alternative options are discussed in 8.2.2 and 8.2.3, so the interest here is in the participants' preferences regarding private entertainment. It generally appears that migrants tend to go to the same places as Greeks do, depending on each individual's lifestyle, age and cultural background: in that sense, trendy bars and nightclubs are as common as tavernas and traditional local coffee shops. Two important observations are relevant.

Firstly, the majority of immigrants in Thessaloniki are 'inserted' into the *dominant* leisure-consumption culture that prevails in Greece today, and thus tend to make use of the same private entertainment spaces. This is particularly true for the groups studied here, both coming from neighbouring states where popular contemporary cultural expressions (commercial music and dance, club culture) do not really differ much from those of the host society, as these countries have also experienced a degree of both Western and Greek cultural imperialism (mostly notable in Albania, where Greek popular artists have occasionally performed in concert halls or nightclubs in Tirana)[6]. It is worth noting that some of the interviewees, especially the youngest ones, would refer to certain city nightclubs, or to Greek pop stars. Many share the Greek habit of going to one of the expensive but popular live-music nightclubs on a Saturday night, or of a long coffee break in the neighbourhood or downtown on a quasi-daily basis. The frequency of such practices might be limited, however, due to heavy work schedules and little free time, which contrast with the habits of the local population, especially its younger sections, as noted by some of the interviewees:

> There are many guys who are rich, I suppose ... They wake up in the morning, at 9 or 10 o'clock, and they go straight to the coffee shop. (Vilco)

The second observation is about private places that function as meeting points (mainly or exclusively) for immigrants. This is an exception to what was described above, but it appears to be quite common among people of an older age, usually males. During the last decade certain coffee shops and bars that attract migrant customers have emerged all over the city; the owners are usually Greek, but increasingly we find migrants taking over. For example, Andreas, an Albanian interviewee, talks about a billiard club where Albanian immigrants gather after work or on weekends to 'play [pool], have company and enjoy' themselves. And, as already mentioned, I personally had the chance to visit a bar in the city centre, which served as a meeting place for a small Bulgarian community who would gather, particularly on Friday and Saturday nights, to have drinks and dance to Greek and Bulgarian music[7].

Nevertheless, apart from *private* places of entertainment, the role of the *public* space is crucial: the open city space, where in general migrants' presence is notable. Given the necessity of generating an income and, in many cases, supporting families back home, on a limited budget that does not allow for frequent going out and consumption, and perhaps also because of different habits and cultural approaches to space, the public places seem to be particularly important in migrants' lives. Within the public urban space, migrants develop leisure practices that somehow 'escape' the market: the neighbourhood itself, some pedestrian zones in urban streets, parks and squares, etc., become places where migrants meet each other, socialise, chat or play. Recent research has showed that immigrants' children are much more involved in sports than Greek children and practice it in outdoor spaces, the neighbourhood itself, parks and fields[8]. The neighbourhood, in particular, has been the primary space of the immigrants' public existence since the beginning, located immediately outside of the private domain of residence. On the other hand, job-finding piazzas too have initially been among the few places where migrants could have a public presence, functioning not only as 'market places' where they would sell directly the only valuable thing they possess in the host country, i.e. their labour, but also as meeting points, places of recreation and socialisation. Finally, as many respondents stated, going for a walk, especially downtown window-shopping or a walk by the seafront (repeatedly mentioned as one of the city's most beautiful parts), has been a basic leisure option for years.

Once again, I am tempted to highlight the dynamic element: in this domain too, things do change over time. The first issue regarding the interviewees' past experiences of space is certainly that of *illegality*: undocumented status denies immigrants the right to a public presence. Irregular migrants are trapped in a social space limited from 'home-to-work'. Hiding so as not to be arrested by the police, as we have seen, and avoiding busy public places, led many migrants towards a lasting 'invisible' existence, suffocating between the private sphere and the workplace:

> Without papers you are afraid ... even in the street we couldn't walk, we were hiding ... [so as] not to be caught by the police, not to walk through places where there were police. (Andreas)
> We were like, from work to home. We couldn't go out to drink a coffee like everybody does, it was work, home. It was very difficult. (Ferin)

Obviously, regularisation may offer immigrants a more visible public existence. But the little free time left after a long working day might hinder migrants' capacity for going out and enjoying themselves long after legal status is obtained, making thus the 'home-to-work' space a permanent situation:

> Only work and home ... There is no time to see how beautiful Greece is. (Raicko)

Secondly, there are the practicalities that emerge from the way the authorities (more correctly: the police) treat immigrants on a daily basis. As we have seen in Chapter 5, even when migrants manage to acquire legal status, frequent controls and arrests continue to be the case for many, also disturbing their everyday routine regarding their leisure time and their experiences of space:

> If I go to the square to use the payphone, they will arrest me and take me to Thermi to check me [the largest police unit to the east] ... Everyday, when I finish work I am here. I may go out to meet a friend, to have a coffee, you know, I may go to a bar in the evening ... and they may arrest me. (Ferin)

Thirdly comes the issue of *discrimination*. Immigrants, especially Albanians, often come across incidents of offensive behaviour, whether in public or private places:

> In the neighbourhood where I used to live, when my children came ... a neighbour had a nephew who wanted to play with our kids, but he wouldn't let him. He said nothing, he just didn't let his nephew play with our children. (Dimitri)
> When we go somewhere ... let's say to a store selling clothes ... you get inside and they treat you like any other customer. From the moment that the discussion goes on and the question 'Where are you from?' comes, when we say [from Albania] ... their behaviour changes. It becomes as if the other person was superior. (Ani)

We have seen, nevertheless, that such incidents gradually fade from migrants' daily experiences; either because the basis of interaction widens to embrace newly formed intercultural relationships, or simply because they become rare cases lost in the vast anonymity of the city. The latter point, for instance, was addressed by migrants who had come to Thessaloniki after spending a period in other (smaller) parts of Greece, where they were more 'exposed' and thus more vulnerable:

> In the city people are different ... They don't care about who you are, if you are an Albanian or not. (Nicolas)

However, neither prejudice nor the way the legal framework is applied function as *exclusionary* mechanisms as such, in the sense of denying migrants the right to access public space itself. By contrast, it appears that the public urban space is being used and enjoyed to a greater extent by immigrants than by locals as leisure culture is increasingly moving towards consumption and as entertainment options are more and more oriented towards the private sphere. The space that remains 'abandoned', to a lesser or a greater extent, by the locals, is gradually 'taken over' and used by newcomers. Perhaps individual migrants will gradually abandon such urban open spaces as their material situation improves and consumerist values prevail. This is something already present in the lifestyles of many of the participants, reflected for instance in the *dominant* leisure culture previously described, or, as put by one of the interviewees (Liliana from Bulgaria), 'Now, gradually, we start behaving like the Greeks.'

Exclusion from *the use* of the public space might come as a consequence of developments that result in new social uses of space. By this I refer to policies and processes of urban regeneration/gentrification which aim to transform the image of the city and specific places within it, in order for it to be used for private consumption, as a tourist attraction, etc. One example from my fieldwork concerned the experiences of Sarakatsani Bulgarians in the square in Thermi, described in the previous section. In his study of the local media discourse, Pavlou (2001: 140-145) explains how immigrants' exclusion from the public space is related to 'city marketing' policies: he looks at public perceptions of the 'proper' use of urban space, which has to be regenerated and therefore 'cleaned' of immigrants, whose presence is 'annoying' and who 'destroy' the public image of specific areas. This kind of discourse is (sometimes) based on existing problems of degradation, but it connects them directly to the presence of distinct social groups (migrants, Roma, beggars, drug-addicts, etc.). The discourse became more hostile in 1997, when Thessaloniki was the Cultural Capital of Europe, and many areas underwent processes of regeneration and reorganisation of their social use. What is actually 'annoying' is the visible face of poverty (Pavlou 2001); in other words, the view of the 'other', who uses space in a different way from 'us'.

Nevertheless, inevitably the presence of immigrants continues to reshape the face of Thessaloniki: certain areas (parks, squares, etc.) become places where immigrants gather in order to meet each other or to look for work. Examples are the Aristotle University campus, Courts Square (Plateia Dikastirion) and the railway station, all in the heart of the city, as well as other strategic points (e.g. motorway junctions, green spaces). This development is also evident at a neighbourhood level in areas with high concentrations of immigrants, where, for instance, the surrounding kiosks sell Albanian, Russian, Bulgarian and other newspapers. The demand for specific types of services on the part of the migrants (e.g. translations, newspapers, special products, food) and the entrepreneurial action of both themselves and of locals, transform the urban landscape in certain streets and neighbourhoods, giving it multicultural characteristics. For example, in the Vardaris area (western part of the centre), in the streets below the main street (Egnatia), there is a growing Chinese market that has emerged during the past few years (mainly clothing stores)[9]. In Courts Square, which functions as a meeting place for migrants from the former Soviet Union, we can observe the development of several small ethnic businesses, ranging from street traders to specialised food stores and ethnic restaurants with self-descriptive, place-specific names (e.g. the 'Caucasus taverna'). I should note that the groups studied here do not exhibit similar tendencies of *visibility* within the city, at least not in such a particular and distinct way; this points to certain aspects of cultural proximity (in terms of food, for instance), as mentioned by many interviewees, but also a degree of *adaptability* to the local environment, especially in the case of Albanians. In general, however, immigrants add new 'colours' and character to the changing urban morphology, and they develop new social uses of space, which acquires a particular meaning for them and becomes their 'place'. In the narratives of many interviewees, the city is 'imagined' as a new home:

> It is more friendly, it is 'warmer', closer to us ... It's a beautiful city. (Emil)
>
> Thessaloniki ... has become a part of my life ... This is my home now ... I adore it. (Valbona)

8 A 'space' for living: socio-cultural integration

This is the last empirical chapter of the thesis, and it deals with a number of additional issues related to the migrants' pathways to incorporation. It starts with the basic issue of welfare, which, although identified as part of the policy/institutional context of immigrants' reception, is treated here separately and is examined from a specific angle. This concerns the extent to which migrants have *access* to certain basic services, and the ways they approach these services, the problems they encounter, etc. In general, the *practices* immigrants develop, collectively and individually, to cope with certain daily matters is the main topic in the discussion to follow. Apart from ways of accessing health and education services, the analysis is concerned with the patterns of solidarity and membership in migrant organisations, the character of informal social networks, and with various aspects of the migrants' everyday lives, ranging from the possession of certain household goods to language practices, strategies to cope with negative stances towards them, and perceptions of identity.

8.1 Access to services and to resources

The welfare of immigrants depends on the existing social-policy framework, the whole set of institutions, measures and provisions constituting the social state in the host country; and on the specific policies targeting the integration of migrants. Obviously, the latter is part of the former, which, in the Greek case, is characterised by late development, limited services, and certain problems of corruption, clientelism, bureaucracy and inefficiency. However, despite the problems and weaknesses, there exists a functioning welfare state based on the insurance and pensions systems, on public health and education for all citizens, and on certain benefits (housing, unemployment, income support, etc.) applying to special categories of the population. This, as elsewhere in Europe, is currently undergoing serious restructuring.

Until the early 2000s, no particular measures for the integration of migrants had been undertaken. Regarding National Insurance and social protection, law 2910/2001 recognised equal rights, as they apply to

Greek citizens, for foreign nationals legally resident in Greece . It was only in 2002 that the government launched a set of measures aiming specifically at integration for the first time. The 'Action Plan for the Social Integration of Immigrants for the Period 2002-2005' includes provisions for the training, labour-market integration and health care of immigrants, the establishment of local centres of social support, and the promotion of cultural exchanges among the various communities. Up to now, however, the outcomes of any implementation of the plan remain obscure. In addition, the ethnocentric spirit and national identity considerations mentioned earlier as characteristic of policy-making in Greece are evident here as well. Ethnic Greek immigrants enjoy special privileges compared to 'aliens', although not all of them enjoy equal rights with Greek citizens, particularly in respect to civil rights and political participation. Nevertheless, despite the lack of relevant provisions, many migrants have been able to benefit from certain public services, whether due to specific legal provisions, gaps in the practical implementation of the policy framework, or, to an extent, informal practices and the positive role of social networks.

In this part of the chapter, the main interest lies in the provision of basic welfare services, that is, public education and health, and the respective pathways of access of the immigrants. The third section deals with additional issues related to the migrants' living conditions, this time in the private sphere. Not only have they managed to access public resources in Greece, but many have succeeded in improving their living standards in many other aspects.

8.1.1 *Immigrants' pathways of access to the national health system*

Access to the national health system has been dependent on registered employment and regular status, which was not the case for the majority of Greece's immigrants throughout the 1990s. In July 2000, the Ministry of Health and Welfare issued a circular on the medical treatment and hospital admission of nationals of countries outside the EU and the European Economic Area. Accordingly, regular immigrants can have access to the national health system as long as they possess a health book issued by the insurance fund they are registered with; in any other case only emergency cases are accepted, and the same applies to undocumented 'aliens'. Ethnic Greek migrants, on the other hand, can benefit from the public health services if they are able to present the necessary documents, which include, for those not insured, a special health book for low-income people. Although only 64.1 per cent of the respondents had social security at the time of the fieldwork, the percentage of those covered by a health book rises to 76 per cent, since dependent family members are covered by the person principally insured.

Even so, since social security stamps are a prerequisite for applying for regularisation or renewal of stay permits, insurance for most of the respondents has been a recent development. In some cases, they had to finance it themselves, or it has been partial, as a result of their informal employment and the unwillingness of employers to pay the social security contributions. Nevertheless, even during this period, there has existed a space for access to basic welfare services. Lack of insurance meant that people had to pay fully for their own medical treatment; this applied to many of my respondents, and it obviously proved too costly for most of them. However, there are many examples of unofficial help from both doctors and clerks at public hospitals or in the private sector. Regarding the latter, contacts and acquaintances have been of particular importance in both accessing the service needed as well as in financial terms. For some of the respondents, it had been their (Greek) boss or a neighbour who introduced them to a doctor. Valbona's testimony below is self-evident:

> When I was pregnant, six months' pregnant, I didn't go to the hospital. I went to a [private] doctor recommended to me by somebody I know, and he didn't get paid. He was a good person.

Others benefited from informal help by hospital staff, especially in the first half of the 1990s. Two characteristic examples are given below:

> I got sick in 1995. I was very ill. I had asthma and I didn't have social security, and I had to call 166 [phone number for urgent cases]. An ambulance came, and they took me to Papanikolaou [a public hospital]. I stayed there for three days, and then the director told me that I should pay. But ... we didn't have the money ... and he said that we definitely had to pay, 160,000 drachmas [480 euros] ... By law, the director was right, anybody without insurance has to pay. But there was another official there and he treated us very well ... he showed pity. My husband was there too, and he [the official] said, 'It's not that important, the money that the director asks for. I am going to have a word with him and you won't pay anything.' ... So it was done ... and we didn't pay anything finally, and I got better, and I had my medicine for free, they gave it to me from the hospital ... And now, since we have arranged the papers and we have got social security, we don't face any problems. (Lela)
>
> There is this Greek doctor who lives upstairs, and she has helped me a lot, with the children. Every time I had to go to the

> hospital for my wife or my kids, she has helped me a lot. (Gjion)

Such attempts at help often had to bend the rules in order to assist people in need, which resulted in interesting anecdotes. Mimoza, one of the Albanian interviewees, had such an experience when her little boy was ill and had to enter the hospital for a few days. Neither she nor her husband possessed a health book at the time to cover the child, and since the procedure requires a formal registration, the hospital reception clerks managed to issue a health book under the boy's name for only three days, as if the boy was a waged employee himself!

Research findings about the various strategies used by immigrants for accessing the national health system while undocumented or uninsured are of particular interest because they uncover 'invisible' aspects of the dynamics of integration. In the first place, some found out about, applied and have been eligible for a special welfare project offering access to health services and some other benefits to low-income people (*Πρόνοια – 'Pronia'*). Such was a Greek-Albanian interviewee's case, who found this way to compensate for not having the opportunity to get social security, given the precarious character of her work (domestic service and childcare):

> I am not insured. I only have *Pronia*. They ask you to present some documents, your ID card, a certificate from the revenue office, a certificate that you are not married and that there are no working members in the family. We got married two months ago and I haven't yet told them. I got my health book last October. (Kaiti)

Obviously, this is not always a viable choice, since it cannot apply to everyone; lack of relevant information, or of access to information (e.g. due to language difficulties) can be an additional factor regarding the limited use of certain benefits and rights that regular immigrants are entitled to. On a more practical level, a common strategy of accessing public hospitals when clandestine was the use of emergency services, as Pandelis recalled of the period he had no documents ('at that time we could only go to the emergency hospitals'). This practice was so widespread among undocumented migrants that the special (border) police started patrolling hospitals, and medical staff are now obliged by law to report undocumented foreigners to the police, although none of the respondents had such an experience.

Finally, an interesting finding concerns Bulgarian immigrants, for whom geographic proximity allows transnational practices regarding medical treatment. Lacking social security in Greece, and obviously not being able to afford the cost of treatment otherwise, many prefer to go to a hospital or doctor in their home country, given that the health system there is cheaper and easily accessible for those who are registered with a Bulgarian social security fund, or who have coverage due to a family member being registered. This strategy was particularly common among older participants.

In sum, access to the Greek national health system depends primarily on legal status and registered employment: although this was the case for a few people in the past, it has gradually become a reality for more and more immigrants in Greece. Regularisation appears to have considerably improved the position of immigrants as far as access to health services and to welfare in general is concerned. There are no signs of systematic discrimination or exclusion, and cases of maltreatment by doctors or hospital staff are quite rare and isolated events. Most of the problems reported by the respondents concerned the malfunctions of the Greek public health system, issues of bureaucracy and some rather isolated events of discriminatory attitudes by employees. Sixteen per cent of the Albanians in the sample and 21.4 per cent of the Bulgarians mentioned problems of offensive treatment and bad-quality services in Greek hospitals.

A way of assessing immigrants' use of health services in Thessaloniki can be offered by taking the example of a particular local hospital in a given period. Raw data on 400 cases of non-EU nationals who received medical treatment between July 2000 and March 2001 have been obtained from the administrative offices of one of the city's most important hospitals (G. Papanikolaou). More than half of the cases concerned Albanian patients, 19 per cent Georgians and 18.3 per cent Russians; the remaining 3.5 per cent was composed of various nationalities, especially Armenians, Bulgarians and Romanians. Despite the presence of some tourists and other transients in this sample, the majority of admissions concerns immigrants who are resident in the city and surrounding places: 57 per cent had a stay permit, and 13.5 per cent possessed documentation applicable to ethnic Greeks. Some 14.3 per cent presented only their passports, 2 per cent had no valid documents at all, and 7 per cent had various other forms of identification (tourist visas, certificates of inter-hospital transfers, etc). Slightly more than one third (36 per cent) were not insured and had to pay the full fee for their treatment. The majority (44.3 per cent) was registered with IKA, while a share of 12.3 per cent were benefactors of the welfare fund for low-income people (the majority ethnic Greeks) and 2.8 per cent were registered with ΟΓΑ. Three people had private insurance, and the remaining cases were subject to special conditions. Despite possible bias embedded in the fact that some of the cases concerned serious incidents (accidents, inter-hospital transfers), it is remarkable that 70 per cent were received by the hospital's emergency services. Not surprisingly, there appears to be a relationship between being insured or not and the type of hospital service received (emergency or not): those without insurance are more likely to use emergency services.

8.1.2 *Public education and the schooling of immigrants' children*

Turning now to education, since the early 1990s, there have been provisions for the education of immigrants' children. Kiprianos (2002) distinguishes two stages in the development of the relevant educational policies: the first period lasted until the mid-1990s and was characterised by an ethnocentric spirit; the second period begins in 1996, when policy-making takes into account the need for intercultural approaches for the first time[1]. In the mid-1990s the government acknowledged that the numbers of 'foreign' pupils in Greek schools were growing, and thus they should be able to register in any school even if their parents were undocumented, according to a statement of the (then) Education Minister G. Papandreou (19 June 1995). In 1999, the government put forward a programme of reception and support classes for the integration of immigrants' children into the Greek educational system. Reception classes consist of two stages: the first one lasts one year and mainly contains language courses and a few compulsory subjects (sports, arts, foreign language); the second provides two extra years of language support parallel to the school programme. Support classes apply to pupils with linguistic difficulties already following the curriculum programme, providing extra hours of language teaching and support. During 1999-2000, 500 reception classes and 701 support classes were functioning all over the country, with a total of about 13,500 foreign pupils attending. A year later, the Ministry of Education established a foundation class programme for foreign pupils without any knowledge of Greek. The Immigration Bill (Law 2910/2001, article 40) recognised equal rights and obligations to 'minor aliens' regarding schooling, participation in educational activities, and documents required for registration. After criticism focusing on the educational exclusion of children whose parents are undocumented, the law allowed registration irrespective of the legal status of parents (Kiprianos 2002) [2]. Recently, the Ministry of Education initiated a project for the 'integration of returning and foreign pupils', which also includes provisions for the teaching of the pupils' mother tongues in specific schools with high participation of migrant children (*Macedonia*, 11 December 2002). The first language would be Russian, and the initial aim was to include about 300 schools in the project by the end of 2004.

Nevertheless, even before the implementation of such measures, and given the limited number of special (intercultural) settings, many 'foreign' children have been able to register in normal state schools. The fieldwork findings show that, at a practical level, few obstacles were posed to the schooling of immigrants' children. About one third (34.8 per cent) of the Albanian respondents and 15.7 per cent of the Bulgarians had children in Greek educational institutions, mostly in preschool, primary and secondary education. Among them, four Albanian and three Bulgarian respondents had children in Greek universities and polytechnics. In four additional cases, the respondents' children had attended a Greek secondary school in the past. If we take into account the fact that many immigrants, particularly Albanians, came at a young age and had got married and had children while in Greece, we can assume that many of the remaining respondents' children were too young to be at school at the time the fieldwork took place. Furthermore, some of the respondents were children themselves when they came, following their parents, and had continued their education in Greece. In respect to this, a small minority had received education in Greece: three Albanians had graduated from a Greek high school, while another seven Albanians and two Bulgarians had studied in a Greek university[3]. The novelty of the phenomenon of large numbers of foreign children in Greek schools created the only notable problem regarding their schooling, which has to do with registration procedures. Registration at school can become a complicated issue in respect to the documents and certificates required, although bureaucratic obstacles are sooner or later overcome:

> For Minas [son's name], we had to get a birth certificate from here, since he was born in Greece, stating that he was born in Greece, in Thessaloniki. We got this one, we had to translate it into Albanian, then we got another paper from the municipality there [in Tirana] stating, 'This person was born in Thessaloniki, Greece'. I brought it here and I had to translate this into Greek. (Lazaros)

In addition, some of the respondents' children had access to the special reception schools mentioned earlier. The daughter of Lela, an Albanian interviewee, who was present during our interview session, spoke herself about her experience after returning to Greece when her parents' documents were issued:

> I had come earlier, for a year. My parents took me with them initially, so I knew a little Greek, but I had forgotten it ... Then we went to this returning migrants' school. They helped us a lot.

> We did the first year's textbook [primary] in order to learn the language, the letters [alphabet], and everything ... We were studying textbooks of previous classes, and then, when we finished this school, we registered normally in the Greek school, and there was not any problem.

The numbers of both 'foreign' and ethnic Greek pupils, especially in primary education, have increased considerably in the last fifteen years and keep rising: in 2002-2003, the total number of children of foreign and ethnic Greek origin in state schools was 130,114, comprising 9 per cent of the total pupil population (*Kathimerini*, 3 January 2004)[4]. The participation of foreign pupils (excluding 'repatriated' ethnic Greeks) in Greek education between 1995-2000 increased by 6.5 percentage points in primary schools, by 1.2 in *Gymnasio*, by 0.3 in technical/professional *Lykeio* and by 0.3 in general *Lykeio* (Kiprianos 2002: Table 1)[5]. Most of the foreign pupils are concentrated in the large urban centres: during 1999-2000 Greater Athens accounted for more than 40 per cent of those attending secondary schools, and Thessaloniki about 16 per cent (*To Vima*, 5 November 2000). In Thessaloniki, between 1999-2002, the number of foreign pupils in secondary education grew by 34.4 per cent (*To Vima*, 5 November 2000; *Macedonia*, 11 February 2002). During 2001-2002, 14,999 foreign and ethnic Greek pupils were studying in prefectural state schools, and their share in the local pupil population was 10 per cent (*Macedonia*, 11 February 2002); about 60 per cent of them were in primary education.

As both the above figures and my fieldwork findings suggest, despite the irregular status of most parents, immigrants' children have not been excluded from education in Greece, at least not in institutional terms. There exist problems, however, regarding the integration of children at school. These are to an extent related to the difficulties arising from their language skills and the process of adaptation into a new educational system. But the widespread prejudices and negative perceptions about migrants in Greece, affecting both teachers and pupils, are factors that should not be underestimated. And there are certainly additional obstacles connected to the socio-economic position of the migrants. The need to enter the labour market at an early age leads many to abandon school before completing basic education, whether this comes as a result of a family strategy or is a personal decision of individual pupils.

Findings suggest that prejudices and/or discrimination at school are certainly a reality but do not practically affect the majority of immigrants' children: in most cases, the latter are well-accepted by other pupils and supported by teachers to overcome linguistic and other difficulties. However, one third of the respondents with children schooled in Thessaloniki complained about unfair treatment: in most of the cases these concerned problematic relationships between pupils, while in a limited number of cases (eighteen), discriminatory attitudes by teachers and pupils' parents were also reported. Such attitudes reflect both the widespread prejudices about immigrants in Greece and the ethnocentric spirit characterising the curriculum programme and the educational system as a whole. The origin of a new pupil is certainly something that attracts attention and creates some sort of distance from the newcomer, especially at an initial stage, but this does not necessarily result in long-term rejection of the 'other' in the classroom[6]:

> He didn't have any problem at all. Well, apart from being told 'Look, he is from Albania,' but these things are unavoidable. (Stavros, talking about his son)
> There are some teachers and some children who say 'They are Albanians,' but not everybody. (Melina, talking about her children)

Indeed, there is evidence that some children adapt very quickly to the new circumstances and some perform exceptionally well. A recent survey on the performance of foreign pupils in high school showed that more than half (52.6 per cent) score above 15 in 20, thus securing university entrance, while 16.6 per cent achieve top marks[7]. Kiprianos (2002) relates this phenomenon to the special importance attributed to education by some foreign pupils or their parents, who see it as a form of capital that will offer better future prospects. Sometimes, the good performance of foreign pupils is even highlighted by teachers as an example to be followed by fellow pupils:

> There was not any injustice at the school, they [the teachers] didn't say 'Look, he's an Albanian,' on the contrary, they were saying, 'Look, he came from a foreign country and he is such a good pupil,' they loved him ... And when I went [to ask about his progress] they were saying 'You should be proud of your kid.' (Lela)

However, the intrinsic ethnocentrism of the Greek educational system, particularly the teaching of certain curriculum subjects and the participation in national celebrations, creates obstacles to the smooth integration of foreign pupils. For instance, during the national holidays all schools organise a parade where the top-ranking pupil carries the Greek flag[8]. In 1999, in Mihaniona, a suburb of Thessaloniki, an Albanian pupil became the flag-bearer, which caused a strong xenophobic reaction that dominated the public and media discourse in the following days. Much of the discourse argued against the right of an Albanian to hold the national flag (see Kapllani & Mai 2005). The event has been repeated since then several times, with the same pupil as well as in other cases. One of the interviewees referred to this incident when talking about his daughter's experience:

> She should be a flag-bearer and she hasn't [been], but I can't complain about this. There was too much fuss about that, not at her school, but earlier, you know, with this event at Mihaniona. (Nikos)

Such nationalistic reactions highlight the contradictions of ethnocentric approaches to education and school life. They reflect the exclusionary character of national identity and the populist discourse that surrounds it (Kapllani & Mai 2005). Similarly, certain curriculum subjects such as history, for instance, are particularly problematic regarding references to sensitive moments in Balkan history from a nationalistic perspective. The testimony quoted below, of Albena, a Bulgarian interviewee, although it might be an isolated case, is characteristic in terms of the practical implications of ethnocentrism in history education:

> Let's say, at the history class, they had a lesson about [the Byzantine Emperor] Vasilios the Bulgarian-slayer ... And a kid who wanted to play ... said, 'I am Vasilios the Bulgarian-slayer.' And my son ... felt offended. Or, for instance, the history teacher ... they had a lesson on the Balkan wars ... and I had told my son about that, when Bulgarians invaded Greece ... which was not good, but he told me 'Mum, the teacher says bad things about Bulgaria and she looks at me.'

Nevertheless, the problems associated with linguistic obstacles and difficulties in adapting are rather more important at a practical level. They may negatively affect the performance and progress of children at school, creating serious delays and in some cases being a reason for not finishing basic education:

> [My son] came a bit later, he registered at school ... but he didn't know a word of Greek ... At school he only sat and listened ... without understanding. (Albena)
> They [the children] faced problems at the beginning, because they ... came here, without speaking the language ... it was difficult. They still face some difficulties ... My son was left behind a little in the beginning. (Melina)

> [My son] quit school, he couldn't make it. He was old when he came ... He didn't finish, he did two years and he stopped. 'I can't,' he said, and he left. (Flora)

Kiprianos (2002), based on an elaboration of statistical trends, reports that a significant number of foreign pupils abandon school (usually after the *Gymnasium*), mostly due to educational difficulties. Moreover, the shares of those continuing to a technical high school are far greater among foreign pupils compared to those of Greeks, who do not consider technical schools as 'good'; the majority of Greeks attend a general high school, which is the route into higher education. One should also take into account the socio-economic condition of migrant families, which in some cases leads children towards exclusion from basic education and early entrance into the labour market in order to add to the family income or be financially independent:

> My son does not go to school. He dropped out when he went to *Gymnasium*. He attended the *Gymnasium* only for one month. He could not make it ... because of the language ... My son said that it was better to look for a job. (Eleni)

In a similar way, the migratory experience itself de facto excluded some from any future educational prospect. Many migrants came at an early age and before finishing high school, especially those from Albania. Young teenagers followed others on the migration path, but were sometimes unaccompanied by parents or older relatives. These people neglected any further education or training out of necessity, and immediately faced harsh employment conditions as unskilled workers in the Greek labour market. Such is the case of Ferin, an Albanian interviewee who was only thirteen when he arrived, together with a group of schoolmates, soon after finishing primary school:

> When I came for the first time, my boss told me, 'Come, I'll register you at school.' ... I didn't come here for school, I came to have a wage, to make some money, so I didn't go. But that was not good, it was stupid that I didn't go.

8.1.3 *Additional issues related to the migrants' living conditions*

> To live here as an immigrant, to be able to pay for a good property, to have a good job, you need to sacrifice. You want to go out, to wear smart clothes, to spend money ... For us, with the wage we get, we can't do that.

The above quote is from my interview with Milen, a young man from Bulgaria: in a few sentences he summarises what is experienced by many migrants and is highlighted in their narratives regarding the kind of life they lead in Thessaloniki. 'Sacrifice' is the crucial word used; and this is partly perceived in material terms, pointing to the conditions and goods that are inevitably linked to what can be characterised as *quality* of life: in Milen's words, a good job, a good house, nice clothes, going out and consumption. The basic spheres of employment, housing, education and health have been covered in my analysis up to now; we have also seen aspects regarding the character of solidarity bonds, interpersonal relationships, as well as entertainment choices, while much earlier in the thesis the social and political reactions, and their practical implications, were addressed. In this section, the focus is on some additional (material) elements of the immigrants' living conditions.

In respect to certain household goods, some 14 per cent of the respondents were lacking basic equipment at the time of the fieldwork (a cooker, a washing machine, or a TV). One in four did not have a landline phone, but this is perhaps misleading since many owned mobile phones. One third had possessions in addition to basic home equipment (videos, DVDs, computers, hi-fi sets, etc). Furthermore, the share of respondents holding a bank account in Greece was slightly below 50 per cent[9]: however, while it exceeds 57 per cent among Albanians, it is only 28.6 per cent among Bulgarian migrants, largely due to Sarakatsani men (only one in twelve has an account) and divorced women (one in nine). Sarakatsani Bulgarians (who keep coming and going) tend not to open a bank account in Greece, while those described as 'elite' migrants, more represented among Bulgarians, also chose to hold bank accounts in their home country. In addition, there appears to be a notable gender divide, reflecting respective differences between the two nationalities (more dependant female migration in the Albanian case)[10]. Generally though, Albanian migrants (usually male heads of households) seem to prefer to entrust their savings to Greek banks. In respect to that, it is worth mentioning a recent decision by the National Bank of Greece to include instructions in the Albanian language at its cashpoint machines, after estimating that nearly 90 per cent of Albanian households (in Greece) are customers of Greek banks, with an average balance of about 15,000 euros (*Eleftherotypia*, 12 September 2004).

Part of the immigrants' savings or earnings are used to support their families back home. Among the respondents, 45.7 per cent said that at the time they were regularly sending money to their relatives, and one in five used to send consumer goods. Remittances seem to depend on household needs and family migration strategies. Those whose spouse and/or children are in the home countries are more likely to remit (65.7 per cent), as well as young migrants below 30 years of age (50 per cent) or families without children (51.1 per cent). The period away from home slightly affects the propensity to remit – 40.3 per cent of those with nine or more years in Greece do so. While remittances appear not to be related to income (migrants earning less than 30 euros a day remit in higher shares – 73.7 per cent), they do though depend on financial security: nearly 60 per cent of those with a bank account send money back home.

Possession of a means of transport was the case for 53.3 per cent of the respondents: 31.2 per cent owned a car, 18.3 per cent had a motorbike and the rest had a bicycle. Differences can be observed on the basis of gender, nationality, ethnic origin, etc. For male Bulgarian immigrants, the Sarakatsani included, the possession of a car in Bulgaria is common; since movement between the two countries is free, they have the legal right to use their car in Greece for a period of six months without having to pay taxes. A typical practice is thus to bring the car and use it until the end of this period, then drive it back and leave it there before taking it to Greece again for another few months. The share of car owners is 37.1 per cent among Bulgarians and 28.3 per cent among Albanians; the latter tend to prefer the motorbike, as 24.6 per cent of them said they have one (but only 5.7 per cent of the Bulgarians). Car ownership is far more common among ethnic Greeks of both nationalities (40 per cent). The shares of female car owners are lower, 26.8 per cent and 31.5 per cent among Albanian and Bulgarian women respectively. The possession of private transport does not seem to reflect spatial 'patterns', i.e. it does not depend on the area of residence or location of the workplace. Municipality residents appear more likely to own a car/motorbike (more than half), while outer-city dwellers seem to be more dependent on public transport or to lead more neighbourhood-based lives. Naturally, this influences common practices, e.g. in things as simple as household shopping: among car/motorbike owners, 42.7 per cent said they go anywhere in the city for shopping, including distant large supermarkets, compared to only 13.8 per cent among those who do not have any transport means.

The percentage of the respondents who go on holiday is high at 74 per cent (higher among Bulgarian migrants, 80 per cent, and ethnic Greeks of both nationalities, 85 per cent). This seems to be a relatively new development. Obviously, the migrants' financial situation plays a role: only 12.5 per cent among those earning 40 euros or more a day said they do not go on holiday (a share which exceeds 20 per cent in all other wage categories). Time, again, is crucial, as more and more migrants move towards long-term settlement, stable jobs, socialisation and full legal status. The shares of those who do not go on holiday

Table 8.1 *Migrants' holiday choices according to their period in Greece (%)*

Holidays	*Period in Greece (years)*				*Nationality & Ethnicity*		
	< 2	*3-4*	*5-8*	*9+*	*Albanians*	*Bulgarians*	*ethnic Greeks*
in Greece	24.1	42.5	55.7	65.2	52.2	50.0	61.2
in Albania/Bulgaria	35.7	34.0	47.5	56.9	42.7	52.9	53.8
no holiday	50.0	34.0	26.2	11.1	29.0	20.0	14.9

drop from 50 per cent among migrants who are in Greece for no more than two years to 11.1 per cent among migrants with nine years or more (Table 8.1). It thus appears that, while holidays are still not an option for many ('We used to go before ... since we came here, no, we don't.'), increasingly some have started enjoying it during the summer ('Last summer we had a better time, we went to the sea ... to Halkidiki.'), by travelling within Greece as well as simply visiting their home countries (which some of the interviewees would not consider as a 'holiday'). Interestingly, the longer migrants are in the country, the more likely they are to travel within Greece on holiday, especially Albanians and ethnic Greeks, as shown in Table 8.1.

To summarise the quantitative dimensions of all these details, including some of the information presented earlier in the thesis also, and to treat them statistically, I have constructed an index composed of basic indicators (ten dichotomous variables) of the migrants' *material* conditions of living – see Table 8.2a below. The new variable (the index scores) is a continuous one and so can be used in both descriptive and exploratory tasks. For instance, to explore differences between the migrant groups, one could compare the average index scores. Accordingly, the data presented in Table 8.2b, confirm the general validity of some of the differences arising from the characteristics of the respondents that have been observed earlier for individual variables. Ethnic Greek Albanians, for instance, appear to be the better-off group, while Bulgarian Sarakatsani seem to be the poorest. Female Albanian migrants are in a relatively worse situation compared to their male compatriots, but it is exactly the opposite for Bulgarian women. Single Albanians appear

Table 8.2a *Details of the immigrants' living conditions: variables used in the index of 'material conditions'*

social security	*health book*	*bank account*	*own transport*	*own property*	*central heating*	*lack equipment*	*extra equipment*	*going out*	*going on holiday*
1=yes 0=no	1=yes[1] 0=no	1=yes 0=no	1=yes[2] 0=no	1=yes 0=no	1=yes 0=no	–1=yes[3] 0=no	1=yes[4] 0=no	1=yes[5] 0=no	1=yes 0=no

Key: [1] have/are covered by a health book; [2] own a car or a motorbike; [3] lack at least one of the following: cooker, washing machine, TV; [4] have at least one of the following: VHS, DVD, PC, Playstation, Air Conditioning; [5] going out at least once a month

Table 8.2b *Details of the immigrants' living condition: comparison of means - living conditions and migrants' characteristics*

		Albanians		*Bulgarians*		*All*	
		Mean	*Std. Dev.*	*Mean*	*Std. Dev.*	*Mean*	*Std. Dev.*
	All	4.5	2.2	3.9	2.5	4.3	2.3
1	ethnic Greek origin	5.1	2.0	3.4	2.7	4.6	2.4
2	female	4.3	2.4	4.3	2.8	4.3	2.6
	male	4.5	2.0	3.6	2.1	4.3	2.1
3	single	4.2	2.0	4.4	1.7	4.2	1.9
	married	4.7	2.2	3.8	2.7	4.4	2.4
	divorced/widowed	–1.0 (N=1)	–	3.5	3.1	3.2	3.2
4	18-29	4.6	1.8	4.3	1.7	4.5	1.8
	30-39	4.9	2.3	4.6	2.2	4.8	2.2
	40-49	3.9	2.6	4.1	3.3	3.9	2.8
	50+	4.3	1.6	2.6	2.7	3.6	2.3
5	primary	3.4	2.5	1.8 (N=4)	2.6	3.1	2.5
	secondary	4.1	2.3	4.0	2.1	4.1	2.2
	technical/professional	4.6	1.5	3.4	2.4	4.0	2.0
	university/postgraduate	5.3	2.0	5.4	2.6	5.3	2.2
6	beginner	2.5	2.82	1.88	1.89	2.27	2.49
	intermediate	4.22	2.02	3.75	1.72	4.08	1.94
	fluent	5.48	1.6	4.7	2.96	5.17	2.25
7	parents/none	4.63	2.03	4.56	2.25	4.61	2.08
	spouse/children	2.85	2.76	2.59	2.46	2.69	2.54
	send remittances	4.06	1.92	3.21	2.34	3.77	2.1
	no remittances	4.79	2.3	4.59	2.44	4.73	2.34

Key: 1=ethnic origin, 2=gender, 3=family status, 4=age, 5=education level, 6=fluency in Greek, 7=members of family in the home countries and propensity to remit on a regular basis.

less favoured than those who are married, but it is the other way round in the Bulgarians' case. Younger people, especially those between 30-39 years old, as well as highly educated immigrants and those who are fluent in Greek, enjoy more satisfactory material conditions. Those who have dependent family members living in the home countries and who send money regularly seem to sacrifice their material well-being in Thessaloniki in order to address family needs 'back home'.

Explanations for such differences should be traced in the varied migration patterns and individual/family migratory projects. But what is captured here as 'material conditions' also includes elements that have to do with consumerist values and Westernised lifestyles. Obviously, much of the respondents' material situation is a function of their financial condition, which, for the majority, depends on their labour-market position and income. Once again, the time factor appears to be important for the material well-being of the migrants. These last two issues could be (partly) 'measured' by the immigrants' wages and the

Table 8.2c *Details of the immigrants' living condition: correlating the 'material conditions' index score*

	Pearson Correlation	*Sig. (2-tailed)*	*N*
years in Greece	0.325	0.000	208
daily wage	0.273	0.001	154

period they have been in Greece, both continuous variables that can be correlated with the 'material conditions' index scores. As Table 8.2c shows, the relationships between these variables appear to be significant, although not particularly strong, due to the multiplicity of factors influencing migrants' living standards and pathways to incorporation. What these (bivariate) correlations indicate is that the respondents' living conditions improve to an extent over time, but they also depend on their income; as we have seen though, the longer a migrant has been in the country, the higher his/her wage tends to be. Additional factors such as social networks and the development of personal relationships with locals, or language skills, as shown earlier in the thesis, also depend on the time immigrants have been in Greece. The impact of regularisation is rather indirect in this case, since the migrants' material well-being primarily depends on their socio-economic situation.

8.2 Patterns of solidarity, agency and identity

Throughout the discussion of the findings, it has become clear that immigrants rely to a significant extent upon personal contacts and relationships in order to access employment, rent a property, etc. Migrant networks not only spread information about the host country or locality prior to emigration, thus functioning as a factor influencing and facilitating the migration decision and journey, but also provide the basis for mutual support *in* Greece, helping immigrants to overcome initial difficulties and further problems and linking them to the home places. As immigrants extend their stay, they increasingly interact with both their co-nationals and the locals. At the same time, networks of a more formal and institutionalised character develop, like various types of migrant/ethnic associations, often, again, in interaction with the citizens and institutions of the host society. In general, both formal and informal migrant networks determine senses of belonging and patterns of membership – in a migrant or ethnic/cultural group, in the sending country, or in the host society – hence they specify the idea of 'community', playing thus a crucial role in the incorporation process. The concept of 'community' is used here in a broad sense. It refers to formal organised networks and establishing communities (associations, ethnic or cultural organisations), but also, most importantly, it points to the informal networks and interpersonal relationships through and by which migrants organise their lives on a daily basis and at a practical level. This section is about the 'social space' for migrants in the city, *space* being here a metaphor referring to relational and organisational aspects of immigrants' incorporation. The section starts with an overview of organised community structures, such as ethnic and cultural associations, and an account of the conditions of participation and membership. It then deals with the nature of relationships developed in the host society.

8.2.1 *Emerging communities: collective organisations and patterns of membership*

Overall, the organisational performance of Albanian and Bulgarian migrants in Thessaloniki has been poor so far, and collective membership appears limited in scale. However, while Albanians have managed to form migrant and ethnic/cultural associations, this has not been the case for Bulgarians, who lack organised community structures – save one 'elite' Greco-Bulgarian organisation and the pre-existing networks of the Sarakatsani. Certainly, this is not a finding *per se*; apart from describing the present situation, one has to acknowledge the short history of immigration to Greece and the late regularisation measures. But a comparison with other migrant groups reveals important differences in the way and the speed by which collectively organised responses emerge: smaller migrant communities, equally 'new', managed to get organised in associations in a relatively short period of time and to achieve higher participation rates[11]. Local organisations of other migrant groups are presented in Table A7 (Appendix A), while Table 8.3 summarises the relevant information collected during the fieldwork for the groups studied here.

Take the Albanians' case first: throughout the past fifteen years, Albanian migrants have managed to establish various associations throughout Greece and at a national level. In these attempts, as mentioned in Section 5.2.2, they were supported by local organisations (left-wing political groups, trade-union bodies and NGOs). In addition, by 2002 there were four Albanophone newspapers and a magazine published in Athens, plus a website created recently, covering not only Albanian, but also Greek news and dedicating significant space to immigrants' issues, legal provisions and rights. At the time of the fieldwork, there were two migrant associations in Thessaloniki: the Albanian Association of Thessaloniki and the Greco-Albanian Association, 'Progress'. There are also a number of ethnic/cultural associations (Northern Epirote, Vlach), the most important of which is the long-es-

Table 8.3 *Immigrants' associations and community networks in Thessaloniki*

Name	*Type & Actions*	*Source*
Albanian Immigrants		
Albanian Association Thessaloniki	Migrant organisation (formed in 1998): campaigns, networking, information, cultural & social events, Albanian language school for migrants' children	information leaflet,
informal chat, observation		
Greco-Albanian Association, 'Progress'	Community association: promoting contact, social & cultural events	informal chat
Drita literary club	Local branch of an Albanian cultural organisation	information leaflet, interviewees
Epirote House (incorporating: Vlachophones' Union, Christians from Vlorë, Himara-Dhermi Union, Union of Friendship between Korçë and Thessaloniki	Federation of community organisations (founded in 1940): registration (initially), information (jobs, housing, legal matters), space for associations meetings/activities, social & cultural events	interview, newspapers,
leaflets, interviewees		
Association of Greeks from Sarandë, Gjirokaster and Delvina	Community association (formed in 1998), social & cultural events, campaigning for citizenship rights	interview
Other associations of ethnic Greek and Vlach Albanians	Community associations	
Several cafés/tavernas (across Thessaloniki)	Meeting points, socialisation	interviewees
Bulgarian Immigrants		
Greek-Bulgarian Friendship Association, 'Kyril and Methodi'	Association active since 1998: promoting contact, supporting Bulgarians in Thessaloniki and Greeks in Bulgaria, social & cultural events	interview
A central café-bar owned by a Bulgarian, several downtown cafés (St Dimitri area, railway station area)	Meeting points, social events	observation, interviewees

tablished federation Epirote House (*Epirotiki Estia*). Some artistic associations also exist (e.g. the *Drita* literary club). In addition, internal Albanian politics are reproduced among migrants in Greece and parties/organisations are likely to have representation in Thessaloniki[12]. Two examples require special attention, due to their size and role, but also because they were the ones more commonly mentioned by respondents: the Albanians' Association and Epirote House.

Epirote House was founded in 1940. It is not a migrant organisation *per se*, but rather a federation of several associations, including community associations of people originating from the Greek region of Epiros and three 'Northern Epirote' unions: (a) Vlachophones, (b) Christians from Vlorë and (c) Himara-Dhermi Union. Before the government managed to develop any policy for immigrants from Albania, Epirote House was issuing a 'registration document', initially to ethnic Greeks but later to non-ethnic-Greek Albanians too. Its main initiatives include advice on legal issues, assistance in health, education and welfare matters, job-finding, support of the ethnic Greek minority in Albania and the establishment of cultural relationships between the two countries. My informants claimed that since the early 1990s, about 145,000 Albanian citizens from all over the country have contacted Epirote House. However, its influence and activity have faded over time, due to the formation of other associations.

The Albanians' Association of Thessaloniki was founded by regular immigrants in 1998, with the support of the Anti-racist Initiative of Thessaloniki. It collaborates with many local organisations, anti-racist groups, political parties, NGOs and trade unions, as well as with other immigrant associations. It functions as an officially recognised institution, representing the Albanians of Thessaloniki in negotiations with local authorities and the government. It has ties with Albanians in the rest of Greece, mainly the Forum of Albanian Immigrants in Athens. Its initiatives include legal advice and social support, organisation of cultural events, celebration of national holidays, participation in cultural festivals and in anti-racist demonstrations. Since March 2001, it has run free courses in the Albanian language for immigrants' children (the teachers are Albanian volunteers).

However, participation rates remain low: only 18.1 per cent of the respondents were members or in contact with the Albanians' Association of Thessaloniki, which seems poor when compared to other migrant groups which are more devoted to maintaining community ties. The interviewees themselves appear aware of this fact and bring it out in their narratives, as Nadi and Adriana did in our joint conversation:

> The Albanians are not that organised ... others have tighter bonds, for instance, the Pontians have very tight bonds ... The Albanians are more individualists, each one for his family. They help each other, of course, there is solidarity, but they don't have that tight bond, with associations ... Let me tell you something that we say in Albania ... those who have tighter bonds are the ones from Korçë ... they come here with all their family, or their relatives. (Adriana)
>
> I know that there are associations here in Thessaloniki, but, how can I explain to you, even myself, I've learned about them accidentally. You can imagine that the majority won't know about them. In the beginning, when my life was only work I

> didn't know ... The Vlachs are more organised ... the Albanian Vlachs. (Nadi)

The quotes above point to a number of issues that were also touched on by other Albanian interviewees. Firstly, the situation of the migrants, in terms of legal status (particularly in the early years), work, free time and family responsibilities, does not allow for frequent participation. Secondly, the Albanian community is large and heterogeneous, so that ties amongst the Albanian population as a whole are weak and information is difficult to spread. Information depends on word of mouth, on certain TV/radio channels running programmes for immigrants and on Albanian newspapers/magazines, especially those published in Athens. Thirdly, membership in general might also be hindered by a certain degree of distrust by Albanians of collective institutions, as commented on by some interviewees, the origins of which have to be traced to the character of the regime under which they lived for years.

There is, though, an important distinction one should make: while *migrant* associations are poorly developed among Albanians in Thessaloniki, *ethnic* or *cultural* unions have emerged since the very beginning, initially assisted by, or incorporated into, existing organisations. Ethnic Greeks and Vlachs, in some cases people originating from the same area, appear much more disposed to form and participate in collective organisations, partly due to their smoother integration patterns, as well as because of strong perceptions of identity dating back to their years in Albania. There are several community associations in Thessaloniki (see Table 8.1), and participation rates among respondents approach 30 per cent. Such associations usually serve to maintain or enhance feelings of identity, sometimes along nationalistic or localist lines, but they also provide a basis for migrants of common origin to meet each other, to celebrate cultural events, to socialise or discuss matters related to their home places. To some extent, they have also managed to campaign (e.g. for citizenship rights) and/or support compatriots in various ways. However, while contact has been the case for many, especially in their early years in Greece, it seems that membership or frequent participation is not a lasting choice for the majority. An example is that of Panoraia, an ethnic Greek Albanian, who gave me the following account of her experience with that kind of association:

> *Epirotiki Estia* ... We contacted them initially, we would get information from there ... We used to be members ... mostly for social support ... it would help us, in the beginning, to find a job, to arrange our papers ... it would show us the way, where we should go for our papers ... consultancy and support ... There

> was another one [association] ... a Northern Epirote had opened it, and we all used to go there ... Because there was a Vlach association here [Vlachs from Gjirokaster], so after this had been established, the Northern Epirotes [ethnic Greeks from Gjirokaster] decided to establish their own association.

On the other hand, *migrant* associations (e.g. the Albanians' Association) have a different function: while, naturally, they operate as an identity-enforcing mechanism, they are more active in providing practical assistance and support, and in campaigning for migrants' rights in general, in collaboration with other migrant communities and with local organisations:

> We don't have much support. Only here, with our association, we are doing something ... I have been a member for the last one and a half years. We cannot make decisions, we only talk about what we face everyday ... the papers, for instance, or about the police ... This is a good thing, everybody should be united so we have a voice ... It's different when you are organised, you can express your complaints ... Our president, together with presidents [of associations of migrants] from other states, the Palestinians, for instance, they went to the ministry and elsewhere, [to campaign] for our problems, for the migrants ... [Our association] has done many things ... It has organised an anti-racist festival, a food festival, it has participated in other initiatives too. We do what we can. (Gjion)

Ethnic Greek Albanians also participate to a relatively high degree in Albanian migrants' associations (19.1 per cent). Membership rates are particularly high among migrants aged between 30-39 years (27.8 per cent) and among those with higher education (30.2 per cent); women, on the other hand, appear less likely to join (14.6 per cent of them do, compared to 19.6 per cent among men). Again, the motives vary, and membership, or contact, does not necessarily mean frequent or active participation: some migrants initially joined the Albanians' Association in order to benefit from specific services, for instance the Albanian language classes the association runs for children:

> I came here because I heard that there was an Albanian language school. My son knows reading and writing Albanian, but my daughter, who was five years old when she came here, didn't know how to read and write. She speaks a little ... So I wanted her to learn Albanian ... I've heard it on the TV, on ET3 channel,

> which I watch every Sunday, there is a program in Albanian. (Dimitri)

The picture varies considerably in the Bulgarians' case. The most important difference is that the community has no official 'representation' in Thessaloniki, despite the operation of two Bulgarian migrant associations in Athens and the publication of a number of newspapers there. There is only an 'elite' organisation, founded in 1998 under the name Greek-Bulgarian Friendship Association, 'Kyril and Methodi'. This maintains ties with the Bulgarian Consulate, and it is active in organising cultural events, in supporting both Bulgarian citizens living in Thessaloniki and Greeks in Bulgaria (students, businessmen); they once invited Bulgarian school children to a summer camp in Greece. However, as admitted by the president in our interview, the association mainly addresses mixed couples and elite migrants (businessmen, musicians, athletes) and only a handful of 'economic migrants' had approached them to date; the founders are themselves a mixed couple who run a private language school and a translation business. Among fieldwork participants, only three people, all women, had approached this association: a music teacher, a swimming coach, and a Sarakatsani woman who is married to a Greek and happens to live close by. On the other hand, ethnic Greeks are necessarily in contact with the Bulgarian Sarakatsani Association: registration with this organisation is a prerequisite for them in order to acquire the special annual visa they are entitled to; but again, membership does not translate into active participation for the majority.

In the absence of an institutionalised voice, a small Bulgarian community is concentrated around a central café-bar owned by a Bulgarian woman. This is primarily a place of meeting, socialisation and entertainment, but it also functions as a space of interaction, where information about jobs and housing circulates, and where newcomers can get useful advice regarding legal procedures and other issues. It is believed that there are similar places in other parts of the city[13]. Liliana's account, although speaking as the owner of the place, is enlightening and explains much:

> There is no solidarity. In Athens it's different ... People have fun, and they gather during the days they don't work ... to exchange information, to speak in their language, to have fun together ... Here they don't ... Because also in Athens, there are more women from Bulgaria who work there without their husbands, and many work as live-ins in houses, so when they have a day off, they go out, they go to these places and they have fun. Here in Thessaloniki, most of the people are together with their

> families, and they don't go out to places that often ... They mostly gather at home ... also to save money ... this is the most important reason.

8.2.2 *Dimensions of interpersonal relationships and informal social networks*

Given the weak organisational performance of the migrant groups studied in Thessaloniki and the limited membership and participation, it is rather migrants' *informal* networks that have played the most important role. Not only did many of the respondents have contacts in Thessaloniki before moving to the city, including relationships with Greek employers and friends who offered assistance in the beginning, but also the geographical patterns of the migrants' settlement in Greece (Section 4.2.2) and to an extent their spatial distribution in the city (Section 7.2.1) has depended on where their friends and relatives were located. In addition, the overwhelming majority made use of such relationships to find employment (Chapter 6), while some had been helped to access housing or health services (sections 7.1.2 and 8.1.1). Even more valuable in migrants' everyday lives, personal ties offered moral and material support at the very human level of socialisation and the spending of free time. As generally observed and has been theorised, social networks function as a source of *social capital* for individuals and households in order to overcome barriers imposed by the market (Portes 1995; see also Sassen 1995) and by an alien environment that sometimes turns hostile. The extent to which networks generate *effective* social capital depends on the size of the community and the density of ties (Portes 1995). To investigate the character of the migrants' social networks in our case, it is useful to pay closer attention to the nature of informal relationships formed and maintained by Albanians and Bulgarians in Thessaloniki, both between themselves and in relation to the local population.

Questionnaire data reveal little on this issue: they inform us that the majority of the respondents socialise mainly with people of the same origin, and nearly 14 per cent said they socialise with compatriots only, while about one in four has friends from other countries too. The age groups that appear more sociable are the youngest (below 30) and the oldest migrants (50 years old or more), reflecting their life phases and the constraints on the rest, who are busier with work and family responsibilities. Interview accounts are more valuable, revealing interesting qualitative elements in addition to highlighting the importance of interpersonal relationships for individual migrants. The extent to which these surpass the level of socialisation and are translated into mutual support and solidarity is a rather controversial issue. While most interviewees agree that there is a certain degree of support, others believe that reciprocity is not that strong. Katerina, an Albanian interviewee, mentioned: 'I would like it if there was more support between each other here, but there is not enough.'; and Vilco, a young Bulgarian man, agreed by telling me that: 'Not everybody does it ... some shut their eyes and pass by.' Interestingly, many of those who claimed that there is no solidarity and support attributed the phenomenon to national characteristics: Albanians described themselves as 'selfish' and 'individualistic' and Bulgarians talked about the 'curse' of not seeking to meet compatriots abroad. By contrast, Ani and Ivan, from Albania and Bulgaria respectively, had different opinions: 'There is this thing, with people from the same country, solidarity,'; 'It's natural ... to help each other.'

The existence of such contradictory perceptions can be explained also by looking at the character of social relationships migrants develop/maintain in Greece, which are either built upon pre-existing contacts/bonds or based on new ties formed in familiar environments (the neighbourhood, the workplace). When referring to 'compatriots', for example, most migrants meant basically or exclusively members of the extended family, and to a lesser degree people from the same town/village. On a second level, the workplace or the neighbourhood are the main places of interaction where new relationships are developed, with compatriots, Greeks or migrants from other countries:

> Well, yes, we help each other. Not everybody ... look ... I won't help you, I will help my sister's husband ... you know, between relatives, then friends, but mostly the relatives ... I don't want to have relationships with other Albanians ... If they are from Korçë, it's OK ... If they are from other places, no. (Andreas)
>
> Well, our Albanian friends, we know them from Albania. We haven't made new friends, only in a single case. (Edri)
>
> My boss helped me when I needed to move, to buy something. We have a friendly relationship ... We go out, have a coffee together, have lunch together ... I have friends from other countries ... I have both Greek and foreigners as close friends ... Not only from work ... Some of my friends were customers at the office. (Adriana)
>
> In my job, I have two or three friends, and we have a nice time ... Russians ... Greeks as well ... I don't have many relationships with [other] Albanians. (Mira)

Often, the relationships migrants maintain/develop in the host country are perceived according to binaries such as 'here and there' or 'now and then': many stressed such differences regarding the kind of relationships and the ways people tend to socialise with each other. On the negative side, it appears that relationships do change in the host country, and sometimes migrants are distanced from each other. The interviewees attributed this to their condition as migrants and the necessities and difficulties imposed by the situation: their work-loaded weekly programmes or their geographical dispersal across the city; some also mentioned factors pointing to the general issue of transition to the market economy and its effects:

> Relationships there used to be friendlier, truer ... but since money came, relationships have changed. (Emil)
> Here people are not so close. It used to be different in Bulgaria. People change when they leave their country ... you have envy starting then, you know, who has made more money. (Liliana)
> Well, one difference is that here they work more, so they can't meet each other that often, as they do in Albania ... relatives ... friends. (Dalina)

Again in contrast to perceptions like the ones above, some interviewees insisted that ties between relatives and friends became stronger abroad. In the words of Emil, from Albania, 'Usually [geographical] distance makes relationships tighter.' So tight that cultural and social differences are often eliminated, and people of different backgrounds are brought together: as a Bulgarian interviewee said, 'Now we all became one ... just because we are in a foreign country,' (Ivan). Many of the migrants interviewed agreed on that; Konstantina's opinion below draws the same picture:

> There are relationships built here ... even friendly ones, between people that wouldn't come into contact there ... just because you are in a foreign land ... I can see how my mother-in-law behaves. She has some relationships with people with whom she wouldn't have come into contact there ... You can't avoid inviting people, so a small community is being formed, also to celebrations, name days ... There is a commitment ... It is imposed because of the situation. (Konstantina)

Although contradictory, both situations might be the case for different individuals. The patterns of socialisation vary considerably according to age, gender, family status, geographical origin, education level or financial situation: families tend to socialise with other families; men with male colleagues, and women with female neighbours or mothers of their children's friends at school. In fact, it was sometimes the same people who argued both cases: migration and the conditions in Thessaloniki are responsible for both distance between people in general, but, on the other hand, they may result in closer bonds and more frequent contact among small groups. In addition, a more dynamic perspective distinguishes, once again, between past and present experiences, attributing the quality of the migrants' interpersonal relationships to the shifts in their legal status and living conditions, or in the responsibilities related to the life course. Some of the interviewees gave such accounts themselves:

> Things were going too fast here and each of us was trying to protect his home and his work ... this is why sometimes we cannot help each other ... if you don't help ... the other person might misunderstand. Competitive relationships are then developed, how much each one earns, etc. As time passes this changes, there are fewer people who stay, they get closer to each other ... When people are illegal, they tend to hide, to avoid others because they don't want to get in trouble ... now this has changed, but there's still not enough solidarity. (Milen)
>
> Well, I'm married ... I have Albanian friends, Greek friends. We go out together, at least we used to go out together, because now, since my child was born, we don't do it that often. (Nadi)

Finally, as made evident in the interview abstracts quoted above and as already mentioned in earlier parts of the thesis, Albanians and Bulgarians in Thessaloniki – like migrants anywhere – inevitably interact with the local population, which gradually results in the breakdown of cultural barriers and prejudices. Nearly 65 per cent of the respondents socialise with Greeks and some have close Greek friends[14]. Spaces of interaction include the neighbourhood, the school, etc., but the workplace appears to be the primary sphere where migrants and locals have the chance to meet, cooperate, talk and socialise. Among the interviewees, the majority of those who referred to close contacts with Greeks were talking about colleagues at work or employment-related acquaintances. It is also interesting how, in some cases, close personal relationships developed between immigrants and their employers, given that economic exploitation is so widespread. In a few instances, the employer's familiarity with the condition of the migrant, or with his/her language and culture, led to the development of personal relationships:

> My boss had been in Germany for twenty-three years, so he knew what it is to be an immigrant. (Adriana)
>
> [My second employer] he spoke Bulgarian, he helped me a lot, apart from that he taught me the job. He also taught me how

> things are here, because we had a different view then, it was different for us. (Milen)

In general though, it is contact between immigrants and locals – socialisation, friendship, even love affairs in a few cases – that appears to beat prejudice in the long run, or as some interviewees put it, 'as they get to know you', especially employers or colleagues at work, neighbours or younger people[15]. The majority of the interviewees themselves seemed to consider common ground more than the distance between themselves and the locals. Migrants of both nationalities referred to the cultural proximity between Greeks and Albanians or Greeks and Bulgarians as a factor facilitating interpersonal contact: a few mentioned a common Balkan identity or tradition, others highlighted age, school, or work. These issues lead us inevitably to an account of the migrants' perceptions of identity, which is given in the following section.

8.2.3 *Daily practices, coping strategies and issues of identity*

However important in relation to their living standards, any account of the material conditions of migrants' lives (as in Section 8.1.3) cannot alone give us a full picture of their incorporation patterns. As mentioned earlier, these patterns may principally reflect their financial situation, crucially determined by their position in the labour market; but they also may point to different consumption values and behaviours as well as to a variety of migratory strategies and plans. Other aspects of the migrants' daily routines, for instance language practices and the use of media, as well as certain strategies immigrants develop to cope in the host country through a (re)negotiation of their identities are also important in shaping migrants' lives in the host country.

Language, to start with, is a crucial issue. Apart from the necessity of speaking and communicating, many migrants tried hard to learn Greek, whether on their own or with the support of others; some also had the opportunity to take a course. To a lesser or a greater extent, language skills improve over time, with positive effects on several aspects of the migrants' everyday lives, as we have already seen[16]. A qualitative account would uncover further elements that play a role regarding non-material aspects of the incorporation process. Mixed language practices, whereby the native language is fused, to a degree, with that of the host society, are certainly among them, indicating the quasi-natural development of transnational daily realities. Also, migrants of ethnic Greek origin, given their 'comparative advantage' in language skills, exhibit a tendency to speak mostly Greek at home. Most importantly, the issue of the so-called 'second generation', the Greek-born or Greek-educated children, brings the language factor to the forefront of the dynamic, long-term character of incorporation. More likely to speak Greek at home, 'foreign', and particularly Albanian, kids impose on their parents the necessity of learning and practicing the language of the host country. The propensity of younger children to use primarily Greek at home and the consequent need of parents to practise the language is apparent in many of the interviewees' relevant statements:

> Well, we mostly speak in Greek, in order to help the children with school ... Sometimes we speak in Albanian too, but even when we speak in Albanian, most of the words are in Greek [she laughs]. Because, whether we want it or not, we live here, so we are going to speak in Greek. Me too, despite that I am older, I have forgotten many words, I don't know how to say certain things [in Albanian] ... and of course, I don't know Greek perfectly, but we speak. (Lela)
> With the children, we mostly speak Greek now, they talk faster in Greek. (Flora)
> We mostly speak Bulgarian [at home], but we also use Greek words, especially with the children. (Kostas)
> [We speak]Bulgarian at home, but we mix it with Greek words. My daughter speaks in Greek most of the time. (Maria)

For the older generation, perhaps more concerned about identity issues, 'losing their origins' appears to be a problem: language was the most important, if not the only, element that most interviewees insisted should be 'preserved' for as long as they were in Greece, speaking both about themselves and also about their children (with the exception of some ethnic Greek Albanians). As mentioned in Section 8.2.1, the Albanians' Association runs Albanian language courses on a weekly basis to combat this loss of language, and for some migrants this was their only reason for approaching the association.

An additional qualitative element is the issue of free time. In sections 7.2.3 and 8.2.2, we have seen aspects of the immigrants' entertainment options and social lives in Thessaloniki. The financial burden, however, does not allow going out frequently, and naturally people need to devote some time to themselves and to their families. I have talked about the 'home-to-work' space that shapes the daily routines of most of the participants, especially the older ones and those who lead family lives; in this respect, there is little difference between migrants and locals. Staying at home is an opportunity to rest and to be with the family; reading, listening to the radio, watching TV, or talking on the phone are the most common daily habits, as well as helping the children with their homework (especially mentioned by female interviewees). Media use, apart from acquiring information on daily matters and/or entertainment, has two additional special functions: it becomes a link with the country of origin and a source of information about issues specific to immigrants in Greece. Again, the sample is characterised by great variety: many read Albanian and Bulgarian newspapers imported from the home countries, or even the Greek dailies, while some also buy the newspapers published by and/or for immigrants in Greece. Younger migrants and those who are more educated, especially those working in offices and qualified jobs, also mentioned the use of the Internet, although this appears very limited overall. Bulgarian migrants living on the outskirts to the north of the city said they can listen to Bulgarian radio stations, and some can get Bulgarian channels on the TV. And there are migrants of both nationalities who can access Albanian or Bulgarian TV channels from Thessaloniki using satellite antennas, although such practices were very rare among my participants.

The extent to which Greek newspapers are read depends on language fluency and free time willingly spent on this, but fieldwork information is rather poor on this issue. On the other hand, there is a wide selection of imported newspapers that are easily accessible and widely read, although some interviewees (especially ethnic Greek Albanians) appeared reluctant or 'not interested', limiting their information about their home places to what their relatives tell them on the phone. Immigrant newspapers published in Athens are also popular, mainly because they publish detailed information on policy developments, legal procedures, entitlement to rights, etc., summarised in their own language. These newspapers also provide a basis for the consolidation of migrant communities, as described in Section 8.2: they have articles specific to immigrants' lives and problems; they offer space for communication and debate on political and cultural issues; they include information on social/cultural events, and give details regarding the activities of associations.

Nevertheless, it is television that seems to be the most widespread entertainment option for the majority, and the basic information source present in many migrant households. The interview material reveals that channel and programme preferences might be very diverse, but the role of television in helping individual migrants to familiarise themselves with the language and the mentality of the host country is important. The interviewees are aware of the negative stereotypes present in the media discourse (see Section 5.2.1), bitterly described by Albanians since they are the 'usual suspects'. But on the other hand, any positive reference to immigrants was mentioned proudly by the interviewees: from little stories of honest foreign workers taking a wallet they found to the police, to the popular 2002 TV series about a love story between an Albanian and his boss's wife (see Chapter 5, footnote

14). Negative images, however, are still commonplace (especially about Albanians) not only in the media discourse, but also most importantly in the public's perception of the immigrant 'other'. How do migrants cope on a daily basis with such stereotypes? The interviewees' narratives reveal a multiplicity of reactions to the host society's xenophobic stances:

> I feel bad ... I am getting angry ... It really hurts me. (Panoraia)
> I don't feel bad, I just don't care ... There are some of our people who get angry ... and ask them, 'Why did you say this?' but I don't care. (Ferin)
> Before, I used to get angry, because you try to prove to yourself that you know, that you have graduated from school, that you have much knowledge and you want to make it here ... and there are some people who put obstacles in your way, who don't let you stand up. (Milen)

What is interesting is the way migrants learn to live with this reality: in their narratives it is clear that they do not feel happy about it, but they do not picture themselves as victims, at least not in the majority of cases. Sometimes they even make fun of the vagueness of the stereotypes about them; I was told some of the common 'jokes' about Albanians by a couple of Albanian participants. An evocative example of such an easy-going approach is given below with Lefteris' sarcastic response to his neighbours' derogatory ignorance:

> I was talking to a neighbour, a racist. He asked me 'Did you have hens in Albania?', 'We did.', 'Did they make eggs?', 'No, they make cows,' I answered.

However, xenophobia, and Albanophobia in particular, is so widespread that many Albanian immigrants have developed a series of strategies in order be accepted and to smooth their relationships with locals. Some have been baptised Orthodox (10.9 per cent of the sample), some have changed their names into Greek ones (16.7 per cent), some simply hide their religious beliefs (4.3 per cent), while others present themselves as of ethnic Greek origin (4.3 per cent)[17]. The role of migrant networks is obvious in such cases: the pioneers had opened a path, which the newcomers followed. Names were crucially indicative of ethnic origin, and a Greek or Orthodox name could be a 'passport' to ethnic Greek status. Names are changed slightly, when there are similar-sounding Greek ones (Illir – Elias), or completely, when they sound foreign or Muslim (Rushan – Ghiorgos, Fatme – Maria); in some cases Christian or Greek-sounding names have been kept without change (Mimoza, Mira, Edi), while names with a Greek version are simply translated (Irena – Erini). Bulgarian migrants too, in some cases, adopt names sounding more 'Greek' (Lioupa – Eleni, Milen – Makis, Vilco – Vaggelis), but this comes after their employers' initiative to call them something easier to pronounce. There are people (of both nationalities) who use a different name at work, or when socialising with Greeks, and their 'real' one at home or among friends and compatriots.

Baptism, on the other hand, appears as a 'uniquely Greek' expression of intercultural relationships between immigrants and locals. The godfathers are Greeks, friends, neighbours, bosses or colleagues, who usually propose the baptism of migrants and/or their children themselves. It is usually Albanians of Muslim, and to a lesser extent Catholic, origin who choose this strategy, not necessarily as a result of religious faith:

> We wanted our children to be baptised, not because we are very religious, but simply because you feel racism in this field too ... so if they are baptised they'll have fewer problems. So, when we went there [to the church], they told us that the mother at least has to be baptised, so it was necessary for me to get baptised ... and I did it, not because I was feeling it. (Edri)

From the immigrants' point of view, this practice is certainly a strategy of adjustment to the host country's culture, in order to 'make things easier' for them or their children. However, in some cases it may reflect actual religious feelings and an internal need to search for their roots, or to discover faith and customs that were banned in the home country. In fact, the rediscovery of religion is a general feature among the populations of the former Eastern Bloc, and is equally present amongst some Bulgarian immigrants as well. The examples below are characteristic:

> I have adopted a few things here because I liked them ... They mostly have to do with customs related to religion, which didn't exist there, since religion was prohibited. All those things that entered our life, the celebrations ... You try to put into your life what was missing ... faith. (Konstantina).
>
> It is important, because ... from the moment I was born, we did not know what religion was, since Hoxha destroyed everything and we had no faith. It is a great emptiness that we still feel these days ... [Now] I go to church, I have been to the monasteries on Mount Athos. (Spyros)

> I always ... felt that I had missed something ... because of the fact I was not baptised ... I grew up in a family of baptised Orthodox, but the issue of religion was ... not a taboo, but we wouldn't talk about that, it didn't exist ... I first entered a church after the death of my grandmother to light a candle, and since then I never stopped doing this ... Ten years later I came here, and I had this thought in my mind, I wanted to get baptised. (Irina)

However, religious expression is not the same for all; while Greece, as a host society, has addressed the needs of those who revert or convert to the Orthodox Church well, other religions, and particularly Muslims, are not easily accepted or welcomed. It is true that a large share of the migrants in Greece originates from countries traditionally belonging to the Eastern Church, and these are even more represented in Thessaloniki. It is also true that the host society's xenophobic perception of Albanians as mainly Muslims is misleading, putting an additional negative element to the image of the 'Albanian': in the Albanian context, 'Muslim' is more of a cultural category than a religious one, and the inheritance from this 'atheist nation' is confirmed by the share of the 'not religious' in my sample, and by the high degree of religious adaptability of Albanians. But the rediscovery of religion, even if only as a point of reference for many, applies also in the case of Muslim Albanians, who, together with migrants from countries sharing the Islamic tradition, face hostility and lack the space to express their beliefs. Among the Albanian respondents, 9.4 per cent said their religious needs were not satisfied in Thessaloniki and 8.7 per cent complained about discriminatory attitudes against them for being Muslims or simply not religious.

One should thus consider that what has been labelled here as 'integration strategies' are to an extent *imposed*. Baptism or name-change partly reflect the power of ethnicity and the continuing (in fact, reemerging) importance of the Orthodox religion in the Greek collective imagination, as well as the xenophobic motives that push employers to call their Albanian employee 'Nikos' rather than 'Ferin', or inspire neighbours to baptise the Albanian children next door. Even when the intentions are good and indicate a willingness to help, the Balkan 'other' is somebody inferior.

Finally, ethnic Greek migrants, despite their privileged position in respect to both legal status and acceptance by the locals, find themselves set into a particular situation of conflicting traditions. Both Greek-Albanians and the Sarakatsani had the same complaint: back home they were the 'Greeks', and in Greece they are the 'Albanians' or the 'Bulgarians'. Stories told by the interviewees highlighted aspects of what some described as 'identity confusion': in their daily interaction with locals, they feel they have to support their Albanian or Bulgarian compatriots, while at the same time they have to (re)confirm and explain their 'Greekness'. However, acculturation and acceptance by the locals appear more straightforward in their case: the higher degree of adaptability and the better conditions observed among ethnic Greek Albanians should be, partly at least, attributed to their more favourable legal status.

As coping strategies, name-change and baptism imply a voluntary shift in the cultural identity of the migrant, an abandonment of the old identity and a rather opportunistic adjustment to what is perceived as the host society's culture and beliefs. This (re)negotiation of identity is not an easy path psychologically or socially; it entails personal and social conflicts, as the 'code switch' is neither simple nor straightforward, and it does not always have the expected outcomes[18]. To an extent, these practices point to the transnational and hybrid experiences lived by many migrants, especially from Albania. Not only when 'Nikos' becomes Ferin when work is finished, or when Orthodox Maria celebrates Easter in Thessaloniki and then, as Fatme, visits her Muslim relatives in Elbasan during Ramadan. Or when ethnic Greek migrants feel confused by being treated as 'Albanians' or 'Bulgarians' in the country they consider their ancestral home, while they were the 'Greeks' in Albania and Bulgaria. More crucially, because these examples are only part of the overall common and simultaneous reference to both 'here' and 'there', to aspects of both cultures that fuse into one, with some elements lost and others gained throughout this process. Albanian migrants, for instance, especially men, referred to '*besa*' as an exclusive feature of what it means to be Albanian. *Besa* is a cultural notion that summarises several virtues of the 'Albanian soul', such as the word of honour, true friendship and 'masculinity'. Bulgarian migrants, on the other hand, would highlight the stubborn nature of Bulgarian people, explaining how it becomes a positive element indicating self-discipline and consistency. At the same time, both would reject certain elements (e.g. talking loudly in the street, or 'being a brute') and adopt new ones they found attractive in the host society (language, religion, traditions, lifestyle, etc.). All these indicate the multiple and fluid character of 'identity', its constant (re)negotiation, and its fragmentation according to the different spheres of life one refers to.

9 Migration and social change: revisiting theory

This chapter addresses the empirical material from a theoretical perspective. Its aims are to summarise the key findings, highlight the main issues raised and frame the basic arguments stemming from the research. This is done in the first part of the chapter, where the migrants' multiple pathways to incorporation are outlined and the main explanatory factors are discussed. Early in the thesis, it was argued that the study of contemporary migration can help us understand broader phenomena. In the case of Greece too, migration is part of a complex set of interconnected social processes, many of which take place in the context of globalisation. On these grounds, the second part of the chapter aims to explore the international relevance of what is taking place in Thessaloniki and to indicate key points as areas for future research. The results are discussed in a comparative theoretical perspective by looking at the experiences of other urban societies beyond the Greek case and by interpreting them in the light of theory: what happens 'here' happens in similar ways in other places too[1]. The chapter ends by identifying the elements indicating the third component in the title of the thesis, i.e. the trends of socio-economic change in relation to migration.

9.1 Fences and bridges: some interpretations

What the research and analysis generally show is that there are no distinct uniform patterns of 'integration' or 'exclusion'. How can we speak about 'exclusion' from the labour market when there are no signs of structural unemployment and the labour-market trajectories of many migrants appear relatively successful? To what extent can 'exclusion' describe the present situation, with increasing numbers acquiring legal status, hence enjoying almost equal access to benefits and services? After all, as we have seen, even without documents, migrants managed not simply to survive, but also to improve their position. Discrimination and negative stereotypes are still in place – but do they really affect immigrants as deeply in daily matters as in the recent past? In contrast, many of the participants express positive reactions, have good relationships with locals and claim feelings of identification with Greece as a host society and with Thessaloniki as 'their place'. Yet, one should be conscious of not idealising positive steps and improvements in individual cases. To what extent can we speak about integration when the majority of immigrants is in an ambivalent legal position of temporary residence? What kind of integration is it that keeps migrants at the bottom of the social hierarchy, doing the 'dirty' jobs for modest rewards? And certainly, xenophobia, despite its decreasing influence on individual experiences, is now well-embedded in the host society's culture, stimulating tensions on certain occasions. Let us recall the recent events that followed a football match between the Albanian and Greek national teams in Tirana (September 2004): thousands of migrants gathered in the streets to celebrate their team's victory, but the reaction of the defeated Greeks resulted in violence in Athens and elsewhere. Not to mention examples from the numerous tragic individual stories that frequently appear in the media: situations of terribly poor conditions, cases of extreme exploitation, accidents in the workplace without compensation, unresolved problems with the leviathan of the Greek state, unjustified expulsions – the list could be endless.

Given the above, different typologies of incorporation can be observed. Some migrants, especially Greek-Albanians, seem to be moving towards assimilation, gradually absorbed by the host society's dominant culture: they maintain minimum contacts with their home places and make plans to stay forever; they try to adapt by socialising mostly with locals and by speaking only Greek at home. Some others are partially integrated: their social lives are based on community contacts and they plan to stay for a set period, whether this might be determined by the accomplishment of projects or by their children's graduation from school. While minority in my sample, there are also apparently a large number of migrants, as shown in other studies[2], that seem to be extremely marginalised and desperate, while a few might be involved in crime and illicit activities. Lastly, especially regarding the groups studied, a figure that might prevail in the future is that of the 'transnational' migrant, who frequently travels back and forth and maintains contacts/relationships in both countries, actually leading a life between 'here' and 'there'. Clearly, there is not an archetypal immigrant in Greece; even the above typologies might apply to one single person's experiences over time, or to different members of a migrant family. During the past fifteen years or so, contradictory forces seem to have been in place. On the one hand, structural, political and institutional processes have been pushing migrants towards the social margin, denying them rights, confining them to exploitation, generating xenophobia. On the other, factors ranging from agency to socialisation and interaction with locals have helped them to overcome difficulties and facilitate their trajectories within the host society. The first two parts of this section are concerned with interpreting such contradictory processes, which ultimately shed light on the two faces of immigrants in Greece, who are at the same time victims and actors. The third part sums up the key explanatory factors in the study of incorporation.

9.1.1 *How 'host' becomes 'hostile': the migrants as victims*

How is the 'other' perceived in the host society? Which is his/her structural position, and why? Answering these questions on the basis of the rather copious empirical material presented in the previous chapters has not been an easy task. In order to interpret the main findings, it is useful to employ two key sociological concepts: roles and stances. On the one hand, the host society has developed particular stances towards immigrants – attitudes and perceptions, but also policy measures and treatment by the authorities. On the other, immigrants came to perform specific roles within the host society, while they have also been denied certain roles. We can identify three basic aspects of the migratory experience that arise out of specific roles and stances, on the basis of which immigrants in Greece are essentially victimised: they are aliens, workers and strangers. These attributes emerge from a complex set of structures and relations embedded in the socio-economic, political-institutional and cultural-ideological spheres. The socio-spatial context forms the terrain upon which these are reflected.

The other as alien is defined by the policy framework and its implementation. The term 'alien' (*αλλοδαπόσ*), extensively used in legal documents and the public discourse, contains certain connotations for the migrants themselves and for Greece as a host society. It came to mean specifically the immigrant – not the 'foreigner' in general – and it is connected to all the attributes the migrant is supposed to entail: they take jobs away from natives, they are responsible for falling wages, they might be criminals; above all, they do not belong to 'us'. In its first phase of development, the *laissez-faire* approach of the legal framework left hundreds of thousands of immigrants without the opportunity to regularise. An alien then was thus de facto 'illegal' (*παράνομοσ*), i.e. someone who unavoidably flouts the law, an offender. Among the factors that have conditioned policy-making during the past decade, the one most apparent at the initial stage has been an institutional-bureaucratic one, characterised by traditional structures and xenophobic attitudes (Baldwin-Edwards & Fakiolas 1999), as analysed in Section 5.1 with respect to the migrants' own experiences. The state was not prepared to deal with the new situation and the initial reaction was marked by blindness, tight control, police brutality, arrests and deportations, as well as by bureaucracy, inefficiency and national-identity considerations. On this basis, aliens became invisible 'non-persons'[3], living in constant hiding and chased by the police. This situation has obviously changed, after two regularisation programmes (that had already taken place before my fieldwork) during which the vast majority of the participants had the opportunity to obtain legal status – not to mention two more limited amnesties that followed my research. Even so, most of the migrants indeed remain 'aliens', since they are doomed to an ambiguous legal position that does not guarantee them viable long-term residence; and there is certainly a minority of immigrants who remain irregular (e.g. recently arrived ones), or who swing back to illegality due to an inability to find registered employment.

However, not all immigrants are necessarily 'aliens'. The selectivity of Greek immigration policy, based on perceptions of national identity, has led to a distinction between good and bad 'others'. Those who belong to 'us' are not treated as 'aliens' because they form part of the nation: they are ethnic Greeks (*ομογενείς*). But even in this case, selectivity has its own hierarchy: different measures are applied to ethnic Greeks from Albania and Bulgaria. Taking also into account the more privileged status of Pontians, it is clear that the fragmented legal framework has contributed to the *ex post* construction of various categories of migrants, with direct effects on both integration processes and the dynamics of migration as such. We have seen, for example, that entitlement to annually renewable visas determined cyclical migration patterns for Sarakatsani Bulgarians. Also, the favourable legal conditions for ethnic Greeks have led 'other' Albanians to the adoption of specific immigration and integration strategies: changing names to sound Greek, presenting themselves as Northern Epirotes and converting to Orthodoxy – the religion of ethnic Greeks – through baptism.

The ideological-cultural reception of the migrants has constructed *the other as stranger*, referring to the concept introduced by Simmel (1950)[4]. The 'stranger' is the 'other within', who is close to 'us' and participates in 'our' society, but whose relationships with the rest of the group are also marked by distance, since s/he does not belong to 'us' and can withdraw at any time. Immigrants are 'strangers' by definition: they are foreigners, i.e. nationals of some other state, they come from a distant place. But they are also 'strangers' in the theoretical sense, because they are 'different'; they possess attributes that are 'strange' to us, differentiating them and portraying them as 'others'. They have to abandon these attributes in order to be able to share 'our' cultural models and adapt to conditions 'here'. When they do not succeed, they become scapegoats, bearing the responsibility for all our misfortunes that supposedly stem from their presence. Immigrants in Greece are perceived as illiterate peasants fleeing from a state of 'backwardness'; they are seen as criminals by birth, and thus untrustworthy. The Balkan 'other' in particular, perhaps precisely because of physical and cultural similarities, has been strategically constructed as someone different, and thus estranged from 'us'.

For a population that has perceived itself as ethnically and culturally homogeneous for nearly a century and that is now confronted directly with the 'other', immigration challenges widespread notions of belonging and perceptions of identity. The emphasis on the supposedly distinctive culture of the 'other' is characteristic of the new racist phenomenon in Europe, which emphasises cultural rather than biological criteria, as in the past[5]. But the position and role of immigrants within the social structure itself contributes to deepening prejudices, uncovering the class-based roots of racism[6]. A segment of the working class is pushed towards the margins and its social condition is linked to its ethnic origin. Thus the term 'immigrant' (or 'alien') comes to signify a specific category, which is ultimately constructed in a paradoxical way, because it contains both unifying and differentiating elements (Balibar & Wallerstein 1990). Despite their heterogeneity, 'immigrants' are defined as a single group, clearly distinguished from 'us'. Interestingly, those participants in the research who have been described as 'elites' *do not* actually think of themselves as 'immigrants'.

The class of the 'other' is thus determined by the productive structures and relations and by their dynamics of change. The 'other' is basically a worker, s/he works hard, doing any job, in harsh conditions and for little money. Occasionally s/he might be judged responsible for the rise in unemployment, the fall of real wages, the expansion of the informal economy. However, there is a particular *space* in the labour market, which has 'accommodated' migrant labour. This space lies on the boundaries between the formal and informal sectors, mostly in the latter – although such boundaries are not marked by distinctive lines. But it *has not* been created by immigration: rather it predated it in different forms and it now expands, taking on new characteristics with the advent of economic restructuring. It took shape because of the increased demand for cheap and flexible labour, primarily by SMEs, on the one hand, and by private households, on the other, for certain labour-intensive productive, but also reproductive, activities. This demand has risen due to a series of factors ranging from the competitive crisis of SMEs to the expansion of the middle classes; it now persists because of the availability of cheap labour offered by migrants and the increasing unwillingness of locals to perform certain types of work. It is characteristic of a context of labour-market segmentation, which it further reinforces and reproduces. Both an outcome and a cause of the contradictions between labour-intensive and capital-intensive activities and formal and informal sectors, labour-market segmentation leads to the polarisation of the labour force, which is more and more expressed along ethnic lines.

The work of immigrants has been crucial for the survival of SMEs. Many businesses in the traditional manufacturing sectors (food and beverages, clothing, etc.) – particularly important in Thessaloniki and northern Greece – have been saved from shutting down or moving abroad, although such trends persist. But immigrants also widely perform 'supporting' or 'assisting' tasks and do the hard work in construction and low-level services at a lower cost: they climb up ladders, they keep the shop, they clean, they load and unload the stock[7]. Given the family character of many SMEs, their employment 'releases' household members from the tasks *they* would normally do. Especially in cities, even the more 'advanced' economic activities, such as the leisure and tourism industries or the financial sector, are in need of this 'supporting' work: somebody has to clean, to deal with repairs, etc. This does not mean of course that the indigenous labour supply for such jobs has disappeared; but it gradually shrinks or moves towards supervisory positions. With rising educational and living standards, locals go for the difficult manual tasks less and less, while fewer will now work there for low wages and without insurance, thereby 'creating' a space for immigrant labour. On the other hand, the demand of households for personal services is mostly related to reproductive activities: housework, cleaning, childminding, caring for the elderly or the disabled. The gendered division of labour, a result of both productive-reproductive relations in the Greek social formation and traditional perceptions of the position of women in society, is reproduced with the work of female migrants who perform the tasks exclusively done by wives, mothers or grandmothers. The employment of migrants counterbalances and further facilitates the exodus of women from home, especially for the middle and upper classes – a trend common across Southern Europe (see King & Zontini 2000). But male immigrants too offer private supporting services related to the household's quality of life at relatively low cost: they do repair work, they paint, they put tiles on the floor or on the roof and look after the garden. Clearly, migrants do the jobs done by household members in the past, or jobs that were not done at all.

These findings suggest that most immigrants perform *specific roles* within the Greek social structure, as servants or manual workers, 'liberating', in a sense, Greek men from repair activities, Greek women from housework, small shop-owners from the toughest manual tasks, etc. and helping small enterprises to stay in business. With migrants doing the hard work, an increased number of locals save valuable time and are now free to deal with their personal development and to engage in leisure activities, which expands socio-economic polarisation at the cultural level (Psimmenos 1995). Migrants, on the other hand, find themselves in a particularly vulnerable position due to institutional and structural factors: both their problematic status (clandestine initially, temporary and ambiguous currently) and the structure of the Greek economy itself, as well as the necessity that led them to emigrate, do not allow them much leeway to avoid such a role. A new 'servant' class has thus been created – working hard, informally hence flexibly, and with very modest financial rewards – which is differentiated *horizontally* from the indigenous labour force simply because it concentrates distinguishable ethnic and cultural characteristics and its members are not citizens. In addition, the imaginary 'space' reserved for migrants in the labour market is translated into the actual space they occupy in the urban geography and the housing market. The studies of Psimmenos (1995; 1998; 2001) and Iosifides & King (1998) on immigrants in Athens draw a dark picture of old, low-quality properties, sometimes long-abandoned or not built for accommodation, in working-class neighbourhoods gradually emptied of their previous inhabitants, which turn into busy and ugly run-down districts forgotten by planners.

Venturing an anachronistic parallelism, it would not be an exaggeration to argue that the living and working conditions of many migrants, especially throughout the 1990s, bring to mind those of the early industrial working class, given the largely different socio-economic context of today (e.g. decreased importance of industrial capital and employment in manufacturing). To paraphrase a saying of Marx (1979: 85), a new class has emerged, which 'has to bear all the burdens of society without enjoying its advantages'. This 'class' though is not *vertically* differentiated from the working class as a whole (even if today such terms and boundaries are rather vague and difficult to define), but it is located at the bottom of the social pyramid, and it is notable because of its ethnic/cultural origin. Of course, clear-cut divisions are simply schematic terms to allow interpretation: the Greek petit entrepreneur or middle-class woman who might employ a migrant can hardly be described as 'capitalists'. But there are obvious exploitative relations between bosses and workers, or 'patrons' and 'servants'. Such exploitative relations are extended in the housing market, and, in a similar way, we could parallel the migrants' conditions to those of the early proletariat (Engels 1993). Immigrants' position in the urban housing markets of today's Greece resembles to an extent the situation prevalent during the first wave of urbanisation in Athens, nearly 150 years ago. 'The emergent working class was thrust into an economy that was ready to exploit them not just as labour but also as tenants. They ... had to adapt to a speculative land and housing market' (Leontidou 1990: 63). Of course, here as well differences are obvious: then the popular strata were coming from rural areas, now many immigrants originate from cities; Athens then was being built, Thessaloniki now expands; the urban economy was at the pre-industrial stage, now it is undergoing trends of post-industrial restructuring. What this argument implies is that the structural position of migrants as a new manual/servile class has a clear spatial face, which also reflects widespread prejudices towards 'aliens' or 'strangers' through discrimination in the housing market.

9.1.2 *Networks, strategies and identity: the migrants as actors*

In the shadow of the state, partly neglecting and largely repressing the immigrants at least until the end of the past decade, the market has crucially conditioned migrants' lives in Greece. The *labour market*, because since the beginning there has never been an issue of work availability, given the shortages in specific sectors, the rising demand for flexibility, the nature of the informal sector, etc. The *housing market*, because it seems to have *counterbalanced* over time problems of discrimination and non-acceptance. But, since the market generates relations of exploitation, how can we explain the gradual improvement of living and working conditions? And what else does the migratory experience entail, apart from work and home? Rather, it is in the *non-market* factors, in the reality of migrants' everyday lives, that we can 'capture' their lifeworld and understand their trajectories in the host society and their pathways to incorporation, especially during the period the majority were irregular, but also in recent years, after repeated regularisation schemes.

The discussion in the previous section touched thus on one side of the coin. It portrayed immigrants in Greece as 'victims': of the legal framework and the way it is implemented; of xenophobia, discrimination and racism; of a segmented labour market that reserves hard and badly paid jobs for them; of socio-spatial structures leading them to low-quality housing in deprived areas. However, the experience of the fieldwork itself and the overall findings of the research came to dissolve another widespread perception of the 'other': that of the marginalised individual who leads a miserable life. In contrast to what is generally believed and despite their vulnerable and legally ambiguous position, immigrants make their own progression within the host society. As shown throughout the analysis, many tend to follow upward social routes. Clearly, it was only when the option of regularisation emerged that a way out of marginalisation became possible. But immigrants have not remained passive in this process. They actively and consciously resisted, struggling not only to survive, but also to change their immediate situation. They developed collective and individual ways to smooth over the difficulties and progress with their lives.

Based on their networks and on informal practices and adaptation strategies, they have managed to organise their lives in various ways.

At the collective level, migrants form associations and get organised in order to claim rights, or to facilitate their needs of socialisation, belonging and identity. As we have seen, organised action has not been the case for the majority of immigrants in the groups studied. Participation in associations remains low among Albanians, while Bulgarians have no organised community in Thessaloniki. The limited time period, the late regularisation measures and the fact that there were no preceding migration streams explain this to some extent. At a grassroots level though, migrants meet together in specific places, forming small informal communities. The networks of migrants provide the basis for solidarity, mutual assistance and socialisation, functioning as sources of information, means of job-finding, ways of accessing the housing market, etc. Social networks seem to become both denser and more open, moving beyond contacts based on kinship or place of origin and expanding towards the broader migrant community and the local population. Relationships with Greeks start in the workplace, often with employers (despite exploitative relations), or in the neighbourhood. They further facilitate migrants' pathways of access to various spheres of social life, from health and welfare services to mainstream entertainment choices. In an almost natural way, the obstacles imposed by prejudice are in practice overcome through everyday life and interaction.

At the individual level, migrants appear conscious of the sacrifices they have to make in order to improve their conditions and/or accomplish their projects. Whether they intend to stay in Greece or go back at some point, whether they have family to support or they simply want to 'live their lives', they appear certain about their decisions and plans. The migratory journey is not necessarily perceived as a mechanistic exodus from economic hardship, but it rather entails a belief that it will help migrants to improve their position, not simply in terms of survival, but also in respect to lifestyle options (see Kosic & Triandafyllidou 2003, on Albanians in Italy). Immigrants cope with reality in various ways: some appear to believe strongly in their own capacities, while others rediscover religion as a source of hope; many build on the 'better days' that will come in the future for them or their children, while others seem to be enjoying life at present. In general, migrants try to adapt and be accepted by developing specific integration strategies: baptism, name-change, learning the language, encouraging children to do well at school, etc. Lacking much in the way of financial resources, they enjoy open public spaces, turning them into lively meeting points. Gradually though, they get accustomed to the dominant Greek entertainment habits. They manage to make their way through closed doors through informal or alternative paths, helped by Greek acquaintances, accessing emergency hospital services, travelling back and forth for health or other reasons, etc. Travel and contact with the home countries and mixed cultural practices facilitate their trajectories in Greece in many ways.

As time passes, and especially when the condition of illegality is replaced by regular status, migrants acquire the self-confidence necessary for them to (re)negotiate their wages and conditions of employment, while some exercise self-employment or entrepreneurship. Entrepreneurship itself can be seen as a strategy for integration. Although there are not particular types of 'ethnic businesses' that are characteristic of these two migrant groups, the limited relevant cases could be possible indicators of a trend that will perhaps be more prominent in the near future. The cultural proximity between Albanians, Bulgarians and Greeks does not allow for the emergence of visible specialised ethnic businesses, as in other cases, apart from a small range of kiosks and shops trading goods from the home countries (Albanian coffee, foreign newspapers, etc.), although in many cases the owners are Greeks. The only distinct type of 'ethnic' enterprise noticed is that of translation businesses, which respond to a demand generated by immigrants, but gradually also covers the needs of locals who have contacts of various kinds with the countries migrants come from (partners, businessmen, investors, students). There are though other, less distinct niches where immigrants increasingly practice self-employment, usually in professions they have done as waged workers, such as undertaking projects in construction, painting and house-repair.

The previous section posed the question of how the host society perceives the 'other'. Here this should be inverted: How do migrants perceive themselves? How do they understand their experience? The diversity of experiences, of smaller or greater difficulties and of individual projects, personal stances or lifestyles imply a variety of reactions. Migrants who experienced exploitation or unfortunate brushes with the police tend to express negative feelings, while those who found things relatively easier appear more positive, or even grateful towards the host country. But whatever the individual migratory journeys, immigrants see themselves as neither victims, nor as 'others'. Although they stress the practical problems generated by the key exclusionary mechanisms (policy, xenophobia, exploitation), the general feedback from most of the participants has been an overall positive assessment of their experience. Among respondents, nearly half of the Albanians and over 60 per cent of the Bulgarians said that they were generally 'satisfied' with their lives, while only 16.7 and 11.5 per cent respectively said they were unhappy. Fulfilment and pride for all that they had managed to achieve 'with their own hands' seem to compensate for earlier harsh conditions. Relationships built with Greeks 'as they get to know you' and personal ways of coping reduce the psychological cost of xenophobic hostility. Feelings of belonging and identification now include Greece and Thessaloniki. The main obstacle to security and long-term plans thus remains the ambiguous legal framework. The interview segments below, a synthesis from various narratives, are characteristic of the multiple ways migrants understand their position and their identity:

> I don't feel a migrant, I feel like a local ... Neither a local, I don't feel this ... between an immigrant and a local ... You are a stranger anyway, but I couldn't say that everything is black ... You even feel a local, some people make you feel like that ... On the other hand, your country attracts you, you cannot avoid this ... I don't feel like a visitor, because my wife and I, we are seriously planning, we are thinking of settling here ...

9.1.3 *Explanatory factors in the study of incorporation*

The empirical findings confirm more or less what has already been pointed out by other studies and by official data. This compensates for the statistical limitations of the quantitative material and allows for generalisations regarding the patterns of incorporation, especially in what concerns the local context, on the basis of the qualitative elements. In general, it seems that the 'price' of Greece's transition to a migrant receiving country was high, and to a great extent it has been paid by the migrants themselves. Although the situation continues to be difficult, the findings indicate a tendency towards stable employment, sometimes better jobs and certainly better working conditions over time. The option of regularisation should be regarded as a turning point in this process. This may be translated into upward social mobility, as it is usually accompanied by longer-term and better-quality housing and an overall improvement in living conditions. My analysis reveals that instead of stable situations of 'exclusion' or 'integration', various patterns of incorporation can be observed. Given the initial aims of the research, its main contribution lies in the explanation of the factors on which incorporation depends. This section aims at summarising key factors and processes, discussing them from a general and comparative perspective.

Firstly, the *characteristics and background* of the migrant population are highly diverse, and this is reflected in the multiplicity of forms and/or degrees of integration at the individual/household level. It appears that factors like gender and age, nationality and ethnicity, cultural or religious origin, as well as pre-migration socio-economic status and human capital, do have a certain weight. For instance, different informal practices have been observed in the ways that Bulgarian and Albanian migrants cope with their daily realities. Ethnic Greeks seem to be a privileged group, due to favourable legal provisions and lower degrees of stigmatisation, in contrast perhaps to the widespread Albanophobia. Clear distinctive lines characterise the labour-market integration of women as compared to that of men. Education, class and status in the home country are sometimes reproduced in the host society, as the differences between 'elite' and other migrants suggest. But although the characteristics of the migrants may influence their pathways to incorporation, they do not produce them as such. Rather, it is the social context in the host country that determines them. It is labour-market structures that confine women in reproductive activities and educated migrants in unskilled manual tasks. It is the Greek national myth and its policy implications that define certain groups as 'unwanted'.

Secondly, the *patterns and dynamics* of migration are also important. On the one hand, individual or family migratory projects and strategies have largely conditioned immigrants' lives in Greece. On the other, proximity and ease of entry have directed migrants to Greece, initially as an immediate solution, but they also determined contact with the places of origin, travel back and forth, cyclical migration, etc., facilitating new and old transnational practices. Historical cross-border relations seem to be taking shape again with the migrants' networks, and not only condition to an extent their routes and settlement in the host country, but they also influence identities and senses of belonging. The Balkan context of transnational migration is given special attention in Section 9.2.2.

Thirdly, the exclusionary logic of immigration policy has conditioned, albeit only partly, immigrants' *relationships with the authorities*. To some extent, this relationship has been problematic because of certain malfunctions in the administration system and the provision of services, such as inefficiency, bureaucracy and delays, which are common in other contexts (Kosic & Triandafyllidou 2003, report on the Italian case) and apply equally to the indigenous populations. *Legal status*, of course, plays a crucial role: when it is obtained, this indicates a turning point in the life of a migrant and not only brings equal rights in accessing welfare, or in the labour market, but also signals or facilitates various other improvements. By contrast, those immigrants who have not managed to regularise, whether as a result of continuing informal employment, or because they are newcomers, find themselves in the vulnerable position of illegality, as described and analysed in several parts of the thesis. However, legal status as such should not be regarded as a panacea, since it is the *productive and employment structures* that ultimately determine the migratory experience. Particularly in

Southern Europe, given the size of the informal economy and the high numbers of illegal immigrants, regularisation cannot alone solve what appears to be a problem embedded in deeper structural factors, i.e. the *labour market* itself (Reyneri 1999; Reyneri & Baganha 1999). Moreover, culturally or ethnically different segments of the population might be excluded, to a lesser or a greater degree, despite their access to rights and services. This is revealed by the experience of other countries in Europe[8] and elsewhere, or from the situation of specific groups, e.g. the Roma who have long been citizens in Southern European states. True, irregular status may confine migrants to the underground economy, but this may go on long after migrants are legalised. After all, this is not necessarily an indicator of social exclusion, at least not in the way it might be perceived in Northern European contexts. In Greece, as in Southern Europe as a whole, the informal sector covers many mainstream economic activities – not necessarily connected to illicit or criminal practices – and informal strategies are traditionally widespread and accepted.

On the other hand, *socio-spatial inequalities*, combined with certain characteristics of immigrants concentrated in specific local settings, may generate conditions of marginalisation, as the studies of Psimmenos (1995; 2001) and Iosifides & King (1998) about Athens reveal. This might even apply to groups who have been subject to more favourable legal provisions, as in the case of Pontian immigrants in western Athens. According to Halkos & Salamouris (2003), the concentration of large numbers of ethnic Greeks from the former Soviet Union in this downgraded, traditionally working-class neighbourhood, together with low language competency and difficulties adapting to the free market system, among other reasons, have contributed to high unemployment rates and exclusion. Thus, apart from legal status, additional measures are necessary, especially at the level of *welfare* and with specific reference to the local context. While in Greece the laissez-faire approach of the state was extended at the level of local government, which is weakly developed anyway, in other Southern European countries more attention has been paid to the social support of immigrants in local contexts. In Catalonia, for example, the *Generalitat*(the autonomous regional government) maintains a strong role in promoting integration (King & Rodriguez-Melguizo 1999).

Place does indeed matter in many ways, since the same groups might have different experiences in different settings, despite the common policy framework and similar patterns of employment at a national level. In the case of Athens, with much more organised and institutionalised *civil-society structures*, polarisation is sharper and more visible at the spatial level. In fact, civil-society organisations, more active in large cities, might be there precisely because social divisions are more intense. In that sense, the observations of King & Rodriguez-Melguizo (1999) and of King & Mai (2004) regarding the crucial role of civil-society institutions in Catalonia and Northern Italy, respectively, can be perceived in terms of supply and demand: they offer valuable services to people in need[9]. In smaller places, with fewer opportunities and weaker forms of organised solidarity, it appears that interaction and informal contact with locals have been easier. This is the case, for instance, in some rural areas of Greece (Kasimis et al. 2003), as well as in towns in the south of Italy (King & Mai 2004).

Migrant networks constitute another factor. They do provide a source of social capital, but their impact on integration might not always be positive. Granovetter (1985) reminds us that it is *weak* ties, rather than *strong* ones, that are usually more effective. Waldinger (1997), studying immigrants in Los Angeles, found that closed social networks might entrap individuals in specific economic niches. Thus, differences in community ties do not necessarily uncover higher or lower 'degrees' of integration. We have seen that immigrants in Thessaloniki rely more on informal contacts than on organised communities, but they increasingly interact with the local population. This might not be the case for other groups, with stronger community institutions but limited access to the wider society, as Cañete (2001) argues in the case of Filipinos in Greece. But the nature of community ties depends not only on specific migrant groups, but also on the local setting. In Athens, for example, there are more and stronger associations, reflecting the patterns of migrants' settlement (much higher concentrations) as well as the capital's centrality in respect to policy-making, a stronger and more diverse civil society, etc. However, the number and size of associations do not necessarily mean higher participation levels, or smoother integration patterns. Generally speaking, the role of formal or informal social networks, together with individual strategies and *transnational* practices, highlight the importance of *agency* in the incorporation process. In our case this has been marked by admirable flexibility and adaptability on the side of the migrants, which seems to be a rule rather than an exception[10].

The *time factor* has been highlighted in several parts of the thesis. The most crucial development time brought during the 1990s was the regularisation programmes, which had an overall positive effect on living standards and to an extent guaranteed better employment conditions and access to basic welfare services. But this seems to have been dependent on additional factors that have also developed over time: the gradual improvement of the migrants' language skills; training or experience acquired in Greece; settlement in Thessaloniki and a sense of identification with the place; the consolidation of locally-based social networks and the emergence of ethnic communities; closer relationships with locals; personal adaptation strategies; and a greater degree of self-confidence, etc. Changes in the dynamics of migration and individuals' migratory plans also played a role: their decision to stay permanently or to return (and when), if they have family at home or if they have cut most attachments to their country of origin, etc.

The important finding about gradual improvement of the migrants' position over time, hence social mobility (see also Hatziprokopiou 2003b), confirms what has been revealed by other studies about Albanians in Thessaloniki (Labrianidis & Lyberaki 2001) and extends these to Bulgarians, whose compatriots in Athens have also been found to enjoy more secure lives after regularisation (Markova 2001). This trend is common in rural settings too (Kasimis et al. 2003), while similar improvements in the migrants' socio-economic conditions have been observed in other countries (e.g. Triandafyllidou & Kosic 2003, and King & Mai 2004, regarding Albanians in Italy). But how does it fit with the conclusions of other researchers, which suggest high levels of exclusion[11]? The 'space' that migrants occupy in the labour market should be perceived as fluid and dynamic, constantly re-supplied by the most vulnerable sections of workers. The migrants who obtain legal status and follow upward social routes might eventually be replaced by clandestine newcomers: a clear distinction should be drawn between legal and illegal migrants, or 'pioneers' and 'newcomers'. This space is thus a pool of labour, not of humans. Migrants themselves form a dynamic section of the labour force and gradually become an organic part of the host society, characterised by a heterogeneity that might reproduce social hierarchies.

Needless to say, it would be naive to simply assume that 'things eventually get better over time'. The extent to which this trend will continue, especially with respect to the second generation, depends on the dynamics of migration, on individual life plans, on the rationalisation of immigration policy with emphasis on integration and long-term residence, but crucially on the transforming structures of local and national economies. In the long run, 'time' might lead to direct competition with locals for the same categories of jobs, whether as a result of migrants' upward social mobility (many second-generation migrants will soon be graduating from Greek universities), or of the increasing precariousness of some locals' position at times of crisis, stimulating hostility and social tensions. Therefore, we should be wary of oversimplified, idealising neoclassical approaches that see the economic success of immigrants as solely dependant on their human and social capital, language fluency and level of 'assimilation' (e.g. Chiswick 1978). Such perspectives overstress the individuals' characteristics and fail to address the dialectical interrelationships between migration, incorporation and social change, and to capture the dynamics of the economic system and the relations of production in the host societies.

Immigrants' trajectories from rejection to survival and then to integration, as evocatively described by King & Mai (2004), are certainly an issue largely underestimated in the literature on migration to Southern Europe. However, the experience of other countries should turn our attention towards potential developments that could possibly reverse the situation that has up to now conditioned the relatively smooth pathways of immigrants in Greece. The forces of globalisation and restructuring can have devastating effects on the fabric of a society and can lead more and more people towards economic ambiguity. These issues are explored in Section 9.2.1.

9.2 From global forces to local lives: dimensions of comparison

The purpose of this part of the discussion is exploratory. The experience of the Southern European immigration model and the limited comparisons drawn in the previous part of the chapter suggest that there are common trends in Greece/Thessaloniki and in other settings. To an extent, some of these trends can be seen as part and parcel of wider international developments that transform national or local contexts of reception. My aim here is to interpret the empirical issues under a theoretical view. Obviously, no detailed analysis can be provided here; the points made could be topics of future research and theorisation. I limit myself to identifying key elements in the way globalisation trends affect, or are manifested in, processes of migration and incorporation in Greece, developing from arguments presented elsewhere (Hatziprokopiou 2004a). The first section aims at exploring the relationship between international trends and economic, political and cultural change in Greece with respect to recent migration. The second locates transnational elements in the unifying Balkan space. The third returns to the local setting and deals with issues of space, evaluating Thessaloniki's recent experience of migration and urban change in the light of history.

9.2.1 Migration and globalisation: Greece, Southern Europe and beyond

To start with, immigration *per se* can be seen as one of the global forces affecting the country. Theoretically, it implies a clash between human rights and national sovereignty, since settlement remains a right of states while movement is regarded as a human right (Soysal 1994; Tapinos 2000: 306). In a globalising world, it becomes increasingly difficult for states to open their borders for various other flows and close them to migrants (Castles 2000). Thus, illegality might have been a key feature in the Greek case, but irregular movements are characteristic of contemporary migration trends on a global scale (Ghosh 1998). This paradox reflects and confirms the contradiction between developed and developing countries, with the former closing their doors to intensifying migratory pressures from the latter. In our case, this contradiction has been connected to the post-1989 developments in the former Eastern Bloc, as most of Greece's immigrants come from the Balkans and especially from one single country, Albania, the least developed country in Europe. Although Greece's experience is situated within the Southern European immigration model (King 2000a), its Balkan dimension points to what has been described as 'regionalism' in global migration patterns (see Baldwin-Edwards 2004b). The proliferation of illegal trafficking networks in the Balkans, which make huge profits by exploiting both the agony of the migrants and the apathy of the West, seems to be a side effect of a globalising speculative capitalism. At the same time, Greece is also affected by today's geopolitical developments, echoed for instance in the growth in numbers of Afghan and Iraqi refugees following recent crises and military interventions[12], while new 'global' migrations like the Chinese (e.g. Pieke 2004) are increasingly represented in the Greek case.

Turning now to the social and political responses to immigration, it appears that the political-institutional and socio-cultural contexts of incorporation reflect to an extent the contemporary crisis in the functions and role of the nation-state and in the collective national imagination. Take immigration policy first. According to Baldwin-Edwards & Fakiolas (1999), Greek immigration policy throughout the 1990s also depended on the country's external relations with the Balkans and the EU. Much of the criticism of the initial Greek response has attacked its repressive and exclusionary logic. This, however, should also be partly attributed to Greece's need to conform to European guidelines (Karydis 1996). The state had to address an immediate problem, but it had also to cope with obligations arising from its membership in the EU and the Schengen Group. Such obligations might be common to all member states, but were perhaps more urgent in Greece due to its geographic location at the south-east corner of the EU, surrounded by 'third' countries. Regarding the Albanian exodus in particular, both Greece's and Italy's 'emergency' responses were largely influenced by EU/Schengen criteria (Baldwin-Edwards 1999). Thus the 'closed doors' and 'non-tolerance' spirit of the 1990s was in accordance with the 'Fortress Europe' ideology. It was not accidental that Law 1975/1991 was characterised by the leader of the French National Front Jean-Marie Le Pen as 'a paradigm for Europe to follow'[13]. One can assume that the revised legal framework is also influenced by the current EU agenda, although from a more realistic perspective aiming at 'immigration management' and combining tight controls with integration measures. It has been argued that Greece's new ways of applying immigration control reflect broader trends of globalisation and restructuring (see Psimmenos & Kasimati 2003).

In that sense, the way Greek immigration policy has developed is indicative of the state's loss of autonomy and retreat to supranational institutions. Moreover, Greece's diplomatic interests in the Balkans, especially regarding its minorities in Albania and Bulgaria, have also conditioned its policy towards immigrants from these countries. This is far more evident in the former case, given the large numbers of people who migrated: the legal framework for Greek-Albanians in Greece has been a tool serving 'Greek political interests ... to maintain the Greek minority in Albania' (Triandafyllidou & Veikou 2002: 203). In general though, the presence of Albanians in the country has become a means of pressuring the Albanian government (see Papailias 2003: 1061-1062). But national identity considerations in policy-making might have also determined the patterns of movement. The granting of citizenship to Pontian Greeks 'returning' from former Soviet states has caused further migrations of Russians, Georgians, Ukrainians, etc., some of which might have been facilitated by cases of corruption in the Greek diplomatic bodies, through which passports were issued to non-ethnic-Greeks, as reported several times in the media.

However, both the polity's emphasis on national identity and especially the social reactions to immigration mirror the changing character and meaning of identity today. The rise of xenophobia and extreme Right activism in Europe, the reawakening of nationalisms and of religious fundamentalisms at the turn of the millennium, although fed by intensifying inequalities and deep political changes, are – indirectly at least – related to this general crisis (see Hobsbawm 1992). On the one hand, globalisation involves a trend towards a homogenised mass culture of consumption; on the other, the previous frameworks of collective reference have been deconstructed: boundaries between 'Left' and 'Right' are not clear anymore, and class identities have lost their past relevance. Theorists like Hobsbawm (1992) and Castells (1997), among others, have associated these trends with the contemporary search for identification with 'imagined communities' of the past: religion, ethnicity and the nation. In Greece too, national identity is transforming with the advent of Europeanisation and the changing world order (see Tsoukalas 1993), but also as it is confronted directly with the 'other' who is now here and among 'us'. Not by chance, religious and nationalistic values re-emerged in the 1990s, in parallel to what was taking place in the Balkans: e.g. the objections to the name of Macedonia, or the support of the (Orthodox) Serbs in Yugoslavia's civil war. Such phenomena have not been unrelated to the rise of economic uncertainty and unemployment, nor to the way Greece experienced the collapse of the Soviet Union internally, as expressed for instance in a government coalition between the Communists and the Right in 1989. The contemporary face of racism in Greece focuses on cultural difference, as in other European countries. The 'right to difference', a left-wing concept, has become an argument used by right-wing intellectuals, who in the Greek case claim the rights of the majority over the minorities that erode 'our' identity and culture. Feelings of superiority towards the Balkan 'other' are built upon perceptions of backwardness, but are reinforced because of the social position and role of immigrants in Greece. Elsewhere in Southern Europe too, one can observe similar expressions of cultural racism 'without colour'[14].

Welfare is another issue particularly relevant to incorporation. The basic problem relates to the (still) uncertain status of migrants in the country, at a time when insurance systems have proved to be inefficient and social-security funds are facing serious fiscal difficulties. The ongoing internal political discussion on the future of insurance systems reflects what Mingione (1997) describes as a deepening crisis of the European varieties of welfare state. In Greece, with its poorly developed social state, welfare restructuring has taken the form of decentralisation and the shift of responsibilities to individual officers, indicating a transition from 'citizens' or 'welfare recipients' to 'clients' (Psimmenos & Kasimati 2003). As we have seen, these trends do not seem to have affected immigrants so far, since the major problems hindering access to services have been illegal status and informal employment. Moreover, as in other European countries, some of the gaps in the policy framework have been covered to an extent by the reaction of civil-society organisations. Apart from international NGOs, smaller initiatives coordinate their activities and build contacts with their European counterparts, while some are supported by EU funding. The experience of the '*Sans Papiers*'[15] movement in France inspired grassroots organisations active in advocacy and campaigning to move beyond traditional left-wing politics and modernise their forms of action.

Since much of what is associated with globalisation has to do primarily with economic trends, it is in the patterns of immigrants' employment that processes of restructuring are more explicitly manifested. The low cost of migrant labour in Greece reflects a rise in the global demand for cheap labour (Psimmenos 1995; 1998; Castles & Miller 1998). Similarly, the demand for flexibility – the cornerstone of economic restructuring – is imposed by the dynamics of the market and by intensifying international competition, which in Greece primarily affects SMEs. Migrant labour crucially offers this much-needed flexibility, but, given the rigidities of the labour market, this takes place within the underground economy. Despite its 'traditional' origins, the informal economy has been revitalised by restructuring processes in Southern Europe as a whole (King & Rybaczuk 1993; Vaiou & Hadjimichalis 1997; Reyneri 1999). Similar trends towards informality and black-market work have been observed across the EU (Williams & Winderbank 1995) and are particularly evident in large cities across the world (Castells 1989; Sassen 1996). The further tertiarisation of urban economies, involving both high-level services and low-skilled 'supporting' or personal services, generate conditions of segmentation in the labour market, as described by Sassen (1991; 1996) in the context of global cities. This leads to the polarisation of the urban labour force, which, with the concentration of migrants at the bottom of the social pyramid, tends to reproduce the contradiction between development and underdevelopment at the level of the city. Similar elements and common trends characterise Mediterranean metropolises (Malheiros & Ribas-Mateos 2002), although their scope is certainly not global. Iosifides & King (1998: 223) argue that increasing social polarisation in Athens brings to mind the hierarchical structure of nineteenth-century industry, while it reflects at the same time contemporary socio-economic restructuring processes in global cities. The socio-spatial implications of such processes, with particular attention to the case of Thessaloniki, are examined in Section 9.2.3.

Thus the employment of migrants in services is part and parcel of the dynamics of economic restructuring (Pugliese 1993). Part of the services offered by immigrants concerns 'reproductive' activities, i.e. domestic work and cleaning, care for children and the elderly, which have traditionally been 'female' jobs. The 'household deficit' for such activities, particularly evident in cities across Southern Europe, has been the outcome of several changes also related to processes of restructuring (King & Zontini 2000). In the EU as a whole, female migrants now offer a cheap form of reproductive work that is crucially very flexible, reproducing the gendered division of labour on 'ethnic' lines (Anderson 2000). On these grounds, Ribas-Mateos (2002) talks about a 'globalised domesticity', arguing that patterns of employment of migrant women in cities reflect the impact of globalisation not only on the process of production, but also on the patterns of reproduction (see also Phizacklea 1998). Changes in lifestyles and life prospects lead to growing and diversifying consumption attitudes, which are crucially connected to the increasing employment of migrants in private/personal services. The studies of Iosifides & King (1998) and Psimmenos (1995; 1998) underline the role of growing personal consumption in the high demand of households for immigrant labour in Athens. Although beyond the scope of the thesis, this partly explains the increased demand for 'pleasure services', currently supplied disproportionately by foreign women (and children) through the trafficking networks: the share of foreign sex workers in Greece increased from 21 per cent in 1991 to nearly 60 per cent in 1996, according to Emke-Poulopoulos (2001: 4). However, the empirical results suggest that together with the 'maid' and the 'prostitute' that King & Zontini (2000) describe as the dominant figures of the female migrant in Southern Europe, in Thessaloniki we can observe a third one: the manufacturing worker. Despite the decreasing importance of industry, or perhaps precisely because of the crisis that certain sectors currently face, employment in manufacturing incorporates considerable shares of migrant women in 'female' industries (e.g. clothing) that are keenly affected by internationalisation and global competition.

Theoretically speaking, the labour-market characteristics of migrants in Greece can be seen as a specific expression of the ongoing antithesis between capital and labour. At a macro level, market forces *do* shape contemporary migration patterns, especially labour-market structures in countries of origin and destination, which are increasingly interdependent (Tapinos 2000). As Sassen (1999) has argued, it is not poverty as such, or overpopulation, that generates migratory flows; Tapinos (2000) reminds us that it is neither the poorer who migrate, nor the least developed countries that are primarily affected by population outflows. It is, rather, relations of dependency, and the restructuring, reorganisation and relocation of economic activity (Sassen 1999). Globalisation and restructuring generate new forms of exploitation, with the deregulation of markets, the 'precarisation' of working regimes, rising unemployment, increasing polarisation between and within countries, etc. (Sassen 1991; 1996; Mingione 1997). Immigrants across the world are one of the groups most affected – in a dual way, since the side effects of globalisation push many to emigrate in the first place. In the emerging world economic order, migrants constitute part of the global proletariat (Cohen 1987; Harris 1995). In fact, they form one of its most mobile sections, a 'transnational working class' (Guarnizo & Smith 1998: 18). Migrants' hard work and flexibility make them 'borrowed men' (and women) 'on borrowed time'[16], as if they are here only to satisfy their employers' needs. As Cohen (1987) has put it, referring to Marx, they are 'free' to sell they only thing they have – their labour – potentially in any part of the globe, although their movement remains dependent on state regulations and border-control regimes.

However, as we move the focus from the macro to the micro, from global processes to concrete phenomena concerning particular migrant groups in specific social formations, we come across a diversity of experiences that cannot be simply attributed to the structural basis of society. Rather they uncover the role of agency or everyday resistance, the factor of social networks and the small things that matter in people's daily lives and in their ways of coping with reality. Increasingly, many of these phenomena today reveal various expressions of transnationalism (Smith & Guarnizo 1998), which can be seen as a form of 'globalisation from below' (Portes 1997). Similar trends can be observed in our case, although they are crucially determined by proximity between the country of destination and the countries of origin, in a regional (Balkan) transnational context.

9.2.2 New bonds: the Balkans as an emerging transnational space

Certain aspects of transnationalism have emerged throughout the analysis. Findings presented at several points in the thesis uncovered transnational strategies practiced by (some of) the participants. These are facilitated by proximity and through the newly formed migrant networks that link localities of origin and destination, which are sometimes built upon historical/cultural bonds between places, as we have seen in the case of Thessaloniki and Korçë. Practices of this kind include remittances, usually sent through informal channels like relatives or compatriots who go back home (Section 8.1.3), to support family members left behind, in some cases spouses and/or children. Many migrants read newspapers brought from the home countries and a small number were involved with Albanian or Bulgarian political parties; one could also assume that many vote in their countries' elections[17]. Visits to home villages/towns are commonplace, whether for holidays or other reasons, such as the issue of certain documents (birth certificates), or access to health services (in the case of Bulgarians). Strategies of cyclical migration – of coming and going on a temporary basis – have been observed among participants, eased by proximity and by factors such as familiarity, contacts, language competency, etc. accumulated over the years. Such practices have a crucial effect on incorporation, since they smooth difficulties and facilitate acculturation.

The increased mobility from Albania and Bulgaria to Greece confirms the scale of 'back and forth' movements. Statistics from the National Tourist Organisation (GNTO) for 2002 counted 1,255,738 and 470,232 arrivals of Albanian and Bulgarian 'tourists' at the borders respectively; Albanians were the third most numerous tourist group that year and Bulgarians were the seventh (see Figure A3, Appendix A). Mobility and contact between countries of origin and destination might go on after the end of the individuals' 'migration cycle': migrants who return home tend to maintain relationships and various forms of contact with Greece. In their study of Albanian return migration, Labrianidis & Hatziprokopiou (2005) found that Albanians returning from Greece and Italy maintain relationships with friends/relatives who are still abroad, while some travel to the host country at least once a year; significant shares have Greek professional partners, and some buy household goods or business equipment from Greece after their return. The dynamics of migration and return are shaped by proximity in a dual sense (Labrianidis & Hatziprokopiou 2005). On the one hand, as long as life prospects are better in Greece the possibility of permanent return is reduced, since proximity allows contacts and visits while abroad. On the other, it might be the other way round, i.e. short-term return with the option of seasonal/cyclical movements for work remaining open. Both possibilities already apply to many migrants from Albania and Bulgaria in Greece, who appear to support livelihoods between places of origin and destination.

Let me recall at this point that, as set out in Chapter 2, migration is just one aspect of post-1989 relations between Greece and the Balkans: another is capital and goods moving in the opposite direction, i.e., from Greece to Balkan countries. In particular, as argued by Labrianidis et al. (2004), a special capital-labour relationship is in place, with inflows of labour being accompanied by outflows of capital (FDI), both reflecting the increased demand of a section of Greek capital, especially SMEs, for cheap and flexible labour. To an extent, the character of the relations between Greece and its northern neighbours can be understood within a context of imperialism, dominance, dependence, etc. Obviously, Greece is neither the only nor the major player in the area; but being a Balkan country itself, it is currently in a relatively privileged position, in many respects. The Balkans function as a 'tank' of cheap labour, a 'reserve army' that can be easily exploited both 'here' and 'there'. Much of the discussion in the thesis, especially in Chapter 6, has analysed how this takes place in the former case. But the latter possibility, i.e. the relocation of Greek companies to Balkan countries, is not unknown to some of the interviewees:

> *Raicko, skilled worker in a metal-processing workshop*: Greeks say, 'You take our jobs, we don't have jobs.' This is not the way it is ... all Greek bosses went to Bulgaria and started businesses there, because they pay less.
> *Valbona, worker in a clothing factory*: The factory used to be a very big one ... now part of it has moved to Bulgaria ... From the three hundred people that were working here when I came, now there are only about sixty left.

Apart from capital movements, there has been a growth in commercial activity. Although Balkan countries constitute secondary trade partners for Greece, trade with the Balkans in the 1990s was highly dynamic, and its share in total imports-exports has been increasing steadily since 1989 (Labrianidis et al. 2004). Not only are certain Greek products now manufactured in Balkan countries, but increasingly they are exported there as well. Favoured by proximity and cultural and human links, Greece has been the first country to enter these new virgin markets (Labrianidis 2000; Kamaras 2001). Naturally, flows of goods and capital are also translated into human mobility. Together with Greek companies moving abroad, there are also movements of Greek citizens who travel back and forth: merchants and distributors, business executives and various categories of professionals, bankers and investors. The Greek presence in the Balkans is currently so strong that some analysts argue for the emergence of a 'Greek capitalist Diaspora' in the region, constituted by a network of corporate entities and individuals (Kamaras 2001). To give an example, according to the National Statistical Institute of Bulgaria (NSIB), among 132,576 people who travelled to Bulgaria for professional reasons during January-September 2002, Greeks had the largest share, 12.9 per cent.

The erstwhile impenetrable northern Greek borders are now easily and frequently crossed for various purposes. The new border dynamics and patterns of mobility bring to mind some of the features of other border zones (e.g. the US-Mexico border, especially the Tijuana area). An interesting example is the long-discussed 'Transborder Free Industrial Zone of Economic Exchange' (ΔΕΒΖΟΣ) that is to be established in the border area of Ormenio in Thrace, at Trigono, a town just eight kilometres from Edirne (Turkey) and ten kilometres from Sviligrad (Bulgaria). Most of the companies planning to move to the area are labour-intensive ones, especially clothing manufacturers (Labrianidis 1998); 60 to 80 per cent of the workers will be coming from Bulgaria on a daily basis[18]. But market dynamics impose new situations long before these are institutionalised: agricultural workers from Macedonia and Bulgaria are already commuting daily or weekly to the border areas of Kilkis, Serres and Drama. Minev et al. (1997) report on Bulgarian fruit-pickers coming and going, especially in the Rodopi region. The municipality of Trigono itself, in conjunction with the Bulgarian municipality of Sviligrad, has already established a job-finding agency to recruit Bulgarian commuters for agricultural work (*Eleftherotypia*, 29 December 2004). All these suggest that the labour markets of Balkan countries are increasingly interdependent; as Minev et al. (1997: 10) argue for the case of Bulgaria and Greece, it is actually the *informal* labour markets that are primarily connected.

It thus seems that we are now at the beginning of a new era for the Balkans; new cross-border relations, interdependence and various types of networks produce dynamics that go further from the Greek investment/Balkan immigration dipole. Tourist mobility, trans-border contact, international students and organised crime provide additional examples. More Greeks are now travelling to the Balkans: between January-September 2002, 266,458 Greeks travelled to Bulgaria for tourist purposes, being the fourth-largest tourist group (NSIB). In 2003, the Greek TV channels were reporting on Greeks from northern towns/villages, including Thessaloniki, visiting places on the other side of the border like Petrich (Bulgaria) or Gevgeli (Macedonia), for shopping, but also for other reasons (e.g. having their teeth filled at low cost by a local dentist). Remote border areas of Greece, poor, emptied by internal migration and 'forgotten' by the state are revitalised not only economically, i.e. due to migrant labour, as Kasimis et al. (2003) suggest, but also demographically, in the context of cross-border mobility. For example, in the above mentioned Trigono area, there is a trend of young people, especially women, leaving for the cities, which results not only in loss of labour force, but also in a growing number of men who 'are left without brides'[19]. Since 2000, 50 mixed marriages have taken place between young locals and Bulgarian women from nearby Sviligrad and 85 children were born. Furthermore, there was a tradition of young Greeks studying in Bulgaria, Yugoslavia and Romania even before the 1980s, which didn't cease after 1989. Recently, there is a trend in Greek universities to attract young Eastern Europeans to study, many of whom come from the Balkans – an issue underestimated in public debates and academic research.

There is, finally, the issue of organised crime and Mafia-type networks, smuggling in guns, tobacco, drugs, oil, pirated CDs, etc.[20]. For rather obvious reasons, relevant information and academic research is scarce and lacks detailed evidence. Such criminal networks also control the trafficking businesses involved in forced prostitution (IOM 2001; 2002). The border cities of Petrich and Sadanski in southern Bulgaria are described as 'the Balkan centres of white slavery' (Emke-Poulopoulos 2001: 15). While in the 1980s most foreign sex workers in Greece were mainly from Asian countries (Thailand, the Philippines), by the mid-1990s the majority were from Central and Eastern Europe and nearly one third were from the Balkans (Emke-Poulopoulos 2001: 4). Not only are women who end up as sex workers in Greece channelled through certain sites in the Balkans, but also there is a trend of Greek men crossing the border to Bulgaria or Macedonia for cheap sexual services.

The relationships, networks and 'back and forth' movements that are being developed in the post-1989 Balkans are indicative of various expressions of transnationalism. After all, the era of globalisation is marked by similar cross-border relationships and integrations at a regional level. Relations of production are stretched across national borders, which are now crossed by various types of flows, new forms of dependency and exchange, and new types and patterns of mobility. The nature of interdependence between Greece and some Balkan countries suggests a migration system characterised by a relationship between capital and labour mobility, fitting to an extent the analysis of Sassen (1999; see Labrianidis et al. 2004). But the bridges built by the human factor should not be underestimated: migrants and their networks establish new bases for social and cultural contact. In that respect, the experience of Greece is not unlike that of other Southern European countries. As the Portuguese geographer Malheiros (2002: 107-108) notes: '... non-formal links resulting from historical and cultural processes ... and specific social relations ... have a strong influence on the establishment of particular geographic interactions'. In the Spanish case, for instance, a similar migration system can be observed, shaped, there as well, by proximity and historical links rooted in Moorish domination and Spanish imperialism (King & Rodriguez-Melguizo 1999). Local sites do matter and transnationalism emerges as a 'multi-local process' (Guarnizo & Smith 1998: 6, 12). The fact that Thessaloniki is not only the base of many of the companies investing in the Balkans (Komninos & Sefertzi 1998), but is also linked to places of origin because of both historical ties and contemporary relationships could thus be seen as an example of what Malheiros (2002: 108) calls 'a new territorial logic' of 'polycentric networks'.

In Eastern Europe 'there is a history of borders moving across people and their communities' and what takes place today is not simply a 'flood from East to West', but a 'much wider field of mobility', with the majority of movements being short-distance and cross-border (Rogers 2000: 8, 10). The Balkan space, fragmented after years of separate national histories and divided by nationalist conflicts, is gradually regaining the unified character it used to have in the years of the Ottoman Empire (see Mazower 2000). The Ottoman area was anyway traversed for work, and the nomadic culture of some particular groups (Vlachs, Sarakatsani) has been shaped by such temporary movements related to pastoral activities. Mai & Schwandner-Sievers (2003) underline the historical precedents of Albanian transnationalism, expressed for instance in the cultural significance of *kurbet* (temporary migration for work). In the early twenty-first century, and despite persisting problems, the Balkans can be pictured as an emerging transnational space, or at least a space of transnational mobility. Perhaps this can be a new way of 'imagining' the Balkans (see Todorova 1997); but certainly, this is the context whereby the processes of migration and the incorporation of migrants in Greece take place. To what extent new and further transnational practices will be generated among Albanian, Bulgarian or other migrants in Greece, and the long-term implications of cross-border movements – especially with the coming EU enlargement – are issues that will become clearer over time.

9.2.3 *Migration and place: Thessaloniki's (second) path to multiculturalism*

Thessaloniki has a rich potential for a crucial role, not only for reasons of proximity. With its long multicultural history, the city has become a new home for immigrants from the Balkans in a period of transforming local geographies and of growing interaction beyond national borders. As has been argued throughout the thesis, the character and direction of incorporation processes reflect to an extent the local social structure, not simply in strictly economic terms, e.g. the productive structures, but generally regarding the wider set of economic, socio-cultural and political-institutional relations. Most importantly, the place of residence is the environment determining the lifeworld of immigrants, i.e. their direct experiences and daily lives. 'Small things', inevitably attached to space, shape migrants' everyday realities far more than abstract social mechanisms. Moreover, the presence of immigrants and their interaction with the local community changes the physiognomy of the city: it challenges established uses of the urban space, altering its landscape, and hence questioning its identity.

During the past two decades or so, the city has been undergoing deep socio-economic and socio-spatial changes. In their analysis of immigrants' exclusion in Athens, Iosifides & King (1998) discuss the extent to which the Greek capital experiences trends similar to those observed in the so-called global cities. According to Sassen (1991; 1996), these include trends towards the tertiarisation of the economy, the restructuring of consumption, the informalisation and precariousness of employment, and intensifying polarisation, which are common in other Mediterranean metropolises (Rome and Milan, Barcelona and Madrid, Lisbon). Such post-modern characteristics in southern cities predated the trends of post-Fordist restructuring as *alternative*, rather than traditional, patterns of urban development (Leontidou 1996). Now these change with the advent of restructuring, with certain implications for both space and people. To an extent, Thessaloniki too exhibits characteristics similar to those observed in global cities, although on a much smaller scale and regional scope. On the one hand, it is undergoing parallel trends, affected by the same processes of internationalisation, economic restructuring and socio-spatial reorganisation. On the other, as the major European cities become nodal centres of the global economy or regional centres of economic importance, Thessaloniki attains a similar function in the south-east corner of Europe, by 'regaining' its Balkan hinterland in an increasingly unified transnational space. At both levels, migration now plays a dynamic role.

The city is expanding in all possible directions. Pollution, traffic and parking are problems even more apparent than in Athens. The key urban trends that Leontidou (1990) identified in the case of Athens are evident here as well: speculation in the housing market, suburbanisation of the middle classes, increasing homogenisation of the urban space with clusters of wealth and poverty speckled across the city. Industrial decline continues with the shutting-down of enterprises, the decentralisation of large industries and the relocation of manufacturers abroad, with Balkan countries being the main destination. As urban economies are increasingly connected to the international environment, the patterns of urban development are transformed, with visible impacts on erstwhile familiar landscapes. Urban planning is directed towards regeneration projects targeting the hosting of European-wide infrastructure, the attraction of dynamic economic activities and the revitalisation of areas marked by technological devaluation (Giannakou & Kafkalas 1999). In Thessaloniki, these trends are reflected, for example, in the Ladadika district, located in the historical centre, and in isolated cases of empty factories, port warehouses or abandoned military camps, which are transformed into cultural and entertainment spaces (mostly private ones). On the other hand, the city attracts institutions with an international character: apart from the long-established International Expo, such examples include the Balkan Exchange Centre, the CEDEFOP and others. Finally, there is a general trend of spatial relocation of economic activity: the leisure industry expands in the historical centre while it also moves towards the eastern suburbs; trade is mostly concentrated downtown (small specialised shops) or on the outskirts of the city (large commercial houses), etc. But old forms are still apparent and coexist with new ones: historical buildings and blocks dating back to the sixties and seventies stand next to post-industrial spaces; high-tech services might be found in areas with labour-intensive workshops; open public spaces continue to be used by people even in zones of private entertainment.

At the same time, Thessaloniki has been at the heart of major events that shook Greece's public life throughout the 1990s. At the beginning of the decade, it was the epicentre of nationalistic demonstrations objecting to the use of the word 'Macedonia' in the name of the neighbouring state. In the mid-1990s, the Church organised massive demonstrations to object to the use of a restored Roman monument (Rotonda) as a cultural centre, as it was planned by the authorities, and finally succeeded in turning it into a temple. When it hosted the Cultural Capital of Europe in 1997, local authorities decided to highlight its Byzantine Orthodox past, neglecting, or at best downplaying, Ottoman and Sephardic traditions. In the early 2000s, the city was shaken again by massive demonstrations organised by the Church against the non-inscription of religious beliefs on the new ID cards issued by the state. Of course, immigrants could not escape being affected in such a xenophobic environment. It was here that severe cases of police brutality took place at several points throughout the 1990s: the most striking example is an incident that took place in 1998, where off-duty policemen tortured an Albanian migrant until he collapsed, while drinking, dancing, singing slogans praising the dictatorship and occasionally firing guns. And it was here (in the suburb of Mihaniona) that a clever Albanian pupil was not allowed to become a flag-bearer, with xenophobic reactions and endless debates on 'what it means to be a Greek'. (Kapllani & Mai 2005).

So, what is the place of immigrants in Thessaloniki? What is the role of space in the dynamics of their incorporation? How does migration fit in with the transformation of urban structures? The previous sections revealed much about the position and role of immigrants in the local economy and society. But as the analysis in Chapter 7 has shown, urban development processes now include the dynamics of migration and incorporation. Space, after all, is a social product; rather than remaining the unchanging scenery of a static social geography, it is transformed accordingly and develops. With respect to the incorporation of immigrants, three key elements need to be stressed: their pathways in the housing market in relation to the transforming social geography of Thessaloniki; their daily experiences of urban space in relation to its changing social use; and the migrants' perceptions of, and identification with, the city, in relation to its character and identity. Here as well, contradictory forces are evident.

Migrants' pathways to the housing market reflect their employment conditions, since they are equally marked by exploitation, discrimination and informality. These apply to other urban cases in Southern Europe, from Athens (Iosifides and King 1998) to various Italian cities (King & Mai 2004; Kosic & Triandafyllidou 2003) and from Barcelona (King & Rodriguez-Melguizo 1999) to Lisbon (Malheiros 2002). In the absence of a strong and open social housing sector, migrants tend to rent old, cheap properties. In many cases, these properties and/or areas were inhabited by refugees from Asia Minor or internal (rural) migrants in the past, which also resembles the historical patterns of settlement in other Mediterranean metropolises [21]. Although traditionally Southern European cities are generally characterised by relatively mixed residential geographies, certain migrant groups exhibit higher degrees of segregation: Moroccans and Filipinos in Barcelona, Cape Verdeans in Lisbon, Chinese in Milan (Malheiros 2002: Table 2). Segregation levels, however, do not necessarily imply socio-spatial exclusion, as Musterd (2003) maintains, taking the case of Amsterdam as an example. He reminds us that social inequalities and polarisation might be more important than residential distributions as such. Thus, even when sharp segregation patterns are not the case, high concentrations of immigrants in *specific* degraded areas might be alarming, as

Halkos & Salamouris (2003) suggest in the case of Pontian ethnic Greeks in western Attica, and Psimmenos (1995; 1998) found for Albanians around Omonia Square in Athens.

However, in the case of Thessaloniki, the analysis has suggested that the processes of incorporation have been rather smooth, in comparison to other urban settings. Although the general features are common, the main difference is simply that social polarisation and segregation patterns are not that sharp. It seems that the relative residential mix of the population is extended and embraces immigrants, despite the exclusionary mechanisms in the housing market. There is no evidence of dense immigrant 'clusters', while Albanians, as we have seen, are 'all over' the city. The 'cheap' districts where migrants tend to live are not necessarily the most deprived ones. Along with rent prices, high concentrations of migrants in specific neighbourhoods reflect the function of migrant networks and the availability of work. This results in a significant presence of immigrants in 'wealthy' areas, indicating what Labrianidis & Lyberaki (2001: 208) have called 'the new social geography of the city', which goes beyond the traditional division between the working-class west and the 'posh' east.

The second issue concerns the social uses of space. The role of urban planning with respect to regeneration/gentrification projects targeting tourist attraction and private investment is crucial in altering social uses of space. 'City marketing' (Pavlou 2001) and the increasing use of certain parts of the urban area for consumption and entertainment exclude migrants, among other vulnerable groups, from the use of particular spaces both symbolically and practically. The authorities tend to relate existing social problems (poverty, prostitution, criminality) to the presence of immigrants, who thus have to be removed. The example of Thermi Square (Section 7.2.2) and the Cultural Capital's policy towards immigrants in 1997, as described by Pavlou (2001), are typical cases; elsewhere in Southern Europe we observe similar conflicts. For instance, in Piazza Garibaldi in Naples, the politics of security and of the image of the historical centre have produced an exclusionary discourse over immigrants' presence in the area (Dines 2002). Similarly, in Athens, the concentration of large numbers of migrants around Omonia Square has been the subject of constant debates and projects for reshaping the face of the area (Psimmenos 1995), especially in the context of building the new underground station and, more recently, the preparation for the Olympics. Such issues of contestation over space bring to mind Lefebvre's concept of 'the right to the city'.

Nevertheless, it seems that in Southern European cities these policies do not always have exclusionary outcomes. As immigrants tend to use public spaces – perhaps forced to, to an extent, by their poor housing conditions – a culture of 'openness' is reproduced, which is familiar to Mediterranean societies where traditionally much activity takes place in the open space (Leontidou 1996). As Malheiros & Ribas-Mateos (2002: 303) put it: 'The tradition of using open spaces by immigrants that frequently live in low-quality and surcharged dwellings is contributing to a change in the appropriation strategies in some Southern European metropolises ... The celebration of cultural diversity and the new multiethnic character of the cities also takes place in the public space.' Processes of restructuring generate simultaneous trends towards both 'privatisation' and 'devaluation' of space and locals increasingly tend to 'consume' leisure/entertainment and abandon places that are 'out of fashion'. As Psimmenos writes on Albanians in Athens, in 'socially dead' places, immigrants organise space in different ways than 'us', developing alternative social uses. Immigrants in Thessaloniki use open spaces in multiple ways: as places of rest, meeting points or job-finding areas.

Thus, on the one hand, market forces determine the socio-spatial integration of immigrants: e.g. concentrations in cheap areas, ethnic entrepreneurship in districts with high migrant presence. On the other, informal processes of settlement, neighbourhood life and socialisation in public spaces condition immigrants' daily experiences of space. Place becomes a crucial component of the migratory experience, and it acquires particular meanings for migrants (King 1995). Their mental map of the destination place reflects their social experiences of space (Iosifides & King 1998), in respect to work and housing, but also socialisation and leisure. For many of the participants in this research, Thessaloniki seems to have been a consciously selected choice, because of history and old cross-border links, as well as proximity and convenience. As a large city, it offers opportunities and ensures anonymity. But still it is not that big; it is contrasted in that respect to Athens, and it is perceived as more humane and 'manageable'. Its virtues – the centre and seafront and its green spaces – are highlighted and defended with strong feelings of identification: this city is now their home.

Inevitably, the image of this city is transforming because of the migrants' presence. The dialectics of incorporation produce 'new cultural encounters' (see King 2000), which are place specific in character and scope. After all, the urban space constitutes a dynamic terrain where identities constantly interact (Papastergiadis 2000: Ch. 1). As in all the new multicultural metropolises across the northern Mediterranean, changes in their landscapes suggest changes in their identity also. In Lisbon, for example, the religion of immigrants not only plays a crucial role in integration, but it is also an important factor of cultural and spatial change – with new 'religion townscapes' transforming the image of the city (Fonseca & Esteves 2002). This is not yet evident in

Thessaloniki, given the cultural background of the majority of its migrants, but it is relevant in the Athens' case, where informal temples are already in place, while the planned building of a mosque has stimulated much controversial debate. Immigrants do play a role in historical and cultural processes regarding the identity of a place. For instance, the role of immigrants in the strengthening of Catalonia's regional identity has been crucial, with an increasing number speaking the Catalan language instead of Castilian Spanish (King & Rodriquez-Melguizo 1999). In Thessaloniki, the interplay between history, identity and contemporary processes of migration and incorporation is of particular interest and importance for the character of the city.

Historically, cosmopolitanism and long-distance interaction shaped the urban character of Southern European societies (Leontidou 1990). This intercultural tradition is now 'rediscovered' in Mediterranean metropolises through immigration (Malheiros & Ribas-Mateos 2002). Thessaloniki was for centuries a multiethnic city of transnational importance at the crossroads between East and West. Early in the thesis, I referred to this aspect of the city's history. Certainly, this was not always marked by peaceful coexistence; but the Jewish majority lived for centuries next to Muslims and Christians (Mazower 2004; Veinstein 1993). Among them, other cultures added to the city's cosmopolitanism: Bulgarians, Albanians, Armenians, Vlachs, Roma, Western Europeans and others (Mazower 2004; Veinstein 1993). Rather than being segregated in closed communities, Thessaloniki's inhabitants used to live together and their daily lives and relationships were based on their locality of origin, neighbourhood contact and professional occupation, rather than on ethnic identification (Mazower 2004).

But the spectres of history haunt present-day developments in another way too. In Greek popular culture of previous decades, Thessaloniki is known as 'the mother of refugees' (προςφυγομάνα), a title that the city acquired with the successful reception of Greek refugee populations from Asia Minor that followed the Greco-Turkish War of 1919-1922. Many of those fleeing from burning Smyrna and other places in Turkey were given temporary shelter in the old caravanserai at the heart of the city; this building currently hosts the city's town hall. In the Ottoman years, caravanserais were the hostels where people would stop for shelter and food for the night. Ribas-Mateos (2001: 36) has intriguingly described the 'Mediterranean migratory space' as a 'new caravanserai' on the road of many migrants towards a better life.

Today, Thessaloniki evolves as an important setting within this space. The city itself becomes a new caravanserai for migrants from the Balkans, Eastern Europe, the former Soviet Union and other parts of the world. What this study reveals is that Albanian and Bulgarian immigrants, along with newcomers of other nationalities, gradually become part of the local community; they might not break their links with their home countries, they might be assimilated or pushed towards the social margin, but they are 'here' and here they build their lives. As 'all urban residents become part of the polis' (Malheiros & Ribas-Mateos 2002: 306), emerging communities turn Thessaloniki into a colourful mosaic. Immigrants become an organic element of the city's life and identity, a structural component of its development, altering both its morphology and its ways of understanding itself. Their presence and action, but crucially their interaction and fusion with the local population, re-establish in the emerging post-modern metropolis of today the image of the multicultural city it had once been.

9.3 Migration, incorporation and change: identifying the trends

What do the findings tell us in general about the dynamics of change in contemporary Greece? Where are the seeds of social and economic transformation to be traced in relation to migration and incorporation? My attempt in this chapter to discuss key findings in relation to international forces and the global-local interaction is only one side of the coin. The other reveals important endogenous developments that suggest that certain elements in the process of immigrants' incorporation are indicative of change within Greek society itself. Obviously, the empirical basis is limited, and my research has not been concerned with capturing such elements. However, the material collected in the thesis and its ensuing analysis provide a basis for describing emerging trends.

Naturally, a first area is the structure and composition of the country's population. A population that was for long perceived as a homogenous entity is now characterised by pluralism and diversity. Greece is now a multicultural society, and this development crucially alters political traditions, cultural beliefs and perceptions of identity. Faced directly with the 'other', national identity is transforming and responds to difference in multiple ways. To an extent, these are reactionary, as the spread of racist and xenophobic feelings and the growing influence of extreme Right parties show. However, current debates on citizenship and senses of belonging suggest that certain things that were unchallenged in the past are now at least discussed. The rhetoric of the public discourse has shifted, and immigration issues are now part of the political agendas of the main parties. Not only has the far Right been growing, but also the range of the pro-migrant voice is expanding to the whole spectrum of the Left. Civil-society organisations are learning how to deal with migrants, how to interact creatively with their associations and, given their limitations, how to inspire participation and collective action. Despite the persistence of xenophobic attitudes, reciprocity between immigrants and locals is growing at an informal level, and there are signs that (some) locals have started to esteem the value of diversity. As interaction increases and the second generation comes into play, hybrid and transnational identities and practices are beginning to emerge.

Education is another field where one can capture change: not only regarding the geographical patterns of school segregation according to the shares of immigrant children, but also due to the specific problems and challenges that arise in respect to both the needs of these pupils and the effective operation of the school system. Multicultural, intercultural and anti-racist approaches to education are beginning to develop, while specific programmes are designed aiming to support immigrant children at school. Relevant debates uncover a necessity for redesigning certain curriculum subjects (history, religious education) and certain school practices (parades).

Another area is that of the economy and the social structure. A particular space has been created for immigrants at the boundaries between the formal and the informal labour market, which keeps them at the bottom of the social hierarchy through processes and relations that turn them into 'servants'. Such a development implies also changes in the class structure within the Greek social formation, which is now characterised by ethnic and cultural difference. This space has a structural function in the way forces of restructuring and internationalisation are affecting specific localities within Greece. However, it is fluid and dynamic and its boundaries are blurred. Individual migrants may find ways out through the acquisition of legal status and the move to the formal labour market: in some cases towards better-paid jobs or even more qualified posts, in others with self-employment and the setting up of ethnic businesses. What these findings reveal in respect to social change is that even under harsh and exploitative conditions, the position of migrants within the host country is not given and may be reversed.

The economic impact of immigration[22] has been rather positive so far, regarding the complementarity of foreign labour, the survival (or even expansion) of certain sectors, growth in consumption, the strengthening of insurance systems and the public budget (through contributions and taxation). In respect to negative outcomes, economic studies tend to emphasise labour-market issues, such as the distorted and short-sighted development path based on labour-intensive activities, the expansion of the informal economy, the replacement of locals by migrants in some sectors, and the impact on indigenous wages. Empirical studies do confirm a low degree of substitution of indigenous labour by foreign workers, in sectors such as agriculture and construction[23]. However, part of the replaced labour force is moving towards better posts or supervisory positions, while the presence of migrants seems to be creating more jobs than those it actually 'takes away'[24]: Say's Law seems to apply so far, suggesting that (labour) supply creates its own demand. As for the rest, these are not exclusively direct effects of immigration as such, but also are a result of the exclusionary policy and the failure of successive governments to regulate the labour market. In addition, immigrants play a key role in policies aiming to keep wages down, by offering motives (and alibis) to employers to move towards the informal sector (Iosifides & King 1998). However, the overall socio-economic effects cannot be limited solely to such 'standard' economic indicators. Background material from my own research and the findings of other studies (e.g. Romaniszyn 1996) suggest that there is a whole range of economic activity addressed especially to immigrants. Specific economic niches have emerged, in some cases with direct involvement of migrants as entrepreneurs: from tavernas or bars serving the migrants, to retail shops selling goods from the sending countries (food and drinks, books and newspapers, DVDs and music, etc.); and from translation offices or travel agencies specialising in the countries where immigrants come from to specialised lawyers dealing with cases of regularisation, expulsion, or human rights.

Then comes the issue of urban transformation. In cities, where restructuring processes are more explicitly manifested, difference and diversity, but also poverty, become more and more apparent at the local spatial level. The emergence and consolidation of new ethnic communities celebrates a de facto multiculturalism, particularly visible in specific localities. The urban space itself is redefined on the basis of new social uses and new geographies. Empty public spaces are revitalised and areas with high immigrant concentrations and/or ethnic businesses acquire a multicultural character. However, the structural position of immigrants has a concrete spatial face, translated into old, bad-quality properties and into sharpening segregation patterns that may confine migrants in specific areas. Even if the findings do not suggest high levels of socio-spatial exclusion of immigrants in Thessaloniki, this might be an issue of concern in the future, as polarisation in the labour market grows and urban inequalities become more intense.

Most of the above elements are policy-relevant; but recent developments suggest that policy approaches change as well. The positive effects of the rationalisation of immigration policy have been pointed out, while new developments include the design of specific measures aiming at integration and non-discrimination legislation according to EU standards. As the final lines of this work are being written, a new immigration law is coming out (Law 3386, published on 25 August 2005 and due to start being applied from 1 January 2006), which, for the first time, explicitly refers to the issue of integration in its title. Practical problems persist, but reflect wider malfunctions in the public sector, which perhaps are experienced more by migrants due to widespread xenophobic attitudes. Together with issues applying specifically to migrants (naturalisation procedures, access to health care and benefits, etc.), these problems underline the necessity for a redefinition of policy, but also of the culture of service delivery. The successive legalisation programmes gave the opportunity to migrants to acquire documents, and thus be entitled to basic rights. However, their ambiguous status in Greece regarding a variety of issues – from long-term residence to pensions and civil rights – constitutes a major problem with respect to welfare. To what extent Greece will manage to integrate migrants at a time of restructuring and social change is both a concern and a challenge for the future.

10 Conclusion: faraway so close

In his account of the diversity and complexity of contemporary migration trends in Europe, Russell King (2002: 94) poses a crucially important question: 'Is migration the exception or the norm?' He answers by pointing out that almost each of us is related to some form of mobility, even if international migration as such concerns a relatively small number of people. The Southern European experience and the Greek case within it, as analysed here, reveal that mobility is only one among many factors that make migrants not really 'different' from the host populations. History is one reason for that. To an extent, the 'other' reminds 'us' of our past, memories of which are still alive for certain sections of the population. Given the obvious differences (setting, patterns, conditions, period), the situation of the migrants has much in common with that of the working class in earlier times. Their experiences of uprooting, survival, discrimination, but also success, bring to mind the pathways of refugees from Asia Minor or the trajectories of internal and international emigrants. Their construction as scapegoats and constant pursuit by the authorities can be paralleled to the experiences of left-wingers until 1975. Each country has a history of stigmatisation of distinct groups, which is now directed towards the immigrants.

Even more crucially, immigrants tell us much about 'our' present. As Tsimouris notes (2003: 15), 'immigrants constitute a mirror through which Greek society watches its own image', although in a distorting and estranging way. It is in this mirror that aspects of social change are reflected. One reason for this relates to the heterogeneity characterising not simply the migrant population as a whole, but also specific migrant groups. The diversity of migratory experiences, despite common patterns and trajectories, reveals differences not only in the characteristics and background of the migrants, but also in their perspectives, plans, expectations and approaches to life. Such diversity constitutes a reality among the host population too, who are not as homogenous as binaristic perceptions of 'us' and 'them' tend to assume, either ethnically or culturally, or in terms of class or lifestyles.

Another factor has to do with the socio-economic and institutional context of reception. Some of the strategies immigrants develop, the extensive reliance on kinship ties and social networks, informality, the use of open spaces, etc., are not as unfamiliar to Greek customs and culture as they could be, say, in Northern Europe. This context, relevant to most Southern European cities, allows what Leontidou (1996: 188) describes as 'polyvalent forms of social integration', for example: 'multiple employment at the individual and family level, moonlighting and a multitude of strategies for income improvement and income sharing, including semi-illegal ones'. Such forms and practices seem to be reproduced in the processes of migrants' incorporation, bringing them even closer to 'us'. In addition, while the underground economy has absorbed migrant labour to a significant degree, it continues to apply to an extent to locals, especially young people, women, pensioners, unskilled workers, etc. Finally, many aspects of the problematic relationship between migrants and the state (public services, regularisation procedures, etc.) might have to do with their specific situation, but they are also connected to the weaknesses of the Greek administration, which affect immigrants and locals alike.

Within this context, the phenomenon of social mobility among migrants should not be surprising: it might apply to them as it does to locals, especially as legal, institutional and cultural obstacles disappear over time. And it depends, again in similar ways as it does in the case of the local population, on constraints and opportunities arising from class, status, education, geographic origin, social networks, and so forth. Moreover, the time factor affects people in similar ways, at least as far as the life course itself is concerned. After all, its unpredictable nature challenges both distinctive lines between 'us' and 'them', as well as neoclassical conceptions of 'rationally acting individuals'. To refer for the last time to the interviewees' narratives, I quote Nadi's simple but evocative comment:

> When you see that you can't have what you need there, then you look for something else. If you can't find this at the place where you live, you are going to look for this somewhere else. Since I could come to Greece, I came here, but I didn't really know ... what exactly I was looking for ... My only thought was to come and work ... Then ... I was thinking to ... have some savings and start my own business in Albania. But time passes and you go on thinking, and then you are suddenly married and have a baby ... You can't anticipate life; nobody can.

Needless to say, we are all affected, although in varying degrees and ways, by the deep structural changes related to globalisation and restructuring. With so many things in common, the question asked earlier has to be rephrased (King 2002: 94): 'Are the migrants therefore still to be regarded as the "Others" who are different from us?' In moral or political terms the answer should be *no*. But in the light of the analysis, it seems that the 'others' become 'strangers', 'aliens' and 'workers', paradoxically rejected by the polity and the society, but much needed for their labour. Thus 'immigrants', as Petrakou (2001) has argued, have been 'constructed' as a distinct category on the basis of the *exclusionary* mechanisms generated in each of the contexts examined in the thesis: the restrictive immigration policy, the spread of xenophobic attitudes, and the particular space migrants occupy in the labour market. Their housing and living conditions in the city are an outcome of the interplay between the above exclusionary processes, which keep them at the bottom of the social hierarchy. Even so, however, within a short period (of only eleven to twelve years at the time of the fieldwork), we can observe a multiplicity of forms and ways of adjustment and of building a life in Thessaloniki. Gradually, immigrants become an organic element of the host society.

The academic (and political) debate on immigrants in Southern European countries, especially in Greece, has been much concerned with the problem of social exclusion. The argument focuses mostly on the tendency of immigrants to work informally, on their illegal status and on a variety of issues ranging from racism to poor living standards, segregation, etc. Albanians in particular, in both Italy and Greece, have been portrayed as one of the most deprived groups, experiencing exclusion and discrimination at several levels. For various reasons, social science seems to reproduce dichotomous perceptions between 'us' and the 'others', whether by treating immigrants as a solid, homogeneous category, as distinct (social, ethnic, cultural) groups, communities or individuals. The migrants are seen as victims (of racism, capitalism, the state), or as a solution (to demographic stagnation or labour shortages) and their situation is regarded as unchangeable. One of my initial concerns when I first undertook this study was to avoid falling into such categorisations. This was not an easy task, and I am still not sure to what extent I have been successful. I had first to overcome my personal illusions and political convictions, without paying the cost of losing my enthusiasm for the general topic of migration and the specific project of the D.Phil. itself.

The experience of the fieldwork and the analysis of the material collected revealed the five key points that have been highlighted in the thesis, which offer an alternative approach that moves beyond binaries between 'us' and 'them'. The first concerns the great *heterogeneity* of the migrant populations, equally apparent in the two nationalities studied here as well as in other migrant groups. Especially in large communities, like the Albanian one, such heterogeneity should be expected, not only regarding its composition, but also with respect to the variety of experiences and trajectories. The second point has to do with the *dynamics of incorporation*. This study has underlined the importance of time, not as a vague category, but in all that it may entail, i.e. the rationalisation of immigration policy, the upward employment mobility and the gradual improvement of living conditions, the development of patterns of socialisation and interaction within each migrant group and between different communities and the local population. The third point is *agency*. Rather than being passive victims of a hostile and alienated environment, migrants take action, whether collectively or individually, formally but mostly informally, and they exhibit admirable capacities of adaptability and flexibility in coping with the difficulties and problems that arise from the institutional and socio-economic context. The fourth point is *place*. The local social structures constitute the context of reception, through which national policies or international forces are filtered. At the base, however, migration remains a social process and a human experience with a place-bounded character and meaning for both migrants and locals. The fifth point concerns *proximity* in the Balkan context and its relevance to the *dynamics of migration* and incorporation; not only it allows various expressions of transnationalism, but also it suggests that immigration to Greece is only part of a wider framework of mobility and exchange in the area. The Balkans have been pictured as an emerging transnational space, whereby we can currently observe diverse types of movement and various kinds of flows, most of which are directly or indirectly related to migration. The processes that we can identify in this regional context are indicative of the way globalisation forces are manifested at a smaller scale.

Rather than searching for single factors and one-way paths leading to integration, the main conclusion is that incorporation is the outcome of a combination of interdependent factors at the level of structures and institutions, on the one hand, and at the level of agency and relationships, on the other. It thus appears that neither 'integration', nor 'exclusion' are definite and stable one-way processes. They are both subject to time, thus they may evolve in parallel directions, and they may be reversed, whether for specific groups or for individual migrants. In addition, it is not only migrants that adjust, but the host society itself is adapting, in conflicting ways, to the new situations imposed by the fact that it is now a multicultural society – and develops as such. The incorporation of immigrants is characterised by a series of *contradictions*, expressed in the diversity of experiences and reflecting broader social mechanisms, processes of economic restructuring, political trends and institutional changes. What this reveals is the key issue of *social change*: Greece, as a host society, is changing anyway, but now it does so because of, and with, the immigrants. Migration becomes part of the dynamics of socio-economic transformation, therefore it should be understood as a 'critical force in history' (Papastergiadis 2000: 53).

In a rapidly transforming reality, where Greece has found itself to have become a multicultural society within a decade or so, no certainties apply. Having said this, I ought to acknowledge the weaknesses of the research presented in the thesis and the limits of the explanations and conclusions to which the analysis have led me. The first weakness relates to the possibility of *bias* concerning the *size of the sample* (rather small) and its *selection* (through 'safe' channels). However, I can point out that my sample's statistical characteristics do not differ much from the more complete official statistics; so I do have some confidence in the non-bias of my sample. In addition, the combination of different sources and methods has hopefully averted the possibility of bias. The over-representation of certain categories of migrants in the sample (e.g. 'elite' migrants, Sarakatsani Bulgarians) allowed me to address these groups as well, largely neglected previously in empirical studies, and to examine similarities and differences in their incorporation patterns. Another category of possible bias has to do with *place*, i.e. the strict focus on Thessaloniki. But the research aimed at capturing the dynamics of incorporation at the local level of the city; as more research takes place in different settings, our knowledge base is enriched, improving our understanding. Given the general aim of the research to both capture individual experiences and explore general 'objective' mechanisms and processes, no other approach is believed to be more relevant and useful than the multi-instrumental, interdisciplinary, combined and comparative methodology used here. If any biases may be found despite the conscious efforts to avoid them, they should rather be attributed to the limitations of the researcher himself, not to the research methods employed. In this connection, I should recall the self-criticism I made in Chapter 3 concerning my own positionality as a member of the host society interviewing immigrants largely through the medium of the Greek language.

The second major weakness relates to the limited comparative basis of the thesis; I have based this on the range of empirical studies that lay within my capabilities. The problem is that the ones concerning Greece focus on a small number of groups (most studies deal with Albanians); thus generalisations of the conclusions to other migrant groups lack empirical evidence and might be based on assumptions. On the other hand, the international dimension has built largely on theory. Research, reading and critical evaluation and incorporation of the vast literature would be impossible; however, the effort made in the thesis is a starting point for future interpretation.

Finally, perhaps the most important weakness stems from the very fact that the *phenomenon is still unfolding*, which suggests that things may change constantly, and it is particularly difficult to make projections at this stage. *Scripta manem*, maybe, but they are often day by day outdated by history. At best, I have described the emerging trends and set out a framework for research and analysis in the future. The empirical findings as such concern the *current* situation, and they are analysed in the light of *current* knowledge. They offer an account of the particular migratory experience of a specific city, which seems to be regaining its old multicultural character in a new context; and of the lives and conditions of a group of migrants to whom I owe this work.

Having outlined the weaknesses, I write a final word regarding what I consider to be the strengths of this research. At an empirical level, this is an up-to-date evidence-based study of Albanian and Bulgarian migrants in Thessaloniki. Apart from simply describing immigrants' characteristics, the thesis has sketched typologies and patterns of incorporation by looking simultaneously at different spheres of migrants' lives and different incorporation contexts. Despite the fact that much research has been done on Albanians, few studies focus on Thessaloniki, while Bulgarian migrants have not been studied much anyway, especially in the context of the city and regarding their various migration patterns. Furthermore, although policy and labour-market issues have been extensively addressed, certain elements have been captured empirically for the first time. These include: the dynamic unfolding of incorporation at several levels over time; the importance of informal networks and practices in the trajectories of immigrants in Greece; some dimensions of the interaction between migrants and locals; the issues of space, its dynamics and its use; and the emergence of transnational elements, regarding networks, practices or aspects of identity, which are to be understood in the context of Balkan transnationalism. The focus on the city itself is important, to address the place-bounded character of the migration experience and the effects on the local setting, given Thessaloniki's history and its multicultural past.

At a methodological level, the research involved combined methodologies and a rich range of sources and types of data, including systematic observation and participation. Through the in-depth interviews, migrants have been given a 'voice', which has been important in order to take their point of view into account, by engaging them as participants in a research about *them*. At an analytical level, the thesis benefits from a dynamic and dialectical account: incorporation is seen as a dynamic process that develops over time; social structures have been analysed without ignoring the role of agency; the dynamics of social change have been explored with respect to both the interaction of immigrants with the host society and wider processes of socio-economic transformation. At a theoretical level, the analysis has developed an international perspective that located the case of Greece within the Southern

European experience and the global map of migration. Aspects of the global-local interaction have been identified, especially within the context of Balkan transnationalism. Finally, the dynamics of incorporation in urban contexts have been generally addressed, in an attempt to explain the links between migration and socio-economic change.

The thesis started with a reference to population movements in the history of Greece. Although contemporary migration processes are taking place within a very different and rapidly transforming environment, the *experience* of the phenomenon at a human level is not that new. The accommodation of refugees from Asia Minor in the 1920s and 1930s, despite early harsh conditions and hostility, has been a success story overall, albeit within the context of nation-building and statal integration. And this was the success of a then poor and politically unstable country. Cultural diversity too has its historical precedents, especially in Thessaloniki where different communities lived together until the recent past, in the context of the Ottoman Empire.

The context of today is globalisation, transnational mobility and the transition towards multiethnic formations and cultural pluralism. The trajectories of Albanian and Bulgarian immigrants in Greece so far have been based largely on informal practices, kinship ties and social networks, which obviously cannot replace social policy. A realistic and inclusive policy framework is certainly necessary, but it is not enough alone. Multicultural coexistence presupposes transnationalist-internationalist practices and perspectives, and a redefinition of the relationship between 'us' and the 'others'. The study of the 'other' uncovers the multidimensional character of identity itself, providing a basis for such a redefinition. After all, the notion of identity, vague and ambiguous, refers to a fragmented and fluid social reality, which essentially reflects the multifaceted social grid, the dialectics between the material world and its image, the clash between structural, institutional and cultural contradictions. Within this complex set of relations that constitute social reality, we are all subjects, actors and participants. Cultural, national or other forms of identification compose the mosaic of the beauty of the world. Multicultural societies may function with the peaceful coexistence of divided communities. The challenge, however, is to explore ways of how we can live together.

Notes

Chapter 2

1 Some of the effects of immigration in the host countries are discussed in the context of the findings. The effects of emigration on the countries of origin are connected to the problems of development and involve a series of issues that are certainly important, but far from the interests of the thesis.
2 Other publications that have been consulted include: Mousourou (1991); Findlay (1996); Papastergiadis (2000); Labrianidis & Lyberaki (2001: Ch. 2-3); Tapinos (2000); and Ammassari & Black (2001).
3 According to classical economic theory (Smith's absolute and Ricardo's comparative advantage), trade and migration are perfect substitutes: a country where labour is in abundance (and hence its cost is low) can either export goods produced through labour-intensive practices or export labour. Neoclassical theory took the argument further: when free trade is established between two countries, the differences in the prices of production factors are reduced and so is, in the long run, the potential for migration.
4 New Growth Theory (e.g. Grossman & Helpman, 1991), for instance, underlines that trade liberalisation should be accompanied by technology transfers to developing countries, which can be achieved through FDI: foreign companies open the path for the introduction of innovations, which might result in technological convergence; this in turn might speed up growth in migrant sending countries, reducing the emigration potential in the long run.
5 In that sense, migration is considered as an investment that the migrant makes, expecting to have net positive returns in either earnings or human capital or both.
6 Despite their differences, the theories of dependency (Frank), uneven (Petras) or unequal (Amin) development and the world-systems school (Wallerstein) can all be seen as historical-structural perspectives inspired, to a lesser or a greater extent, by Marxist economic theory.
7 World systems theory stresses the distinction between core, periphery and semi-periphery, according to the different position and role of countries in the international division of labour, which is dominated by the capitalist mode of production (Wallerstein 1974). Rather than referring to a *global economy*, it assumes a *world system*, based on a dynamic world economy that is increasingly integrating. Its weak point is the rather economistic logic of analysis, almost totally ignoring cultural factors.
8 This is primarily concerned with the implications of a homogenising mass-media based culture for national identities and local communities. Rather than implying a specific school of thought, this approach is drawn out of a special edition of *Theory, Culture and Society* (Featherstone 1990), with contributions from many well-known

social theorists (Robertson, Bauman, A. D. Smith, Touraine, Appadurai, J. Friedmann, Wallerstein, and others). As a weakness, this analysis is limited in focusing on the negative effects of homogenisation, ignoring other factors and neglecting processes of differentiation.

9 The theoretical insights of D. Harvey (1989), A. Giddens (1991) and R. Robertson (1992) are relevant here. They all develop a historical worldview linking globalisation to modernity; human society gradually moves towards an interconnected world and a respective global consciousness of people.

10 This approach sees globalisation as the result of the development and expansion of the capitalist mode of production, which embraced the globe exponentially after the 1970s' crisis (Ross & Trachte 1990).

11 For an account of the sceptics' view, see the introduction in Held & McGrew (1999).

12 This distinction stems from the different meanings of the terms 'international' (implying that sovereign nation-states are the crucial actors in the international scene) and 'global' (suggesting that states are losing importance, while supranational institutions and market forces prevail).

13 The terms 'capitalism', 'capitalist system', etc. have their origins in the tradition of classical political economy and the Marxist intellectual heritage, and, despite the fact that they refer to politically loaded concepts, they are widely used today in different social science disciplines (sociology, political economy, critical human geography, etc.) without a need for precise definitions. As employed throughout the thesis, basically in this chapter and in Chapter 9, the terms describe, in abstract terms, the present system of economic organisation, which has been evolving over the past five centuries or so, passing from different stages of development and with many national or regional variations. In general, its key characteristics can be summarised in three basic elements: the domination of the free market, capital accumulation and wage labour.

14 See Hobsbawm (1992). Castells (1998: 2) locates the reasons for the collapse of the Eastern Bloc in 'the inability of statism to manage the transition to the information age'; this is a rather simplistic explanation, overemphasising exogenous developments and ignoring internal problems and political oppression.

15 Key factors indicating the decline of the nation-state are: regional integrations and increasing economic interdependence; internationalisation of national economies and abolition of most forms of protectionism; prevalence of policies promoting privatisations and dismantling the social state; adoption of common rules at the international level and transfer of many decision-making procedures to supranational institutions; international migration, formation of new minorities and deterritorialisation of culture; awakened nationalisms and regionalisms; decreasing citizen participation and trust towards the state.

16 S. Strange refers to the 'Westfailure system', pointing to the international system of nation-states that emerged in nineteenth-century Europe during the period that succeeded the Treaty of Westphalia.

17 These are obviously connected, representing different aspects of a single process. The distinction is rather methodological, addressing both the socio-economic basis (the capitalist world system) and the cultural roots (modernity, as a system of thought and civilisation) of globalisation in history.

18 Since the discovery of America and early modern technological advances, people's perception of the world has changed dramatically: not only did we realise that the Earth is not flat and rotates, but also our knowledge expanded and we achieved an increasingly more universalistic awareness. However, the discovery of the 'other' has passed through the violent path that characterises human history.

19 Lenin's account of imperialism located its chief characteristics in the domination of financial over industrial capital, the role of MNCs in the global scene, and the inequalities generated in a global system in which the development of certain regions produced the underdevelopment of others. Playing with words, we could argue that globalisation today may be seen as the 'highest stage of imperialism'.

20 History, of course, is linear only when looking back. We could learn the lesson that the greatest steps are taken after radical breaks with the 'norms' of linear historical development.

21 'Fordism' refers to the system of production organisation prevalent in the West during the twentieth century; it depended on monopoly capitalism and national development and was characterised by standardised industrial production in large units, directed to mass consumption. It was established on the basis of a Keynesian social contract guaranteeing full employment and prevailed as a model antagonistic to the Soviet one, with which though it had much in common in terms of economic development.

22 Although the account of King & Rybaczuk (1993) lies in the context of new productive structures and migratory trends in Southern Europe, it reflects broader changes and more general trends.

23 Castells (1983: 307) distinguishes between the Marxian term 'mode of production' (i. e. 'the way surplus is appropriated') and the term 'mode of development' i.e. ('the way surplus is increased'). I. Ramonet, editor of *Le Monde Diplomatique*, has evocatively compared the industrial revolution, which replaced the human hand through the use of machines, to the present-day information revolution, which is replacing the human mind through the use of computers, with multiplying social and economic effects.

24 Changes in the characteristics and synthesis of the 'bourgeoisie' and especially the 'proletariat' make the Marxian definition of class difficult to apply to the new context. Neo-Gramscian views suggest the emergence of a 'transnational capitalist class', a global ruling elite, mobile across core areas of the world economy (Sklair 2001). But what used to be the 'working class' in the past (proletarian = s/he who has no possession of other production means than her/his labour power) is now a fragmented notion, including various and very different social groups: office employees and blue-collar workers, highly paid manual specialists and low-paid service workers, part-time workers and the unemployed.

25 Changing consumption patterns and the increasing demand for services by middle and lower strata represent the consumption effect of the restructuring process. The shift of demand towards quality and the homogenisation of consumption patterns point to the emergence of consumerism as the dominant ideology/culture of contemporary capitalism. As the 'ruling class' increasingly dominates the livelihood and lifestyle of other social groups within and beyond the sphere of economic production (Touraine 1971), consumerism becomes the global ideology of the masses (Sklair 2001).

26 The division between a formal and an informal economic sector, resulting in primary and secondary labour markets, is not that distinctively apparent in real life; it is rather a theoretical abstraction to explain polarisation in the labour market (Piore 1979; for more details see Section 2.1.1).

27 The emergence of NGOs as major actors in social policy and practice is rather contradictory. While they seem to operate as an alibi for the reduction of the welfare state, replacing some of its old functions, they also appear as a response to this crisis, offering social protection to social groups that are vulnerable, or targeting countries that are too weak to confront globalisation forces. Thus, despite questions concerning corruption and/or relations with governments, one should acknowledge that many

NGOs are historically linked to 'new' social movements of the 1960s and 1970s, and directly participate in today's struggles, forming also part of the anti-globalisation movement.

28 In addition, as Papastergiadis (2000: 78) notes, 'the bulk of global trade is focused on speculative options, future shares, insurance, finance and real estate, rather than the commodity market.' This obviously favours developed countries, whose economies are based on an advanced financial sector, while developing countries depend on material production (and mostly have urgent material needs).

29 Hirst & Thompson (1996) have challenged this argument by stressing that most TNCs are legally domiciled in developed countries (mainly Europe, USA, Japan). Sklair's (1999) response emphasises the fact that most TNCs operate outside their home countries, express the interests of those who control them (rather than national ones) and develop global strategies (rather than focusing on 'foreign investment').

30 Partial exceptions are the countries that joined the European Union in 2004 and the ones scheduled to join in 2007, although income polarisation and serious economic problems are characteristic of them too.

31 Such as the Newly Industrialising Countries, particularly the so-called East Asian 'tigers'; also, to different extents, Mexico, Brazil and Chile (where, however, inequalities remain intense); finally, India, and particularly China, which has emerged as a global economic actor with rapid growth rates and extreme contradictions.

32 I owe this expression to my friend G. Ververis; it refers to contradictory trends that can be seen as opposite sides of the same coin. For instance, in the political-cultural field, we may face a homogenising mass culture (Americanisation, McDonaldisation, etc.), but we also witness trends of individual or collective quests for 'safe' identities and 'imagined communities' (religion, nationalism, etc.).

33 See Castles & Miller (1998), Muus (2001), Findlay (1995) and King (2002).

34 See for instance: King (1995); Castles & Miller (1998); Koser & Lutz (1998); Castles (2000); Tapinos (2000); Urzúa (2000); Papastergiadis (2000); Muus (2001).

35 An important aspect of this changing geography is that contemporary migration is not solely directed towards the industrial centres and the big cities of the developed world, but, increasingly, towards important sites in developing countries. The emergence of Southern Europe as a new destination for migrants is also indicative of the 'changing global map of migration' (King 2000a).

36 Services have become the basic sector of immigrant employment in the developed world. This has led scholars to stress the 'post-industrial' character of contemporary migrations, in contrast to the industrial migration of the post-war era (Pugliese 1993). The rise in the global demand for a cheap labour force functions, in the developed countries, as a pull factor for immigration, by creating employment opportunities for migrants even when unemployment is high (Piore 1979; Castles & Miller 1998).

37 According to the definitions by Esping-Andersen (1990).

38 The brief analysis that follows draws mainly from Mousourou (1993); King & Rybaczuk (1993), King et al. (1997), King (2000a).

39 The underground economy in Southern Europe originates from traditional productive structures and informal employment arrangements, further supplemented by trends of restructuring and strategies of flexibility, as well as by the expansion of illicit activities (Vaiou & Hadjimichalis 1997: 52-53).

40 Informal economic activities in Greece are also stimulated by clientelist relations between political parties and the private sector, as well as by widespread practices of tax evasion and non-adoption of labour norms by many individuals and firms, due to the high costs of taxation and of social-security contributions (Fakiolas 2000: 62). In ad-

dition, the family character of many of the numerous small companies further facilitates informal employment arrangements on the basis of kinship.

41 Average monthly household spending increased by approximately 18 per cent during the period from 1993-1994 to 1998-1999 (NSSG, Family Budget Survey: Table 3).

42 The rest had not declared. Results are from a survey by the National Centre for Social Research, reported in the newspaper *Eleftherotypia* (3 March 2002).

43 Nevertheless we should stay sceptical towards early 'enthusiastic' exaggerations, like that of Sarris & Zografakis (1999), who suggested – despite a lack of reliable data – that immigration in the 1990s has contributed 1.5 per cent to the growth of the Greek GDP, with overall positive effects in the growth of private investment, in decreasing (!) consumer prices, and in job creation, and thus in the general prosperity (see criticism by Labrianidis & Lyberaki 2001: 141-143).

44 During the fieldwork, I 'discovered' (and included in my study) the migration of Sarakatsani ethnic Greeks from Bulgaria; their numbers must be small, and I have not been able to locate any official data concerning them.

45 Figures are for the 'Real Population'. What the NSSG calls 'Usual Resident Population' is counted at about 10,934,000 people, of whom 761,800 are foreign passport holders and nearly 644,000 come from countries other than the EU-15 and EEA, Malta, Cyprus, Monaco and Andorra, and also excluding North America, Oceania and Japan (see Table A3 in Appendix A). Among this last category, the share of Albanians approaches 70 per cent, and Bulgarians come in second place with 5.6 per cent.

46 It is beyond the scope of the thesis to examine Greek immigration policy in detail, since much has already been written about that (see for instance: Kourtovic 1994; Lazaridis 1996; Karydis 1996; Baldwin-Edwards & Fakiolas 1999; Triandafyllidou 2000; Baldwin-Edwards 2001; Kourtovic 2001; Georgoulas 2001; Fakiolas 2003; Sitaropoulos 2003). This section offers an introduction to the development of the policy framework, which is necessary in order to understand incorporation processes as analysed later in the thesis – starting from its effects on the migrants' daily lives in Chapter 5.

47 An initial provision aimed at excluding migrants from neighbouring countries, but this was withdrawn following criticism and mobilisation of trade unions, NGOs, anti-racist groups and migrant associations.

48 See, for instance: Baldwin-Edwards & Fakiolas (1999); Baldwin-Edwards (2001); Fakiolas (2003).

49 The data are from the newspaper article by P. Galati in the newspaper *Kathimerini* (26 June 2004).

Chapter 3

1 For instance, Samers (1998) has proposed instead the term 'negotiation', meaning more or less the same thing, i.e. the ways migrants approach the dominant languages, labour markets, social services and administration bodies, failing though to capture the dynamic interaction of structural and institutional factors. 'Integration', on the other hand, as used in the previously mentioned studies of Musterd et al. (2000) or King & Rodriguez-Melguizo (1999), does not differ much from what I call incorporation. Furthermore, Heckman (2004: 4) offers a holistic approach by defining integration as a process of 'inclusion of migrants in the core institutions, relations and statuses in the receiving country', which is indeed an interactive process between migrants and the receiving society.

2 This includes over 130 titles published between 1970-2001, around sixty of them in Greek and the vast majority of the remainder in English.

3 See for instance Psimmenos (1995; 1998) on undocumented Albanians; Romaniszyn (1996) on Polish immigrants; Minev et al. (1997); Markova & Sarris (1997) and Markova (2001) on Bulgarians; Lazaridis & Romaniszyn (1998) on Albanians and Poles; Iosifides & King (1998) on Albanians, Filipinos and Egyptians; Droukas (1998) on Albanians; Lazaridis (1999) on ethnic Greek and 'other' Albanians; Lazaridis & Wickens (1999) on Albanians and EU citizens; Cañete (2001) on Filipino migrants; Labrianidis & Lyberaki (2001) on Albanians.

4 See for instance Vaiou & Hadjimichalis (1997) on 'cities, regions and informal labour', or various chapters in several edited volumes on 'social exclusion' (Kassimati 1998; Sakis Karagiorgas Foundation 1998) and 'identity' (Kostandopoulou et al. 1999), among other publications.

5 For example, the research of Psimmenos (1995; 1998) on social exclusion of Albanians in Athens provided a thorough analysis of the mechanisms of migrants' marginalisation, underestimating though the early phase of migration at the time (early 1990s). The research of Labrianidis & Lyberaki (2001) on Albanians in Thessaloniki was the first major work to 'see' the migrants' pathways to integration, followed by my own contribution (Hatziprokopiou 2003b), derived from fieldwork for this thesis.

6 See previous footnote. Also of relevance here is the economistic logic apparent in some studies, despite their analytical thoroughness (e.g. Linardos-Rylmon 1993; Lianos et al. 1996; or even Labrianidis & Lyberaki 2001). Pointing out, for instance, that the jobs migrants do are mostly in the informal sector and 'would not be done' without foreign labour is certainly true and useful, but – apart from downplaying the issue of exploitation – assumes either that migration is temporary, or that migrants (and their children) will *always* perform these kind of jobs.

7 Of 1,470 people surveyed in 1997-1998, 40 per cent had employed migrants. The sample was structured according to the basic geographical and demographic characteristics of the population.

8 E.g. highly skilled professionals who escape the average 'labour migrant' category in Greece, migrants who took Greek language courses, ethnic Greek (Sarakatsani) Bulgarians.

9 In general, throughout the fieldwork, several insights have arisen about how the questionnaire could have been better designed: for instance, some questions could have had a simpler answer format in order to be coded more easily, while some other questions could have been completely avoided.

10 Some basic textbooks on statistics have been particularly useful in order to refresh knowledge from my undergraduate years and to understand better the procedures and tests I wanted to apply (Kindis 1984; Paraskevopoulos 1990; Heiman 1996). On how to work with SPSS, I relied upon both general and specialised introductory books (Bryman & Cramer 1997; Bryman 2001: Ch. 11-12; Robson 2002: Ch. 13), and also consulted the Help tool of the statistical package itself. Quantitative data are discussed throughout the analysis and basic results are summarised in tables and figures.

11 When I refer to fieldwork findings though, 'Greater Thessaloniki' includes a suburban village to the north (Liti, administratively outside the Thessaloniki area). This is where the snowball effect brought me: the (Bulgarian) participants I spoke to there used to commute on a daily basis and most of their activities, relationships, etc., were in the centre of the city.

12 NSSG, National Accounts, regional data. All data used here are from various tables, publications and online material of the National Statistical Service of Greece, unless stated otherwise.

13 Table A4 in Appendix A illustrates the main local socio-economic indicators during 1991 and 2001.

Chapter 4

1 Two people from Albania became Protestants, after being converted by American missionaries in the early 1990s, while one Bulgarian woman is Muslim, belonging to the Muslim minority of the south-eastern part of Bulgaria.
2 Albanian women form a share of 42.1 per cent in the survey of Labrianidis & Lyberaki (2001). Census data (2001) count the share of women at 40.5 per cent among all Albanians in Thessaloniki, but only 23.8 per cent among those employed. Among Albanian regularisation applicants in 1998, only 18.3 per cent were women (Cavounidis & Hatzaki 1999). By contrast, the shares of women among Bulgarian migrants are significantly higher: 75 per cent in Markova's (2001) first sample, 54 per cent in the aggregate census data, 43.7 per cent among the employed Bulgarians and 46.2 per cent in regularisation applications.
3 It is worth noting that relatively large shares of divorced or separated women were also found in Markova's study of Bulgarian immigrants in Athens (2001: 256).
4 The findings of King et al. (2003) about many Albanian migrants in the United Kingdom who had spent some years in Greece suggest that this may be a more general trend among Albanian migrants in Greece as a whole.
5 Female migration to Greece appears to be following a 'tradition' of inter-ethnic marriages as well, in some cases, as an outcome of relationships formed between Greek students in Bulgaria and local women. However, the boundaries between such cases of 'love migration' and the bride-trade, trafficking and the illicit activities forcing women into prostitution are not that clear anymore: a simple Internet search on this issue can lead to commercial websites involved literally in a 'bazaar' of Eastern European women whose dreams for a better future might be easily exploited by profit-making networks.
6 This particular individual may be an exception in my study, but it further confirms the fact of pre-1989 mobility in the Bulgarian case, supporting the argument about a 'tradition' in Greco-Bulgarian marriages. The existence of the Greek-Bulgarian Friendship Association, 'Kyril and Methodi' in Thessaloniki, and of a similar organisation in Athens, where members are mostly mixed couples of Greeks (usually men) married to Bulgarians, offers additional proof of this trend (see Section 8.2.1).
7 The narratives of the migrants interviewed reveal to an extent what numbers hide, such as the feelings and experiences of being 'clandestine'. Valbona, an Albanian participant told me 'It's all very complicated ... I was feeling scared, I can say. I was very nervous, anyway ... I didn't know what the future would be,' before bursting into tears.
8 These cases are counted under the category 'illegal entry' in Table 4.4, whereas those who had to pay appear in 'illegal entry (trafficking)'.
9 Only one Greek-Albanian respondent came as a seasonal worker: this could be proof of the inefficiency of the bilateral agreement on recruiting seasonal workers signed in 1997 between Greece and Albania, but it is most likely to be related to the geographic (urban) scope of my research: the agreement had to do with seasonal work in agriculture mostly, that is, in rural areas, and thus it is not applicable here.
10 Four Albanians had worked in Italy before coming to Greece; all had relatives in Greece and three decided to come during 1996-1997, when the first amnesty programme was announced by the government. Information about the regularisation programme through friends was a factor for the only Bulgarian respondent who had

been to a different country (Spain) before re-emigrating to Greece. Two young women, one Albanian of ethnic Greek origin and one Bulgarian whose father is a Greek citizen, had been studying abroad (in Romania and Germany, respectively) before joining their families in Greece.

11 On networks between cities and the commercial routes linking places in the Ottoman Balkans, see for instance Todorov (1986), Katsiardi-Hering (2003) and Stoianovich (2003).

12 Both Vlachs and non-Grecophone Orthodox Albanians are considered 'ethnic Greeks' (*Voreioepirotes*) by the Greek state, and those who were in a position to prove their roots have been treated favourably.

13 The regional position of Korçë in what is now the south-eastern corner of Albania and its economic role were improved in the aftermath of the devastation of Moschopolis (1770s), a city that had been an important merchant town in this part of the Balkans and one of the centres of Vlach culture for centuries.

14 In the context of Bulgarian migration, a similarly interesting case for future research might be Plovdiv (again a city with a strong Vlach element in the past) given the commercial links and the parallel cultural and social development with Thessaloniki (see Miteva 2001). According to my findings, Plovdiv and its surroundings is the second major region of origin of Bulgarian migrants to Thessaloniki, which contrasts with Markova's (2001) evidence that most Bulgarians in Athens come from northern cities.

Chapter 5

1 For instance, the Greek ombudsman reported several problems regarding the detention conditions of those awaiting expulsion in the General Police Directorate of Attica and other police departments (Cert. N. 1956, 10 December 2001): not only was the period of detention often longer than the six months stipulated by law, but also the hygiene conditions were bad and the numbers of people detained exceeded the capacity of the place where they were kept.

2 The survey questioned a random sample of 2,000 people who called the 1464 telephone helpline operated by the Centre for Citizens' Support (*ΚΕΠ*, a body of the Ministry of the Interior) to ask for information about the procedures of the second regularisation during summer 2001 (*Eleftherotypia*, 1 August 2001: 46).

3 Problems of a similar nature continued to exist after the revision of the legal framework (Law 2910/2001) and they were highlighted in a report of the Greek ombudsman entitled 'Suggestions for the simpler, more effective and fair realisation of the policy of Law 2910/2001', that was sent to the Ministry of the Interior on 23 September 2003 (cert. N. 4603).

4 In addition, under the provisions of the new law, the application fee required for the issue of a work permit (separate from the stay permit) was set at 294, 440 or 880 euros for permits lasting 1-2 years, 2-6 years and more than 6 years, respectively (*Eleftherotypia*, 29 May 2001: 59).

5 The cost of buying all of the 250 social security stamps required was calculated as follows in 2001: about 1,380 euros for the IKA fund, 1,430 euros for TEBE and 293 euros for *ΟΓΑ* (*Eleftherotypia*, 31 May 2001: 20).

6 Such conditions produce further difficulties and create space for exploitation and corruption. Some migrants (those who can afford it) may pay a lawyer to prepare their applications and submit them on their behalf, so that they can escape both the endless queues and the loss of days out of work; there have been reported cases of lawyers and 'counselling offices' financially exploiting the situation (*Eleftherotypia*, 28

May 2001; 22 January 2003; 13 July 2003). Lawyers are given priority in public service departments between 11 a.m. and 1 p.m. (on the basis of a law dating back to 1955), so applicants who are still in the queue have to wait longer or come again the next day. Another issue has been the emergence of illegal businesses producing and issuing forged documents (e.g. *Imerisia*, 21 June 2003).

7 The survey was based on questionnaires distributed to public servants in 29 public sector bodies, as part of a project entitled 'Investigation of problems in serving migrants, returnees, refugees', realised by the Institute of Urban Environment and Human Potential of Panteion University (Athens) during the first trimester of 2003 and under the supervision of Panteion professors P. Getimis and X. Petrinioti. The preliminary findings quoted here were published in *Eleftherotypia* (1 July 2004). The research highlights an interesting contradiction between the stances and the values of public servants: negative perceptions, particularly towards specific nationalities (Albanians, 58.2 per cent; Romanians, 32.4 per cent; and Bulgarians, 29.7 per cent) coexisted with values such as the need to combat racism, to promote social solidarity, to support human rights, to protect individual liberties, to fight poverty. Researchers interpret this on the basis of the problems involved in the process itself, most of which are mentioned above.

8 The National Commission for Human Rights, in its 2001 report, talks about 'bad detention conditions', 'inadequate legal support' and 'racist treatment' by Greek police officers towards aliens arrested for lacking documents (2002: 45-47). Amnesty International's 2003 report on Greece denounces cases of 'torturing' and 'ill-treatment' of alien detainees 'during arrest and in custody'.

9 Another two parties deserve special reference due to their short-lasting influence during the 1990s. The first, *ΔΗ.Κ.ΚΙ.*, split from PASOK, representing its populist left wing. It combined a working-class rhetoric with 'patriotic' ideology, but it has never seriously included immigrants in its agenda apart from general statements against governmental policy; ultimately it has seen its electoral power diminishing, and it did not participate in the last elections. 'Political Spring', *ΠΟΛ.ΑΝ.*, split from New Democracy led by a former Minister of Foreign Affairs, who was the first Greek official to 'welcome' ethnic Greeks when the Albanian border opened (the separation of his group caused the fall of the conservative government in 1993); although not directly xenophobic, it induced a nationalistic discourse particularly popular at the time of the demonstrations for the 'Macedonian cause' (early 1990s), but since then its influence has gradually faded until the last election, when the 'turncoats' rejoined the party.

10 *ΛΑ.Ο.Σ* are the Greek initials for 'People's Orthodox Alert'. Logging on to the party's website, we read (in Greek): 'The People's Orthodox Alert was formed on the 14th of September 2000 with the aim of changing the rotten political climate and having reborn, for all of us, the ideals of Faith, Religion and Family...' Among the banners appearing on the screen, there is one stating: 'Yellow card for unemployment, bogus immigrants and non-meritocracy'.

11 The Balkan Neighbours Project, which monitors national media in Albania, Bulgaria, Greece, Macedonia, Romania, Serbia and Turkey, produces a quarterly report on the perceptions of the Balkan 'other' and of internal minorities as they appear in the press; the autumn 1996 report for Greece featured negative stereotypes in mainstream newspapers, particularly of Albanians (Lenkova 1996).

12 The Greek state objected to the right of the Former Yugoslav Republic of Macedonia to use the name 'Macedonia' and certain symbols, because they 'belong' to the Greek national inheritance, and could be used for 'minority claims'; apart from an economic embargo that injured the two countries' diplomatic relations, the issue in Greece led to a reawakening of nationalism, which was extremely popular and successful in terms of mobilisation. Greco-Turkish relations reached the razor's edge at the end of

1995 when a group of Turks landed on the deserted rocky island of Imia (or Kardak, in Turkish) and raised the Turkish flag.

13 It is worth interpreting this in relation to what Lipovac (1993: 36) calls 'a love-hate relationship' between Greece and Western Europe. Accordingly, this relationship is manifested in traditional feelings of inferiority towards the West (due to economic and political dependency, historically), that are played out through perceptions of 'justification' (400 years of Ottoman rule) and attitudes of 'devaluation' of the Western world as opposed to the Greek ('dumb Westerners' or '*koutofragkoi*' in Greek, reference to the glorious ancient past). In a similar way, within the new post-1989 Balkan context, such feelings and attitudes reappear in the reverse: now 'we' have found somebody to exploit, somebody who depends on 'us' for survival and/or politico-economic stability, thus somebody towards whom 'we' can feel superior.

14 It is worth mentioning here the example of a recent TV drama series that touched the issue directly, although in a rather romantic manner, telling the story of the forbidden love between a young Albanian worker and his employer's wife in a rural setting ('Love Came From Far Away', 2002). The series lasted for a year on one of the most popular TV channels, and despite its heavy reliance on clichés and stereotypes, it has certainly been an exception to the rule regarding migrants' portrayal on Greek TV, therefore it is very likely to have had a positive impact on common perceptions; it certainly made a good impression on many of the interviewees, who mentioned it with an element of pride. More recently, a young Albanian girl was included among the participants in the 2004 series of the 'Fame Story' reality show. Obviously, such examples indicate a degree of 'absorption' of immigrants by the dominant culture; but they certainly reflect a change of attitude in the Greek media.

15 Apart from long established institutions (mainstream parties, trade unions, the Church) and a few branches of international organisations, the emergence of civil-society groups in Greece not only came at a quite late stage, but its presence, influence and capacity to mobilise was – and still is – marginal. Thus, the development of organised civil society coincided with the transformation of Greece into a host society; it is connected to factors ranging from the decline of the welfare state or the decentralisation of public services, to the expansion of the role of international NGOs globally, the availability of resources and funding (e.g. from the EU), and the decline of traditional forms of political participation, mobilisation and protest (traditional left-wing and working-class politics). Governmental research in 2000 found that 45 per cent of registered NGOs were employing waged staff, and that waged employment in the sector accounted for 3.3 per cent of the total; nearly 45 per cent of the NGOs surveyed were based in Attica and one fifth in Central Macedonia (Ministry of Labour and Social Security 2002: 73-74).

16 Ministry of Labour and Social Security, National Action Plan for Employment 2002, Pillar II, 7th Guiding Line: Combating discrimination and promoting social inclusion through access to employment.

17 Think-tanks, research institutes, NGOs, grassroots initiatives, left-wing groups, trade unions, etc.

Chapter 6

1 Percentages from now on are among those working (N=198), unless stated otherwise.

2 '*Personal services*' refers to work offered directly to individuals and households: domestic service, cleaning, private care, casual maintenance and repair work (gardening, painting, roofing, tiling, etc.). A share of those working in the '*maintenance and*

repair' sector is actually employed by individuals and households as well. The reason for treating them separately is because in this case they are employed as waged workers by private specialised businesses (as cleaners, electricians, plumbers, etc.), or they are regular workers (maintenance, repair, cleaning) in companies and other institutions (e.g. university).

3 '*Other services*' includes educational institutions (music or language schools), business companies (accountancies, investment, web design), and other services (translations, architects, NGOs) and refer to migrants doing both white- and blue-collar work (Table 6.1; for details see Table A6 in Appendix A).

4 One fifth (ten people) of those in manufacturing work in such small workshops (four in metallurgy and another four in carpentry). Of the remaining 40, one fourth work in factories producing metal machinery, another fourth in clothing factories, five people in furniture and bathroom equipment, three in oil, plastics and chemicals, another three in shoe factories, and two in food and beverages. The remaining seven have not specified (see Table A6, Appendix A).

5 'Other services' for men include musicians, language tutors, economists, an engineer, an architect, a public servant; for women, music and language tutors, office workers, translators, economists, a university professor, a doctor, a lawyer, a web designer, a swimming coach.

6 The larger businesses run by immigrants are two companies offering specialised business and trading services and a translation office. Of the women entrepreneurs, one runs a café-bar and the other a restaurant. Family businesses include two retail shops, a jewellery store and a small clothing manufacturer. Among the self-employed women, there is a hairdresser, a painter undertaking tasks together with her husband, a shop-keeper, a web designer and two music tutors. Self-employed men work mostly in construction, while there are also two craftsmen, an architect, a kiosk owner and a corner-shop owner.

7 Where relevant, the amounts earned were converted from drachmas into euros. For the respondents who stated their monthly salary, daily wages have been calculated by dividing this amount by twenty working days. In the few cases where respondents stated their hourly rate of pay this was multiplied by eight hours of work per day. Forty people did not state the exact amount they earn, but said their payment was 'very low', 'high' or 'unstable/not fixed/depends' and were processed in SPSS under the relevant categories ('less than 20', '40+', 'not fixed', respectively). In four cases, there was no response. Statistical procedures (e.g. means, correlation) were based on exact amounts, excluding those not working.

8 As a basis for comparison, IKA statistics (September 2003) tell us that the average daily wage of (insured) construction workers in Thessaloniki was 46.4 euros (about 2.5 euros below the national one). Obviously the level of productivity is not taken into account when drawing such comparisons on the basis of individual immigrants' experiences.

9 Given an initial lack of detailed knowledge on these matters, the relevant section of the questionnaire was not designed to capture such specificities. The exact numbers of migrants who followed the above pathways of access to social security remain obscure, apart from a few notes kept during the interviews when a special reference was made by the respondents themselves.

10 Information on that concerns about 80 per cent of the sample (N=166), and 76 per cent stated the exact period they had been working at their current occupation.

11 This information (employment history) is impossible to present here in a systematic way, due to the variety of different tasks performed by a single person. The relevant answer format in the questionnaire allowed for multiple responses. Of the results presented, I have excluded 53 cases of people who have been doing the same job-type

since the beginning, as well as 5.3 per cent of missing data: each different occupation performed by a single individual has been counted only once. The high percentage aggregates reflect the multiple responses inherent in the questions asked about different jobs done.

12 This idea came from a conference presentation by Pajo (2001), theorising from the Albanian case.

13 The only respondent who worked as a public servant is an ethnic Greek Albanian who was granted Greek citizenship and who acknowledged the role of intermediaries (people he knew in responsible posts) in assisting in his recruitment.

14 Immigrants' health problems, often caused by hard work in insecure environments and bad living conditions, is a crucial issue surprisingly underestimated in the literature on migration to Greece. The daily press often reports on 'occupational accidents' of migrants at work. According to data from the Labour Watch Service of the Ministry of Labour, the number of immigrants dying in occupational accidents in construction and manufacturing rose from 20 in 2000 to 39 in 2001 and reached 40 in 2002, which is attributed mainly to the nature of the jobs performed, the limited safety measures undertaken by employers and the low skills migrant workers generally have (*Eleftherotypia*, 18 January 2004).

15 See Jahn & Straubhar (1999).

Chapter 7

1 However, cases with diverse housing conditions have been included in this category. Ground floors in outer Thessaloniki buildings should not always be considered as 'inappropriate', neither are they less popular among locals. At the other end of the spectrum, there are examples of people who lived in wagons or sheds converted into rooms situated in the courtyards of the factories where they work, without water and with outdoor self-made toilets. Or the unique case of a Sarakatsan man who comes for short periods of work and, in order to save money (to finance his daughters' studies at a Greek university, as he told me), he sleeps in his car and accommodates his other needs at the homes of his more settled compatriots.

2 For instance, those employed in white-collar and highly skilled positions, those who are employers or self-employed and those who earn 40 euros or more a day are more likely to have their own property, to live on upper floors, or to enjoy central heating and a larger housing space.

3 Refer back to Section 3.3 for definitions of these geographical units. There is a possibility of slight spatial bias, related to the overrepresentation of central Thessaloniki and certain neighbourhoods in the way the sample was generated; but my findings do not contrast much with the 2001 census data, which however do not include disaggregated information on the distribution of the specific migrant groups studied here (see Figure A2 in Appendix A).

4 The fact that the residential distribution of Bulgarian immigrants exhibits higher concentrations in a particular area might reflect bias in the selection of the sample. This was to an extent intended and has been useful in order to address, on the one hand, the special case of the Bulgarian Sarakatsani, and, on the other, to examine the interplay between migration and socio-spatial dynamics at the neighbourhood level.

5 At the beginning of the 1990s, research on the housing market in Thessaloniki showed that about 70 per cent of the households in the conurbation lived in their own accommodation (Velentzas et al. 1996: Ch. 7.4), which implies lower degrees of residential mobility among the local population, at least at the time that most immigrants arrived.

6 One possible exception that should be noted here has to do with the background and socio-economic status of the migrants. Those in the sample who have been described as 'elite' migrants, people of high educational level who do specialised, qualified jobs (scientists, artists, etc.) – proportionally far more highly represented among Bulgarian immigrants – expressed different cultural values in respect to leisure and thus preference for different types and places of entertainment (theatre, opera, etc.).

7 On bars and cafés that function as small 'community centres' see also Section 8.2.1. Some of these places might be used as meeting points for people from the same area, town or village in the home country, although nothing like that was encountered during the fieldwork.

8 Survey by the Paediatric Clinic of the Regional General Hospital at Athens (*Ta Nea*, 3 May 2004: N58).

9 During the fieldwork, I personally witnessed the expansion of a small 'Chinatown' in Thessaloniki, counting four shops (shoes and clothing mainly) on the main street in 2000, twenty-one in 2002, while many more had mushroomed in the surrounding streets by my last visit in 2003.

Chapter 8

1 As early as 1992 a ministerial council recognised the necessity for establishing reception/support classes for immigrants, based on the related provisions applying to ethnic Greeks. In 1996, an educational law (2413/1996) raised the issue of intercultural education for the first time, acknowledging the needs of children with 'educational, social and cultural particularities' and the consequent necessity for the establishment of 'intercultural schools' (Chapter 1, articles 34-37). This provision allowed for the recognition of foreign communities' schools (Polish, Russian), but left the responsibility for the foundation of intercultural schools to local authorities, community organisations and the Church.

2 Regarding this, there seems to exist an ongoing conflict between the Ministry of the Interior and the legal framework. I. Sotirhou, in *Eleftherotypia*, 29 December 2003, reports on a memorandum sent by the Minister of the Interior to the Ministry of Education, calling on state schools to expel the children of undocumented migrants, which is against both the law and the Constitution and was denounced by the ombudsman; Education officials insist on facilitating enrolment procedures for these children.

3 This finding points also to a trend which is not specifically revealed by the fieldwork material, neither is it supported by available official statistics: the numbers of foreign students in Greek universities have grown immensely during the past decade. The principal countries of origin happen to coincide with the countries many immigrants come from: Albania and other Balkan and Eastern European or former Soviet countries, as well as Asian, African and Western European countries.

4 Of them 75.5 per cent are of 'foreign' origin, 42.7 per cent have spent six years or more in the country, 10.7 per cent were born in Greece; 72.4 per cent were born in Albania, 3 per cent in Bulgaria, 2.2 per cent in Georgia, 2.1 per cent in Russia, 1.5 per cent in Ukraine, 1.2 per cent in Romania and 1.1 per cent in Armenia. 31,873 children are of 'ethnic Greek' origin: 15.4 per cent were born in Greece, 22.6 per cent in Georgia, 19.6 per cent in Russia, 8.2 per cent in Kazakhstan; Greek-Albanian pupils form 13.6 per cent, while 5.3 and 2.1 per cent are children of returning migrants from Germany and the USA respectively. The newspaper reported on a study by the Institute of Diaspora Greeks' and Intercultural Education (*ΙΠΟΔΕ*).

5 Secondary education in Greece is broken into two stages: '*Gymnasio*' refers to junior high school (the first three years of secondary school) and its completion ends the nine years of obligatory education. After that, pupils might go on to a general *Lykeio*, or senior high school (final three years), which leads to *Apolytyrion* (Lyceum degree) and includes preparation for university entry; or they can attend a technical/professional *Lykeio*.

6 A survey by KAPA Research done on behalf of UNICEF with a sample of 2,343 Greek parents, teachers and pupils in Athenian and Thessalonikan schools uncovered the following stances towards foreign pupils: their presence at school is considered 'positive' by just 11 per cent of parents, but by 72 per cent of pupils (*Imerisia*, 20 March 2001).

7 The research was carried out by the *ΙΠΟΔΕ* and the results were published in *Kathimerini* (5 December 2003, article by A. Lakasas); the survey was based on a countrywide sample of 35,049 foreign pupils (more than one third of their total population), taking into account second- and third-year senior high school examinations.

8 This happens on two occasions: on the 28th of October, when the refusal of Greece to allow (Fascist) Italian troops into the country in 1940 is celebrated; and the 25th of March, a day commemorating the symbolic initiation of the Greek struggle for independence from the Ottoman Empire in 1821.

9 It should be noted that the relevant question was aimed at information about individuals, not households; thus the figure might appear lower due to dependent family members expressing their personal situation.

10 Only 36.8 per cent of women have an account. Interestingly, while among Albanians the share of women having an account is lower (39 per cent, compared to 65 per cent among men), among Bulgarians it is the other way round (about one third of women, compared to only 22.3 per cent among men).

11 Apart from relying solely on the accounts of the interviewees, much of the information presented in this section is based on informal chats, observation, brochures and leaflets published by migrant associations and other organisations, etc. In three cases (Epirote House, Association of Greeks from Sarandë, Gjirokaster and Delvina, Kyril and Methodi), I conducted personal interviews with the associations' leaders. All this material also provided a basis for a comparison between the Thessaloniki experience of Albanian and Bulgarian migrants and the situation in Athens and elsewhere, regarding other migrant groups as well. In that respect, several of the texts written by community representatives in the second part of the volume edited by Marvakis et al. (2001: 333-388) have been particularly helpful, especially the overviews by E. Markova and K. Kuka on the Bulgarian and Albanian cases, respectively.

12 Both the Socialist and the Democratic parties of Albania have representation in Thessaloniki, as well as the Greek minority's party (*Omonia*) and other organisations. Six respondents said they are or used to be in contact with one of the above. I personally was present at a demonstration against the NATO bombings of Yugoslavia during the Kosovo events, where a local (Albanian) member of the Democratic Party tried to discourage Albanian protesters from taking part. Representatives of both Epirote House and the Association of Greeks from Sarandë, Gjirokaster and Delvina informed me about minority politics in Albania and said they had contacts with members of the Greek minority party.

13 This was mentioned by two younger interviewees and the owner of the café described above herself. It appears though that these places, strategically located near the railway station and the area around St Dimitrios Church, where many Bulgarian migrants live, were owned by Greeks.

14 A higher share (74.6 per cent) of ethnic Greek migrants in particular tend to interact with locals, perhaps due to language and less prejudice towards them. The percen-

tage of women socialising with Greeks is lower than that of men (55.3 and 70.5 per cent, respectively), which points both to the differences between male and female employment (e.g. female domestic workers and carers who work alone) and the family division of labour (as women bear most of the weight of housework and child-care duties).

15 An interesting example is reported in *Kathimerini* (17 October 2004: 34). Data from the Athens Council Registration Service reveal that during 2003 and the first eight months of 2004, about 10 per cent of the marriages that took place in the capital were mixed ones. The majority are foreign women marrying Greek men, while the chief nationalities are Albanians, Ukrainians and Bulgarians.

16 Obviously, ethnic Greek migrants might be in a more advantaged position in this respect, but language fluency might also depend on education received in Greece as well as on factors stemming from the individuals' characteristics (age, self-study, socialisation with Greeks).

17 I have to acknowledge the possible reluctance of the respondents to tell the whole truth to somebody coming from the host society. In my interview with Ferin, for example, it only came out that this was his real name near the end of our conversation; for the most part I called him by the name he had introduced himself with in the beginning: Nikos. In the survey presented in Labrianidis & Lyberaki (2001: 174), the percentage of the (Albanian) respondents using Greek names is as high as 34 per cent.

18 Interestingly, quantitative data show no positive relationship between the migrants' well-being and the adoption of such integration strategies. By contrast, respondents who practiced such strategies received on average lower wages and had a lower average score in the 'index of material conditions' (results for the Albanian section of the sample). Obviously, quantitative accounts of material elements of this kind might hide positive aspects at other levels (e.g. inter-ethnic contact). But again, this finding indicates a relationship only, not causality: it might be the most deprived among the migrants who choose to change their name, pass for ethnic Greeks, get baptised or hide their religious beliefs.

Chapter 9

1 It is impossible to include here numerous cases for extensive comparisons: this is not a comparative study anyway. The point is, on the one hand, to see what happens in Athens and other places in Greece and to highlight similarities and differences. On the other hand, it is important to evaluate the findings of this case study in the light of what is known about other settings; a reference to theory is therefore appropriate, enriched with examples from the Southern European urban experience of migration.

2 For instance, Karydis (1996), Psimmenos (1995), Kourtovic (2001), Halkos & Salamouris (2003).

3 See Iosifides & King (1998); also King & Mai (2004) on Albanians in Italy.

4 Migrants can be understood as 'strangers', as proposed by Papastergiadis (2000: Ch. 3); Lazaridis & Wickens (1999) have offered such an interpretation specifically for the Greek case.

5 See Mousourou (1993); also Anthias & Lazaridis (1999: 1-12).

6 See Balibar & Wallerstein (1990), especially chapters 12 ('The class-based racism') and 13 ('Racism and crisis') by E. Balibar.

7 Obviously, agriculture is also a sector concentrating large numbers of migrant workers. Given the urban focus of the research however, it is not accounted here. For details on that, see Lianos et al. (1996) and Kasimis et al. (2003).

8 E.g. Turks in Germany, North Africans in France, Bangladeshis or Black Caribbeans in the United Kingdom, etc., despite differences in the legal position of these groups in each of these countries.

9 Primarily Moroccans in the former case and Albanians, among other migrant groups, in the latter.

10 Other groups, in Greece or in other countries, develop similar strategies. Polish immigrants in Athens, for instance, learn the language, get baptised, take Greek names, build relationships with locals, go on holiday in the host country, etc. (Romaniszyn 1996). Kosic & Triandafyllidou (2003) and King & Mai (2004) observed similar strategies among Albanians in Italy.

11 See, for instance, Anthias & Lazaridis (1999) on the Southern European experience. On Greece, see Psimmenos (1995; 1998), Iosifides & King (1998), Lazaridis (1999), Lazaridis & Psimmenos (2000).

12 Fakiolas (2003: 548) reports on an information note issued by the Ministry of Public Order on 15 November 2002: among nearly 219,600 migrants arrested for illegal entry/residence in 2001, 4.8 per cent were Iraqis and 1.9 per cent were Afghans; the share of Iraqis in 2000's arrests was lower (4.4 per cent), while Afghans were not represented in that year's arrests (at least not in significant shares).

13 See *Deltio Thielis*, magazine of the Network of Movements for Social and Political Rights (May 1998).

14 E.g. Daly & Barot (1999) on Tunisians in Italy, or Trimikliniotis (1999) on immigrants in Cyprus.

15 The origins of the movement lie in an August 1996 event, when three hundred undocumented migrants from Africa were violently evicted by riot police from St Bernard's Church in northern Paris, where they had found sactuary for several months. It currently has expanded to a network of grassroots organisations ('collectives') supporting and campaigning for undocumented migrants ('sans papiers', as commonly referred to in French) with 'branches' across France and in several other EU countries (for more information, see: pajol.eu.org).

16 This is a phrase Smart (1997) uses to describe the role of migrants to Canada in Alberta's agriculture. Despite notable differences in migration contexts and patterns, this distant case does not differ much from the way migrants in Greece function as flexible labour, e.g. in construction or personal services.

17 In respect to this, the (Greek) Macedonian Press Agency reported on 21 October 2001 that about 260 Bulgarian nationals living in Thessaloniki were expected to vote in the Bulgarian national election of 11 November 2001 at the city's Bulgarian Consulate.

18 The idea is to provide incentives for companies to move there instead of relocating abroad, thus helping them to escape the unstable environments of Balkan countries without losing the asset of low-cost labour. The gains for the local community – among the poorest regions in the EU – are obvious, but overall benefits for the national economy are also expected, by keeping economic activity within the country. The infrastructure was supposed to start being built in 2002, while similar initiatives are being designed for other northern border regions, on the basis of the institutional framework 'Free Zones of Economic Exchange', EU Regulation 2913/92, Article 166. For further details see Labrianidis (1998).

19 Reported in *Eleftherotypia*, 29 December 2004.

20 See, for instance, *Eleftherotypia*, 21 November 2004, article by G. Linardos.

21 High concentrations of migrants in specific working-class districts of Athens that hosted refugees and internal migrants in the past have been noted in the studies of Psimmenos (1995; 1998) and Halkos & Salamouris (2003). Similarly, in Barcelona's central districts, Morrocans tend to 'replace' Andalusian immigrants (King & Rodriguez-Melguizo). In northern Italian cities, immigrants occupy spaces previously inhabited by migrants from the south (King & Mai, 2004).

22 For a theoretical account of the economic impact of immigration see for instance Borjas (1994) and Jahn & Straubhaar (1999). The issues touched on here are those addressed by studies looking specifically at the Greek case: e.g. Lianos (1996; 2003), Fakiolas (1999), Labrianidis & Lyberaki (2001), Lyberaki & Pelagidis (2000), Sarris & Zografakis (1999).

23 E.g. Lianos et al. (1996); Labrianidis & Lyberaki (2001).

24 See Sarris & Zografakis (1999); also Labrianidis & Lyberaki (2001).

Bibliography

Alexiou, Th. (1999), 'Waged labour and social exclusion', *Theseis* 69: 25-49. (In Greek.)

Allen, J. (1996), 'Post industrialism/postfordism', in S. Hall, D. Held, D. Hubert & K. Thompson (eds.), *Modernity: an Introduction to Modern Societies*, 536-555. Oxford: Blackwell.

Amitsis, G. & G. Lazaridis (eds.) (2001), *Legal and Socio-Political Dimensions of Immigration to Greece*. Athens: Papazisis. (In Greek.)

Ammassari, S. & R. Black (2001), 'Harnessing the potential of migration and return to promote development: applying concepts to West Africa', *Sussex Migration Working Papers*, Sussex Centre for Migration Research, University of Sussex, July 2001.

Amnesty International (2003), Amnesty International Report 2003 (January-December 2002): Greece. www. amnesty.org.

Anderson, B. (2000), Doing the Dirty Work: the Global Politics of Domestic Labour. London: Zed Books.

Anthias, F. & G. Lazaridis (eds.) (1999), *Into the Margins: Migration and Exclusion in Southern Europe*. Aldershot: Ashgate.

Baganha, M. I. & M. L. Fonseca (eds.) (2004), *New Waves: Migration from Eastern to Southern Europe*. Lisbon: Luso-American Foundation & Metropolis Portugal.

Baldwin-Edwards, M. (1999), 'Where free markets reign: aliens in the twilight zone', in M. Baldwin-Edwards & J. Arango (eds.), *Immigrants and the Informal Economy in Southern Europe*, 1-15. London: Frank Cass.

Baldwin-Edwards, M. (2001), 'An analytic commentary on the Greek immigration bill, 2000', *Mediterranean Migration Observatory Working Paper Series*, no. 2, February 2001. Athens: MMO-Panteion University.

Baldwin-Edwards, M. (2004a), 'Albanian emigration and the Greek labour market: economic symbiosis and social ambiguity', *South East Europe Review for Labour and Social Affairs* 7 (1): 51-65.

Baldwin-Edwards, M. (2004b), 'Mediterranean migrations; regionalisms versus globalisation', *Finisterra: Revista Portuguesa de Geografia* 34 (77): 9-20.

Baldwin-Edwards, M. & R. Fakiolas (1999), 'Greece: the contours of a fragmented policy response', in M. Baldwin-Edwards & J. Arango (eds.), *Immigration and the Informal Economy in Southern Europe*, 186-204. London: Frank Cass

Baldwin-Edwards, M. & C. Safilios-Rothschild (1999), 'Immigration and unemployment in Greece: perceptions and realities', in N. Bermeo (ed.), *The Social Consequences of Unemployment in Southern Europe*, special issue of *South European Society and Politics* 4 (2): 206-221.

Balibar, E. & I. Wallerstein (1990), *Race, Nation, Classe: les Identités Ambigües*. Paris: Editions La Decouverte.

Bauböck, R. (2002), 'How migration transforms citizenship: international, multinational and transnational perspectives', *IWE Working Paper Series*, no. 24, February 2002. Vienna: Österreichichische Akademie der Wissenschaften-IWE.

Borjas, G. J. (1994), 'The economics of immigration', *Journal of Economic Literature* 32: 1667-1717.

Bourdieu, P. (1977), *Outline of a Theory of Practice*. Cambridge: Cambridge University Press.

Bryman, A. (2001), *Social Research Methods*. Oxford: Oxford University Press.

Bryman, A. & D. Cramer (1997), *Quantitative Data Analysis with SPSS for Windows: a Guide for Social Scientists*. London: Routledge.

Budd, L. (1998), 'Territorial competition and globalisation: Scylla and Charybdis of European cities', *Urban Studies* 35 (4): 663-685.

Cañete, L. Y. (2001), 'The Filipino community in Greece at the end of the 20th century', in Ath. Marvakis, D. Parsanoglou & M. Pavlou (eds.), *Immigrants in Greece*, 277-304. Athens: Ellinika Grammata. (In Greek.)

Castells, M. (1989), *The Informational City: Information Technology, Economic Restructuring and the Urban-Regional Process*. Oxford: Basil Blackwell.

Castells, M. (1996), *The Information Age: Economy, Society and Culture. Vol. 1. The Rise of the Network Society*. Oxford: Blackwell Publishers.

Castells, M. (1997), *The Information Age: Economy, Society and Culture. Vol. 2. The Power of Identity*. Oxford: Blackwell Publishers.

Castells, M. (1998), *The Information Age: Economy, Society and Culture. Vol. 3. End of Millennium*. Oxford: Blackwell Publishers.

Castles, S. (2000), 'International migration at the beginning of the 21st century: global trends and issues', *International Social Science Journal* 52 (165): 269-281.

Castles, S. (2001), 'Migration and community formation under conditions of globalisation', paper presented at the conference 'Reinventing Society in the New Economy'. University of Toronto, 9-10 March 2001.

Castles, S. & M. J. Miller (1998), *The Age of Migration: International Population Movements in the Modern World*. 2nd edn. London: Macmillan.

Castles, S., H. Booth & T. Wallace (1984), *Here for Good: Western Europe's New Ethnic Minorities*. London: Pluto Press.

Cavounidis, J. & M. Hatzaki (1999), *Aliens who Applied for the Card of Temporary Residence: Nationality, Gender and Spatial Distribution*. Athens: National Institute for Employment (EIE). (In Greek.)

Chiswick, B. R. (1978), 'The effects of Americanization on the earnings of foreign-born men', *Journal of Political Economy* 86: 897-921.

Chronaki, Z., C. Hadjimichalis, L. Labrianidis & D. Vaiou (1993), 'Diffused industrialisation in Thessaloniki: from expansion to crisis', *International Journal of Urban and Regional Research* 17(2): 178-194.

Cohen, R. (1987), *The New Helots: Migrants in the International Division of Labour*. Aldershot: Gower.

Daly, F. & R. Barot (1999), 'Economic migration and social exclusion: the case of Tunisians in Italy', in F. Anthias & G. Lazaridis (eds.), *Into the Margins: Migration and Exclusion in Southern Europe*, 35-53. Aldershot: Ashgate.

Damanakis, M. (1997), *The Education of Returning Migrant and Alien Migrant Pupils in Greece: a transcultural perspective*. Athens: Gutemberg. (In Greek.)

Dines, N. (2002), 'Immigration, urban regeneration and contested space: the case of Piazza Garibaldi in Naples', paper presented at the 'Rights to the City' conference, Rome, 29 May-1 June 2002.

Droukas, E. (1998), 'Albanians in the Greek informal economy', *Journal of Ethnic and Migration Studies* 24 (2): 347-365.

Emke-Poulopoulos, I. (2001), 'Trafficking in women and children: Greece, a country of destination and transit', *Mediterranean Migration Observatory Working Paper Series*, no. 2, August 2001. Athens: MMO-Panteion University.

Engels, F. (1952), *The Condition of the Working Class in England*. Edited and introduced by D. McLellan. Oxford: Oxford University Press.

Esping-Andersen, G. (1990), *The Three Worlds of Welfare Capitalism*. Cambridge: Polity Press.

Fakiolas, R. (1995), 'Italy and Greece: from emigrants to immigrants', in Cohen, R. (ed.), *The Cambridge Survey of World Migration*, 313-315. Cambridge: Cambridge University Press.

Fakiolas, R. (1999), 'Socio-economic effects of immigration to Greece', *Journal of European Social Policy* 9 (3): 211-229.

Fakiolas, R. (2000), 'Migration and unregistered labour in the Greek economy', in King, R., Lazaridis, G. & Tsardanidis Ch. (eds.), *Eldorado or Fortress? Migration in Southern Europe*, 57-78. London: Macmillan Press.

Fakiolas, R. (2003), 'Regularising undocumented immigrants in Greece: procedures and effects', *Journal of Ethnic and Migration Studies* 29 (3): 535-561.

Fakiolas, R. & R. King (1996), 'Emigration, return, immigration: a review and evaluation of Greece's postwar experience of international migration', *International Journal of Population Geography* 2: 171-190.

Fakiolas, R. & L. Maratou-Alipranti (2000), 'Foreign female immigrants in Greece', *Papers: Revista de Sociologia* 60: 101-117.

Fassmann, H. & R. Münz (eds.) (1994), *European Migration in the late 20th Century*. Aldershot: IIASA/Edward Elgar.

Featherstone, M. (1990), *Global Culture: nationalisms, globalisation and modernity*. Special issue of *Theory Culture and Society* 7 (2-3). London: Sage Publications.

Ferrera, M. (1996), 'Il modello sud-europeo di welfare state', *Rivista Italiana di Scienza Politica* 1: 67-101.

Findlay A. (1996), 'Extra-Union migration: the South-North perspective', in: P. Rees, J. Stillwell, A. Convey & M. Kupiszewski (eds.), *Population Migration in the European Union*, 29-55. Chichester: John Wiley and Sons.

Findlay, A. M. (1995), 'Skilled transients: the invisible phenomenon', in R. Cohen (ed.), *The Cambridge Survey of World Migration*, 515-22. Cambridge: Cambridge University Press.

Fonseca, M. L. & A. Esteves (2002), 'Migration and new religion townscapes in Lisbon', in M. L. Fonseca, J. Malheiros, N. Ribas-Mateos, P. White & A. Esteves (eds.), *Immigration and Place in Mediterranean Metropolises*, 255-289. Lisbon: Luso-American Foundation & Metropolis Portugal.

Fonseca, M. L., J. Malheiros, N. Ribas-Mateos, P. White & A. Esteves (eds.) (2002), *Immigration and Place in Mediterranean Metropolises*. Lisbon: Luso-American Foundation & Metropolis Portugal.

Fröbel, F., J. Heinrichs & O. Kreye (1983), *The New International Division of Labour*. Cambridge: Cambridge University Press.

Georgoulas, St. (2001), 'The new immigration social policy in Greece and its legitimisation', in Ath. Marvakis, D. Parsanoglou & M. Pavlou (eds.), *Immigrants in Greece*, 199-226. Athens: Ellinika Grammata. (In Greek.)

Ghosh, B. (1998), *Huddled Masses and Uncertain Shores: Insights into Irregular Migration*. London: Martinus Nijhoff Publishers.

Giannakou, A. & G. Kafkalas (1999), 'Trends of spatial distribution of the tertiary sector and the regulation of urban development: lessons from the case of Thessaloniki', in

D. Oikonomou & G. Petrakos (eds.), *The Development of Greek Cities: Interdisciplinary Perspectives of Urban Analysis and Policy*, 93-115. Volos: Thessaly University Press & Gutemberg. (In Greek.)

Giddens, A. (1991), *The Consequences of Modernity*. Cambridge: Polity Press.

Giner, S. (1985), 'Political economy, legitimation and the State in Southern Europe', in R. Hudson & J. Lewis (eds.), *Uneven Development in Southern Europe: Studies in Accumulation, Class, Migration and the State*, 309-350. London: Methuen.

Glarnetatzis, Y. (2001), 'An insight on the antiracist movement in Greece: the case of the Anti-racist Initiative of Thessaloniki', in Ath. Marvakis, D. Parsanoglou & M. Pavlou (eds.), *Immigrants in Greece*, 391-399. Athens: Ellinika Grammata. (In Greek.)

Glytsos, N. (1995), 'Problems and policies regarding the socio-economic integration of returnees and foreign workers in Greece', *International Migration* 33 (2): 155-176.

GNTO (Greek National Tourism Organisation) *Tourism Statistics* (various tables). www.gnto.gr. [accessed May 2004] (pages also available in English).

Gorz, A. (1980), *Adieu au proletariat*. Paris: Galilée.

Granovetter, M. (1985), 'Economic action and social structure: the problem of embeddedness', *American Journal of Sociology* 91: 481-510.

Greek Human Rights Commission (2002), *Report 2001*. Athens: Ethniko Typografeio. (In Greek.)

Grossman, G. M. & E. Helpman (1991), *Innovation and Growth in the Global Economy*. Cambridge MA: MIT Press.

Guarnizo, L. E. & M. P. Smith (1998), 'The locations of transnationalism', in M. P. Smith & L. E. Guarnizo (eds.), *Transnationalism from Below, Comparative Urban and Community Research*, 3-31. New Brunswick: Transaction Publishers.

Habermas, J. (1984), *The Theory of Communicative Action*, vol. 1. Boston MA: Beacon.

Hadjimichalis, C. (1994), 'The fringes of Europe and EU integration: a view from the South', *European Urban and Regional Studies* 1 (1): 19-29.

Hadjiyanni, A., K. Kallas & A. Papadopoulos (1999), 'Employment trajectories of university graduates in Greece: forms and strategies of matching social networking and educational capital for integrating into urban and rural labour markets', paper presented at the Regional Studies Association International Conference 'Regional Potentials in an Integrating Europe', University of the Basque Country, Bilbao, 18-21 September 1999.

Halkos, G. & D. Salamouris (2003), 'Socio-economic integration of ethnic Greeks from the former USSR: obstacles to entry into the Greek labour market', *Journal of Ethnic and Migration Studies* 29 (3): 519-534.

Harris J.R. & M. P. Todaro (1970), 'Migration, unemployment and development: a two-sector analysis', *American Economic Review* 60: 126-142.

Harris, N. (1995), *The New Untouchables*. London: Penguin.

Harvey, D. (1989), *The Condition of Postmodernity*. Oxford: Blackwell.

Hatziprokopiou, M., K. Velentzas & B. Brahimi (2001), 'Immigrant labour in Greece: characteristics and conditions of employment', *Annuaire de l'Universtité de Sofia 'St Kliment Ohridski', Faculté des Sciences Economiques et de Gestion*, t. 1: 293-306.

Hatziprokopiou, P. (2003a), 'Aspects of alterity in contemporary Greece: Albanian migrants and the multiple identities of the ΦOtherΦ ', paper presented at the International Sociological Conference 'Alterity and Society', Athens, 7-9 May 2003. (In Greek.)

Hatziprokopiou, P. (2003b), 'Albanian immigrants in Thessaloniki, Greece: processes of economic and social incorporation', *Journal of Ethnic and Migration Studies* 29 (6): 1033-1057.

Hatziprokopiou, P. (2004a), 'Balkan immigrants in the Greek city of Thessaloniki: local processes of incorporation in international perspective', *European Urban and Regional Studies* 11 (4): 321-338.

Hatziprokopiou, P. (2004b), 'Immigration and the transforming urban space: from Balkans to Thessaloniki', in *7th Panhellenic Geographic Conference Proceedings*, vol. 1, 87-94. Mytilini: University of the Aegean-Geography Department. (In Greek.)

Heckman, F. (2004), 'Integration and integration policies: IMISCOE network feasibility study' (draft version, November 2004), paper presented at the 1st Annual IMISCOE Conference, Coimbra, 3-6 December 2004.

Heiman, G. W. (1996), *Basic Statistics for the Behavioral Sciences*. 2nd edn. Boston: Houghton Mifflin Company.

Held, D. & A. MacGrew (1999), *Global Transformations: Politics, Economics and Culture*. Oxford: Polity Press.

Hettne, B. (1990), *Development Theory and the Three Worlds*. London: Longman.

Hirst, P. & G. Thompson (1996), *Globalisation in Question*. Cambridge: Polity Press.

Hobsbawm, E. (1992), *Nations and Nationalism since 1789: Programme, Myth, Reality*. Cambridge: Cambridge University Press.

ICAP (2003), *Thessaloniki Business Guide 2003: Economic Analysis*. www.icap.gr/thessaloniki/data/economic/index.htm.

IKA (Foundation of Social Insurance) (2003), *IKA Monthly Employment Data, September 2003*. www.ika.gr.

IOM (International Organisation for Migration) (2001), *Victims of trafficking in the Balkans: a study of trafficking in women and children for sexual exploitation to, through and from the Balkan region*. Vienna/Geneva: IOM.

IOM (International Organisation for Migration) (2002), *Trafficking for sexual exploitation: the case of the Russian Federation*. IOM Migration Research Series, no. 7 (report by D. M. Hughes). Geneva: IOM.

Iosifides, Th. & R. King (1998), 'Socio-spatial dynamics and exclusion of three immigrant groups in the Athens conurbation', *South European Society and Politics* 3 (3): 205-229.

Jahn, A. & Th. Straubhaar (1999), 'A survey of the economics of illegal migration', in M. Baldwin-Edwards & J. Arango (eds.), *Immigration and the Informal Economy in Southern Europe*, 16-42. London: Frank Cass.

Judd, Ch. M., E. R. Smith & L. Kidder (1991), *Research Methods in Social Relations*. Fort Worth: Harcourt Brace Jovanovich College Publishers.

Kafetzis, P., E. Michalopoulou, E. Manologlou & P. Tsartas (1998), 'Empirical dimensions of xenophobia', in E. Michalopoulou, P., Tsartas, M. Giannisopoulou, P. Kafetzis & E. Manologlou (eds.), *Macedonia and the Balkans: Xenophobia and Development*, 171-222. Athens: EKKE & Alexandria. (In Greek.)

Kafkalas, G., A. Loukaki, S. Manos, P. Tarani, V. Fourkas & D. Foutakis (1996), *Mechanisms of Internationalization of European Cities, Cyberspace, and the Role of Thessaloniki*. Research Project Final Report, Spatial Development Research Unit, Department of Urban and Spatial Planning and Regional Development, Faculty of Architecture, Aristotle University of Thessaloniki. (In Greek.)

Kamaras, A. (2001), 'A Capitalist Diaspora: the Greeks in the Balkans', *The Hellenic Observatory Discussion Paper Series*, Discussion Paper no. 4. London: London School of Economics and Political Science.

Kapllani, G. & N. Mai (2005), 'Greece belongs to Greeks! the case of the Greek flag in the hands of an Albanian student', in R. King, N. Mai and S. Schwandner-Sievers (eds.), *The New Albanian Migration*, 153-172. Brighton: Sussex Academic Press.

Karydis, V. (1996), *The Criminality of Immigrants in Greece: Issues of Theory and Anti-Crime Policy*. Athens: Papazisis. (In Greek.)

Kasimati, K. (ed.) (1998), *Social Exclusion: the Greek Experience*. Athens: KEKMOKOP-Panteion University & Gutemberg. (In Greek.)

Kasimati, K., V. Maos, N. Glytsos, V. Agtzidis, M. Vergeti & A. Ragousis (1992), *Pontian Immigrants from the former Soviet Union: their Social and Economic Integration*. Athens: Ministry of Culture, General Secretariat of Greeks Abroad & KEKMOKOP-Panteion University. (In Greek.)

Kasimis, Ch., A. Papadopoulos & E. Zacopoulou (2003), 'Migrants in rural Greece', *Sociologia Ruralis* 43 (2): 167-184.

Katsiardi-Hering, O. (2003), 'Greek commercial networks', in S. Asdrahas (ed.), *Greek Economic History, 15th-19th Century*, vol. 1, 461-481. Athens: Bank of Piraeus Cultural Foundation. (In Greek.)

Katsikas, H. (1998), 'Exclusion from education – rejection from work: the case of the children of Pontian immigrants from the former USSR', in Sakis Karagiorgas Foundation (eds.), *Social Inequalities and Social Exclusion*, 444-454. Athens: Exandas & Sakis Karagiorgas Foundation. (In Greek.)

Katsoridas, D. (1994), *Foreign (?), workers in Greece*. Athens: Iamos. (In Greek.)

Kindis, A. (1984), *Statistical and Econometric Methods*. Athens: Gutemberg. (In Greek.)

King, R. (1995), 'Migration, globalisation and place', in D. Massey & P. Jess (eds.), *A Place in the World? Places, Cultures and Globalisation*, 5-53. Milton Keynes: Open University & Oxford University Press.

King, R. (2000a), 'Southern Europe in the changing global map of migration', in R. King, G. Lazaridis & Ch. Tsardanidis (eds.), *Eldorado or Fortress? Migration in Southern Europe*, 1-26. London: Macmillan Press.

King, R. (2000b), 'Generalisations from the history of return migration', in B. Ghosh (ed.), *Return Migration: Journey of Hope or Despair?*, 7-55. Geneva: IOM/UN.

King, R. (2002), 'Towards a new map of European migration', *International Journal of Population Geography* 8 (2): 89-106.

King, R. (ed.) (2001), *The Mediterranean Passage: Migration and New Cultural Encounters in Southern Europe*. Liverpool: Liverpool University Press.

King, R. & N. Mai (2004), 'Albanian immigrants in Lecce and Modena: narratives of rejection, survival and integration', *Population, Society and Place*, 10 (6): 455-477.

King, R. & I. Rodriguez-Melguizo (1999), 'Recent immigration to Spain: the case of Moroccans in Catalonia', in F. Anthias and G. Lazaridis (eds.), *Into the Margins: Migration and Exclusion in Southern Europe*, 55-82. Aldershot: Ashgate.

King, R. & K. Rybaczuk (1993), 'Southern Europe and the international division of labour: from emigration to immigration', in R. King (ed.), *The New Geography of European Migration*, 175-206. London: Belhaven Press.

King, R. & E. Zontini (2000), 'The role of gender in the South European immigration model', *Papers, Revista de Sociologia* 60: 35-52.

King, R., A. Fielding & R. Black (1997), 'The international migration turnaround in Southern Europe', in R. King and R. Black (eds.), *Southern Europe and the New Immigrations*, 1-25. Brighton: Sussex Academic Press.

King, R., Th. Iosifides & L. Myrivili (1998), 'A migrants' story: from Albania to Athens', *Journal of Ethnic and Migration Studies* 24 (1): 159-175.

King, R., G. Lazaridis & Ch. Tsardanidis (eds.) (2000), *Eldorado or Fortress? Migration in Southern Europe*. London: Macmillan Press.

King, R., N. Mai & M. Dalipaj (2003), *Exploding the Migration Myths*. London: Fabian Society & Oxfam.

Kiprianos, P. (2002), 'Les immigrés en Grèce: Politiques éducatives et trajectoires scolaires', paper presented at the conference 'Etudes balkaniques: état des savoirs et pistes de recherche', Paris, 19-20 December 2002.

Kivisto, P. (2001), 'Theorising transnational immigration: a critical review of current efforts', *Ethnic and Racial Studies* 24 (4): 549-577.

Klein, J-L (1997), 'L'espace local a l'heure de la globalisation: la part de la mobilisation sociale', *Cahiers de Geographie du Quebec* 41 (114): 367-377.

Koiliari, A. (1997), *Foreigner in Greece: migrants, language and social integration*. Thessaloniki: Paratiritis. (In Greek.)

Komninos, N. & E. Sefertzi (1998), 'Neo-industrialisation and peripherality: evidence from regions in Northern Greece', *Geoforum* 29 (1): 37-49.

Koniordos, M. (1994), 'Employment and Greek immigration policy', in H. Theodoroupoulos & A. Sykiotou (eds.), *The Rights of Migrant Workers and their Families*, 167-174. Athens: Marangopoulos Foundation for Human Rights & Estia Bookshop. (In Greek.)

Konstandopoulou, Hr., L. Maratou-Alipranti, D. Germanos & Th. Oikonomou (eds.) (1999), *'Us' and the 'Others': Reference to the Trends and the Symbols*. Athens: EKKE & Typothito-G. Dardanos. (In Greek.)

Koser, K. & H. Lutz (eds.) (1998), *The New Migration in Europe: Social Constructions and Social Realities*. London: Macmillan.

Kosic, A. & A. Triandafyllidou (2003), 'Albanian immigrants in Italy: migration plans, coping strategies and identity issues', *Journal of Ethnic and Migration Studies* 29 (6): 997-1014.

Kourtovic, I. (1994), 'The legal framework for migrant workers in Greece', in H. Theodoroupoulos & A. Sykiotou (eds.), *The Rights of Migrant Workers and their Families*, 182-193. Athens: Marangopoulos Foundation for Human Rights & Estia Bookshop. (In Greek.)

Kourtovic, I. (2001), 'Immigrants: between the Law and legitimisation (criminality report)', in Ath. Marvakis, D. Parsanoglou & M. Pavlou (eds.), *Immigrants in Greece*, 163-198. Athens: Ellinika Grammata. (In Greek.)

Kupiszewski, M. (1996), 'Extra-Union migration: the East-West perspective', in Ph. Rees, J. Stillwell, A. Convey & M. Kupiszewski (eds.), *Population Migration in the European Union*, 13-37. Chichester: John Wiley and Sons.

Labrianidis, L. (1998), 'The Creation of the Free Cross-border Industrial Zone of Economic Exchange in Thrace', *Market Without Borders* 3 (4): 265-280. (In Greek.)

Labrianidis, L. (2000), 'The restructuring of the Balkans and the role of Greece: a critical approach', in G. Petrakos (ed.), *The Development of the Balkans*, 371-396. Volos/Athens: Thessaly University Press & Gutenberg. (In Greek.)

Labrianidis, L. & A. Lyberaki, in collaboration with P. Tinios & P. Hatziprokopiou (2001), *Albanian Immigrants in Thessaloniki: Paths of Prosperity and Overviews of their Public Image*. Thessaloniki: Paratiritis. (In Greek.)

Labrianidis, L., A. Lyberaki, P. Tinios & P. Hatziprokopiou (2004), 'Inflow of migrants and outflow of FDI: Aspects of interdependence between Greece and the Balkans', *Journal of Ethnic and Migration Studies* 30 (6): 1183-1208.

Labrianidis, L. & P. Hatziprokopiou (2005), 'The Albanian migration cycle: migrants tend to return to their country of origin after all', in R. King, N. Mai & S. Schwandner-Sievers (eds.), *The New Albanian Migration*, 93-117. Brighton: Sussex Academic Press.

Lash, S. & J. Urry (1994), *Economies of Sign and Space*. London: Sage.

Lazaridis, G. (1996), 'Immigration to Greece: a critical evaluation of Greek policy', *New Community* 22 (2): 335-348.

Lazaridis, G. (1999), 'The helots of the new millennium: ethnic-Greek Albanians and ΦotherΦ Albanians in Greece', in F. Anthias & G. Lazaridis (eds.), *Into the Margins: Migration and Exclusion in Southern Europe*, 105-121. Aldershot: Ashgate.

Lazaridis, G. & Poyago-Theotoky, J. (1999), 'Undocumented migrants in Greece: issues of regularization', *International Migration* 37 (4): 715-740.

Lazaridis, G. & I. Psimmenos (2000), 'Migrant flows from Albania to Greece: economic, social and spatial exclusion', in R. King, G. Lazaridis & Ch. Tsardanidis (eds.), *Eldorado or Fortress? Migration in Southern Europe*, 170-185. London: Macmillan.

Lazaridis, G. & K. Romaniszyn (1998), 'Albanian and Polish undocumented workers in Greece: a comparative analysis', *Journal of European Social Policy* 8 (1): 5-22.

Lazaridis, G. & E. Wickens (1999), ' ΦUsΦ and the ΦothersΦ: ethnic minorities in Greece', *Annals of Tourism Research* 26 (3): 639-655.

Lefebvre, H. (1996), 'The right to the city', in *Writings on Cities*, selected, translated and introduced by E. Kofman & E. Lebas, 61-181. Cambridge: Blackwell.

Lenin, V. I. (1976), *Imperialism: the Highest Stage of Capitalism*. Athens: Themelio. (In Greek.)

Lenkova, M. (1996), 'Balkan Neighbours: report for Greece, October-December 1996', *Balkan Neighbours Project*. Sofia: ACCESS Association.

Leontidou, L. (1990), *The Mediterranean City in Transition: Social Change and Urban Development*. Cambridge: Cambridge University Press.

Leontidou, L. (1996), 'Alternatives to modernism in (Southern), urban theory: exploring in-between spaces', *International Journal of Urban and Regional Research* 20 (2): 178-195.

Lianos T., A. Sarris & L. Katseli (1996), 'Illegal migration and local labour markets: the case of northern Greece', *International Migration* 34 (3): 449-484.

Lianos Th. (2001), 'Illegal immigrants in Greece and their choice of destination', *International Migration* 39 (2): 3-28.

Lianos, Th. (2003), *Contemporary Immigration to Greece: an Econometric Investigation*, in collaboration with P. Papakonstantinou. Centre for Planning and Economic Research (KEPE), Studies, n. 51. Athens: KEPE. (In Greek.)

Linardos-Rylmon, P. (1993), *Foreign Workers and the Labour Market in Greece*. Athens: INE-GSEE. (In Greek.)

Lipietz, A. (1987), *Mirages and Miracles: the Crisis in Global Fordism*. London: Verso.

Lipovac, Th. (1993), 'Orthodox Christianity and nationalism: two aspects of the modern Greek political culture', *Greek Review of Political Science* 2: 31-47. (In Greek.)

Lyberaki, A. & Th. Pelagidis (2000), *The 'Fear of the Foreigner' in the Labour Market: Tolerances and Prejudices in Development*. Athens: Polis. (In Greek.)

Maalouf, A. (1998), *Les Identités Meurtieres*. Paris: Grasset.

Mai, N. & S. Stephanie Schwandner-Sievers (2003), 'Albanian migration and new transnationalisms', *Journal of Ethnic and Migration Studies* 29 (6): 939-948.

Malheiros, J. (2002), 'Ethni-cities: residential patterns in the Northern European and Mediterranean metropolises – implications for policy design', *International Journal of Population Geography* 8: 107-134.

Malheiros, J. & N. Ribas-Mateos (2002), 'Immigration and place in northern Mediterranean cities: issues for debate', in M. L. Fonseca, J. Malheiros, N. Ribas-Mateos, P. White & A. Esteves (eds.), *Immigration and Place in Mediterranean Metropolises*, 293-308. Lisbon: Luso-American Foundation and Metropolis Portugal.

Mann, M. (1993), 'Nation-states in Europe and other continents: diversifying, developing, not dying', *Daedalus* 132 (3): 115-139.

Maratou-Alipranti, L. (2002), 'Foreign labour in Greece: trends and problems of social integration', in D. Karantinos, L. Maratou-Alipranti & E. Fronimou (eds.), *Dimensions of*

Social Exclusion in Greece: Basic Issues and Identification of Policy Priorities, vol. 1, 275-306, Athens: EKKE. (In Greek.)

Markou, G. (1994), 'School integration problems of returning migrant pupils', *Greek Review of Social Research* 84-85: 132-168. (In Greek.)

Markova E. & A. H. Sarris (1997), 'The performance of Bulgarian illegal immigrants in the Greek labour market', *South European Society and Politics* 2 (2): 57-77.

Markova, E. (2001), 'The presence of Bulgarian immigrants in the Greek labour market and in Greek society', in Ath. Marvakis, D. Parsanoglou & M. Pavlou (eds.), *Immigrants in Greece*, 247-276, Athens: Ellinika Grammata. (In Greek.)

Marvakis, Ath., D. Parsanoglou & M. Pavlou (2001), 'Immigrants in Greece: Φproblems Φ, social phenomena and subjects', in Ath. Marvakis, D. Parsanoglou & M. Pavlou (eds.), *Immigrants in Greece*, 13-28. Athens: Ellinika Grammata. (In Greek.)

Marvakis, Ath., D. Parsanoglou & M. Pavlou (eds.) (2001), *Immigrants in Greece*. Athens: Ellinika Grammata. (In Greek.)

Marx, K. (1979), *The German Ideology*, vol. 1. Athens: Gutemberg. (In Greek.)

Marx, K. (1997), *Capital: a Critique of Political Economy*, vol. 1. New York: Vintage Books.

Massey, D. S., J. Arango, G. Hugo, A. Koaouci, A. Pellegrino & J. E. Taylor (1993), 'Theories of international migration: a review and appraisal', *Population and Development Review* 19 (3): 431-466.

Mavreas, K. (1998), 'Dimensions of social exclusion: Pontian and Northern Epirote refugees in Greece', *Greek Review of Social Research* 96-97: 185-218. (In Greek.)

Mazower, M. (2000), *The Balkans*. London: Phoenix Press.

Mazower, M. (2004), *Salonica, City of Ghosts: Christians, Muslims and Jews 1430-1950*. London: HarperCollins.

Meintanis, E. (1994), 'The Europeanisation of immigration politics. Greece: the European laggard', paper presented at the Sussex European Institute Research-in-Progress Seminars, University of Sussex, 11 May 2004.

Mendieta, E. (2001), 'Invisible cities: a phenomenology of globalisation from below', *City* 5 (1): 7-26.

Minev, D., M. Zheliaskova, M. Ketsetzopoulou & N. Bouras (1997), 'The labour migration from Bulgaria to Greece: parameters, factors, consequences', paper presented at the conference 'Non-military Aspects of Security in Southern Europe: Migration, Employment and Labour Markets', Santorini, 19-21 September 1997.

Mingione, E. (1995), 'Labour market segmentation and informal work in Southern Europe', *European Urban and Regional Studies* 2 (2): 121-43.

Mingione, E. (1997), 'The Current Crisis of Intensive Work Regimes and the Question of Social Exclusion in Industrialised Countries', *WZB Sozialforschung Discussion Papers*, FS I 97-105. Berlin: Wissenschaftszentrum fur Sozialforschung.

Ministry of Labour and Social Security (2002), *National Action Plan for Employment 2002*. Athens: Ministry of Labour and Social Security. (In Greek.)

Miteva, I. (2001), 'Thessaloniki and Plovdiv and the parallel historical, cultural and social development, 18th-20th century', *Etudes Balkaniques* 37 (1): 169-170.

Moskov, K. (1978), *Thessaloniki 1700-1912: Anatomy of the Retailers' City*. Athens: Stohastis. (In Greek.)

Mousourou, L. (1991), *Migration and Immigration Policy in Greece and Europe*. Athens: Gutemberg. (In Greek.)

Mousourou, L. (1993), *From Gastarbeiters to the Spirit of Schengen*. Athens: Gutemberg. (In Greek.)

Murray, R. (1989), 'Fordism and post-fordism', in S. Hall & M. Jacques (eds.), *New Times: the Changing Face of Politics in the 1990s*. London: Lawrence & Wishart.

Musterd, S., C. Kesteloot, A. Murie & W. Ostendorf (2000), *Urban Social Exclusion and Modes of Integration: Literature Review*. Amsterdam: Fourth RTD Framework Programme, TSER, Urbex Series No. 1.

Musterd, S. (2003), 'Segregation and integration: a contested relationship', *Journal of Ethnic and Migration Studies* 29 (4): 623-641.

Muus, Ph. (2001), 'International migration and the European Union: trends and consequences', *International Journal of Criminal Policy and Research* 9: 31-49.

Naxakis, H. & M. Hletsos (eds.) (2001), *Migrants and Migration: Economic, Political and Social Aspects*. Athens: Patakis. (In Greek.)

Network of Movements for Social and Political Rights (1998), *Deltio Thielis* magazine, text by Ch. Bakelas, vol. 11, May 1998, 52-55. (In Greek.)

NSSG (National Statistical Service of Greece) (1999), *Justice Statistics*. Athens: NSSG. (In Greek.)

NSSG (National Statistical Service of Greece) (2003), *Greece in Numbers*. Athens: NSSG. (In Greek.)

NSSG (National Statistical Service of Greece) *Census 2001* (various tables); *Family Budget Surveys, 1998-1999* (table 3); *Labour Force Surveys, 1998-2003, by trimester* (various tables); *National Accounts* (first table). www.statistics.gr. [accessed October 2004] (pages also available in English).

Pajo, E. (2002), 'Preliminary notes on Albanian migration as social mobility', paper presented at the Annual Comparativists Day, UCLA Centre for Comparative Analysis, Los Angeles, 3-5 January 2001.

Papadopoulou, A. (2002), 'Kurdish asylum seekers in Greece: the role of networks in the migration process', UNU/WIDER conference on 'Poverty, International Migration and Asylum', Helsinki, 27-28 September 2002.

Papalias, P. (2003), ' ΦMoney of *kurbet* is money of bloodΦ: the making of a ΦheroΦ of migration at the Greek-Albanian border', *Journal of Ethnic and Migration Studies* 29 (6): 1059-1078.

Papastergiadis, N. (2000), *The Turbulence of Migration: Globalisation. Deterritorialisation and Hybridity*. Cambridge: Polity Press.

Paraskevopoulos, I. (1990), *Statistics, Applied to Behavioural Sciences*, vol. 1. *Descriptive Statistics*. Athens. (In Greek.)

Pavlou, M. (2001), 'The Φsmugglers of fearΦ: racist discourse and immigrants in the press of a potential metropolis', in Ath. Marvakis, D. Parsanoglou & M. Pavlou (eds.), *Immigrants in Greece*, 127-162. Athens: Ellinika Grammata. (In Greek.)

Petrakou, E. (2001), 'The construction of immigration in Greek society', in Ath. Marvakis, D. Parsanoglou & M. Pavlou (eds.), *Immigrants in Greece*, 31-55. Athens: Ellinika Grammata. (In Greek.)

Petrinioti, X. (1993), *Immigration to Greece: a first recording, classification and analysis*. Athens: Library of the Institute of International Relations & Odysseas. (In Greek.)

Petronoti, M. (2001), 'Ethnic mobilisation in Athens: steps and initiatives towards integration', in J. Tillie & A. Rogers (eds.), *Multicultural Policies and Modes of Citizenship in European Cities*, 41-60. Aldershot: Ashgate.

Petronoti, M. & A. Triandafyllidou (2003), *Recent immigration flows to Greece*. A special issue of the bibliography of social sciences on Modern Greek society of the National Institute for Social Research. Athens: EKKE & National Book Centre.

Phizakclea, A. (1998), 'Migration and globalisation: a feminist perspective', in K. Koser & H. Lutz (eds.), *The New Migration in Europe: Social Constructions and Social Realities*, 21-38. London: Macmillan.

Pieke, F. (2004), 'Chinese Globalization and Migration to Europe', *Centre for Comparative Immigration Studies Working Paper Series* WP n. 94, CCIS, University of California San Diego, March 2004.

Piore, M. J. (1979), *Birds of Passage: Migrant Labor and Industrial Societies*. Cambridge MA: Cambridge University Press.

Portes, A. (1995), 'Economic sociology and the sociology of immigration: a conceptual overview', in A. Portes (ed.), *The Economic Sociology of Immigration: Essays on Networks, Ethnicity and Enterpreneurship*, 1-41. New York: Russell Sage Foundation.

Portes, A. (1997), 'Globalisation from below: the rise of transnational communities', *ESRC Transnational Communities Programme Working Paper Series*, WPTC-98-01. New York: Princeton University.

Potts, L. (1990), *The World Labour Market: a History of Migration*. London: Zed Books.

Psimmenos, I. (1995), *Immigration from the Balkans, Social Exclusion in Athens*. Athens: Papazisis-Glory Books. (In Greek.)

Psimmenos, I. (1998), 'Creating spaces of social exclusion: the case of Albanian clandestine immigrants at the centre of Athens', in K. Kasimati (ed.), *Social Exclusion: the Greek Experience*, 221-273. Athens: KEKMOKOP & Gutemberg. (In Greek.)

Psimmenos, I. (2001), New employment regimes and clandestine immigrants in Metropolitan Athens', in Ath. Marvakis, D. Parsanoglou & M. Pavlou (eds.), *Immigrants in Greece*, 95-126. Athens: Ellinika Grammata. (In Greek.)

Psimmenos, I. & K. Kasimati (2002), 'Shifting work identities and oppositional work narratives: the case of domestic and construction Albanian immigrants in Greece', paper presented at the conference 'Albanian Migration and the new Transnationalisms', University of Sussex, Brighton 6-7 September 2002.

Psimmenos, I. & K. Kasimati (2003), 'Immigration control pathways: organisational culture and work values of Greek welfare officers', *Journal of Ethnic and Migration Studies* 29 (2): 337-372.

Pugliese, E. (1993), 'Restructuring of the labour market and the role of the Third World migrations in Europe', *Environment and Planning D – Society and Space* 11 (5): 513-522.

Ratcliffe, P. (1999), 'Housing inequality and ΦraceΦ: some critical reflections on the concept of Φsocial exclusionΦ ', *Ethnic and Racial Studies* 22 (1): 1-22.

Reyneri, E. (1999), 'Immigration and the underground economy in the new receiving South European countries: manifold perverse effects, manifold deep-rooted causes', presented at theEuropean Socio-Economic Research Conference, Brussels 28-30 April 1999.

Reyneri, E. & M. Baganha (1999), 'New migrants in South European Countries and their insertion in the underground economy', in E. Reyneri, M. Baganha, A. Dal Lago & S. Laacher (eds.), *Migrants' Insertion in the Informal Economy, Deviant Behaviour and the Impact on Receiving Societies*. Comparative Reports. MIGRINF project funded by DG XII of the European Commission, Contract no. SOE2-CT95-3005, mimeo.

Ribas-Mateos, N. (2001), 'Revising migratory contexts: the Mediterranean caravanserai', in R. King (ed.), *The Mediterranean Passage: Migration and New Cultural Encounters in Southern Europe*, 22-40. Liverpool: Liverpool University Press.

Ribas-Mateos, N. (2002), 'Women of the South in Southern European cities: a globalised domesticity', in M. L. Fonseca, J. Malheiros, N. Ribas-Mateos, P. White & A. Esteves (eds.), *Immigration and Place in Mediterranean Metropolises*, 33-52. Lisbon: Luso-American Foundation & Metropolis Portugal.

Rifkin, J. (1995), *The End of Work: the Decline of the Global Labour Force and the Dawn of the Post-Market Era*. New York: G. P. Putnam's Sons.

Robertson, R. (1992), *Globalisation: Social Theory and Global Culture*. London: Sage.

Robson, C. (2001), *Real World Research*. 2nd edn. Malden: Blackwell Publishing.

Rogers, A. (2000), 'A European space for transnationalism?', *Transnational Communities Programme Working Paper Series*, WPTC-2K-07. *ESRC* TC Programme, Institute of Social and Cultural Anthropology, University of Oxford.

Romaniszyn, K. (1996), 'The invisible community: undocumented Polish workers in Athens', *New Community* 22 (2): 321-333.

Room, G. J. (1999), 'Social exclusion. solidarity and the challenge of globalisation', *International Journal of Social Welfare* 8: 166-174.

Ross, R. J. & K. C. Trachte (1990), *Global Capitalism: the new leviathan*. Albany: State University of New York Press.

Sakis Karagiorgas Foundation (eds.) (1998), *Social Inequalities and Social Exclusion*. Conference Proceedings. Athens: Sakis Karagiorgas Foundation & Exandas. (In Greek.)

Salt, J. (1992), 'Current and future international migration trends affecting Europe', in Council of Europe (ed.), *People on the Move: New Migration Flows in Europe*, 41-81. Strasbourg: Council of Europe Press.

Samatas, M. (2003), 'Greece in ΦSchengenlandΦ: blessing or anathema for citizens' and foreigners' rights?', *Journal of Ethnic and Migration Studies* 29 (1): 141-156.

Samers, M. (1998), 'Immigration, Φethnic minoritiesΦ and Φsocial exclusionΦ in the European Union: a critical perspective' *Geoforum* 29 (2): 123-144.

Sarris, A. H. & S. Zografakis (1999), 'A computable general equilibrium assessment of the impact of illegal immigration on the Greek economy', *Journal of Population Economics* 12: 155-182.

Sassen, S. (1991), *The Global City: New York, London, Tokyo*. Princeton: Princeton University Press.

Sassen, S. (1995), 'Immigration and local labor markets', in A. Portes (ed.), *The Economic Sociology of Immigration: Essays on Networks, Ethnicity and Entrepreneurship*, 87-127. New York: Russell Sage Foundation.

Sassen, S. (1996a), 'New employment regimes in cities: the impact on immigrant workers', *New Community* 22 (4): 579-594.

Sassen, S. (1996b), *Losing Control? Sovereignty in an Age of Globalization*. New York: Columbia University Press.

Sassen, S. (1999), *The Mobility of Labor and Capital: a Study in International Investment and Labor Flow*. 2nd edn. Cambridge: Cambridge University Press.

Sayer, A. (2000), 'System, lifeworld and gender: associational versus counterfactual thinking', *Sociology* 34 (3): 707-725.

School, J. (1998), 'A multi-country approach to study the determinants of migration', paper presented at the UN-IOM Technical Symposium on International Migration and Development, The Hague, 29 June-3 July 1998.

Silver, H. (1994), 'Social exclusion and social solidarity: three paradigms', *International Labour Review* 133 (5-6): 531-578.

Simmel, G. (1950), 'The Stranger', in K. H. Wolff (ed.), *The Sociology of Georg Simmel*. New York: The Free Press of Glencoe.

Sintès, P. (2002), 'Les Albanais en Grèce: Le rôle des réseaux préexistants', paper presented at the conference 'Etudes balkaniques: état des savoirs et pistes de recherche', Paris, 19-20 December 2002.

Sitaropoulos, N. (2003), *Immigration law and management in Greece: towards an exodus from underdevelopment and a comprehensive immigration policy*. Centre for International and European Economic Law, Working Paper no. 3. Athens: Ant. N. Sakkoulas Publishers.

Sklair, L. (1999), 'Competing conceptions of globalisation', *Journal of World Systems Research* 5 (2): 143-163.

Sklair, L. (2001), *The Transnational Capitalist Class*. Oxford: Blackwell.

Smart, J. (1997), 'Borrowed men on borrowed time: globalisation, labour migration and local economies in Alberta', *Canadian Journal of Regional Science* 21 (2): 141-156.

Smith, M. P. & L. E. Guarnizo (eds.) (1998), *Transnationalism from Below. Comparative Urban and Community Research*, vol. 6. New Brunswick: Transaction Publishers.

Solé, C. (1995), 'Portugal and Spain: from exporters to importers of labour', in R. Cohen (ed.), *The Cambridge Survey of World Migration*, 316-320. Cambridge: Cambridge University Press.

Solé, C. (1999), 'The impact of immigration on South European new receiving societies', in E. Reyneri, M. Baganha, A. Dal Lago & S. Laacher (eds.), *Migrants' Insertion in the Informal Economy, Deviant Behaviour and the Impact on Receiving Societies*. Comparative Reports. MIGRINF project funded by DG XII of the European Commission, Contract no. SOE2-CT95-3005, mimeo.

Soysal-Nuhoglu, Y. (1994), *Limits of Citizenship: Migrants and Postnational Membership in Europe*. Chicago: The University of Chicago Press.

Stark, O. (1991), *The Migration of Labor*. Cambridge MA: Basil Blackwell.

Stoianovich, T. (2003), 'Market types and mechanisms', in S. Asdrahas (ed.), *Greek Economic History, 15th-19th century*, vol. 1, 483-513. Athens: Bank of Piraeus Cultural Foundation. (In Greek.)

Strange, S. (1999), 'The Westfailure system', *Review of International Studies* 25 (3): 345-354.

Swanson, J. C. (1979), 'The consequences of emigration for economic development: a review of the literature', in R. E. Rhoades (ed.), *The Anthropology of Return Migration*, special issue of *Papers in Anthropology* 20 (1): 39-55.

Symeonidou, H. (1999), 'Multicultural differences and the welfare state in Southern European countries: the case of Greece', in Ch. Konstandopoulou, L. Maratou-Alipranti, D. Germanos & Th. Oikonomou (eds.), *'Us' and the 'Others': Reference to the Trends and the Symbols*, 303-316. Athens: EKKE & Typothito-G.Dardanos. (In Greek.)

Tapinos, G. (2000), 'Globalisation, regional integration, international migration', *International Social Science Journal* 52 (165): 297-306.

Tapinos, G. & D. Delaunay (2000), 'Can one really talk of the globalisation of migration flows?', in OECD (eds.), *Globalisation, Migration and Development, Social Issues – Employment*. Paris: OECD.

Tastsoglou, E. & L. Maratou-Alipranti (eds.) (2003), *Gender and International Migration: Focus on Greece*. Special issue of the *Greek Review of Social Research* 110 A.

Theodoroupoulos, H. & A. Sykiotou (eds.) (1994), *The Rights of Migrant Workers and their Families*. Athens: Marangopoulos Foundation for Human Rights & Estia Bookshop. (In Greek.)

Todorov, N. (1986), *The Balkan City, 15th-19th century: Socio-Economic and Demographic Development*, vol. 2. Athens: Themelio. (In Greek.)

Touraine, A. (1971), *The Post-Industrial Society. Tomorrow's Social History: Classes, Conflicts and Culture on the Programmed Society*. New York: Random House.

Touraine, A. (2000), 'A method for studying social actors', *Journal of World Systems Research* 6 (3): 900-918.

Triandafyllidou, A., A. Mikrakis & M. Calloni (1997), 'New Greek nationalism', *Sociological Research Online* 2 (1). www.socresonline.org.uk/2/1/7.html.

Triandafyllidou, A. (1996), 'Greek migration policy: a critical note', *Review of Modern Greek Studies* 1 (1): 15-22.

Triandafyllidou, A. (2000), 'Racists? Us? Are you joking? The discourse of social exclusion of immigrants in Greece', in R. King, G. Lazaridis & Ch. Tsardanidis (eds.), *Eldorado or Fortress? Migration in Southern Europe*, 186-206. London: Macmillan.

Triandafyllidou, A. (2002), 'Greece', in Walter, J. (ed.), *Racism and cultural diversity in the mass media: an overview of research and examples of good practice in the EU member states, 1995-2000*, 149-170. Vienna: European Monitoring Centre on Racism and Xenophobia & European Research Centre on Migration and Ethnic Relations.

Triandafyllidou, A. & M. Veikou (2002), 'The hierarchy of Greekness: ethnic and national identity considerations in Greek immigration policy', *Ethnicities* 2 (2): 189-208.

Trimikliniotis, N. (1999), 'Racism and new migration to Cyprus: the racialisation of migrant workers', in F. Anthias & G. Lazaridis (eds.), *Into the Margins: Migration and Exclusion in Southern Europe*, 139-178. Aldershot: Ashgate.

Tsiakalos, G. (1998), 'Social exclusion: definitions, context and meaning', in K. Kasimati (ed.), *Social Exclusion, the Greek experience*, 39-64. Athens: KEKMOKOP-Panteion University & Gutemberg. (In Greek.)

Tsiakalos, G. (2000), *Guide to Anti-racist Education*. Athens: Ellinika Grammata. (In Greek.)

Tsimouris, G. (2003), 'The imaginary construction of the nation, the classification of alterity and the positions of migrants in Greek society and the labour market: intense relationships', paper presented at the International Sociological Conference 'Alterity and Society', Athens, 7-9 May 2003. (In Greek.)

Tsoukalas, C. (1993), 'Greek national identity in an integrated Europe and a changing world order', in H. Psomiades & S. Thomadakis (eds.), *Greece, the New Europe and the Changing International Order*, 57-78. New York: Pella.

Tsoulouvis, L. (1996), 'Urban planning, social policy and networks of urban inequality and social exclusion in Greek cities', *International Journal of Urban and Regional Studies* 20 (4): 718-732.

UNHCR (United Nations High Commission for Refugees) (2003), *Asylum Applications Lodged in Industrialised Countries: Levels and Trends, 2000-2002*. Geneva: UNHCR Population Research Unit.

UNPD (United Nations Population Division) (2002), *International Migration Report 2002*. New York: United Nations.

Urzúa, R. (2000), 'International migration, social science and public policy', *International Social Science Journal* 19 (3): 421-429.

Vaiou, D. & K. Hadjimichalis (1997), *With the Sewing Machine in the Kitchen and the Poles in the Fields: Cities, Regions and Informal Labour*. Athens: Exandas. (In Greek.)

Veikou, M. (1998), 'Forced immigration: aspects of social exclusion and the voluntary acceptance of inequalities', in Sakis Karagiorgas Foundation (eds.), *Social Inequalities and Social Exclusion*, 479-487. Athens: Exandas & Sakis Karagiorgas Foundation. (In Greek.)

Veinstein, G. (1993), *Salonique, 1850-1918: la 'Ville des Juifs' et le Réveil des Balkans*. Paris: Éditions Autrement – Serie Memoires no. 12.

Velentzas, K., N. Kalogirou, S. Karagianni, E. Katsikas, N. Papamihos. M. Hatziprokopiou & K. Hlomoudis (1996), *The Housing Market in the Thessaloniki Conurbation*. Thessaloniki: Paratiritis. (In Greek.)

Vergopoulos, K. (1999), *Globalisation: the Great Chimera*. Athens: Nea Synora-A.A. Livanis. (In Greek.)

Vertovec, S. & R. Cohen (eds.) (1999), *Migration, Diasporas and Transnationalism*. Cheltenham: Edward Edgar Publishers.

Waldinger, R. (1997), 'Social capital or social closure? Immigrant networks in the labor market', *Lewis Center for Regional Policy Studies Working Paper Series*, n. 26, School of Public Policy and Social Research, UCLA.

Wallerstein, I. (1974), *The Modern World System*. New York: Academic Press.

Williams, C. C. & J. Winderbank (1995), 'Black market work in the European Community: peripheral work for peripheral localities', *International Journal of Urban and Regional Research* 19 (1): 23-38.

Zlotnik, H. (1999), 'Trends in international migration since 1965, what existing data reveal', *International Migration* 37: 21-61.

Appendix A Additional tables and figures

All tables and figures are my own elaboration of data from the sources stated.

Figure A1 *Age structure (%), fertility and mortality (per 1,000) of the Greek population, 1971-2001*

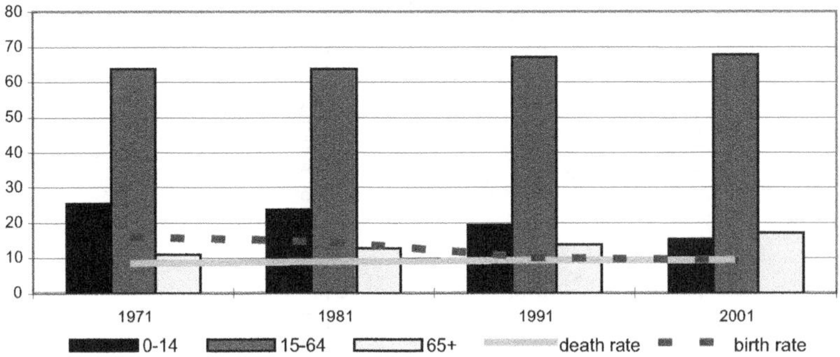

Source: NSSG, censuses 1971, 1981, 1991, 2001, as presented in NSSG (2003: tables Iα, Iγ).

Table A1 *Foreign nationals employed in 2001, by sector and sex*

Sector	*Employed Foreign Nationals*		
	% men	*% women*	*all*
agriculture & cattle-breeding, fishery, forestry	19.8	12.4	68,682
mining	0.2	0.0	648
manufacturing	13.7	7.9	46,553
energy	0.2	0.0	569
construction	35.1	0.9	96,003
trade & repair, hotel & catering	13.8	19.9	61,497
transport & storage, communication	3.2	1.7	10,721
banking & finance	0.3	0.6	1,506
other services	6.6	51.8	80,488
n.a.	7.1	4.8	25,007
total	**270,771**	**120,903**	**391,674**

Source: NSSG, Census 2001: Employed Aliens.

Table A2 *Foreign nationals in Greece, top 21 nationalities*

Country of Citizenship	All	% by Nationality	%Women[1]	Women%[2]	Country of Citizenship	All	% by Nationality	%Women[1]	Women%[2]
dual nationality	89,207	–	55.4	–	Ukraine	14,149	1.8	74.3	2.9
foreign nationality	796,713	–	45.2	–	Poland	13,378	1.7	54.1	2.0
Albania	443,55	55.7	41.0	50.5	Pakistan	11,192	1.4	4.4	0.1
Bulgaria	37,230	4.7	59.6	6.2	Australia	9,677	1.2	52.7	1.4
Georgia	23,159	2.9	56.9	3.7	Turkey	8,297	1.0	47.7	1.1
Romania	23,066	2.9	42.9	2.7	Italy	7,953	1.0	50.2	1.1
USA	22,507	2.8	51.1	3.2	Egypt	7,846	1.0	22.4	0.5
Cyprus	19,084	2.4	52.7	2.8	Armenia	7,808	1.0	53.3	1.2
Russian Fed	18,219	2.3	62.1	3.1	India	7,409	0.9	7.2	0.2
UK	15,308	1.9	57.9	2.5	Iraq	7,188	0.9	29.6	0.6
Germany	15,303	1.90	57.4	2.4	Canada	6,909	0.9	51.7	1.0

[1] %women = percentage of women within nationality. [2] women% = female migrants by nationality

Source: NSSG, Census 2001, Real population by country of citizenship

Table A3 *Regional distribution and structure of the migrant population*

	Regional Distributions					*Shares in regional population*	*Shares in migrant population*	
	total population	*foreign nationals**	*migrants***	*Albanians*	*Bulgarians*		*Albanians*	*Bulgarians*
Greece	**10,934,097**	**761,813**	**644,126**	**438,036**	**35,104**	**5.89**	**68.00**	**5.45**
East Macedonia & Thrace	5.6	2.0	2.0	1.3	3.9	2.1	45.2	10.5
Central Macedonia	17.2	13.1	13.9	11.6	13.9	4.8	56.8	5.4
in which: Thessaloniki	*9.9*	*8.8*	*9.2*	*7.2*	*8.4*	*5.5*	*53.5*	*5.0*
Western Macedonia	2.7	1.2	1.2	1.5	0.2	2.7	86.3	1.0
Thessaly	6.8	4.2	4.6	5.8	3.4	4.0	86.3	4.0
Epirus	3.1	2.1	2.2	3.1	0.2	4.2	95.2	0.6
Ionian islands	1.9	2.6	2.4	3.1	0.9	7.5	86.3	1.9
Central Greece	6.6	4.6	5.0	5.6	6.2	4.4	76.2	6.9
Western Greece	1.9	1.4	1.6	1.6	1.4	4.9	69.9	5.0
Peloponnese	5.5	6.3	6.8	6.1	16.2	7.4	60.7	12.9
Attica	35.6	48.6	50.4	47.3	29.2	8.3	63.8	3.2
in which: Athens	*25.7*	*36.1*	*36.9*	*33.2*	*24.8*	*8.5*	*61.3*	*3.7*
Piraeus	*5.1*	*5.4*	*5.9*	*5.9*	*2.2*	*6.9*	*67.6*	*2.0*
Northern Aegean	1.9	1.3	1.2	1.2	1.8	3.8	64.7	8.1
Southern Aegean	2.7	3.7	3.5	3.3	3.1	7.6	63.8	4.7
Crete	5.4	5.3	5.2	4.0	14.8	5.6	52.4	15.6

* Excluding people with dual citizenship. ** As before, also excluding nationals of former EU-15 and EEA countries, as well as Cyprus, Malta, Monaco, Andorra, USA, Canada, Japan, Oceania

Note: There is an amount of missing data

Source: NSSG, Census 2001 (tables given to EUROSTAT), Usual Resident Population.

Figure A2 *Non-EU citizens in Greater Thessaloniki*

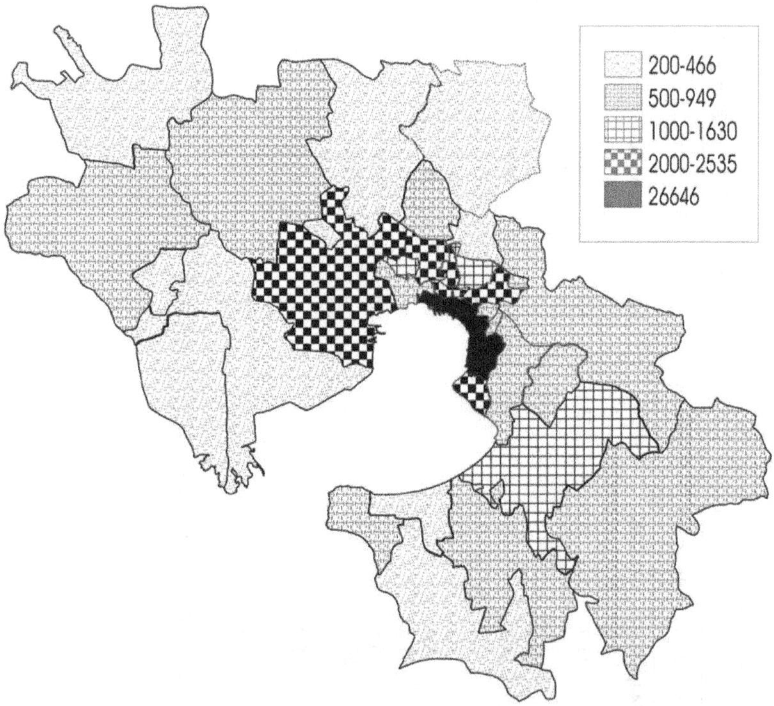

Source: NSSG, Census 2001, Usual Resident population

Table A4 *Thessaloniki Prefecture, key socio-economic indicators, 1991, 2001*

	Census 1991			*Census 2001*		
	total	*men*	*women*	*total*	*men*	*women*
Total Population	**946,864**	**48.2**	**51.8**	**1,057,825**	**48.4**	**51.6**
Age structure						
15-29	25.2	–	–	23.8	–	–
30-34	32.5	–	–	32.2	–	–
35-65	38.0	–	–	38.1	–	–
65+	10.7	–	–	14.1	–	–
Education level						
Postgraduate	0.6	0.9	0.3	1.1	1.4	0.8
University	7.8	8.9	6.8	10.7	10.9	10.5
Polytechnic	1.7	1.7	1.8	3.8	3.6	3.9
Other post-secondary	0.5	0.6	0.4	4.3	4.1	4.5
Secondary	28.1	29.5	26.8	30.8	32.6	29.1
Three years' secondary	11.1	11.7	10.5	11.6	12.7	10.6
Primary	36.4	35.5	37.2	28.0	26.8	29.1
Not finished primary but literate	9.6	8.6	10.5	7.7	6.6	8.7
Illiterate	4.3	2.6	5.9	2.1	1.4	2.8

	Census 1991			Census 2001		
	total	*men*	*women*	*total*	*men*	*women*
Total Labour Force	**372,652**	**64.8**	**35.2**	**457,138**	**60.6**	**39.4**
Sector of employment						
agriculture	6.0	7.1	4.0	4.8	4.8	4.9
mining	0.1	0.2	0.0	0.1	0.1	0.0
manufacturing	23.4	21.7	26.5	17.9	18.7	16.6
water, electricity, gas	0.4	0.5	0.2	0.4	0.6	0.2
construction	6.2	9.5	0.2	7.4	11.7	0.9
trade, repair	16.9	17.8	15.2	17.0	17.4	16.3
hotels & restaurants	3.3	3.6	2.8	5.4	5.2	5.8
transport, storing, communication	5.8	8.1	1.6	5.9	8.1	2.3
financial organisations, real estate management	6.1	5.3	7.5	8.8	7.1	11.4
public administration, defence, insurance	5.9	6.3	5.0	5.1	5.7	4.3
education services	5.9	3.8	9.7	6.8	4.3	10.8
health & welfare	4.6	2.8	7.7	4.9	2.9	8.0
other services	3.5	2.9	4.6	4.9	3.2	7.5
young, not classified	12.0	10.4	14.9	10.5	10.3	10.9
Position at work						
employers	9.4	11.7	5.1	12.3	14.8	8.3
self-employed	21.3	25.7	13.3	12.3	14.7	8.6
waged	59.4	55.6	66.3	67.7	64.9	72.0
assistants	3.6	2.1	6.3	2.6	1.2	4.8
not declared	6.3	4.9	8.9	5.1	4.4	6.2
Unemployment rate by age group						
Total unemployment	7.6	5.9	10.8	11.4	9.6	14.2
10-19	–	23.5	30.4	–	44.9	49.1
20-24	–	15.7	21.9	–	23.9	26.5
25-29	–	8.5	12.6	–	13.0	16.1
30-44	–	3.4	5.5	–	6.5	10.3
45-64	–	3.0	4.3	–	5.4	11.1
65+	–	1.4	3.0	–	0.0	0.0
Unemployment composition by age group						
10-19	–	13.1	16.3	–	11.4	7.9
20-24	–	28.8	35.9	–	24.0	22.8
25-29	–	18.9	19.8	–	18.9	19.1
30-44	–	22.2	20.6	–	28.1	32.2
45-64	–	16.8	7.4	–	17.5	18.1
65+	–	0.3	0.1	–	0.0	0.0

Source: NSSG, Censuses 1991 and 2001, various tables

Table A5 *Pro-migrant civil-society organisations in Thessaloniki*

*Organisation**	*Type & Action*	*Source*
Social & Welfare Services		
Médecins Sans Frontières	*NGO: Open polyclinic*	leaflet, interviewee
Doctors of the World	*NGO: Open polyclinic*	leaflet, interviewee
Greek Red Cross	*Charity: Consultancy, support*	leaflet

*Organisation**	*Type & Action*	*Source*
Centre for the Reception and Support of Immigrants and Refugees		
INTEGRA action for 'Employment' Community initiative (run by MAKINE)	*European project: Consulting, advocacy, information, legal support*	visits, informal chats, leaflet, interviewees
Epirote House	*Federation of community associations: registration, consultancy, legal support*	interview, interviewees
Refugees' Reception Centre	*NGO : food and shelter, social services, legal support*	leaflet
Church: various parishes	*Food and shelter, material & moral support*	interviewees
Greek Language Courses		
Aristotle University of Thessaloniki	*Language courses*	leaflet
Odysseas	*NGO, free language courses, theatre group*	visits, observation, informal chats, interviewees
NELE (Prefecture Committee for People's Education)	*Local administration: Free language courses*	leaflets, interviewees
Steki sto Viologiko: social centre	*Free language courses*	visits, informal chats, observation, interviewees
Advocacy & Campaign		
Macedonian Institute of Labour (independent body of the Thessaloniki labour centre)	*Trade-union body: Research, vocational training, providing space for INTEGRA and Odysseas*	leaflet, website
Antigone: information and documentation centre (national focus of EUMC, part of the RAXEN Network)	*NGO, European project: information, documentation, research*	website
Local committee against racism and xenophobia	*Advocacy (long inactive)*	leaflet, observation
SOS Racism	*Advocacy (long inactive)*	leaflet, observation
Amnesty International, Thessaloniki Branch	*NGO: advocacy, human rights' watch*	Campaign brochures
Anti-racist Initiative of Thessaloniki	*Left-wing organisation: campaigns, advocacy, networking, support of associations & individuals*	participation, observation, campaign brochures, interviewees
YRE: Youth Against Racism in Europe	*Left-wing group: campaigns, advocacy*	campaign brochures
Black Sun Collective: None is illegal	*Anarchist group: campaigns, advocacy*	campaign leaflet

* The list is by no means complete; I only included organisations for which I had obtained first-hand information.

Source: fieldwork findings, as stated in the third column

Table A6 *Detailed profession of immigrants by sector of employment*

	A	*B*	*C*	*D*	*E*	*F*	*G*	*H*	*I*	*J*	*K*	*L*	*Total*	*%*
shoes & clothing manufacturers	13	–	–	–	–	–	–	–	–	–	–	–	**13**	6.3
metal machinery factories	10	–	–	–	–	–	–	–	–	–	–	–	**10**	4.8
oil, plastics & chemicals	5	–	–	–	–	–	–	–	–	–	–	–	**5**	2.4
bathroom equipment manufacturers	3	–	–	–	–	–	–	–	–	–	–	–	**3**	1.4
other manufacturers	9	–	–	–	–	–	–	–	–	–	–	–	**9**	4.3
carpenters & other craftsmen	6	–	–	–	–	–	–	–	–	–	–	–	**6**	2.9
metal processing workshops	4	–	–	–	–	–	–	–	–	–	–	–	**4**	1.9
drivers	–	1	–	–	–	1	–	–	–	–	–	–	**2**	1.0
construction workers, builders	–	32	–	–	–	–	–	–	–	–	–	–	**32**	15.4
general manual workers*	–	–	6	6	–	–	–	2	–	1	–	–	**15**	7.2
electricians & plumbers	–	–	–	6	–	–	–	–	–	–	–	–	**6**	2.9
domestic service & cleaning	–	–	14	–	–	–	–	–	–	–	–	–	**14**	6.7
carers	–	–	11	–	–	–	–	–	–	–	–	–	**11**	5.3
hairdressers, beauticians	–	–	2	–	–	–	–	–	–	–	–	–	**2**	1.0
store assistants, retail shopkeepers	–	–	–	–	–	10	–	–	–	–	–	–	**10**	4.8
assistant workers in trade companies	–	–	–	–	–	7	–	–	–	–	–	–	**7**	3.4
assistants in petrol stations	–	–	–	–	–	3	–	–	–	–	–	–	**3**	1.4
assistants in bakeries & confectioneries	–	–	–	–	–	4	–	–	–	–	–	–	**4**	1.9
waiters/assistants in fast-food/restaurants	–	–	–	–	9	–	–	–	–	–	–	–	**9**	4.3
waiters/assistants in café-bars**	–	–	–	–	7	–	–	–	–	–	–	–	**7**	3.4
businessmen & entrepreneurs	–	–	–	–	2	2	2	–	–	1	–	–	**7**	3.4
specialised professionals	1	–	–	–	–	–	2	2	1	1	1	–	**8**	3.8
white-collar employees***	–	–	–	–	–	–	1	–	–	2	1	–	**4**	1.9
public servants	–	–	–	–	–	–	–	2	–	–	–	–	**2**	1.0
music & language teachers	–	–	–	–	–	–	–	2	3	–	–	–	**5**	2.4
unemployed	–	–	–	–	–	–	–	–	–	–	–	6	**6**	2.9
retired	–	–	–	–	–	–	–	–	–	–	–	2	**2**	1.0
housewives	–	–	–	–	–	–	–	–	–	–	–	2	**2**	1.0
Total	**51**	**33**	**33**	**12**	**18**	**27**	**5**	**8**	**4**	**5**	**2**	**10**	**208**	100.0
%	24.5	15.9	15.9	5.8	8.7	13.0	2.4	3.8	1.9	2.4	1.0	4.8	100.0	

*general assistants, repairing, cleaning, painting
** plus one hotel room-service person
*** translation
A. manufacturing; B. construction; C. personal services; D. maintenance & repair; E. hotel, leisure & catering; F. trade & retail; G. financial & business services; H. university & public sector; I. other education; J. translations; K. other services; L. unemployed & inactive
Source: fieldwork findings

Table A7 *Community organisations of other migrant groups in Thessaloniki*

Name or Description	*Type and/or Actions*
organisations incorporating migrants of various nationalities	
Steki Metanaston: 'Immigrants' Place' Café and meeting place, provides space for several associations' meetings & activities, also hosts the Anti-racist Initiative of Thessaloniki.	
International Federation of Foreign Women	?
established communities & associations	
Armenian Orthodox Church 'Virgin Mary' & Armenian General Benevolent Union	Church and Community association (dating back to the nineteenth century, but supporting new Armenian immigrants)
Pan-African Congress, northern Greece branch[1]	Campaign organisation
Friends of Africa Association[1]	Cultural association
Union of African Students of Macedonia1	Student society
Community of Nigerians in Thessaloniki and northern Greece[1]	Migrant organisation
Sudanese Assocation[1]	Migrant organisation
Union of Congolese students[1]	Student society
Union of Palestinian students	Student society
KASAPI: Filipino Association, northern Greece branch	Migrant organisation
Community of Yugoslavians in Thessaloniki[2]	Community, socialisation and cultural celebrations
Community of Afghan refugees	asylum-seekers' informal community, campaigning
other migrant groups[3]	
Turkish and Iraqi Kurds	They have small communities in Thessaloniki (dating back in the 1980s). Many are organised alongside radical political groups (Turkish Kurds in the PKK, and Iraqi Kurds in the Revolutionary Party of Kurdistan), protesting and campaigning for their cause and raising funds by selling political publications in Greek.
Pontian ethnic Greeks from former Soviet Republics	Various associations of Pontian Greeks from the former USSR, many pre-existing Pontian unions/ associations, some newly formed by migrants, according to place of origin or locally-based
other citizens of countries of the former Soviet Union	Georgians, Russians and Ukrainians in particular, who have relatively sizeable communities in Thessaloniki, are likely to have formed associations. During the fieldwork I was told by a Georgian woman about the existence of a Georgian immigrants' association

Name or Description	*Type and/or Actions*
Chinese (& other migrants from South-East Asian countries)	There is a small but growing Chinese community, mostly engaged in trade (imports & retail) of clothes and, to a lesser extent, shoes. Migrants from China, and also other South-East Asian countries, are increasingly involved in street trade, of either clothes (in open markets and local bazaars) or cheap electronic gadgets (both in local bazaars and downtown).

Note: The table does not include nationals of EU member states (EU-15 and Cyprus), North America and Japan, despite the strong presence of citizens from some of these countries: for instance, the American, German and Italian schools of Thessaloniki enrol both Greek pupils and children from the respective countries, while I also came across an institution where Japanese kids living in the city were taught their native tongue. There is also a small Spanish-speaking community around the local branch of the Cervantes Institute. There are also many Cypriots who work or study with various associations and societies.

[1] Despite their small size, the presence of African students and migrants from various countries is increasingly visible. Many are involved in street trade (African artefacts, electronic gadgets, pirated CDs). There are a couple of African music clubs in town, owned jointly by Africans and Greeks.

[2] I was told this by a Serbian woman working at Liliana's Bulgarian café. There also existed an initiative supporting Bosnian Serbs during the recent Balkans war, with which however I never came into contact.

[3] Only 'visible' communities have been included here, i.e. those about which I had information or I could observe. It is not certain whether or not other migrants groups (e.g. Polish, Ukrainians, Pakistanis) who have established associations in Athens have managed to develop organised community structures in Thessaloniki; the state of other migrant groups (e.g. Indians, Egyptians) is also unknown.

Source: fieldwork findings (NGOs, magazines, leaflets, informal chats, observation)

Figure A3 *Albanian and Bulgarian 'tourists' 1994-2002 ('000s and % of total tourists)*

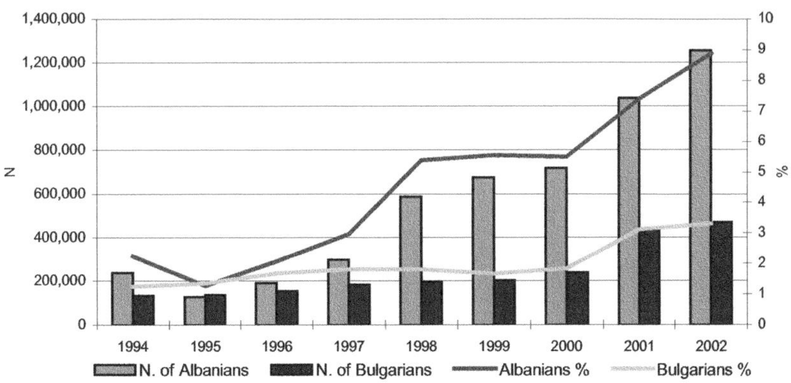

Source: Greek National Tourism Organisation, arrivals of travellers at the borders by nationality

Appendix B1 The questionnaire

ΕΡΩΤΗΜΑΤΟΛΟΓΙΟ

ΜΕΤΑΝΑΣΤΕΣ ΑΠΟ ΒΑΛΚΑΝΙΚΕΣ ΧΩΡΕΣ ΣΤΗ ΘΕΣΣΑΛΟΝΙΚΗ
Ζητήματα Κοινωνικού Αποκλεισμού και Κοινωνικής Ένταξης
στοιχεία μετανάστευσης,
συνθήκες κατοίκησης και εργασίας,
συνθήκες ζωής στην Ελλάδα

α/α ερωτηματολογίου: ________ τόπος διεξαγωγής: ________________ ημερομηνία: ___/___/___

Ερευνητής:
Πάνος Αρίων Χατζηπροκοπίου
Υποψήφιος διδάκτορας
Sussex European Institute
Πανεπιστήμιο του Sussex
Μεγάλη Βρετανία

τίτλος διδακτορικής διατριβής:
«Παγκοσμιοποίηση και σύγχρονη μετανάστευση στις νοτιοευρωπαϊκές πόλεις: Κοινωνική ένταξη και κοινωνικός αποκλεισμός των μεταναστών στη Θεσσαλονίκη»

Α. ΠΡΟΣΩΠΙΚΑ ΔΕΔΟΜΕΝΑ

Α1. Υπηκοότητα: Αλβανική ☐ Βουλγαρική ☐ Ρουμάνικη ☐

Α2. Εθνικότητα (εθνική καταγωγή):

Α3. Τόπος διαμονής πριν τη μετανάστευση:

Α4. Φύλο: 0-ΑΝΤΡΑΣ ☐ 1-ΓΥΝΑΙΚΑ ☐

Α5. Ηλικία:

Α6. Οικογενειακή κατάσταση:
i- άγαμος-η ☐
ii- έγγαμος-η ☐
iv- διαξευγμένος-η/χήρος-α ☐
iii- αριθμός παιδιών: ______

Α7. Μέλη νοικοκυριού:

	i- στη Θεσσαλονίκη	ii- στην πατρίδα	iii- αλλού (που)
α- γονείς			
β- σύζυγος			
γ- παιδιά			
δ- αδέρφια			
άλλος (ποιος):			

Συνεχίστε στην επόμενη σελίδα

Β. ΣΤΟΙΧΕΙΑ ΜΕΤΑΝΑΣΤΕΥΣΗΣ:
ΕΙΣΟΔΟΣ ΣΤΗΝ ΕΛΛΑΔΑ ΚΑΙ ΑΦΙΞΗ ΣΤΗ ΘΕΣΣΑΛΟΝΙΚΗ

Β1. Λόγοι που αφήσατε τη χώρα σας (παρακαλώ ιεραρχείστε):
i- οικονομικοί λόγοι* ☐
ii- πολιτικός πρόσφυγας ☐
iii- ελληνική καταγωγή ☐
άλλο (τι): ______

* π.χ. ανεργία, χαμηλότερο βιοτικό επίπεδο, δυσκολότερες συνθήκες ζωής, χειρότερες συνθήκες απασχόλησης, χαμηλότεροι μισθοί

Β2. Λόγοι που ήρθατε στην Ελλάδα (παρακαλώ ιεραρχείστε):
i- οικονομικοί λόγοι* ☐
ii- είναι εύκολο να μπεις στη χώρα ☐
iii- είναι κοντά στην πατρίδα ☐
iv- ενδιάμεσος σταθμός για κάπου αλλού ☐
v- ομογενής ☐
άλλο (τι): ______

* π.χ. καλύτερες συνθήκες απασχόλησης-καλύτερες δουλειές, ευκολότερο να βρεις δουλειά νόμιμα/παράνομα, υψηλότεροι μισθοί, ανώτερο βιοτικό επίπεδο

Β3. Πότε ήρθατε για πρώτη φορά στην Ελλάδα;

Β4. Στο διάστημα της συνολικής παραμονής σας στην Ελλάδα, βρεθήκατε στη χώρα σας για μεγάλη περίοδο (άνω των τριών μηνών) για να ξαναεπιστρέψετε στη συνέχεια στην Ελλάδα;
0-ΝΑΙ ☐ 1-ΟΧΙ ☐
α) Αν ΝΑΙ, για πόσο διάστημα; ______ α) για ποιο λόγο; ______

Β5. Υπήρξατε ποτέ μετανάστης σε άλλη χώρα (εκτός της Ελλάδας);
0-ΝΑΙ ☐ 1-ΟΧΙ ☐
α) Αν ΝΑΙ, ποια; ______ β) χρονική περίοδος: ______
Σχόλια:

Β6. α) Μέσο εισόδου στην Ελλάδα την πρώτη φορά που ήρθατε:
i- με τα πόδια ☐
ii- με αυτοκίνητο ☐
iii- με λεωφορείο ☐
iv- με τρένο ☐
άλλο (διευκρινίστε): ______
β) Συνήθως, όταν πηγαίνετε στην πατρίδα σας και επιστρέφετε ξανά στην Ελλάδα, τι μέσο χρησιμοποιείτε;

Β7. Τρόπος εισόδου στην Ελλάδα κατά την πρώτη άφιξή σας (νομικό καθεστώς):
i- με άδεια παραμονής ☐
ii- με τουριστική βίζα: ☐
iii- ως εποχιακός εργάτης ☐
iv- ως ομογενής ☐
v- παράνομη είσοδος: ☐
άλλο (διευκρινίστε): ______
α) Σχόλια (π.χ., αν πληρώσατε για την απόκτηση visa ή για την «μεταφορά» σας στην Ελλάδα, αν ήρθατε ως εξαρτημένο μέλος οικογένειας μετανάστη που ήδη βρισκόταν νόμιμα στη χώρα, αν παντρευτήκατε Έλληνα-ίδα, κλπ.): ______

Β8. α) Λόγοι εγκατάστασης στη Θεσσαλονίκη και ιστορία εγκατάστασης μέχρι να έρθετε εδώ:
1ος ______
2ος ______
3ος ______
β) Σε ποια μέρη της Ελλάδας ζήσατε προτού εγκατασταθείτε στη Θεσσαλονίκη;
______

Συνεχίστε στην επόμενη σελίδα

B9. Αρχικές επαφές που σας βοήθησαν αρχικά να εγκατασταθείτε, ή σας επηρέασαν σχετικά με την απόφασή σας να έρθετε στην Ελλάδα (σε περίπτωση περισσότερων από μία απάντηση, παρακαλώ ιεραρχήστε: 1,2,κλπ):
i- συγγενείς ☐
ii- φίλοι και γνωστοί (συμπατριώτες) ☐
iii- Έλληνες γνωστοί-εργοδότες ☐
άλλοι (ποιοι): ____________
Σχόλια: ____________

B10. Είστε κάτοχος νόμιμων εγγράφων αυτήν την περίοδο;
0-ΝΑΙ ☐ 1-ΟΧΙ ☐
α) Αν ΝΑΙ, έχετε:
1. λευκή κάρτα ☐
2. πράσινη κάρτα ☐
3. δελτίο καταγραφής ☐
4. βεβαίωση πράσινης κάρτας ☐
5. δελτίο ταυτότητας (ομογενείς) ☐
6. visa ☐ τι είδους: ____________
7. έχω κάνει πρόσφατα αίτηση και περιμένω ☐
β) Αν ΟΧΙ, για ποιο λόγο δεν έχετε καταφέρει να προμηθευτείτε νόμιμα χαρτιά;
____
Σχόλια: ____________

Γ. ΣΥΝΘΗΚΕΣ ΚΑΤΟΙΚΙΑΣ

Γ1. Περιοχή κατοικίας: α) από πότε ζείτε εκεί;

Γ2. Άλλοι άνθρωποι που ζουν μαζί σας:
α) Σύνολο ατόμων που κατοικείτε στο ίδιο σπίτι: ____________
β) Προσδιορίσετε τη σχέση σας μαζί τους:
μέλη νοικοκυριού ☐ άλλοι συγγενείς ☐ συμπατριώτες φίλοι ☐
άλλοι (ποιοί): ____________

Γ3. α) Τύπος κατοικίας (αν είστε φιλοξενούμενος σε σπίτι συγγενή/φίλου/γνωστού/εργοδότη, παρακαλώ συμπληρώστε το κουτάκι και εξηγείστε):

	i- σήμερα	ii- την πρώτη φορά που ήρθατε
i- ξενοδοχείο	☐	☐
ii- ενοικιαζόμενο διαμέρισμα	☐	☐
iii- ιδιόκτητο διαμέρισμα	☐	☐
iv- φιλοξενούμενος (πού)	☐ ____________	☐ ____________
άλλο (διευκρινίστε):	____________	____________

β) Πόσα δωμάτια έχει (εκτός κουζίνας) [____]
γ) Εάν νοικιάζετε διαμέρισμα, πόσο νοίκι πληρώνετε [____________]

Γ4. α) Γνωρίζετε αν συμπατριώτες σας κατοικούν στην ίδια περιοχή;
0-ΝΑΙ ☐ 1-ΟΧΙ ☐
β) Γνωρίζετε αν μετανάστες από άλλες χώρες κατοικούν στην ίδια περιοχή;
0-ΝΑΙ ☐ 1-ΟΧΙ ☐

Γ5. Κατά τη γνώμη σας, αισθανθήκατε ποτέ κάποιου είδους διάκριση ψάχνοντας για κατοικία (ή όσον αφορά π.χ. την αντιμετώπιση του ιδιοκτήτη προς το άτομό σας, κλπ.);
0-ΝΑΙ ☐ 1-ΟΧΙ ☐
α) Αν ΝΑΙ, με ποιόν τρόπο; ____________

Συνεχίστε στην επόμενη σελίδα

Γ6. Πώς θα περιγράφατε γενικά τις σχέσεις σας με τους γείτονές σας;
0-Φιλικές ☐ 1-Εχθρικές ☐ 2-Ουδέτερες ☐
Σχόλια:

Γ7. α) Γενικά είσθε ικανοποιημένος-η από την σημερινή σας κατοικία;
0-ΝΑΙ ☐ 1-ΟΧΙ ☐ 2-ΟΥΔΕΤΕΡΟ ☐
β) … από την γειτονιά/ περιοχή σας;
0-ΝΑΙ ☐ 1-ΟΧΙ ☐ 2-ΟΥΔΕΤΕΡΟ ☐
Θέλετε να κάνετε κάποια σχόλια σχετικά (πιθανά προβλήματα, θετικά στοιχεία κλπ.);

γ) Αισθάνεστε ότι η σημερινή σας κατοικία είναι γενικά περισσότερο ικανοποιητική από οποιαδήποτε άλλη που έτυχε να κατοικήσετε;
i- στη Θεσσαλονίκη 0-ΝΑΙ ☐ 1-ΟΧΙ ☐
ii- στην Ελλάδα γενικά 0-ΝΑΙ ☐ 1-ΟΧΙ ☐
iii- στην πατρίδα σας 0-ΝΑΙ ☐ 1-ΟΧΙ ☐
Σχόλια: __________

Γ8. Ιστορία κατοίκησης στη Θεσσαλονίκη (δώστε συνοπτικές πληροφορίες για τις διάφορες κατοικίες που κατά καιρούς μείνατε στη Θεσσαλονίκη: περιοχές-γειτονιές-δρόμοι, τύπος σπιτιού):

Δ. ΣΥΝΘΗΚΕΣ ΕΡΓΑΣΙΑΣ

Δ1. α) Σημερινή απασχόληση (επάγγελμα, βασικές ασχολίες, περιγραφή εργοδότη, τύπος και μέγεθος επιχείρησης, κλάδος): __________

Επιχειρηματικότητα. Σε περίπτωση που είστε αυτοαπασχολούμενος, ο/η ίδιος-α, η κάποιο μέλος της οικογένειάς σας στου/στης οποίου-ας την επιχείρηση εργάζεσθε, παρακαλώ δώστε περισσότερες λεπτομέρειες (στοιχεία επιχείρησης, βασικοί πελάτες, προβλήματα στην αρχή, σημερινά προβλήματα, κλπ.): __________

β) Τύπος απασχόλησης: i- εποχιακή/περιστασιακή ☐
ii- ημιαπασχόληση ☐
iii- μόνιμη ☐

Δ2. α) Τόπος εργασίας (περιοχή-γειτονιά):
β) περίοδος απασχόλησης στη συγκεκριμένη θέση (μέχρι σήμερα):

Δ3. α) μισθός (διευκρινίστε): __________ β) ώρες απασχόλησης: __________
γ) υπάρχει συμβόλαιο εργασίας; 0-ΝΑΙ ☐ 1-ΟΧΙ ☐
δ) είστε ασφαλισμένος; 0-ΝΑΙ ☐ 1-ΟΧΙ ☐

Δ4. Πως βρήκατε τη σημερινή σας εργασία; Γενικότερα, πως βρίσκετε δουλειά στην Ελλάδα;

	α) <u>σημερινή θέση εργασίας</u>	β) <u>γενικά</u>
i- Μόνος	☐	☐
ii- φίλοι-συγγενείς	☐	☐
iii- «πιάτσες»	☐	☐
iv- αγγελία	☐	☐
v- ΟΑΕΔ	☐	☐
	άλλο (διευκρινίστε): __________	άλλο (διευκρινίστε): __________

Συνεχίστε στην επόμενη σελίδα

Δ5. Επαγγελματική ιστορία στην Ελλάδα (αν κάνετε πολλές δουλειές, τότε περιγράψτε γενικά τις πιο σημαντικές, εκείνες που διήρκεσαν για αρκετά μεγάλο χρονικό διάστημα, ή τις βασικές δουλειές που κάνατε τα τελευταία 5 χρόνια): ______

Σχόλια: ______

Δ6. Υπήρξατε ποτέ άνεργος για περίοδο μεγαλύτερη από ένα μήνα;
0-ΝΑΙ ☐ 1-ΟΧΙ ☐ 2-για πόσο χρονικό διάστημα; ______
Σχόλια:

Δ7. Είχατε ποτέ την εμπειρία διακρίσεων κατά την αναζήτηση εργασίας ή στον ίδιο το χώρο εργασίας; Νοιώσατε ποτέ διαφορετική αντιμετώπιση σε σχέση με τους Έλληνες συναδέλφους σας;
0-ΝΑΙ ☐ 1-ΟΧΙ ☐
α) Από ποιους;
1- Εργοδότες ☐
2- Συναδέλφους ☐
Άλλους (διευκρινίστε): ______
β) Με ποιόν τρόπο; ______
Σχόλια: ______

Δ8. α) Γενικά, είστε ικανοποιημένος-η από τη σημερινή σας απασχόληση;
0-ΝΑΙ ☐ 1-ΟΧΙ ☐ 2-ΟΥΔΕΤΕΡΟ ☐
Σχόλια:
β) Γενικά είσθε ικανοποιημένος-η από τις συνθήκες εργασίας που συναντήσατε στην Ελλάδα;
0-ΝΑΙ ☐ 1-ΟΧΙ ☐ 2-ΟΥΔΕΤΕΡΟ ☐
Σχόλια: ______

Δ9. Εργαζόσασταν στην πατρίδα σας προτού έρθετε στην Ελλάδα;
0-ΝΑΙ ☐ 1-ΟΧΙ ☐
α) Αν, ΝΑΙ, περιγράψτε την τελευταία σας απασχόληση στην πατρίδα σας (επάγγελμα, θέση εργασίας, κλάδος): ______

Δ10. Επίπεδο εκπαίδευσης και επαγγελματικά προσόντα:
i- δημοτικό ☐
ii- γυμνάσιο ☐
iii- λύκειο ☐
iv- τεχνική/επαγγελματική ☐ διευκρινίστε: ______
v- τεχνολογικό ινστιτούτο (ΤΕΙ) ☐
vi- Πανεπιστήμιο (ΑΕΙ) ☐
vii- Μεταπτυχιακά ☐
επιπλέον προσόντα: ______
Σχόλια: ______

Δ11. Εκπαίδευση/κατάρτιση στην Ελλάδα (σεμινάρια, πανεπιστημιακή, τεχνολογική ή τεχνική εκπαίδευση κατάρτιση, και οποιαδήποτε άλλη εκπαίδευση έτυχε να έχετε στην Ελλάδα). Αν έχετε παρακολουθήσει μαθήματα εκμάθησης της ελληνικής γλώσσας συμπληρώστε το κουτάκι και δώστε επιπλέον λεπτομέρειες:
0-μαθήματα ελληνικής γλώσσας ☐: ______
1-Εκπαίδευση-κατάρτιση: ______

Συνεχίστε στην επόμενη σελίδα

Δ12. α) Χρήση της ελληνικής γλώσσας:

	i- ελάχιστη	ii- ικανοποιητική	iii- άριστη
1- Ομιλία-κατανόηση	☐	☐	☐
2- Γραφή	☐	☐	☐

β) Μιλάτε άλλες γλώσσες, εκτός της μητρικής σας γλώσσας και των ελληνικών; Ποιες; (περιγράψτε επίπεδο γνώσης της γλώσσας):
ΝΑΙ ☐ ΟΧΙ ☐ ______

Ε. ΣΥΝΘΗΚΕΣ ΖΩΗΣ ΣΤΗΝ ΕΛΛΑΔΑ

Ε1. α) Μέλη του νοικοκυριού που εργάζονται:______
β) Μέσο μηνιαίο εισόδημα νοικοκυριού κατά την τρέχουσα περίοδο (διευκρινίστε αν πρόκειται για το ατομικό σας ή το συνολικό οικογενειακό εισόδημα): [______]

Ε2. Γενικά, πως δαπανείτε το εισόδημά σας;
Μπορείτε να δώσετε ένα μέσο ποσό ή ποσοστό του εισοδήματός σας που ξοδεύεται για:
i- λογαριασμούς (ΟΤΕ, ΔΕΗ) ☐ [______]
ii- εξοπλισμό νοικοκυριού ☐
iii- τραπεζικές καταθέσεις ☐ [______]
iv- επενδύσεις στην Ελλάδα ☐
v- διασκέδαση-ψυχαγωγία ☐
vi- εμβάσματα στην πατρίδα ☐ [______]
άλλο (τι;):

Ε3. α) Αν στέλνετε εμβάσματα στην πατρίδα σας, για ποιο σκοπό προορίζονται τα χρήματα;
i- για συντήρηση οικογένειας ☐
ii- για αγορά/βελτίωση κατοικίας ☐
ii- για επένδυση ☐ τι είδους; ______
άλλο (διευκρινίστε): ______
β) Εκτός από εμβάσματα, στέλνεται καταναλωτικά αγαθά ή είδη εξοπλισμού νοικοκυριού στην πατρίδα;
0-ΝΑΙ ☐ 1-ΟΧΙ ☐

Ε4. Εξοπλισμός νοικοκυριού:
α) Οδηγάτε (εδώ):
i- αυτοκίνητο ☐ ii- μηχανάκι ☐ iii- ποδήλατο ☐
β) Στο σπίτι έχετε: i- κεντρική θέρμανση ☐ αν όχι, τι; ______
ii- τηλέφωνο ☐
iii- ηλεκτρική κουζίνα ☐
iv- πλυντήριο ☐
v- ραδιόφωνο ☐
vi- τηλεόραση ☐
άλλο (διευκρινίστε): ______

Ε5. α) Έχετε βιβλιάρια ενσήμων και υγείας στην Ελλάδα;
1- βιβλιάριο ενσήμων ☐ 2- βιβλιάριο υγείας ☐
β) Εάν προκύψει ανάγκη για ιατρική περίθαλψη, συνήθως πώς στο αντιμετωπίζετε;
i- πάω σε (δημόσιο) νοσοκομείο ☐
ii- πάω σε ιδιωτική κλινική ☐
iii- επισκέπτομαι (ιδιωτικό) ιατρείο ☐
γ) Υπάρχουν περιπτώσεις που συναντάται προβλήματα όσον αφορά την ιατροφαρμακευτική σας περίθαλψη (εξετάσεις, νοσηλεία, κλπ.); Μπορείτε να αναφέρεται ορισμένα από αυτά;
______

Συνεχίστε στην επόμενη σελίδα

E6. Τα παιδιά σας (αν έχετε) πηγαίνουν σχολείο (στην Ελλάδα);
0-ΝΑΙ ▢ 1-ΟΧΙ ▢ α) Αν , ΝΑΙ, σε ποια τάξη; ____________
β) Σε ποιο σχολείο (σχολείο-περιοχή); ____________
γ) Σας ανέφεραν ποτέ κάποιο παράπονο διακριτικής αντιμετώπισης εξαιτίας της καταγωγής/ του θρησκεύματός τους; 1-ΝΑΙ, στο σχολείο ▢ 2-ΝΑΙ, στη γειτονιά ▢
δ) Από ποιους; i- δασκάλους ▢ ii- άλλα παιδιά ▢ iii- γονείς παιδιών ▢
Σχόλια:

E7. Επαφές και σχέσεις με άλλους (συμπατριώτες, μετανάστες άλλων εθνικοτήτων, Έλληνες). Προσδιορίστε το είδος της σχέσης (συγγενείς, φίλοι, γείτονες, συνάδελφοι, κλπ.):
____
____

E8. Θεωρείτε τον εαυτό σας θρησκευόμενο;
0-ΝΑΙ ▢ 1-ΟΧΙ ▢ α) Αν, ΝΑΙ, ποιο είναι το θρήσκευμά σας; ____________
β) Αισθάνεστε ότι οι θρησκευτικές σας ανάγκες ικανοποιούνται
1-στη Θεσσαλονίκη; 0-ΝΑΙ ▢ 1-ΟΧΙ ▢
2-στην Ελλάδα γενικά; 0-ΝΑΙ ▢ 1-ΟΧΙ ▢
γ) Είχατε ποτέ την εμπειρία διακρίσεων/διαφορετικής αντιμετώπισης εξαιτίας του θρησκεύματός σας;
0-ΝΑΙ ▢ 1-ΟΧΙ ▢
Σχόλια: ____________

E9. α) Συμμετέχετε σε συλλογικούς φορείς στην Ελλάδα;
0-ΝΑΙ ▢ 1-ΟΧΙ ▢ β) διευκρινίστε και δώστε σύντομη περιγραφή:
i- Συλλόγους μεταναστών ▢: ____________
ii- Πολιτισμικούς συλλόγους ▢ ____________
iii- Συνδικαλιστικούς φορείς ▢: ____________
iv- Πολιτικές οργανώσεις ▢: ____________
άλλο (τι): ____________
Σχόλια: ____________
____

E10. Συνήθως που κάνετε τα καθημερινά σας ψώνια (σε τι είδους μαγαζιά και σε ποια περιοχή);
i- σε συνοικιακά μαγαζιά ▢ ____________
ii- σε σουπερμάρκετ της γειτονιάς/περιοχής σας ▢ ____________
iii- σε μεγάλα σουπερμάρκετ ▢ ____________
Σχόλια: ____________

E11. α) Βγαίνετε έξω να διασκεδάσετε στον ελεύθερο χρόνο σας; Πόσο συχνά;
i- Τουλάχιστον μια φορά το 15θήμερο ▢
ii- Τουλάχιστον μια φορά το μήνα ▢
iii- Σπάνια ▢
β) Συνήθως πού;
i- στη γειτονία ▢
ii- στο κέντρο ▢
iii- αλλού (πού): ____________
Σχόλια:
____

E12. Πηγαίνετε διακοπές (μόνος-η ή με την οικογένειά σας);
0-ΝΑΙ ▢ 1-ΟΧΙ ▢
α) Συνήθως που πηγαίνετε (διευκρινίστε); i- στην Ελλάδα ____________
ii- στην πατρίδα ____________
αλλού (που;) ____________
β) πότε ήταν η τελευταία φορά;

Συνεχίστε στην επόμενη σελίδα

Ε13. Ποια είναι η γνώμη σας για τη συμπεριφορά/την αντίληψη των ντόπιων (ανθρώπων, υπηρεσιών, οργανισμών) προς τους συμπατριώτες σας (απαντήστε μονάχα αν είστε σίγουροι, με σύντομη διευκρίνιση-σχολιασμό);

	0-φιλική	1-εχθρική	2-ουδέτερη
i- Δημόσιες υπηρεσίες και οργανισμοί	☐	☐	☐
ii- Αστυνομία	☐	☐	☐
iii- ΜΜΕ	☐	☐	☐
iv- Εργοδότες	☐	☐	☐
v- Συνδικαλιστές	☐	☐	☐
vi- Θεσσαλονικείς	☐	☐	☐
vii- Έλληνες γενικά	☐	☐	☐
viii- Μειονοτικές ομάδες (Τσιγγάνοι-μουσουλμάνοι):	☐	☐	☐
ix- Μετανάστες άλλων εθνικοτήτων:	☐	☐	☐

Σχόλια: ____________________

Γ14. Πιστεύετε ότι η συμπεριφορά των παραπάνω (από –α- έως -η-) είναι διαφορετική όσον αφορά μετανάστες άλλων εθνικοτήτων (απαντήστε μονάχα αφόσον έχετε παρατηρήσει φαινόμενα διαφορετικής αντιμετώπισης ή έχετε ακούσει/γνωρίζετε για την αντίληψη των ντόπιων σε σχέση με ορισμένες κατηγορίες μεταναστών);

0-ΝΑΙ ☐ 1-ΟΧΙ ☐

α) Αν, ΝΑΙ, αναφέρετε κάποιες εθνικότητες μεταναστών που, κατά τη γνώμη σας χαίρουν διαφορετικής αντιμετώπισης και να περιγράψετε συνοπτικά σε τι συνίσταται αυτή:

____

Σχόλια: ____________________

Γ15. Χρειάστηκε εσείς να κάνετε κάτι για να γίνετε ευκολότερα αποδεκτοί από τους ντόπιους (π.χ. ορισμένοι Αλβανοί δήλωναν ελληνικά ονόματα προκειμένου να έχουν την «προνομιακή» μεταχείριση των βορειοηπειρωτών); Μπορείτε να περιγράψετε συνοπτικά κάποιες από τις σχετικές σας προσπάθειες;

____

____

ΣΤ. ΕΠΙΠΛΕΟΝ ΠΛΗΡΟΦΟΡΙΕΣ

ΣΤ1. Γενικά, είστε ικανοποιημένος από τη ζωή σας στη Θεσσαλονίκη;

0-ΝΑΙ ☐ 1-ΟΧΙ ☐ 2-ΟΥΔΕΤΕΡΟ ☐

Σχόλια: ____________________

ΣΤ2. Μελλοντικά σχέδια (αν δώσετε περισσότερες από μία απαντήσεις, παρακαλώ ιεραρχείστε):

i- να συνεχίσω να ζω στη Θεσσαλονίκη ☐
ii- να μετακομίσω σε άλλη πόλη/ της Ελλάδας ☐ που; ____________
iii- να μεταναστεύσω σε άλλη χώρα ☐ που; ____________
iv- να επιστρέψω στην πατρίδα μου ☐
v- Δεν ξέρω ☐

ΣΤ3. Μελλοντικά επαγγελματικά σχέδια:

i- να συνεχίσω στην τωρινή μου εργασία ☐
ii- να ψάξω για καλύτερη δουλειά ☐
iii- να ξεκινήσω τη δική μου δουλειά ☐

Σχόλια: ____________________

ΣΤ4. Θα θέλατε να προσθέσετε κάτι που κατά τη γνώμη σας αξίζει να τονιστεί και δεν αναφέρθηκε αλλού;

Σας ευχαριστώ για τη συμμετοχή σας

QUESTIONNAIRE

IMMIGRANTS FROM BALKAN COUNTRIES IN THESSALONIKI
Issues of Social Exclusion and Social Integration
Information on migration,
Housing and working conditions,
Living conditions in Greece

Questionnaire N. : ________ Place: ________________ Date: ___/___/____

Researcher:
Panos Arion Hatziprokopiou
DPhil Candidate
Sussex European Institute
University of Sussex
United Kingdom

Title of DPhil Thesis:
«Globalisation, Migration and Socioeconomic change in contemporary Greece: Processes of social incorporation of Albanian and Bulgarian immigrants in Thessaloniki»

A. PERSONAL DATA

1. Nationality: Albanian ☐ Bulgarian ☐ Romanian ☐
2. Ethnicity (ethnic origin):
3. Place of residence before emigration:
4. Sex: 0-MALE ☐ 1-FEMALE ☐
5. Age:
6. Family Status: i- single ☐ ii- married ☐ iii- divorced/widowed ☐ iii- N. of children: _______
7. Household members:

	i- in Thessaloniki	ii- at home country	iii- other (where?)
a- parents			
b- spouse			
c- children			
d- brothers/sisters			
e- other (who):			

Please, continue in the next page

B. MIGRATION DATA:
ENTRY IN GREECE AND ARRIVAL TO THESSALONIKI

B1. Reasons for leaving your country of origin (please put in order):
- i- Economic reasons* ☐
- ii- Political refugee ☐
- iii- Greek origin ☐
- Other (what) __________

* π.χ. unemployment, lower living standards, difficult life conditions, worse employment conditions, lower wages, etc.

B2. Reasons for coming to Greece (please put in order):
- i- Economic reasons* ☐
- ii- Easy to enter the country ☐
- iii- Close to my country ☐
- iv- Transit station for somewhere else ☐
- v- Ethnic Greek origin ☐
- other (what): __________

* unemployment, lower living standards, difficult living conditions, worse employment conditions, lower wages, etc.

B3. When was the first time that you came to Greece?

B4. Since you came in Greece, have you been back to your country for a long period (of more than 3 months) and then returned to Greece?
0-YES ☐ 1-NO ☐
α) If YES, for how long? ________ α) what was the reason? ________

B5. Have you ever emigrated to a country other than Greece?
0-YES ☐ 1-NO ☐
α) If YES, which? ________ β) period (Dates): ________
Comments:

B6. α) Means of entry into Greece the first time you came:
- i- on foot ☐
- ii- by car ☐
- iii- by coach ☐
- iv- by train ☐
- other (specify): ________

β) When you go back to your country and then return to Greece, what of the above means of transport do you usually use??

B7. Mode of entry into Greece the first time you came (legal status):
- i- stay permit ☐
- ii- tourist visa ☐
- iii- seasonal worker ☐
- iv- ethnic Greek ☐
- v- illegal entry ☐
- other (specify): ________

α) Comments (e.g., if you paid to obtain a visa or for your 'transportation' in Greece, if you came as a dependent family member of an immigrant already in Greece, if you married a Greek citizen, etc.):
____

B8. α) Reasons for settling in Thessaloniki and history of settlement before coming here:
1st ________
2nd ________
3rd ________
β) Where in Greece have you lived before coming to Thessaloniki? ________
____

Please, continue in the next page

B9. Initial contacts that helped you initially to settle, or that influenced you in respect to your decision to come to Greece (in case of more than one answers, please order: 1,2, etc):

- i- relatives ☐
- ii- friends and acquaintances (compatriots) ☐
- iii- Greek acwuaintances-employers ☐
- others (who?): ______

Comments: ______

B10. Do you currently have legal documentations?

0-YES ☐ 1-NO ☐

α) if YES, you have:

1. white card ☐
2. green card ☐
3. registration card ☐
4. green card certificate ☐
5. ID card (ethnic Greeks) ☐
6. visa ☐ which type: ______
7. I have applied but it has not been issued yet ☐

β) if NO, what is the reason why you have not been able to obtain legal documents?

______

Comments: ______

Γ. HOUSING CONDITIONS

Γ1. Area of Residence: α) Period you live there?

Γ2. Other people living with you:

α) Total number of people living in the same house: ______

β) Please specify the type of your relationship with them:

household members ☐ other relatives ☐ friends/compatriots ☐

other (who): ______

Γ3. α) Type of residence (if you a guest the place of a relative/friend/employer, please tick the box and explain):

	i- <u>today</u>	ii- <u>the first time you came</u>
i- hotel	☐	☐
ii- rented flat	☐	☐
iii- own property	☐	☐
iv- guest (where)	☐	☐
other (specify):	______	______

β) How many rooms does it have? [____]

γ) If you rent the property, how much do you pay for rent? [________]

Γ4. α) Do you know if people of the same nationality as yours live in the area?

0-YES ☐ 1-NO ☐

β) Are you aware of immigrants from other nationalities living in the area?

0-YES ☐ 1-NO ☐

Γ5. In your opinion, have you ever felt some sort of discrimination while looking for accommodation (or regarding the landlords' attitude towards you, etc.)?

0-YES ☐ 1-NO ☐

α) If YES, in which way? ______

Please, continue in the next page

Γ6. How would you describe your relations with your neighbours?
0-friendly ☐ 1-Hostile ☐ 2-Neutral ☐
Comments:

Γ7. α) In general, are you satisfied from your current accommodation?
0-YES ☐ 1-NO ☐ 2-NEUTRAL ☐
β) … from your neighbourhood/area?
0-YES ☐ 1-NO ☐ 2-NEUTRAL ☐
Would you like to make any comments regarding possible problems, positive elements, etc?

γ) Do you feel that your current accommodation is in general more satisfactory than any other you had lived?
i- in Thessaloniki 0-YES ☐ 1-NO ☐
ii- in Greece, generally 0-YES ☐ 1-NO ☐
iii- in your home country 0-YES ☐ 1-NO ☐
Comments:

Γ8. History of residence in Thessaloniki (please give brief information about the various places you have lived in Thessaloniki: districts-neighbourhoods-streets-property type):

Δ. EMPLOYMENT CONDITIONS

Δ1. α) Current occupation (profession, main duties, employers' description, type & size of company, sector):

Entrepreneurship. In case you are self-employed, yourself, or some other member of your family to whose company you work, please give further details (company type, main customers, problems initially, problems today, etc.):

β) Type of Employment: i- seasonal/occasional ☐
ii- part-time ☐
iii- permanent ☐

Δ2. α) Location of workplace (area - neighbourhood):
β) period of employment in current occupation (up to now):

Δ3. α) wage (specify): ____ β) daily hours of work: ____
γ) do you have an employment contract? 0-YES ☐ 1-NO ☐
δ) do you have social security? 0-YES ☐ 1-NO ☐

Δ4. How did you find your present job? In general, how do you find work in Greece?

	α) current position	β) in general
i- Alone	☐	☐
ii- friends-relatives	☐	☐
iii- «piazzas»	☐	☐
iv- vacancy ad	☐	☐
v- Jobcentre	☐	☐
other (specify):	____	other (specify): ____

Please, continue in the next page

Δ5. Employment history in Greece (if you have changed many jobs, please describe in general the most important ones, those lasting for a significant period, opr the basic jobs you have been doing during the last 5 years): __________

Comments: __________

Δ6. Have you ever been unemployed for a period longer than one month?
0-YES ☐ 1-NO ☐ 2-for how long? __________
Comments:

Δ7. have you ever had any experience of discrimination while looking for a job, or at the workplace itself? Have you ever felt to be treated in a different way than your Greek colleagues?
0-YES ☐ 1-NO ☐
α) From whom?
1- Employers ☐
2- Colleagues ☐
Others (specify): __________
β) In which way? __________
Comments: __________

Δ8. α) In general, would you say that you are satisfied from your current occupation?
0-YES ☐ 1-NO ☐ 2-NEUTRAL ☐
Comments:
β) In general, would you say that you are satisfied form the conditions of employment in Greece?
0-YES ☐ 1-NO ☐ 2-NEUTRAL ☐
Comments: __________

Δ9. Did you use to work at your home country before coming to Greece?
0-YES ☐ 1-NO ☐
α) If, YES, please describe your last occupation in your home country (profession, position, sector):
____

Δ10. Επίπεδο Education level and professional qualifications:
i- primary ☐
ii- gymnasium ☐
iii- lyceum ☐
iv- technical/professional ☐ specify: __________
v- polytechnic ☐
vi- University ☐
vii- Postgraduate ☐
additional qualifications: __________
Comments: __________

Δ11. Education/training in Greece (seminars, university, technological or technical education/training, and any other form of education you happened to receive in Greece). If you have followed classes of Greek language, please tick the box and give additional details:
0-Greek language courses ☐: __________
1-Education-training: __________

Please, continue in the next page

Δ12. α) Use of Greek language:

	i- beginner	ii- intermediate	iii- fluent
1- speach-understanding	☐	☐	☐
2- writing	☐	☐	☐

β) Do you speak any languages other than your mother tongue and Greek? Which? (please indicate level of knowledge of the language):
YES ☐ NO ☐ ____________________

E. LIVING CONDITIONS IN GREECE

E1. α) Household members working: ________
β) Average monthly household income during the current period (specify If this concerns your personal or household income): [________]

E2. In general, how do you spend your income?
Could you give an average amount or percentage that you spend on:
i- Bills ☐ [________]
ii- household equipment ☐
iii- bank account ☐ [________]
iv- investment in Greece ☐
v- leisure-entertainment ☐
vi- remittances at home ☐ [________]
other (what?):

E3. α) In case that you send remittances to your home country, which is the reason you do that?
i- to support family ☐
ii- to buy/improve house ☐
ii- to invest ☐ what sort of investment? ____________________
other (specify): ____________________
β) Apart from remittances, do you send consumer goods at your home country?
0-YES ☐ 1-NO ☐

E4. Household equipment:
α) Do you drive (in Greece):
i- a car ☐ ii- a motorbike ☐ iii- a bicycle ☐
β) At home you have: i- central heating ☐ If not, what? ____________
ii- telephone ☐
iii- oven ☐
iv- washing machine ☐
v- radio ☐
vi- television ☐
other (specify): ____________________

E5. α) Do you have insurance book and health book in Greece?
1- insurance book ☐ 2- health book ☐
β) in case you face a need for medical treatment, how do you usually deal with that?
i- I go to a (public) hospital ☐
ii- I go to a private clinic ☐
iii- I visit a (private) GP ☐
γ) have you encountered any problems in respect to your medical treatment (tests, hospitalisation, etc.)? Could you mention some of those?
____

Please, continue in the next page

E6. If you have children, do they go to school (in Greece)?
0-YES ☐ 1-NO ☐ α) If , YES, in which year? ______
β) in which school (school-area)? ______
γ) Have they ever complained about any incident of differential treatment because of their origin or religion? 1-YES, at school ☐ 2-YES, at the neighbourhood ☐
δ) from whom? i- teachers☐ ii- other children ☐ iii- children's parents ☐
Comments:

E7. Contacts and relationships with others (compatriots, migrants of other nationalities, Greeks). Please specify the type of the relationship (relatives, friends, neighbours, colleagues, κλπ.):
______
______

E8. Would you consider yourself a religious person??
0-YES ☐ 1-NO ☐ α) If, YES, which is your religion? ______
β) Do you feel that your religious needs are satisfied
1-in Thessaloniki? 0-YES ☐ 1-NO ☐
2-generally in Greece? 0-YES ☐ 1-NO ☐
γ) Have you ever had any experience of discrimination/differential treatment because of your religion?
0-YES ☐ 1-NO ☐
Comments: ______

E9. α) Do you participate in any collective organisation here in Greece?
0-YES ☐ 1-NO ☐ β) please specify and briefly describe:
i- Migrant Associations ☐: ______
ii- Cultural Organisations ☐ ______
iii- Trade Union Bodies ☐: ______
iv- Political Organisations ☐: ______
other (what): ______
Comments: ______
______

E10. Where do you usually do your daily shopping (what types of shops, which area)?
i- neighbourhood stores ☐ ______
ii- wider area small supermarkets ☐ ______
iii- large supermarkets ☐ ______
Comments: ______

E11. α) Do you go out on your free time? How often?
i- At least once in 15 days ☐
ii- At least once in a month ☐
iii- rarely ☐
β) Where do you usually go?
i- at the neighbourhood ☐
ii- downtown ☐
iii- other (where): ______
Comments: ______

E12. Do you go holiday alone or with your family)?
0-YES ☐ 1-NO ☐
α) Where do you usually go (specify)? i- in Greece ______
ii- at home country ______
other (where?) ______
β) when was the last time?

Please, continue in the next page

E13. What do you think about the attitude/perception of the locals (people, services, institutions) towards your compatriots (please answer only if you are sure, including brief specification-comment)?

	0-friendly	1-hostile	2-neutral
i- public services	☐	☐	☐
ii- Police	☐	☐	☐
iii- Media	☐	☐	☐
iv- Employers	☐	☐	☐
v- Trade-Unionists	☐	☐	☐
vi- Thessaloniceans	☐	☐	☐
vii- Greeks in general	☐	☐	☐
viii- Minority groups (Gypsies-Muslims):	☐	☐	☐
ix- Migrants of other nationalities:	☐	☐	☐

Comments: ____________________

Γ14. Do you believe that the attitude of the above (from i to vii) is different regarding immigrants of other nationalities (please answer only if you have observed incidents of different treatment, or you have heard/you know about the locals' perceptions regarding certain categories of migrants)?

0-YES ☐ 1-NO ☐

α) If, YES, please state some migrant nationalities who you believe receive different treatment and describe briefly in which way this takes place:

____

Comments: ____________________

E13. Have you ever felt being in the need to do something in order to be more acceptable by the locals (π.χ. some Albanians give Greek names in order to have the 'privileged' treatment that applies to the ethnic Greeks)? Can you give some details/ make comments on this?

____

____

ΣΤ. ADDITIONAL INFORMATION

ΣΤ1. In general, are you satisfied from your life in Thessaloniki?

0-YES ☐ 1-NO ☐ 2-NEUTRAL ☐

Comments: ____________________

ΣΤ2. Future plans (If you give more than one answers, please put in order):

i- stay in Thessaloniki ☐
ii- move to some other place in Greece ☐ πoυ? __________
iii- migrate to another country ☐ πoυ? __________
iv- return back to my country ☐
v- Don't know ☐

ΣΤ3. Future employment plans:

i- stay in present occupation ☐
ii- look for a better job ☐
iii- start my own business ☐
Comments: ____________________

ΣΤ4. Would you like to give some additional information or to comment on a particular issue that you think is essential but it has not touched elsewhere in the questionnaire?

Thank you for your participation

Appendix B2 The interview guide

A. Interview
Date, time, place, name of the interviewee, tape number, language skill level.

B. Demographic Profile
Gender, birth date, birthplace, ethnic background, religion, education, marital status, number of children, previous occupations in country of origin.

Notes

C. Migration Dynamics

C1 Why did you choose to migrate to Greece?
C2 When did you first migrate to this country?
C3 When you first came, what route did you take and what means of transport did you use (boat, foot, bus, combination etc.)?
C4 What was your entry point into Greece?
C5 Did you migrate alone, or with other members of your family (state which ones), or with a group of friends?
C6 What were your reactions when you first arrived?
C7 Who helped you settle in when you first arrived?
C8 Apart from (state place of interview), where else in this country have you lived and/or worked?
C9 Why did you choose (state place of interview)?
C10 Have you also migrated to other countries? (State which ones, when and for how long.)
C11 How would you compare those experiences of migration to the current one?
C12 Have you been back to Albania/Bulgaria since your first migration? If so, for how long, and how many times? Was your return migration forced or voluntary?
C13 If you have returned, what route and means of transport have you used (air, boat, train, bus, shared taxi, etc.)?
C14 How do you see yourself here (immigrant, tourist, visitor, refugee ...)?

D. Exclusion

Exclusion/discrimination in the labour market

D1 What kind of jobs have you performed in Greece? What is your current job? Have you ever been unemployed for a long period (in Greece)? Please describe your working experiences.

D2 Were you able to get a job according to your educational qualifications and experience? Please explain.

D3 How did you find these jobs? How did you find your current job?

D4 How is your relationship with your employer? How is your employer treating you?

D5 How many hours do you usually work? How often do you have a break? How long is it?

D6 Are you satisfied with your current job and your payment? What payment is given to a Greek or another migrant worker for the same job? Did you have any bad experiences (e.g. not receive your payment)?

D8 Do you work with other migrants? How is your relationship with them?

D9 Do you belong to any trade union or professional association? Please explain.

D10 When you were working, did you experience any advances of a sexual nature from your employer? Please describe your experiences.

Exclusion from formal networks of support and citizenship rights/discrimination in approaching social welfare institutions

D11 What was your legal status when you first arrived in Greece?

D12 What is your legal status at the moment? (Do you possess a White or Green Card or other documentation for Greece?)

D13 Was it easy to issue your legal papers? Did you encounter any difficulties? Please explain.

D14 For how long is your card valid? How often do you have to renew it?

D15 Are you satisfied with your legal status at the moment?

D16 Did you receive any support or help from a Greek state agency in issuing legal papers?

D17 Are you registered with a social security fund or not? Please explain.

D18 Do you have access to health services? Are you registered with a doctor?

D19 Did you encounter any problems in registering your children at school? Please explain.

D20 Are your children treated the same as Greek children at school by teachers and by other children?

Housing exclusion/discrimination in the housing market

D21 Where do you live? In what other areas of the city have you lived in the past?

D22 What type of accommodation do you live in? Please describe the property. How many people do you live with?

D23 Do you own the property or are you renting it?

D24 Why did you choose this particular accommodation?

D25 What is easy to find a place to live? Did you encounter any difficulties in renting a property? Please describe your personal experiences.

D26 Are you satisfied with your accommodation? Would you like to move somewhere else? If yes, explain why and state where would you like to move.

D27 Do any other compatriots or members of other ethnic groups reside in this area?

Exclusion/inclusion from/in informal networks of support, ethnic solidarity

D28 Do Albanian/Bulgarians support one another in Greece? If they do, please explain in which ways they do so. Is it different in Albania/Bulgaria?

D29 Have you received any help from the neighbourhood?

D30 Do you belong to an Albanian/Bulgarian association or another migrant or anti-racist movement?

D31 Why did you decide to become a member (motivation), and what are you gaining from your participation? Has the association helped you in any way? Please explain.

D32 What kind of activities does the association promote and what action has been taken so far to achieve its goals? For example, has the association made any formal complaints to the government? Has it mobilised you to protest? Has it promoted cultural activities in the host country? Please explain.

D33 Are there any other ethnic associations apart from the one that you belong to? If yes, what are their names? Are there any differences between the association you belong to and the others? Please explain.

E. Racism and Identity

E1 Do you like it here (Greece)? Why?

E2 Please describe to me any incidents where you felt you were being unfairly treated. Who treated you unfairly and in what way? Please explain.

E3 Did you experience unfair treatment in the following areas: accessing welfare institutions (e.g. to get a benefit, enrol in a pension scheme, access to health care); education (schools); labour market, police, neighbourhood, shops, streets, other? Please describe your experience in each case.

E4 Did your friends have any similar experiences?

E5 How do you react when you are being treated unfairly?

E6 Have you ever been a victim of violence (e.g. physical, verbal) in Greece? Please describe your experiences (when, where and what happened?).

E7 Has any member of your family or a friend of yours ever been a victim of (physical and/or verbal) violence in Greece?

E8 What do you think about the treatment of Albanians/Bulgarians in Greece? Is it fair? Why? How should things be?

E9 What do you like/not like about Greeks?

E10 In what respect are they different from Albanians/Bulgarians? In what respect are they similar?

E11 Do you socialise mainly with people from your own country, with Greeks, or with other migrants? Have you got Greek friends? What do you like doing together?

E12 How do you relate to Greeks? What is your relationship with them (e.g. close friendship, baptism, etc)?

E13 What do you like doing together with other Albanians/Bulgarians? Is it different from what you like doing with Greeks? Why?

E14 How do Albanians/Bulgarians relate to one another in Greece? Is it different from Albania/Bulgaria?

E15 What do you think about the other Albanians/Bulgarians here?

E16 Have you ever had a Greek partner? Would it be a problem? Why? Was it different from having an Albanian/Bulgarian partner? Why?

E17 Do you have friends of other nationalities (excluding Albanians/Bulgarians and the host society)?

E18 What do you like about Albania/Bulgaria? Are there any particular aspects (values) of the Albanian/Bulgarian way of life which you value?

E19 Are there any particular aspects (values) of the Albanian/Bulgarian way of life which contrast with the Greek way of life? Which ones? Why?

E20 What adjectives do the Greeks use (employers, neighbours, media) in everyday life to refer to Albanian/Bulgarian (and ethnic Greek) migrants? Name both positive and negative ones.

E21 Do you consider that these adjectives are representative of the Albanians/Bulgarians (ethnic Greek) character and or behaviour?

E22 Who is using these expressions?

E23 How do they affect you? In which ways? Please explain.

E24 How do people react when you mention to them that you come from Albania/Bulgaria?

E25 Are you aware of any jokes about Albanian/Bulgarian migrants?
E26 What differentiates the Albanians/Bulgarians from the Greeks and ethnic Greeks?
E27 Are you proud to be Albanian/Bulgarian?
E28 What does it mean to be Albanian/Bulgarian in Greece for you?
E29 What is important for you to preserve of your country and its culture in the host country? Please explain.
E30 What Albanian/Bulgarian aspects and elements would you like your children to maintain?
E31 Do you speak Albanian/Bulgarian at home? And outside?
E32 Do you practice your religion? Is this important for you? How often do you attend religious meetings? Did you encounter any problems?
E33 Were there any occasions where you had to hide the fact that you are Albanian/Bulgarian (and present yourself as an ethnic Greek)? Please describe your experiences.
E34 What are the elements which differentiate Albanians/Bulgarians from ethnic Greeks?
E35 (For ethnic Greeks) How do you feel when people treat you as an Albanian/Bulgarian?

F. Media and Cultural Inclusion/Exclusion
F1 Do you watch/listen to/read Greek television/radio/newspapers? Which ones?
F2 What do you like watching on television?
F3 How do you spend your free time?
F4 Who do you go with (if not answered before)?
F5 What about news? Do you read/watch it on Greek media?
F6 How about when they talk about Albanians/Bulgarians, what do you think of that?
F7 Do you think it is a fair representation? In what respect?
F8 Do you remember any programme in particular?
F9 Do you think that what the media says corresponds to what Greek people think?
F10 Do you think that what the media says influences the way people behave with you?
F11 What about other foreign people living and working in Greece, are they portrayed differently or similarly? Please explain.
F12 What do you like doing during your free time? Do you go out? Where would you usually go?
F13 Do you go on holiday? Where? How often?

Section on Albanian/Bulgarian Media
F14 Do you have access to television and press from Albania/Bulgaria? Which ones are available here?

F15 Are there any local Albanian/Bulgarian newspapers produced here?
F16 Do Albanian/Bulgarian people refer to these? Please explain.
F17 What do you find in Albanian/Bulgarian media produced in Greece that you cannot find in Albanian/Bulgarian media produced in Albania/Bulgaria?
F18 How about the Internet?

G. Future Plans

G1 Where do you see yourself in ten years' time? What is your intention for the future? Stay in this place in Greece/ move to another place in Greece (state where)/ move to another country (state which one)/ return to Albania/Bulgaria.
G2 How long are you planning to stay in Greece? Why?
G3 If your plan is to return to Albania/Bulgaria, what are your plans for resettling there (employment, business, family reasons etc.)? Do you currently send money to your country? For what purpose?
G4 When would you plan to return? And would you plan to go back to the place of your origin, or to another place?(Where?)
G5 In general, what did you expect your migration experience to be in Greece? And how did it work out?

Printed and bound by CPI Group (UK) Ltd, Croydon, CR0 4YY
17/09/2025
14737698-0001